AF539432

Women and International Action

INTERNATIONAL ENCYCLOPAEDIA OF WOMEN

Volume 5

Women and International Action

By

Dr. Digumarti Bhaskara Rao
Reader and Research Director
R.V.R. College of Education
D-43 (277) S.V.N. Colony
Guntur – 522 006
Andhra Pradesh (India)

&

Mrs. Digumarti Pushpa Latha
Executive Member
Care Welfare Society
Guntur – 522 006
Andhra Pradesh (India)

D P H

DISCOVERY PUBLISHING HOUSE PVT. LTD.
NEW DELHI-110 002

Published by:
Tilak Wasan

DISCOVERY PUBLISHING HOUSE PVT. LTD.
4831/24, Ansari Road, Prahlad Street
Darya Ganj, New Delhi-110002 (India)
Phone: +91-11-23279245, 43764432
Fax: +91-11-23253475
E-mail: parul.wasan@gmail.com
discoverypublishinghouse@gmail.com
info@discoverypublishinggroup.com
web: www.discoverypublishinggroup.com

Edition: **2011**
ISBN: 978-81-8356-911-8 (Set)

International Encyclopaedia of Women (5 Vols. Set)
Authors

Printed at:
Mehra Offset Press
Delhi

Contents

Foreword

Women and men are equal in every human concern in this World. They are equally competing in almost all spheres of work and power and are equally achieving the set goals. Culture, economy and polity may be barriers to women in certain parts of the globe, still women are marching ahead with great conviction and confidence to keep themselves on par with their counter parts in every affair.

This International Encyclopaedia of Women is touching every area concerned to women. Volume 1 explains the status of the world's women, Volume 2 discusses the role of education in women's empowerment, Volume 3 discusses the challenges and advancement of women, Volume 4 outlines the family health, and Volume 5 presents the details of the international instruments applicable for the development of women.

This Encyclopedia will meet the requirements of planners, researchers, educationists and activists.

Dr. Digumarti Bhaskara Rao
Mrs. Digumarti Pushpa latha
R. V.R College of Edication
Nagarjuna University,
Guntur 522006 (India)

Acknowledgements

We are thankful to the United Nations and its various commissions, agencies, divisions and departments, the UNESCO, Paris, the UNESCO Institute for Education, Hamburg, the United Nations Centre for Human Rights, Geneva, the UNESCO, Dakar, the International Institute for Population Sciences, Bombay, the Organisation of African Unity; and the United Nations Information Centre, New Delhi for extending their kind cooperation in providing us with the necessary material on our request for the preparation of this International Encyclopaedia of Women.

Volume 1 of the Encyclopaedia contains the material taken from *The World's Women 1995: Trends and Statistics*, United Nations. We thank Prof. Ann Marie Erb-Leoncavallo, Associate Information Officer, Department of Public Information, United Nations, New York for sending the above cited material along with some other valuable documents with the necessary permission to cite material with due credit.

Volume 2 contains the material obtained from Carolyn Medel-Anonueva, ed., *Women, Education and Empowerment: Pathways Towards Autonomy*, UNESCO Institute for Education, Carolyn Medel-Anonueva, ed, *Women Reading the World: Policies and Practices of Literacy in Asia*, UNESCO Institute for Education, Namtip Aksornkool, *Daughters of the Earth,* UNESCO; Cynthia Guttman, *In Our Own Hands,* UNESCO; *The African Conference on the Empowerment of Women through Functional literacy and the Education of the Girl Child*, Kampala: We thank Prof. Cendrine Sebastiani, Publications Department, UNESCO Institute for Education; Prof. Francoise Pinzon, Global Action Programme on Education For All, UNESCO; The Organisers of the African conference on the Empowerment of Women for sending the material for use in our work.

Volume 3 contains the material obtained from *Worldwide Facts and Statistics About the Status of Women,* Committee for the '95 World conference on Women, *Women: Challenges to the Year 2000*, United Nations; *Fourth World Conference on Women, The Advancement of*

Women: Notes for Speakers, United Nations, etc. We are thankful to the concerned Personnel of United Nations Department of Public Information, New York, United Nations Information Centre, New Delhi; Committee for the '95 World Conference on Women, New York; and East- West centre, Honolulu for their kind material support.

Volume 4 contains the material obtained from International Institute for Population Science, *National Family Health Survey (MCH and Family Planning) India, 1992-93*, IIPS. We are thankful to the IIPS, Bombay, Government of India; East-West Centre, and Population Research Centres in India for their valuable cooperation.

Volume 5 contains the material taken from *The International Bill of Human Rights*, United Nations, *Discrimination Against Women: The Convention and The Committee*, UN Centre for Human Rights, Geneva, *Harmful Traditional Practices Affecting the Health of Women and Children*, UN Centre for Human Rights, *The Nairobi Foreword-Looking Strategies for the Advancement of Women*, United Nations (as adopted by the World Conference to Review and Appraise the Achievements of the United Nations Decade for Women: Equality, Development and Peace, Nairobi, Kenya, 15-16 July 1995), and *The Flatform for Action*, United Nations, We are thankful to the United Nations for using these international instruments on women.

We are also thankful to many scholars, researchers, teachers, administrators and friends working on women around the globe who helped us in gettings the necessary information and material on women to prepare this International Encyclopaedia of Women.

Dr. Digumarti Bhaskara Rao
Ms. Digumarti Pushpa Latha

Overview of the World's Women

Issues of gender equality are moving to the top of the global agenda but better understanding of women's and men's contributions to society is essential to speed the shift from agenda to policy to practice. Too often, women and men live in different worlds—worlds that differ in access to education and work opportunities, and in health, personal security and leisure time. *The World's Women 1995* provides information and analyses to highlight the economic, political and social differences that still separate women's and men's lives and how these differences are changing.

How different are these worlds? Anecdote and misperception abound, in large part because good information has been lacking. As a result, policy has been ill-informed, strategy unfounded and practice unquestioned. Fortunately, this is beginning to change. It is changing because advocates of women's interests have done much in the past 20 years to sharpen people's awareness of the importance of gender concerns. It is changing because this growing awareness has, by raising new questions and rephrasing old, greatly increased the demand for better statistics to inform and focus the debate. And it is changing because women's contributions—and women's rights—have moved to the centre of social and economic change.

The International Conference of Population and Development, held in Cairo in 1994, was a breakthrough. It established a new consensus on two fundamental points:

—Empowering women and improving their status are essential to realizing the full potential of economic, political and social development.

—Empowering women is an important end in itself. And as women acquire the same status, opportunities and social, economic and legal rights as men, as they acquire the right to reproductive health and the right to protection against genderbased violence, human well-being will be enhanced.

The International Conference on Population and Development drew together the many strands of thought and action initiated by two decades of women's conferences. It was also the culmination of an active effort by women's groups to lobby international forums for women's issues. At the United Nations Conference on Environment and Development in Rio de Janeiro in 1992, nongovernmental organizations pushed for understanding the link between women's issues and sustainable development. At the World Conference on Human Rights in Vienna in 1993, women's rights were finally accepted as issues of international human rights.

At the Population Conference and later at the World Summit for Social Development, held in Copenhagen in 1995, the terms of discourse shifted. Not only were women on the agenda—women helped set the agenda. The empowerment of women was not merely the subject of special sessions about women's issues. It was accepted as a crucial element in any strategy seeking to solve social, economic and environmental problems. And building on the advances made in the recognition of women's human rights at the World Conference in Vienna, women's human rights became a focus of the debate in Cairo. The rights approach, advanced by women's groups, was added to the core objectives of development policy and the movement for women's equality.

To promote action on the new consensus, this edition of *The World's Women* builds on the first, presenting statistical summaries of health, schooling, family life, work and public life. Each has to be seen in proper context, however. Yes, there have been important changes in the past 25 years and women have generally made steady progress, but it is impossible to make sweeping global statements. Women's labour force participation rates are up in much of the world, but down in countries wracked by war and economic decline. Girls' education is improving, but there are hundreds of millions of illiterate women and girls who do not complete primary schooling, especially in Africa and southern Asia.

It is also important to look at a range of indicators. Women's political participation may be high in the Nordic countries, but in employment Nordic women still face considerable job segregation and wage discrimination. Women's higher education may be widespread in western Asia, but in many of those countries there are few or no women in important political positions and work opportunities are largely limited to unpaid family about.

It is also important to look at a range of indicators. Women's political participation may be high in the Nordic countries, but in employment Nordic women still face considerable job segregation and wage discrimination. Women's higher education may be widespread in western Asia, but in many of those countries there are few or no women in important political positions and work opportunities are largely limited to unpaid family labour.

The World's Women presents few global figures, focusing instead on country data and regional averages (see the box on regional trends). There are myriad differences among countries in every field and *The World's Women* tries to find a meaningful balance between detailed country statements and broad generalization. Generalizations are primarily drawn at the regional and subregional levels where there is a high degree of uniformity among countries. For all the topics covered, *The World's Women* has tapped as many statistical sources as possible, with detailed references as a basis for further study. Specialized studies are used when they encompass several countries, preferably in more than one region, so as to avoid presenting conclusions relevant in only one country.

Indicators relevant to specific age groups are crucial to understanding women's situation. The Programme of Action of the International Conference on Population and Development identified equality for the girl-child as a necessary first step in ensuring that women realize their full potential and become equal partners with men. This edition of *The World's Women* responds to this concern by highlighting the experience of the girl-child. Evidence of prenatal sex selection and differences in mortality, health, school enrolment and even work indicates that girls and boys are not treated equally.

The experience of the elderly is more difficult to describe from the few available data. Although elderly people constitute a valuable component of societies' human resources, data on the elderly are insufficient for regional generalizations. Considering that the number of elderly are growing rapidly in all regions, this gap needs to be addressed.

Regional trends

Latin America and the Caribbean

* Fertility has declined significantly—dropping 40 per cent or more over the past two decades in 13 of the region's 33 countries. The total fertility rate has fallen from 4.8 to 3.2. But adolescent fertility remains high—13 per cent of all births are to mothers below age 20. In Central America, 18 per cent.

* Maternal mortality has declined in most countries of Latin America but the incidence of unsafe abortion in South America is the highest in the world.

* Literacy has reached 85 per cent or more across most of the region, and girls outnumber boys at both secondary and tertiary levels of education.

* Latin America's recorded labour force participation rate for women (34 per cent) is low, but in the Caribbean it is much higher (49 per cent).

* Latin America's and the Caribbean are as urbanized as the developed regions, with 74 per cent of the population in urban areas. But the rate of growth is much higher—2.5 per cent a year compared with 0.9 per cent—which strains housing, water and sanitation and other infrastructure.

Sub-Saharan Africa

* Minimal progress is seen in the basic social and economic indicators. Health and education gains have faltered in the face of economic crises and civil strife. Literacy remains the lowest in the world, 43 per cent of adult women and 67 per cent of adult men, and the difference between women's and men's literacy rates is the highest.

* Fertility is the highest in the world at about six children per woman.

* Women's labour force participation has dropped throughout the past two decades—the onlv region where this occurred.

* Urban areas are growing at a rate of 5 per cent a year, but with new housing and economic growth at a standstill, many live in poverty and squalor. Africa's urban migrants are predominantly male, shifting the sex ratio in rural areas to 106 women per 100 men.

* Estimated HIV infection rates continue to soar, and unlike any other region, the per centage of women infected with HIV is estimated to be as high if not higher than the per centage of men. In Uganda and in Zambia, the life expectancy of both women and men has already declined because of the disease, and eight other countries are beginning to see similar effects.

Northern Africa and western Asia

* In the past two decades, many countries in the region have invested in girl's education—bringing the primary -secondary enrolment ratio for girls to 67 in northern Africa (from 50 in 1970) and 84 in western Asia, and raising women's literacy to 44 per cent in the region. But women's illiteracy in northern Africa remains high, and girls' enrolment still lags behind boys."

* Women are entering the labour force in increasing number—up from 8 per cent in 1970 to 21 in 1990 in northern Africa and from 22 to 30 per cent in western Asia. Still, these numbers are the lowest in the world. Also low is women's share of decision-making positions in government and business.

* Marriage among girls aged 15--19 has declined significantly in northern Africa and to a lesser degree in western Asia-—from 38 per

cent to 10 per cent in northern Africa and from 24 per cent to 17 per cent western Asia. Teenage fertility, however, remains fairly high.

* Fertility—which was traditionally high—has declined significantly in the past 20 years, especially in northern Africa. It remains high (with total fertility rates over 5) in several countries in western Asia. These countries also have low female literacy.

Southern Asia

* Many health and education indicators remain low. Although it has risen by 10 years in the past two decades, life expectancy remains lower in southern Asia than in any other region but sub-Saharan Africa—58 for both women and men. Equal life expectancies are also exceptional—in all other regions, women have an advantage of several years.

* One in 35 women dies of pregnancy-related complications. Maternal mortality has declined but still remains high.

* Nearly two thirds of adult women are illiterate and the per centage of girls enrolled in primary and secondary levels of schooling is far below all other regions except sub-Saharan Africa.

* Women continue to marry early—41 per cent of girls aged 15-19 are already married—and adolescent fertility remains high.

* More women are counted in the labour force but most are still relegated to unpaid family labour or low-paying jobs. Although women's representation at the highest levels of government is generally weakest in Asia, four of the world's 10 current women heads of state or government hold office in this region.

Eastern and South-eastern Asia

* Development indicators continue to improve. Infant mortality has declined significantly in south-eastern Asia in the past two decades.

* Literacy is nearly universal in most countries for men but not for women. However, girls and boys now have nearly equal access to primary and secondary education.

* Adolescent marriage rates in eastern Asia are the lowest in the world—only 2 per cent of women and less than 1 per cent of men aged 15-19 are married—and household size is shrinking.

* Eastern Asia reports the largest average decline in fertility, from 4.7 to 2.3, and its contraceptive use now exceeds that of developed regions. Fertility has also declined in south-eastern Asia, but is still generally higher than in eastern Asia.

* Women's participation in the labour force is as high as in developed regions—approximately 55 per cent.

Developed regions

* Basic health and education indicators generally indicate high levels of well-being but in eastern Europe some show signs of deterioration. Currently, women in 13 countries have a life expectancy of 80 years of more and 11 more countries are expected to reach that level after the year 2000. Men's life expectancy has increased little during the past two decades in eastern Europe, however, partly due to a rise in death rates for middle--aged men. Women's life expectancy in eastern Europe has increased much less than in other regions.

* Fertility continues to fail—from 2.3 in 1975 to 1.9 in 1995. But teenage pregnancy is relatively high in some countries—Bulgaria, the Republic of Moldova, Ukraine and the United States.

* Traditional family structure and size are changing. People are marrying later or not at all, and marriages are less stable. Remarriage rates have dropped—especially for women—and single parent families now make up 10—25 per cent of all families. The population is ageing and becoming increasingly female as it does.

* Women's labour force participation increased significantly for regions outside of eastern Europe from 38 per cent in 1970 to 52 per cent in 1990. In eastern Europe, where women's labour force participation was already 56 per cent in 1970, the increase was small (to 58 per cent).

* Women continue to earn less than men—in manufacturing, women's average wage is three quarters that of men's. And women and men tend to work in different jobs—women in clerical, sales and services, and men in production and transport. And men commonly do work which is accorded higher pay and status. For example, the majority of school administrators are men while most teachers are women, and the majority of hospital consultants are men while most nurses are women.

* Women work longer hours than men in the majority of these countries—at least 2 hours longer than men do in 13 out of 21 countries studied. Much of the unpaid work is done by women—for example, women contribute roughly three quarters of total child care at home.

Education for empowerment

In the Programme of Action of the International Conference on Population and Development, education is considered one of the most important means to empower women with the knowledge, skills and self—confidence necessary to participate fully in development processes. Educated women marry later, want fewer children, are more likely to use effective methods of contraception and have greater means to improve their economic livelihood.

Through widespread promotion of universal primary education, literacy rates for women have increased over the past few decades—to at least 75 per cent in most countries of Latin America and the Caribbean and eastern and south—eastern Asia. But high rates of illiteracy among women still prevail in much of Africa and in parts of Asia. And when illiteracy is high it almost always is accompanied by large differences in rates between women and men.

At intermediate levels of education, girls have made progress in their enrolment in school through the second level. The primary—secondary enrolment ratio is now about equal for girls and boys in the developed regions and Latin America and the Caribbean and is approaching near equality in eastern, south—eastern and western Asia. But progress in many countries was reversed in the 1980s, particularly among those experiencing problems of war, economic adjustment and declining international assistance—as in Africa, Latin America and the Caribbean, and eastern Europe.

In higher education enrolments, women equal or exceed men in many regions. They outnumber men in the developed regions outside western Europe, in Latin America and the Caribbean and western Asia. Women are not as well represented in other regions, and in sub—Saharan Africa and southern Asia they are far behind—30 and 38 women per 100 men.

The Framework for Action to implement the World Declaration on Education for All states that it is urgent to improve access to education for girls and women—and to remove every obstacle that hampers their active participation. Priority actions include eliminating the social and cultural barriers the discourage—or even exclude—girls and women from the benefits of regular education programmes.

Seeking influence

Despite progress in women's higher education, major obstacles still arise when women strive to translate their high—level education into social and economic advancement. In the world of business, for example, women rarely account for more than 1 to 2 per cent of top executive positions. In the more general category of administration and management including middle levels, women's share rose in every region but one between 1980 and 1990. Women's participation jumped from 16 to 33 per cent in developed regions outside Europe. In Latin America, it rose from 18 to 25 per cent.

In the health and teaching professions—two of the largest occupational fields requiring advanced training—women are well represented in many countries but usually at the bottom levels of the status and wage hierarchy.

Similarly, among the staff of an international group of agriculture research institutes, women's participation at the non—scientific and trainee levels is moderate, but there are few women at management and senior scientific levels.

The information people receive through news papers, radio and television shapes their opinions about the world. And the more decision—making positions women hold in the media, the more they can influence output—breaking stereotypes that hurt women, attracting greater attention to issues of equality in the home and in public life, and providing young women with new images, ideas and ideals. Women now make up more than half of the communications students in a large number of countries and are increasingly visible as presenters, announcers and reporters, but they remain poorly represented in the more influential media occupations such as programme managers and senior editors.

In the top levels of government, women's participation remains the exception. At the end of 1994 only 10 women were heads of state or government; of these 10 countries only Norway had as many as one third women ministers or subministers. Some progress has been made in the appointment of women to ministerial or subministerial positions but these positions are usually tenuous for them. Most countries with women in top ministerial positions do not have comparable representation at the subministerial level. And in other countries, where significant numbers of women have reached the subministerial levels, very few have reached the top. Progress for women in parliaments has also been mixed and varies widely among regions. It is strongest in northern Europe, where it appears to be rising steadily.

Missing from this summary is women's remarkable advance in less traditional paths to power and influence. The importance of the United Nations Decade for Women and international women's conferences should not be underestimated, for these forums enabled women to develop the skills required for exercising power and influence, to mobilize resources and articulate issues and to practise organizing, lobbying and legislating. Excluded from most political offices, many women have found a voice in non—governmental organizations (NGOs) at the grass roots, national and international levels. NGOs have taken issues previously ignored— such as violence against women and rights to reproductive health—and brought them into the mainstream policy debate.

Since the women's conference in Nairobi in 1985, many grass—roots groups have been working to create new awareness of women's rights, including their rights within the family, and to help women achieve those rights. They have set agendas and carved out a space for women's issues.

And as seen in recent United Nations conferences, NGOs as a group can wield influence broad enough to be active partners With governments in deciding national policies and programmes.

Reproductive health-reproductive freedom

With greater access to education, employment and contraception, many women are choosing to marry later and have fewer children. Those who wait to marry and begin child—bearing have better access to education and greater opportunities to improve their lives. Women's increased access to education, to employment and to contraception, coupled with declining rates of infant mortality, have contributed to the worldwide decline in fertility.

The number of children women bear in developed regions is now below replacement levels at 1.9 per women. In Latin America and in most parts of Asia it has also dropped significantly. But in Africa women still have an average of six children and in many sub—Saharan African countries women have as many or more children now than they did 20 years ago.

Adolescent fertility has declined in many developing and developed countries over the past 20 years. In Central America and sub—Saharan Africa, however, rates are five to seven times higher than in developed regions. Inadequate nutrition, anaemia and early pregnancies threaten the health and life of young girls and adolescents.

Too many women lack access to reproductive health services. In developing countries maternal mortality is a leading cause of death for women of reproductive age. WHO estimates that more than half a million women die each year in childbirth and millions more develop pregnancy—related health complications. The deteriorating economic and health conditions in sub—Saharan Africa led to an increase in maternal mortality during the 1980s, where it remains the highest in the world. An African woman's lifetime risk of dying from pregnancy-related causes is 1 in 23, while a North American woman's is 1 in 4,000. Maternal mortality also increased in some countries of eastern Europe.

Pregnancy and childbirth have become safer for women in most of Asia and in parts of Latin America. In developed countries attended delivery is almost universal, but in developing countries only 55 per cent of births take place with a trained attendant and only 37 per cent in hospitals or clinics. Today new importance is being placed on women's reproductive health and safe motherhood as advocates work to redefine reproductive health as an issue of human rights.

The Programme of Action of the International Conference on Population and Development set forth a new framework to guide government actions in population, development and reproductive health—and to measure and evaluate programmes designed to realize these objectives. Instead of the traditional approach centered on family planning and population policy objectives, governments are encouraged to develop client—centered management information systems in population and development and particularly reproductive health, including family planning and sexual health programmes.

Fewer marriages—smaller households

Rapid population changes, combined with many other social and economic changes, are being accompanied by considerable changes in women's household and family status. Most people still marry but they marry later in life, especially women. In developing regions, consensual unions and other non-formal unions remain prevalent, especially in rural areas.

As a result of these changes, many women— many more women than men—spend a significant part of their life without a partner, with important consequences for their economic welfare and their children's.

In developed regions, marriage has become both less frequent and less stable, and cohabitations is on the rise. Marriages preceded by a period of cohabitations have clearly increased in many countries of northern Europe. And where divorce once led quickly to remarriage, many postpone marriage or never remarry.

Since men have higher rates of remarriage, marry at an older age, and have a shorter life expectancy, most older men are married, while many older women are widows. Among women 60 and older, widowhood is significant everywhere—from 40 per cent in the developed regions and Latin America to 50 per cent in Africa and Asia. Moreover, in Asia and Africa, widowhood also affects many women at younger ages.

Between 1970 and 1990 household size decreased significantly in the developed regions, in Latin America and the Caribbean and in eastern and south—eastern Asia. Households are the smallest in developed regions, having declined to an average of 2.8 persons per household in 1990. In eastern Asia the average household size has declined to 3.7, in south—eastern Asia to 4.9. In Latin American countries the average fell to 4.7 persons per household, and in the Caribbean to 4.1. In northern African countries household size increased on average from 5.4 to 5.7.

In developed countries the decline in the average household size reflects an increase in the number of one—person households, especially among unmarried adults and the elderly. In developing regions the size of the household is more affected by the number of children, although a shift from extended households to nuclear households also has some effect.

Household size remains high in countries where fertility has not yet fallen significantly—for instance, in some of the African and western Asian countries.

Work—paid and unpaid

Women's access to paid work is crucial to their self—reliance and the economic well—being of dependent family members. But access to such work is unequal between women and men. Women work in different occupations than men, almost always with lower status and pay.

In developing countries many women work as unpaid family labourers in subsistence agriculture and household enterprises. Many women also work in the informal sector, where their remuneration is unstable, and their access to funds to improve their productivity is limited at best. And whatever other work women do, they also have the major responsibility for most household work, including the care of children and other family members.

The work women do contributes substantially to the well—being of families, communities and nations. But work in the household—even when it is economic—is inadequately measured, and this subverts policies for the credit, income and security of women and their families.

Over the past two decades, women's reported economic activity rates increased in all regions except sub—Saharan Africa and eastern Asia, and all of these increases are large except in eastern Europe, central Asia and Ocean. In fact, women's labour force participation increased more in the 1980s than in the 1970s in many regions. In contrast, men's economic activity rates have declined everywhere except central Asia.

The decline in women's reported labour force participation in sub—Saharan Africa stands out as an exception—dropping from a high of 57 per cent in 1970 to 54 per cent in 1980 to 53 per cent in 1990.

In 1990 the average labour force participation rate among women aged 15 and over ranged from a high of 56—58 per cent in eastern and central Asia and eastern Europe to a low in northern Africa of 21 per cent. The participation rates of men vary within a more limited range of 72—83 per cent. Because so many women in developing countries work in agriculture and informal household enterprises where their contributions are underreported, their recorded rates of economic activity should be higher in many cases. The estimated increase in southern Asia—from 25 per cent of women economically active in 1970 to 44 per cent in 1990—may be due largely to changes in the statistical methods used rather than to significant changes in work patterns.

Although work in subsistence production is crucial to survival, it goes largely underreported in population and agricultural surveys and censuses.

Most of the food eaten in agricultural households in developing countries is produced within the family holding, much of it by women. Some data show the extent of women's unreported work in agriculture. In Bangladesh, India and Pakistan, government surveys using methods to improve the measurement of subsistence work, report that more than half of rural women engage in such activities as tending poultry or cattle, planting rice, drying seeds, collecting water and preparing dung cakes for fuel. Direct observation of women's activities suggests that almost all women in rural areas contribute economically in one way or another.

The informal sector—working on own -account and in small family enterprises—also provides women with important opportunities in areas where salaried employment is closed or inadequate. In five of the six African countries studied by the Statistical Division of the United Nations Secretariat, more than one third of women economically active outside agriculture work in the informal sector, and in seven countries of Latin America 15-20 per cent. In nine countries in Asia the numbers vary—from less than 10 per cent of economically active women in western Asia to 41 per cent in the Republic of Korea and 65 per cent in Indonesia.

Although fewer women than men participate in the labour force, in some countries—including Honduras, Jamaica and Zambia—more women than men make up the informal sector labour force. In several other countries, women make up 40 per cent or more of the informal sector

In addition to the invisibility of many of women's economic activities, women remain responsible for most housework, which also goes unmeasured by the System of National Accounts. But time—use data for many developed countries show almost everywhere that women work at least as many hours each week as men, and in a large number of countries they work at least two hours more than men. Further, the daily time a man spends on work tends to be the same throughout his working life. But a woman's working time fluctuates widely and at times is extremely heavy—the result of combining paid work, household and child—care responsibilities.

Two thirds to three quarters of household work in developed regions is performed by women. In most countries studied, women spend 30 hours or more on housework each week while men spend around 10 hours. Among household tasks, the division of labour remains clear and definite in most countries. Few men do the laundry, clean the house, make the beds, iron the clothes. And most women do little household repair and maintenance. Even when employed outside the home, women do most of the housework.

Efforts to generate better statistics

The first world conference on women in Mexico in 1975 recognized the importance of improving statistics on women. Until the early 1980s women's advocates and women's offices were the main forces behind this work. Big efforts had not yet been launched in statistical offices—either nationally or internationally.

The collaboration of the Statistical Division of the United Nations Secretariat with the International Research and Training Institute for the Advancement of Women (INSTRAW) —beginning in 1982—on a training programme to promote dialogue and understanding between policy makers and statisticians, laid the groundwork for a comprehensive programme of work.

By the time of the world conference in Nairobi in 1985 some progress was evident. The Statistical Division compiled 39 key statistical indicators on the situation of women for 172 countries, and important efforts at the national level included the preparation of *Women and Men* in Sweden, first published in 1984 and with sales of 100,000.

Since Nairobi numerous developments have stregthened and given new momentum to this work. The general approach in development strategy has moved from women in development to gender and development. The focus has shifted from women in isolation to women in relation to men—to the roles each has, the relationships between them and different impacts of policies and programmes.

In statistics the focus has likewise moved from attention to women's statistics to gender statistics. There now is a recognition, for example, that biases in statistics apply not only to women but also to men—in their roles as husbands and fathers and in their roles in the household. That recognition reaches beyonds the disaggregation of data by sex to assessing statistical systems in terms of gender. It asks:

—Do the topics investigated on statistics and the concepts and definitions used in data collection reflect the diversities of women's and men's lives?

—Will the methods used in collecting data take into account stereotypes and cultural factors that might produce bias?

—Are the ways data are compiled and presented well suited to the needs of policy makers, planners and others who need such data?

The first World's Women: Trends and Statistics, issued in 1991, presented the most comprehensive and authoritative compilations of global indicators on the status of women ever available. The book's data have informed debates at international conferences and national policy meetings and provided a resource to the press and others. Its publication greatly contributed to the understanding of data users and created, for the first time, a substantial global audience for statistical genderbased information. This audience has demanded, in turn, more and better data. The book also stimulated more work on the compilation of statistics and led to The World's Women 1995 being prepared as an official conference document for the Fourth World Conference on Women in Beijing in 1995.

As gender issues receive greater priority in the work programmes of international organizations, support to the Statistical Division of the United Nations Secretariat and to national efforts to improve this work have gathered strength at UNFPA, UNICEF, UNDP, WFP, UNIFEM and INSTRAW, among others, ILO, FAO, WHO, UNESCO and UNHCR are also rethinking statistical recommendations and guidelines in their work to better understand women's activities and situations, and products of this change are evident in The World's Women 1995.

The World's Women 1995 shows considerable development in the statistics available on women and men—and in ways of presenting them effectively. But it also points to important needs for new work—to be addressed in the Platform for Action of the Fourth World Conference on Women. Some problems identified by the first world conference—such as the measurement of women's economic contribution and the definition of the concepts of household and household head—are still unresolved. But significant improvements have been made in many areas. Data users know much more today than 20 years ago about how women's and men's situations differ in social, political and economic life. And consumers of data are also asking many more questions that are increasing the demand for more refined statistics. Still other areas not commonly addressed in the regular production of official statistics have only begun to be explored: the male role in the family, women in poverty and women's human rights, including violence against women.

Important in today's more in-depth approach are:

—Identification of the data needed to understand the disparities in the situation, contributions and problems of women and men.

—Evaluation of existing concept and methods against today's changed realities.

—Development of new concepts and methods to yield unbiased data.

—The preparation of statistics in formats easily accessible to a wide array of users.

None of this is easy—or without cost. Every step requires considerable efforts and expertise. All require integrated approaches that pull together today's often fragmented, specialized efforts and take a fresh look at methods and priorities—in, say, education, employment, criminal justice, business, credit and training. All require a broader, more integrated treatment of social and economic data. And all require special efforts to improve international comparability. But required above all—for true national, regional and global assessments of the social, political and economic lives of women and men—is agreement on what the key issues are and support for how to address them.

The objectives is always to produce timely statistics on women and men that can inform policy, refine strategy and influence practice. After two decades of efforts, improved gender statistics are doing much to inform policy debate and implementation. But to proved truly effective monitoring at all leaves requires continuity and reinforcing the dialogue between statisticians and the consumers of statistics—policy makers, researchers, advocates and the media.

1

Women at A Glance

Few causes promoted by the United Nations have generated more intense and widespread support than the campaign to promote and protect the equal rights of women. The Charter of the United Nations was the first international agreement to proclaim gender equality as a fundamental human right. Over the years the Organization has helped create an historic legacy of internationally agreed strategies, standards, programmes and goals to advance the status of women worldwide. While progress has been achieved, as the following statistics indicate, much work remains to be done.

Status of Women

- Women have not achieved equality with men in any country.
- Of the world's 1.3 billion poor people, it is estimated that nearly 70 per cent are women.
- Between 75 and 80 per cent of the world's 27 million refugees are women and children.
- Women's life expectancy, educational attainment and income are highest in Sweden, Canada, Norway, USA and Finland.
- The Fourth World Conference on Women, held in Beijing, China from 4-15 September 1995, resulted in agreement by 189 delegations on a five-year plan to enhance the social, economic and political empowerment of women, improve their health, advance their education and promote their reproductive rights.
- Over 100 countries have announced new initiatives to further the advancement of women as a result of the Beijing Women's Conference.
- The 1979 UN Convention on the Elimination of All Forms of Discrimination against Women, often described as a Bill of Rights for Women, has now been ratified by 154 countries.

Political Participation

- The first country to grant women the right to vote was New Zealand in 1893.
- Only 24 women have been elected heads of state or government in the century.
- Women hold 10.5 per cent of the seats in the world's parliaments.
- In early 1995, Sweden formed the world's first cabinet to have equal numbers of men and women.
- Of the 185 highest-ranking diplomats to the United Nations, seven are women.
- The percentage of female cabinet ministers worldwide has doubled in the last decade, from 3.4 in 1987 to 6.8 per cent in 1996.

Women and Education

- Of the world's nearly one billion illiterate adults, two-thirds are women
- Two-thirds of the 130 million children worldwide who are not in school are girls.
- During the past two decades the combined primary and secondary enrollment ratio for girls in developing countries increased from 38 per cent to 78 per cent.

Women and the Economy

- The majority of women earn on average about three-fourths of the pay of males for the same work, outside of the agricultural sector, in both developed and developing countries.
- In most countries, women work approximately twice the unpaid time men do.
- Women make up 31 per cent of the official labour force in developing countries and 46.7 per cent worldwide.
- Rural women produce more than 55 per cent of all food grown in developing countries.
- The value of women's unpaid housework and community work is estimated at between 10-35 per cent of GDP worldwide, amounting to $ 11 trillion in 1993.
- Women hold 35.1 per cent of professional posts in the United Nations Secretariat including 17.9 per cent in senior management.
- By the year 2000, there will be as many women employees as men in many industrialized nations.

Women and Population

- Women outlive men in almost every country.

- There are slightly fewer women than men in the world— 98.6 women for every 100 men.
- Out-of-marriage births have increased more than 50 per cent in the last 20 years in developed countries.
- One is every four households in the world is now headed by a woman.
- The life expectancy of women has gone up. In 1992, the average woman lived to be 62.9 years in developing countries compared to 53.7 years in 1970. In industrialized countries, women's average life expectancy in 1992 was 79.4 years, up from 74.2 in 1970.
- By 2025, the proportion of women aged 60 or older will almost double in East and South-East Asia, Latin America and the Caribbean, and North Africa.

Women and Health

- Women are becoming increasingly affected by HIV.Today about 42 per cent of estimated cases are women, and the number of infected women is expected to reach 15 million by the year 2000.
- An estimated 20 million unsafe abortions are performed worldwide every year, resulting in the deaths of 70,000 women.
- Approximately 585,000 women die every year, over 1,600 every day, from causes related to pregnancy and childbirth. In sub-Saharan Africa, 1 in 13 women will die from pregnancy or childbirth related causes, compared to 1 in 3,300 women in the United States.
- Globally, 43 per cent of all women and 51 per cent of pregnant women suffer from iron-deficiency anemia.

Women and Violence

- Each year an estimated two million girls suffer the practice of female genital mutilation.
- Worldwide, 20 to 50 per cent of women experience some degree of domestic violence during marriage.
- The primary victims of today's armed conflicts are civilian women and their children, not soldiers.
- The use of rape as a weapon of war has become more evident. In Rwanda from April 1994 to April 1995, estimates of the number of women and girls raped range from 15,700 to over 250,000.
- Rapes during recent conflicts in the former Yugoslavia and Rwanda are being investigated with a view to prosecution by International Tribunals established by the United Nations.

2

Human Rights

Introduction

Five major United Nations legal instruments exists to define and to guarantee the protection of human rights: the Universal Declaration of Human Rights (1984), the International Covenant on Civil Economic, Social and Cultural Rights (1966), the International Covenant on Civil and Political Rights (1966) and the two Operational Protocols to the latter Covenant. The Declaration is a manifesto with primarily moral authority. The Covenants are treaties binding on the States which ratify them. Together they constitute the document known as the International Bill of Human Rights.

Preparation of an International Bill of Rights was a fundamental preoccupation of the United Nations. The Charter of the United Nations, agreed to in San Francisco in 1945, in seven different articles declared United Nations support for human rights and set up a Human Rights Commission. In its first session in January 1946, the General Assembly called for the Commission to work towards "the formulation of an international bill of rights". When the Commission on Human Rights began its work in February 1947, this item was its first priority.

The members of the Commission were immediately divided over whether the Bill should take the form of a proclamation or a treaty. As a compromise, they decided that the Bill should have three parts: a declaration proclaiming general principles, a "covenant or covenants" embodying these principles in a form which would be binding on States which ratified them, and "measures of implementation" or provisions for review of the way in which States carried out their covenant obligations. In less than two years, the Commission sent to its superior bodies, the Economic and Social Council and the General Assembly, a completed draft of a Universal Declaration of Human Rights. On 10 December 1948, the General Assembly adopted the Universal Declaration of Human Rights by a vote of 48 in favour, eight abstentions and no dissensions.

The same day, the Assembly adopted a resolution urging that the Commission continue giving priority to drafting a treaty which would give legal force to the Declaration. In 1951, the Commission produced a draft covenant which it sent to its parent body, the Economic and Social Council. Seeing the difficulties in embodying in one covenant two different categories of rights, the Council urged the General Assembly to approve the drafting of two covenants. The Assembly agreed, and requested the Commission to proceed. The Commission complied and produced two draft covenants—one on economic, social and cultural rights, the other on civil and political rights, the latter with an optional protocol, and providing also for measures of review of implementation of the Covenant provisions. On 16 December 1966, the Assembly voted unanimously to adopt the three instruments and open them for signature. The instruments, after their ratification by 35 United Nations Member States, entered into force in 1976.

On 15 December 1989, by a vote of 59 in favour to 26 against, with 48 abstentions, the General Assembly adopted the Second Optional Protocol to the International Covenant on Civil and Political Rights, aiming at the abolition of the death penalty. This Second Optional Protocol came into force in July 1991.

The UNIVERSAL DECLARATION OF HUMAN RIGHTS is the basic international statement of the inalienable and inviolable rights of all members of the human family. It is intended to serve as "the common standard of achievement for all peoples and all nations" in the effort to secure universal and effective recognition and observance of the rights and freedoms it lists.

The two COVENANTS relating to human rights provide internal protection for specified rights and freedoms. Both Covenants recognize the right of peoples to self-determination. Both have provisions barring all forms of discrimination in the exercise of human rights. Both have the force of law for the countries which ratify them.

The first treaty,the COVENANT ON ECONOMIC, SOCIAL AND CULTURAL RIGHTS, recognizes the right to work and to free choice of employment, to fair wages, to form and join unions, to social security and to adequate standards of living conditions for their people. States reports on their progress in promotion of these rights are reviewed by a committee of experts appointed by the Economic and Social Council.

The COVENANT ON CIVIL AND POLITICAL RIGHTS recognizes the right of every human person to life, liberty and security of person, to privacy, to freedom from cruel, inhuman or degrading treatment and from torture,to freedom from slavery, to immunity from arbitrary arrest, to a fair trial, to recognition as a person before the law, to immunity from retroactive sentences, to freedom of thought, conscience and religion, to freedom of opinion and expression, to liberty of movement, including the right to emigrate, to peaceful assembly and to freedom of association.

The Covenant on Civil and Political Rights sets up a Human Rights Committee to consider progress reports from States which have ratified the Covenant. The Committee may also hear complaints by such States that other States which have ratified the Covenant have failed in upholding the obligations under the Covenant.

Under the OPTIONAL PROTOCOL to the Civil and Political Covenant, individuals under certain circumstances may file complaints of human rights violations by ratifying States.

Under the SECOND OPTIONAL PROTOCOL to the Civil and Political Covenant, States must take all necessary measures to abolish the death penalty.

The Declaration is accepted almost universally as a gauge by which Governments can measure their progress in the protection of human rights. In United Nations organs, the Declaration has an authority surpassed only by the Charter. It is invoked constantly not only in the General Assembly, but also in the Security Council and other organs. It is quoted in international legal instruments, including the Council of Europe's Convention for the Protection of Human Rights and Fundamental Freedoms (1950), the Japanese Peace Treaty (1951), the Special Statute for the status of Trieste (1954), the Constitution of the Organization of African Unity (1963) and the Final Document of the Conference on Security and Co-operation in Europe (1975), signed at Helsinki by 35 States. It is invoked in a score of national constitutions. It has inspired and sometimes become part of many countries' national legislation, and has been cited with approval in national courts.

UNIVERSAL DECLARATION OF HUMAN RIGHTS

Preamble

Whereas recognition of the inherent dignity and of the equal and inalienable rights of all members of the human family is the foundation of freedom, justice and peace in the world,

Whereas disregard and contempt for human rights have resulted in barbarous acts which have outraged the conscience of mankind, and the advent of a world in which human beings shall enjoy freedom of speech and belief and freedom from fear and want has been proclaimed as the highest aspiration of the common people,

Whereas it is essential,if man is not to be compelled to have recourse, as a last resort, to rebellion against tyranny and oppression, that human rights should be protected by the rule of law,

Whereas the it is essential to promote the development of friendly relations between nations,

Whereas the peoples of the United Nations have in the Charter reaffirmed their faith in fundamental human rights, in the dignity and worth of the human person and in the equal rights of men and women and have determined to promote social progress and better standards of life in larger freedom.

Whereas Member States have pledged themselves to achieve, in co-operation with the United Nations, the promotion of universal respect for and observance of human rights and fundamental freedoms,

Whereas a common understanding of these rights and freedoms is of the greatest importance for the full realization of this pledge,

Now, therefore, The General Assembly Proclaims

This Universal Declaration of Human Rights as a common standard of achievement for all peoples and all nations, to the end that every individual and every organ of society, keeping this Declaration constantly in mind, shall strive by teaching and education to promote respect for these rights and freedoms and by progressive measures, national and international, to secure their universal and effective recognition and observance, both among the peoples of Member States themselves and among the peoples of territories under their jurisdiction.

Article 1

All human beings are born free and equal in dignity and rights. They are endowed with reason and conscience and should act towards one another in a spirit of brotherhood.

Article 2

Everyone is entitled to all the rights and freedoms set forth in this Declaration, without distinction of any kind, such as race, colour, sex, language, religion, political or other opinion, national or social origin, property, birth or other status.

Furthermore, no distinction shall be made on the basis of the political, jurisdictional or international status of the country or territory to which a person belongs, whether it be independent, trust, non-self-governing or under any other limitation of sovereignty.

Article 3

Everyone has the right to life, liberty and security of person.

Article 4

No one shall be 4held in slavery or servitude: slavery and the slave trade shall be prohibited in all their forms.

Article 5

No one shall be subjected to torture or to cruel, inhuman or degrading treatment or punishment.

Article 6

Everyone has the right to recognition everywhere as a person before the law.

Article 7

All are equal before the law and are entitled without any discrimination to equal protection of the law. All are entitled to equal protection against any discrimination in violation of this Declaration and against any incitement to such discrimination.

Article 8

Everyone has the right to an effective remedy by the competent national tribunals for acts violating the fundamental rights granted him by the constitution or by law.

Article 9

No one shall be subjected to arbitrary arrest, detention or exile.

Article 10

Everyone is entitled in full equality to a fair and public hearing by an independent and impartial tribunal, in the determination of his rights and obligations and of any criminal charge against him.

Article 11

1. Everyone charged with a penal offence has the right to be presumed innocent until proved guilty according to law in a public trial at which he has had all the guarantees necessary for his defence.
2. No one shall be held guilty of any penal offence on account of any act or omission which did not constitute a penal offence, under na-

tional or international law, at the time when it was committed. Nor shall a heavier penalty be imposed than the one that was applicable at the time the penal offence was committed.

Article 12

No one shall be subjected to arbitrary interference with his privacy, family, home or correspondence, nor to attacks upon his honour and reputation. Everyone has the right to the protection of the law against such interference or attacks.

Article 13

1. Everyone has the right to freedom on movement and residence within the borders of each state.
2. Everyone has the right to leave any country, including his won, and to return to his country.

Article 14

1. Everyone has the right to seek and to enjoy in other countries asylum from persecution.
2. This right may not be invoked in the case of prosecutions genuinely arising from non-political crimes or from acts contrary to the purposes and principles of the United Nations.

Article 15

1. Everyone has the right to a nationality.
2. No one shall be arbitrarily deprived of his nationality nor denied the right to change his nationality.

Article 16

1. Men and women of full age, without any limitation due to race, nationality or religion, have the right to marry and to found a family.
   They are entitled to equal rights as to marriage, during marriage and at its dissolution.
2. Marriage shall be entered into only with the free and full consent of the intending spouses.
3. The family is the natural and fundamental group unit of society and is entitled to protection by society and the State.

Article 17

1. Everyone has the right to own property alone as well as in association with others.
2. No one shall be arbitrarily deprived of his property.

Article 18

Everyone has the right to freedom of thought, conscience and religion: this right includes freedom to change his religion or belief, and freedom, either alone or in community with others and in public or private, to manifest his religion or belief in teaching, practice, worship and observance.

Article 19

Everyone has the right to freedom of opinion and expression; this right includes freedom to hold opinions without interference and to seek, receive and impart information and ideas through any media and regardless of frontiers.

Article 20

1. Everyone has the right to freedom of peaceful assembly and association.
2. No one may be compelled to belong to anssociation.

Article 21

1. Everyone has the right to take part in the government of his country, directly or through freely chosen representatives.
2. Everyone has the right of equal access to public service in his country.
3. The will of the people shall be the basis of the authority of government; this will shall be expressed in periodic and genuine elections which shall be by universal and equal suffrage and shall be held by secret vote or by equivalent free voting procedures.

Article 22

Everyone, as a member of society, has the right to social security and is entitled to realization, through national effort and international cooperation and in accordance with the organization and resources of each State, of the economic, social and cultural rights indispensable for his dignity and the free development of his personality.

Article 23

1. Everyone has the right to work, to free choice of employment, to just and favourable conditions of work and to protection against unemployment.
2. Everyone, without any discrimination, has the right to equal pay for equal work.
3. Everyone who works has the right to just and favourable remunera-

tion ensuring for himself and his family an existence worthy of human dignity, and supplemented, if necessary, by other means of social protection.

4. Everyone has the right to form and to join trade unions for the protection of his interests.

Article 24

Everyone has the right to rest and leisure, including reasonable limitation of working hours and periodic holidays with pay.

Article 25

1. Everyone has the right to a standard of living adequate for the health and well-being of himself and of his family, including food, clothing, housing and medical care and necessary social services, and the right to security in the event of unemployment, sickness, disability, widowhood, old age or other lack of livelihood in circumstances beyond his control.
2. Motherhood and childhood are entitled to special care and assistance. All children, whether born in or out of wedlock, shall enjoy the same social protection.

Article 26

1. Everyone has the right to education. Education shall be free, at least in the elementary and fundamental stages. Elementary education shall be compulsory. Technical and professional education shall be made generally available and higher education shall be equally accessible to all on the basis of merit.
2. Education shall be directed to of the human personality and to the strengthening of respect for human rights and fundamental freedoms. It shall promote understanding, tolerance and friendship among all nations, racial or religious groups, and shall further the activities of the United Nations for the maintenance of peace.
3. Parents have a prior right to choose the kind of education that shall be given to their children.

Article 27

1. Everyone has the right freely to participate in the cultural life of the community, to enjoy the arts and to share in scientific advancement and its benefits.
2. Everyone has the right to the protection of the moral and material interests resulting from any scientific, literary or artistic production of which he is the author.

Article 28

Everyone is entitled to a social and international order in which the rights and freedoms set forth in this Declaration can be fully realized.

Article 29

1. Everyone has duties to the community in which alone the free and full development of his personality is possible.
2. In the exercise of his rights and freedoms, everyone shall be subject only to such limitations as are determined by law solely for the purpose of securing due recognition and respect for the rights and freedoms of others and of meeting the just requirements of morality, public order and the general welfare in a democratic society.
3. These rights and freedoms welfare may in no case be exercised contrary to the purposes and principles of the United Nations.

Article 30

Nothing in this Declaration may be interpreted as implying for any State, group or person any right to engage in any activity or to perform any act aimed at the destruction of any of the rights and freedoms set forth herein.

INTERNATIONAL COVENANT ON ECONOMIC, SOCIAL AND CULTURAL RIGHTS

Preamble

The States Parties to The Present Covenant

Considering that, in accordance with the principles proclaimed in the Charter of the United Nations, recognition of the inherent dignity and of the equal and inalienable rights of all members of the human family is the foundation of freedom,justice and peace in the world,

Recognizing that these rights derive from the inherent dignity of the human person.

Recognizing that, in accordance with the Universal Declaration of Human Rights, the ideal of free human beings enjoying freedom from fear and want can only be achieved if conditions are created whereby everyone may enjoy his economic, social and cultural rights, as well as his civil and political rights,

Considering the obligation of States under the Charter of the United Nations to promote universal respect for, and observance of, human rights and freedoms,

Realizing that the individual, having duties to other individuals and to the community to which be belongs, is under a responsibility to strive for the promotion and observance of the rights recognized in the present Covenant,

Agree upon the following articles:

PART 1

Article 1

1. All peoples have the right of self-determination. By virtue of that right they freely determine their political status and freely pursue their economic, social and cultural development.
2. All peoples may, for their own ends, freely dispose of their natural wealth and resources without prejudice to any obligations arising out of international economic co-operation, based upon the principle of mutual benefit, and international law. In no case may a people be deprived of its own means of subsistence.
3. The States Parties to the present Covenant, including those having responsibility for the administration of Non-Self-Governing and Trust Territories, shall promote the realization of the right of self determination, and shall respect that right, in conformity with the provisions of the Charter of the United Nations.

PART II

Article 2

1. Each State Party to the present Covenant undertakes to take steps, individually and through international assistance and co-opearation, especially economic and technical, to the maximum of its available resources, with a view to achieving progressively the full realization of the rights recognized in the present Covenant by all appropriate means, including particularly the adoption of legislative measures.
2. The States Parties to the present Covenant undertake to guarantee that the rights enunciated in the present Covenant will be exercised without discrimination of any kind as to race, colour, sex, language, religion, political or other opinion, national or social origin, property, birth or other status.
3. Developing countries, with due regard to human rights and their national economy, may determine to what extent they would guarantee the economic rights recognized in the present Covenant to non-nationals.

Article 3

The States Parties to the present Covenant undertake to ensure the equal right of men and women to the enjoyment of all economic, social and cultural rights set forth in the present Covenant.

Article 4

The States Parties to the present Covenant recognize that, in the enjoyment of those rights provided by the State in conformity with the present Covenant, the State may subject such rights only to such limitations as are determined by law only is so far as this may be compatible with the nature of these rights and solely for the purpose of promoting the general welfare in a democratic society.

Article 5

1. Nothing in the present Covenant may be interpreted as implying for any State, group or person any right to engage in any activity or to perform any act aimed at the destruction of any of the rights or freedoms recognized herein, or at their limitation to a greater extent that is provided for in the present Covenant.
2. No restriction upon or derogation from any of the fundamental human rights recognized or existing in any country in virtue of law, conventions, regulations or custom shall be admitted on the pretext that the present Covenant does not recognize such rights or that it recognizes them to a lesser extent.

PART III

Article 6

1. The States Parties to the present Covenant recognize the right to work, which includes the right of everyone to the opportunity to gain his living by work which he freely chooses or accepts, and will take appropriate steps to safeguard this right.
2. The steps to be taken by a State Party to the present Covenant to achieve the full realization of this right shall include technical and vocational guidance and training programmes, policies and techniques to achieve steady economic, social and cultural development and full and productive employment under conditions safeguarding fundamental political and economic freedoms to the individual.

Article 7

The States Parties to the present Covenant recognize the right of everyone to the enjoyment of just and favourable conditions of work which ensure, in particular:

(a) Remuneration which provides all workers, as a minimum, with:
  (i) Fair wages and equal remuneration for work of equal value without distinction of any kind, in particular women being guaranteed conditions of work not inferior to those enjoyed by men, with equal pay for equal work;
  (ii) A decent living for themselves and their families in accordance with the provisions of the present convenant;
(b) Safe and healthy working conditions;
(c) Equal opportunity for everyone to be promoted in his employment to an appropriate higher level, subject to no considerations other than those of seniority and competence;
(d) Rest, leisure and reasonable limitation of working hours and periodic holidays with pay, as well as remuneration for public holidays.

Article 8

1. The States Parties to the present Covenant undertake to ensure:
  (a) The right of everyone to form trade unions and join the trade union of his choice, subject only to the rules of the organization concerned, for the promotion and protection of his economic and social interests. No restrictions may be placed on the exercise of this right other than those prescribed by law and which are necessary in a democratic society in the interests of national security or public order or for the protection of the rights and freedoms of others;
  (b) The right of trade unions to establish national federations or confederations and the right of the latter to form or join international trade-union organizations;
  (c) The right of trade unions to function freely subject to no limitations other than those prescribed by law and which are necessary in a democratic society in the interests of national security or public order or for the protection of the rights and freedoms of others;
  (d) The right to strike, provided that it is exercised in conformity with the laws of the particular country.
2. This article shall not prevent the imposition of lawful restrictions on the exercise of these rights by members of the armed forces or of the police or of the administration of the State.
3. Nothing in this article shall authorize State Parties to the International Labour Organisation Convention of 1948 concerning Freedom of Association and Protection of the Right to Organize to take legislative measures which would prejudice, or apply the law in such

a manner as would prejudice, the guarantees provided for in that Convention.

Article 9

The States Parties to the present convenient recognize the right of everyone to social security, including social insurance.

Article 10

The States Parties to the present Convenant recognize that:

1. The widest possible protection and assistance should be accorded to the family, which is the natural and fundamental group unit of society,particularly for its establishment and while it is responsible for the care and education of dependent children. Marriage must be entered into with the free consent of the intending spouses.
2. Special protection should be accorded to mothers during a reasonable period before and after childbirth. During such period working mothers should be accorded paid leave or leave with adequate social security benefits.
3. Special measures of protection and assistance should be taken on behalf of all children and young persons without any discrimination for reasons of parentage or other conditions. Children and young persons should be protected from economic and social exploitation. Their employment in work harmful to their morals or health or dangerous to life or likely to hamper their normal development should be punishable by law. States should also set age limits below which the paid employment of child labour should be prohibited and punishable by law.

Article 11

1. The States Parties to the present Covenant recognize the right of everyone to an adequate standard of living for himself and his family, including adequate food, clothing and housing, and to the continuous improvement of living conditions. The States Parties will take appropriate steps to ensure the realization of this right, recognizing to this effect the essential importance of international co-operation based on free consent.
2. The States Parties to the present Covenant, recognizing the fundamental right of everyone to be free from hunger, shall take, individually and through international co-operation, the measures, including specific programmes, which are needed:
   (a) To improve methods of production, conservation and distribution of food by making full use of technical and scientific knowl-

edge, by disseminating knowledge of the principles of nutrition and by developing or reforming agrarian systems in such a way as to achieve the most efficient development and utilization of natural resources;

(b) Taking into account the problems of both food-importing and food-exporting countries, to ensure an equitable distribution of world food supplies in relation to need.

Article 12

1. The States Parties to the present Covenant recognize the right of everyone to the enjoyment of the highest attainable standard of physical and mental health.
2. The steps to be taken by the States Parties to the present Covenant to achieve the full realization of this shall include those necessary for:
   (a) The provision for the reduction of the stillbirth-rate and of infant mortality and for the healthy development of the child;
   (b) The improvement of all aspects of environmental and industrial hygiene;
   (c) The prevention, treatment and control of epidemic, endemic, occupational and other diseases;
   (d) The creation of conditions which would assure to all medical service and medical attention in the event of sickness.

Article 13

1. The States Parties to the present Covenant recognize the right of everyone to education. They agree that education shall be directed to the full development of the human personality and the sense of its dignity, and shall strengthen the respect for human rights and fundamental freedoms. They further agree that education shall enable all persons to participate effectively in a free society, promote understanding, tolerance and friendship among all nations and all racial, ethnic or religious groups, and further the activities of the United Nations for the maintenance of peace.
2. The States Parties to the present Covenant recognize that, with a view to achieving the full realization of this right:
   (a) Primary education shall be compulsory and available free to all;
   (b) Secondary education in its different forms, including technical and vocational secondary education, shall be made generally available and accessible to all be every appropriate means, and in particular by the progressive introduction of free education;
   (c) Higher education shall be made equally accessible to all,on the

basis of capacity, by every appropriate means, and in particular by the progressive introduction of free education;

(d) Fundamental education shall be encouraged or intensified as far as possible for those persons who have not received or completed the whole, period of their primary education;

(e) The development of a system of schools at all levels shall be actively pursued, an adequate fellowship system shall be established, and the material conditions of teaching staff shall be continuously improved.

3. The States Parties to the present Covenant undertake to have respect for the liberty of parents and, when applicable, legal guardians to choose for their children schools, other than those established by the public authorities, which conform to such minimum educational standards as may be laid down or approved by the State and to ensure the religious and moral education of their children in conformity with their won convictions.

4. No part of this article shall be construed so as to interfere with the liberty of individual and bodies to establish and direct educational institutions, subject always to the observance of the principles set forth in paragraph 1 of this article and to the requirement that the education given in such institutions shall conform to such minimum standards as may be laid down by the State.

Article 14

Each State Party to the present Covenant which, at the time of becoming a Party, has not been able to secure in its metropolitan territory or other territories under its jurisdiction compulsory primary education, free of charge, undertakes, within two years, to work out and adopt a detailed plan of action for the progressive implementation, within a reasonable number of years,to be fixed in the plan, of the principle of compulsory education free of charge for all.

Article 15

1. The States Parties to the present Covenant recognize the right of everyone:

(a) To take part in cultural life;

(b) To enjoy the benefits of scientific progress and its applications;

(c) To benefit from the protection of the moral and material interests resulting from any scientific, literary or artistic production of which he is the author.

2. The steps to be taken by the States Parties to the present Covenant to achieve the full realization of this right shall include those neces-

sary for the conservation, the development and the diffusion of science and culture.

3. The States Parties to the present Covenant undertake to respect the freedom indispensable for scientific research and creative activity.
4. The States Parties to the present Covenant recognize the benefits to be derived from the encouragement and development of international contacts and co-operation in the scientific and cultural fields.

PART IV

Article 16

1. The States Parties to the present Covenant undertake to submit in conformity with this part of the Covenant report on the measures which they have adopted and the progress made in achieving the observance of the rights recognized herein.
2.
   (a) All reports shall be submitted to the Secretary-General of the United Nations, who shall transmit copies to the Economic and Social Council for consideration in accordance with the provisions of the present Covenant.

   (b) The Secretary-General of the United Nations shall also transmit to the specialized agencies copies of the reports, or any relevant parts therefrom, from States Parties to the present Covenant which are also members of these specialized agencies in so far as these reports, or parts therefrom, relate to any matters which fall within the responsibilities of the said agencies in accordance with their constitutional instruments.

Article 17

1. The States Parties to the present Covenant shall furnish their reports in stages, in accordance with a programme to be established by the Economic and Social Council within one year of the entry into force of the present Covenant after consultation with the States Parties and the specialized agencies concerned.
2. Reports may indicate factors and difficulties affecting the degree of fulfilment of obligations under the present Covenant.
3. Where relevant information has previously been furnished to the United nations or to any specialized agency by any State Party to the present Covenant, it will not be necessary to reproduce that information, but a precise reference to the information so furnished will suffice.

Article 18

Pursuant to its responsibilities under the Charter of the United Nations in the field of human rights and fundamental freedoms, the Economic and Social Council may make arrangements with the specialized agencies in respect of their reporting to it on the progress made in achieving the observance of the provisions of the present Covenant falling within the scope of their activities. These reports may include particulars of decisions and recommendations on such implementation adopted by their competent organs.

Article 19

The Economic and Social Council may transmit to the Commission on Human Rights for study and general recommendations or, as appropriate, for information the reports concerning human rights submitted by States in accordance with articles 16 and 17, and those concerning human rights submitted by the specialized agencies in accordance with article 18

Article 20

The States Parties to the present Covenant and the specialized agencies concerned may submit comments to the Economic and Social Council on any general recommendation under article 19 or reference to such general recommendation in any report of the Commission on Human Rights or any documentation referred to therein.

Article 21

The Economic and Social Council may submit from time to time to the General Assembly reports with recommendations of a general nature and a summary of the information received from the States Parties to the present Covenant and the specialized agencies on the measures taken and the progress made in achieving general observance of the rights recognized in the present Covenant.

Article 22

The Economic and Social Council may bring to the attention of other organs of the United Nations, their subsidiary organs and specialized agencies concerned with furnishing technical assistance any matters arising out of the reports referred to in this part of the present Covenant which may assist such bodies in deciding, each within its field of competence, on the advisability of international measures likely to contribute to the effective progressive implementation of the present Covenant.

Article 23

The State Parties to the present Covenant agree that international action for the achievement of the rights recognized in the present Covenant includes such methods as the conclusion of conventions, the adoption of recommendations, the furnishing of technical assistance and the holding of regional meetings and technical meetings for the purpose of consultation and study organized in conjunction with the Governments concerned.

Article 24

Noting in the present Covenant shall be interpreted as impairing the provisions of the Charter of the United Nations and of the constitutions of the specialized agencies which define the respective responsibilities of the various organs of the United Nations and of the specialized agencies in regard to the matters dealt with in the present Covenant.

Article 25

Noting in the present Covenant shall be interpreted as impairing the inherent right of all peoples to enjoy and utilize fully and freely their natural wealth and resources.

PART V

Article 26

1. The present Covenant is open for signature by any State Member of the United Nations or member of any of its specialized agencies, by any State Party to the Statute of the International Court of Justice, and by any other State which has been invited by the General Assembly of the United Nations to become a party to the present Covenant.
2. The present Covenant is subject to ratification. Instruments of ratification shall be deposited with the Secretary-General of the United Nations.
3. The present Covenant shall be open to accession by any State referred to in paragraph 1 of this article.
4. Accession shall be effected by the deposit of an instrument of accession with the Secretary-General of the United Nations.
5. The Secretary-General of the United Nations shall inform all States which have signed the present Covenant or acceded to it of the deposit of each instrument of ratification or accession.

Article 27

1. The present Covenant shall enter into force three months after the date of the deposit with the Secretary-General of the United Nations of the thrity-fifth instrument of ratification or instrument of accession. .
2. For each state ratifying the present Covenant or acceding to it after the deposit of the thirty-fifth instrument of ratification or instrument of accession, the present Covenant shall enter into force three months after the date of the deposit of its won instrument of ratification or instrument of accession.

Article 28

The provisions of the present Covenant shall extend to all parts of federal States without any limitations or exceptions.

Article 29

1. Any State Party to the present Covenant may propose an amendment and file it with the Secretary-General of the United Nations. The Secretary-General shall thereupon communicate any proposed amendments to the States Parties to the present Covenant with a request that they notify him whether they favour a conference of States Parties for the purpose of considering and voting upon the proposals. In the event that at least one third of the States Parties favours such a conference, the Secretary-General shall convene the conference under the auspices of the United Nations. Any amendment adopted by a majority of the States Parties present and voting at the conference shall be submitted to the General Assembly of the United Nations for approval.
2. Amendments shall come into force when they have been approved by the General Assembly of the United Nations and accepted by a two-thirds majority of the States Parties to the present Covenant in accordance with their respective constitutional processes.
3. When amendments come into force they shall be binding on those States Parties which have accepted them, other States Parties still being bound by the provisions of the present Covenant and any earlier amendment which they have accepted.

Article 30

Irrespective of the notifications made under article 26, paragraph 5, the Secretary-General of the United Nations shall inform all States referred to in paragraph 1 of the same article of the following particulars:

(a) Signatures, ratifications and accessions under article 26;

(b) The date of the entry into force of the present Covenant under article 27 and the date of the entry into force of any amendments under article 29.

Article 31

1. The present Covenant, of which the Chinese, English, French, Russian and Spanish texts are equally authentic, shall be deposited in the archives of the United Nations.
2. The Secretary-General of the United Nations shall transmit certified copies of the present Covenant to all States referred to in article 26.

INTERNATIONAL COVENANT ON CIVIL AND POLITICAL RIGHTS

Preamble

The States Parties to the Present Covenant

Considering that, in accordance with the principles proclaimed in the Charter of the United Nations, recognition of the inherent dignity and of the equal and inalienable rights of all members of the human family is the foundation of freedom, justice and peace in the world,

Recognizing that these rights derive from the inherent dignity of the human person,

Recognizing that, in accordance with the Universal Declaration of Human Rights, the ideal of free human beings enjoying civil and political freedom and freedom from fear and want can only be achieved if conditions are created whereby everyone may enjoy his civil and political rights, as well as his economic, social and cultural rights,

Considering the obligation of States under the Charter of the United Nations to promote universal respect for, and observance of,human rights and freedoms,

Realizing that the individual, having duties to other individuals and to the community to which he belongs,is under a responsibility to strive for the promotion and observance of the rights recognized in the present Covenant,

Agree upon the following articles:

PART I

Article 1

1. All peoples have the right of self-determinations. By virtue of that

right they freely determine their political status and freely pursue their economic, social and cultural development.

2. All peoples may, for their own ends, freely dispose of their natural wealth and resources without prejudice to any obligations arising out of international economic co-operation, based upon the principle of mutual benefit, and international law. In no case may a people be deprived of its own means of subsistence.
3. The States Parties to the present Covenant,including those having responsibility for the administration of Non-Self-Governing and Trust Territories, shall promote the realization of the right of self-determination, and shall respect that right, in conformity with the provisions of the Charter of the United Nations.

PART II

Article 2

1. Each State Party to the present Covenant undertakes to respect and to ensure to all individuals within its territory and subject to its jurisdiction the rights recognized in the present Covenant, without distinction of any kind, such as race, colour, sex,language, religion, political or other opinion,national or social origin, property, birth or other status.
2. Where not already provided for by existing legislative or other measures, each State Party to the present Covenant undertakes to take the necessary steps, in accordance with its constitutional processes and with the provisions of the present Covenant, to adopt such legislative or other measures as may be necessary to give effect to the rights recognized in the present Covenant.
3. Each State Party to the present Covenant undertakes:
   (a) To ensure that any person whose rights or freedoms as herein recognized are violated shall have an effective remedy, notwithstanding that the violation has been committed by persons acting in an official capacity;
   (b) To ensure that any person claiming such a remedy shall have his right there to determined by competent judicial, administrative or legislative authorities, or by any other competent authority provided for by the legal system of the State, and to develop the possibilities of judicial remedy;
   (c) To ensure that the competent authorities shall enforce such remedies when granted.

Article 3

The States Parties to the present Covenant undertake to ensure the equal right of men and women to the enjoyment of all civil and political rights set forth in the present Covenant.

Article 4

1. In time of public emergency which threatens the life of the nation and the existence of which is officially proclaimed, the States Parties to the present Covenant may take measures derogating from their obligations under the present Covenant to the extent strictly required by the exigencies of the situation, provided that such measures are not inconsistent with their other obligations under international law and do not involve discrimination solely on the ground of race, colour, sex, language, religion or social origin.
2. No derogation from articles 6,7,8 (paragraphs 1 and 2), 11,15,16 and 18 may be made under this provision.
3. Any State Party to the present Covenant availing itself of the right of derogation shall immediately inform the other States Parties to the present Covenant, through the intermediary of the Secretary-General of the United Nations, of the provisions from which it has derogated and of the reasons by which it was actuated. A further communication shall be made, through the same intermediary, on the date on which it terminates such derogation.

Article 5

1. Nothing in the present Covenant may be interpreted as implying for any State, group or person any right to engage in any activity or perform any act aimed at the destruction of any of the rights and freedoms recognized herein or at their limitation to a greater extent than is provided for in the present Covenant.
2. There shall be no restriction upon or derogation from any of the fundamental human rights recognized or existing in any State Party to the present Covenant pursuant to law, conventions, regulations or custom on the pretext that the present Covenant does not recognize such rights or that it recognizes them to a lesser extent.

PART III

Article 6

1. Every human being has the inherent right to life. This right shall be protected by law. No one shall be arbitrarily deprived of his life.
2. In countries which have not abolished the death penalty, sentence of

death may be imposed only for the most serious crimes in accordance with the law in force at the time of the commission of the crime and not contrary to the provisions of the present Covenant and to the Convention on the Prevention and Punishment of the Crime of Genocide. This penalty can only be carried out pursuant to a final judgement rendered by a competent court.

3. When deprivation of life constitutes the crime of genocide, it is understood that nothing in this article shall authorize any State Party to the present Covenant to derogate in any way from any obligation assumed under the provisions of the Convention on the Prevention and Punishment of the Crime of Genocide.
4. Anyone sentenced to death shall have the right to seek pardon or commutation of the sentence. Amnesty, pardon or commutation of the sentence of death may be granted in all cases.
5. Sentence of death may be imposed for crimes committed by persons below eighteen years of age and shall not be carried out on pregnant women.
6. Nothing in this article shall be invoked to delay or to prevent the abolition of capital punishment by any State Party to the present Covenant.

Article 7

No one shall be subjected to torture or to cruel,inhuman or degrading treatment or punishment. In particular, no one shall be subjected without his free consent to medical or scientific experimentation.

Article 8

1. No one shall be held in slavery; slavery and the slave-trade in all their forms shall be prohibited.
2. No one shall be held in servitude.
3. (a) No one shall be required to perform forced or compulsory labour;
   (b) Paragraph 3
   (a) shall not be held to preclude, in countries where imprisonment with hard labour may be imposed as a punishment for a crime, the performance of hard labour in pursuance of a sentence to such punishment by a competent court;

   (c) For the purpose of this paragraph the term "forced or compulsory labour" shall not include:

   (i) Any work or service, not referred to in sub-paragraph (b), normally required of a person who is under detention in consequence of a lawful order of a court, or of a person during conditional release from such detention;

(ii) Any service of a military character and, in countries where conscientious objection is recognized, any national service required by law of conscientious objectors;

(iii) Any service exacted in cases of emergency or calamity threatening the life or well-being of the community;

(iv) Any work or service which forms part of normal civil obligations.

Article 9

1. Everyone has the right to liberty and security of person. No one shall be subjected to arbitrary arrest or detention. No one shall be deprived of his liberty except on such grounds and in accordance with such procedure as are established by law.
2. Anyone who is arrested shall be informed, at the time of arrest, of the reasons for his arrest and shall be promptly informed of any charges against him.
3. Anyone arrested detained on a criminal charge shall be brought promptly before a judge or other officer authorized by law to exercise judicial power and shall be entitled to trial within a reasonable time or to release. It shall not be the general rule that persons awaiting trial shall be detained in custody, but release may be subject to guarantees to appear for trial, at any other stage of the judicial proceedings, and should occasion arise, for execution of the judgment.
4. Anyone who is deprived of his liberty by arrest or detention shall be entitled to take proceedings before a court, in order that court may decide without delay on the lawfulness of his detention and order his release if the detention is not lawful.
5. Anyone who has been the victim of unlawful arrest or detention shall have an enforceable right to compensation.

Article 10

1. All Persons deprived of their liberty shall be treated with humanity and with respect for the inherent dignity of the human person.
2. (a) Accused persons shall, save in exceptional circumstances, be seg regated from convicted persons and shall be subject to separate treatment appropriate to their status as unconvicted persons;

   (b) Accused juvenile persons shall be separated from adults and brought as speedily as possible for adjudication.
3. The penitentiary system shall comprise treatment of prisoners the essential aim of which shall be their reformation and social rehabilitation. juvenile offenders shall be segregated from adults and be accorded treatment appropriate to their age and legal status.

Article 11

No one shall be imprisoned merely on the ground of inability to fulfil a contractual obligation.

Article 12

1. Everyone lawfully within the territory of a State shall, within that territory, have the right to liberty of movement and freedom to choose his residence.
2. Everyone shall be free to leave any country, including his own.
3. The above-mentioned rights shall not be subject to any restrictions except those which are provided by law, are necessary to protect national security, public order (*ordre public*), public health or morals or the rights and freedoms of others, and are consistent with the other rights recognized in the present Covenant.
4. No one shall be arbitrarily deprived of the right to enter his own country.

Article 13

An alien lawfully in the territory of a State Party to the present Covenant may be expelled thereform only in pursuance of a decision reached in accordance with law and shall, except where compelling reasons of national security otherwise require, be allowed to submit the reasons against his expulsion and to have his case reviewed by, and be represented for the purpose before, the competent authority.

Article 14

1. All persons shall be equal before the courts and tribunals. In the determination of any criminal charge against him, or of his rights and obligations in a suit at law, everyone shall be entitled to a fair and public hearing by a competent, independent and impartial tribunal established by law. The press and the public may be excluded from all or part of trial for reasons of morals, public order (*ordre public)* or national security in a democratic society, or when the interest of the private lives of the parties so requires, or to the extent strictly necessary in the opinion of the court in special circumstances where publicity would prejudice the interests of justice; but any judgement rendered in a criminal case or in a suit at law shall be made public except where the interest of juvenile persons otherwise requires or the proceedings concern matrimonial disputes or the guardianship of children.
2. Everyone charged with a criminal offence shall have the right to be presumed innocent until proved guilty according to law.

3. In the determination of any criminal charge against him, everyone shall be entitled to the following minimum guarantees, in full equality:
   (a) To be informed promptly and in detail in a language which he understands of the nature and cause of the charge against him;
   (b) To have adequate time and facilities for the preparation of his defence and to communicate with counsel of his own choosing;
   (c) To be tried without undue delay:
   (d) To be tried in his presence, and to defend himself in person or through legal assistance of his own choosing; to be informed, if he does not have legal assistance, of this right; and to have legal assistance assigned to him,in any case where the interests of justice so require, and without payment by him in any such case if he does not have sufficient means to pay for it;
   (e) To examine, or have examined,the witnesses against him and to obtain the attendance and examination of witnesses on his behalf under the same conditions as witnesses against him;
   (f) To have the free assistance of an interpreter if he cannot understand or speak the language used in court;
   (g) Not to be compelled to testify against himself or to confess guilt.
4. In the case of juvenile persons, the procedure shall be such as will take account of their age and the desirability of promoting their rehabilitation.
5. Everyone convicted of a crime shall have the right to his conviction and sentence being reviewed by a higher tribunal according to law.
6. When a person has by a final decision been convicted of a criminal offence and when subsequently his conviction has been reversed or he has been pardoned on the ground that a new or newly discovered fact shows conclusively that there has been a miscarriage of justice, the person who has suffered punishment as a result of such conviction shall be compensated according to law, unless it is proved that the non-disclosure of the unknown fact in time is wholly or partly att tributable to him.
7. No one shall be liable to be tried or punished again for an offence for which he has already been finally convicted or acquitted in accordance with the law and penal procedure of each country.

Article 15

1. No one shall be held guilty of any cirminal offence on account of any act or omission which did not constitute a criminal offence, under national or international law, at the time when it was com-

mitted. Nor shall a heavier penalty be imposed than the one that was applicable at the time when the criminal offence was committed. If, subsequent to the commission of the offence, provision is made by law for the imposition of a lighter penalty, the offender shall benefit thereby.

2. Noting in this article shall prejudice the trial and punishment of any person for any act or omission which, at the time when it was committed, was criminal according to the general principles of law recognized by the community of nations.

Article 16

Everyone shall have the right to recognition everywhere as a person before the law.

Article 17

1. No one shall be subjected to arbitrary or unlawful interference with his privacy, family, home or correspondence, nor to unlawful attacks on his honour and reputation.
2. Everyone has the right to the protection of the law against such interference or attacks.

Article 18

1. Everyone shall have the right to freedom of thought, conscience and religion. This right shall include freedom to have or to adopt a religion or belief of his choice, and freedom, either individually or in community with others and in public or private, to manifest his religion or belief in worship,observance, practice and teaching.
2. No one shall be subject to coercion which would impair his freedom to have or to adopt a religion or belief of his choice.
3. Freedom to manifest one's religion or beliefs may be subject only to such limitations as are prescribed by law and are necessary to protect public safety, order, health or morals or the fundamental rights and freedoms of thers.
4. The States Parties to the present Covenant undertake to have respect for the liberty of parents and, when applicable, legal guardinas to ensure the religious and moral education of their children in conformity with their own convictions.

Article 19

1. Everyone shall have the right to hold opinions without interference.
2. Everyone shall have the right to freedom of expression; this right shall include freedom to seek, receive and impart information and

ideas of all kinds, regardless of frontiers, either orally, in writing or in print, in the form of art, or through any other media of his choice.

3. The exercise of the rights provided for in paragraph 2 of this article carries with it special duties and responsibilities. It may therefore be subject to certain restrictions,but these shall only be such as are provided by law and are necessary:
   (a) For respect of the rights or reputations of thers:
   (b) For the protection of national security or of public order *(ordre public)* or of public health or morals.

Article 20

1. Any propaganda for war shall be prohibited by law.
2. Any advocacy of national, racial or religious hatred that constitutes incitement to discrimination, hostility or violence shall be prohibited by law.

Article 21

The right of peaceful assembly shall be recognized. No restrictions may be place on the exercise of this right other than those imposed in conformity with the law and which are necessary in a democratic society in the interests of national security or public safety, public order *(ordre public),* the protection of public health or morals or the protection of the rights and freedoms of others.

Article 22

1. Everyone shall have the right to freedom of association with others including the right to form and join trade unions for the protection of his interests.
2. No restrictions may be placec on the exercise of this right other than those which are prescribed by law and which are necessary in a democratic society in the interests of national security of public safety, public order (*ordre public),* the protection of public health or morals or the protection of the rights and freedoms of others. This article shall not prevent the imposition of lawful restrictions on members of the armed forces and of the police in their exercise of this right.
3. Nothing in this article shall authorize States Parties to the International Labour Organisation Convention of 1948 concerning Freedom of Association and Protection of the Right of Organize to take legislative measures which would prejudice, or to apply the law in such a manner as to prejudice. the guarantees provided for in that Convention.

Article 23

1. The family is the natural and fundamental group unit of society and is entitled to protection by society and the State.
2. The right of men and women of marriageable age to marry and to found a family shall be recognized.
3. No marriage shall be entered into without the free and full consent of the intending spouses.
4. States Parties to the present Covenant shall take appropriate steps to ensure equality of rights and responsibilities of spouses as to marriage, during marriage and at its dissolution. In the case of dissolution, provision shall be made for the neceessary protection of any children.

Article 24

1. Every child shall have, without any discrimination as to race, colour, sex, languae, religion, national or social origin, property or birth, the right to such measures of protection as are required by his status as a minor, on the part of his family, society and the State.
2. Every child shall be registered immediately after birth and shall have a name.
3. Every child has the right to acquire a nationality.

Article 25

Every citizen shall have the right and the opportunity, without any of the distinctions mentioned in article 2 and without unreasonable restrictions:

(a) To take part in the conduct of public affairs, directly or through freely chosen representatives;

(b) To vote and to be elected at genuine periodic elections which shall be by universal and equal suffrage and shall be held by secret ballot, guaranteeing the free expression of the will of the electors;

(c) To have access, on general terms of equality, to public service in his country.

Article 26

All persons are equal before the law and are entitled without any discrimination to the equal protection of the law. In this respect, the law shall prohibit any discrimination and guarantee to all persons equal and effective protection against discrimination on any ground such as race, colour, sex, language, religion, political or other opinion, national or social origin, property, birth or other status.

Article 27

In those States in which ethnic, religious or linguistic minorities exist, persons belonging to such minorities shall not be denied the right, in community with the other members of their group, to enjoy their own culture, to profess and practise their own religion, or to use their own language.

PART IV

Article 28

1. There shall be established a Human Rights Committee (hereafter referred to in the present Covenant as the Committee). It hsall consist of eighteen members and shall carry out the function herein after provided.
2. The Committee shall be composed of nationals of the States Parties to the present Covenant who shall be persons of high moral character and recognized competence in the field of human rights, consideration being given to the usefulness of the participation of some persons having legal experience.
3. The members of the Committee shall be elected and shall serve in their personal capacity.

Article 29

1. The members of the Committee shall be elected by secret ballot from a list of persons possessing the qualifications prescribed in article 28 and nominated for the purpose by the States Parties to the present Covenant.
2. Each State Party to the present Covenant may nominate not more than two persons. These persons shall be nationals of the nominating State.
3. A person shall be eligible for renomination.

Article 30

1. The initial election shall be held no later than six months after the date of the entry into force of the present Covenant.
2. At least four months before the date of each election to the Committee, other than an election to fill a vacancy declared in accordance with article 34, the Secretary-General of the United Nations shall address a written invitation to the States Parties to the present Covenant to submit their nominations for membership of the Committee within three months.
3. The Secretary-General of the United Nations shall prepare a list in

alphabetical order of all the persons thus nominated, with an indication of the States Parties which have nominated them, and shall submit it to the States Parties to the present Covenant no later than one month before the date of each election.

4. Elections of the members of the Committee shall be held at a meeting of the States Parties to the present Covenant convened by the Secretary-General of the United Nations at the Headquarters of the United Nations. At that meeting, for which two thirds of the States Parties to the present Covenant shall constitute a quorum, the persons elected to the Committee shall be those nominees who obtain the largest number of votes and an absolute majority of the votes of the representatives of States Parties Present and voting.

Article 31

1. The Committee may not include more than one national of the same State.
2. In the election of the Committee, consideration shall be given to equitable geographical distribution of membership and to the rep4resentation of the different forms of civilization and of the principal legal systems.

Article 32

1. The members of the Committee shall be elected for a term of four years. They shall be eligible for re-election if renominated. However, the terms of nine of the members elected at the first election shall expire at the end of two years; immediately after the first election, the names of these nine members shall be chosen by lot by the Chairman of the meeting referred to in article 30, paragraph 4.
2. Elections at the expiry of office shall be held in accordance with the preceding articles of this part of the present Covenant.

Article 33

1. If, in the unanimous opinion of the other members, a member of the Committe has ceased to carry out his functions for any cause other than absence of a temprory character, the Chairman of the Committee shall notify the Sectetary-General of the United Nations, who shall then declare the seat of that member to be vacant.
2. In the event of the death or the resignation of a member of the Committee, the Chairman shall immediately notify the Secretary-General of the United Nations, who shall declare the seat vacant from the date of death or the date on which the resignation takes effect.

Article 34

1. When a Cacancy is declared in accordance with article 33 and if the term of office of the member to be replaced does not expire within six months of the declaration of the vacancy, the Secretary General of the United Nations shall notify each of the States Parties to the present Covenant, which may within two months submit nominations in accordance with article 29 for the purpose of filling the vacancy.
2. The Secretary-General of the United Nations shall prepare a list in alphabetical order of the persons thus nominated and shall submit it to the States Parties to the present Covenant. The election to fill the vacancy shall then take place in accordance with the relevant provisions of this part of the present Covenant.
3. A member of the Committee elected to fill a vacancy declared in accordance with article 33 shall hold office for the remainder of the term of the member who vacated the seat on the Committee under the provisions of that article.

Article 35

The members of the Committee shall, with the approval of the General Assembly of the United Nations, receive emoluments from United Nations resources on such terms and conditions as the General Assembly may decide, having regard to the importance of the Committee's responsibilities.

Article 36

The Secretary-General of the United Nations shall provide the necessary staff and facilities for the effective performance of the functions of the Committee under the present Covenant.

Article 37

1. The Secretary-General of the United Nations shall convene the initial meeting of the Committee at the Headquarters of the United Nations.
2. After its initial meeting, the Committee shall meet at such times as shall be provided its rules of procedure.
3. The Committee shall normally meet at the Headquarters of the United Nations or at the United nations Office at Geneva.

Article 38

Every member of the Committee shall, before taking up his duties, make a solemn declaration in open committee that he will perform his functions impartially and conscientiously.

Article 39

1. The Committee shall elect its officers for a term of two years. They may be re-elected.
2. The Committee shall establish its own rules of procedure, but these rules shall provide, *inter alia*, that:
   (a) Twelve members shall constitute a quorum;
   (b) Decisions of the Committee shall be made by a majority vote of the members present.

Article 40

1. The States Parties to the present Covenant undertake to submit reports on the measures they have adopted which give effect to the rights recognized herein and on the progress made in the enjoyment of those rights:
   (a) Within one year of the entry into force of the present Covenant for the States Parties concerned;
   (b) Thereafter whenever the Committee so requests.
2. All reports shall be submitted to the Secretary-General of the United Nations, who shall transmit them to the Committee for consideration. Reports shall indicate the factors and difficulties, if any, affecting the implementation of the present Covenant.
3. The Secretary-General of the United Nations may, after consultation with the Committee, transmit to the specialized agencies concerned copies of such parts of the reports as may fall within their field of competence.
4. The Committee shall study the reports submitted by the States Parties to the present Covenant. It shall transmit its reports, and such general comments as it may consider appropriate, the States Parties. The Committee may also transmit to the Economic and Social Council these comments along with the copies of the reports it has received from States Parties to the present Covenant.
5. The States Parties to the present Covenant may submit to the Committee observations on any comments that may be made in accordance with paragraph 4 of this article.

Article 41

1. A State Party to the present Covenant may at any time declare under this article that is recognizes the competence of the Committee to receive and consider communications to the effect that a State Party claims that another State Party is not fulfiling its obligations under

the present Covenant. Communications under this article may be received and considered only if submitted by a State Party which has made a declaration recognizing in regard to itself the competence of the Committee. No communication shall be received by the Committee if it concerns a State Party which has not made such a declaration. Communications received under this article shall be dealt with in accordance with they following procedure:

(a) If a State Party to the present Covenant considers that another State Party is not giving effect to the provisions of the present Covenant,it may, by written communication, bring the matter to the attention of that State Party. Within three months after the receipt of the communication, the receiving State shall afford the State which sent the communication an explanation or any other statement in writing clarifying the matter, which should include, to the extent possible and pertinent, reference to domestic procedures and remedies taken, pending, or available in the matter.

(b) If the matter is not adjusted to the satisfaction of both States Parties concerned within six months after the receipt by the receiving State of the initial communication, either State shall have the right to refer the matter to the Committee, by notice given to the Committee and to the other State.

(c) The Committee shall deal with the matter referred to it only after it has ascertained that all available domestic remedies have been invoked and exhausted in the matter, in conformity with the generally recognized principles of international law. This shall not be rule where the application of the remedies is unreasonably prolonged.

(d) The Committee shall hold closed meetings when examining communications under this article.

(e) Subject to the provisions of sub-paragraph (c), the Committee shall make available its good offices to the States Parties concerned with a view to a friendly solution of the matter on the basis of respect for human rights and fundamental freedoms as recognized in the present Covenant.

(f) In any matter referred to it, the Committee may call upon the States Parties concerned, referred to in sub-paragraph (b), to supply any relevant information.

(g) The States Parties concerned, referred to in sub-paragraph (b), shall have the right to be represented when the matter is being considered in the Committee and to make submissions orally and/or in writing.

(h) The Committee shall, within twelve months after the date of receipt of notice under sub-paragraph (b), submit a report:

(i) If a solution within the terms of sub-paragraph (e) is reached, the Committee shall confine its report to a brief statement of the facts and of the solution reached;

(ii) If a solution with the terms of sub-paragraph (e) is not reached, the Committee shall confine its report to a brief statement of the facts; the written submissions and record of the oral submissions made by the States parties concerned shall be attached to the report.

In every matter, the report shall be communicated to the States Parties concerned.

2. The provisions of this article shall come into force when ten States Parties to the present Covenant have made declarations under paragraph 1 of this article. Such declaration shall be deposited by the States Parties with the Secretary-General of the United Nations, who shall transmit copies thereof to the other States Parties. A declaration may be withdrawn at any time by notification to the Secretary-General. Such a withdrawal shall not prejudice the consideration of any matter which is the subject of a communication already transmitted under this article; no further communication by any State Party shall be received after the notification of withdrawal of the declaration has been received by the Secretary-General, unless the State Party concerned had made a new declaration.

Article 42

1. (a) If a matter referred to the Committee in accordance with article 41 is not resolved to the satisfaction of the States Parties con cerned, the Committee may, with the prior consent of the States Parties concerned, appoint an *ad hoc* Conciliation Commission(hereinafter referred to as the Commission). The good offices of the Commission shall be made available to the States Parties concerned with a view to an amicable solution of the matter on the basis of respect for the present Covenant;

(b) The Commission shall consist of five persons acceptable to the States Parties concerned. If the States,Parties concerned fail to reach agreement within three months on all or part of the composition of the commission, the members of the Commission concerning whom no agreement has been reached shall be elected by secret ballot by a two-thirds majority vote of the

Committee from among its memebers.

2. The members of the Commission shall serve in their personal capacity. They shall not be nationals of the States Parties concerned, or of a State not party to the present Covenant, or of a State Party which has not made a declaration under article 41.
3. The Commission shall elect its own Chairman and adopt its own rules of procedure.
4. The meetings of the Commission shall normally be held at the Head-quarters of the United Nations or at the United Nations Office at Geneva. However, they may be held at such other convenient places as the Commission may determine in consultation with the Secretary-General of the United Nations and the States Parties concerned.
5. The secretariat provided in accordance with article 36 shall also service the commissions appointed under this article.
6. The information received and collated by the Committee shall be made available to the Commission and the Commission may call upon the States Parties concerned to supply any other relevant information.
7. When the Commission has fully considered the matter, but in any event not later than twelve months after having been seized of the matter, it shall submit to the Chairman of the Committee a report for communication to the States Parties concerned:
   (a) If the Commission is unable to complete its consideration of the matter within twelve months, it shall confine its report to a brief statement of the status of its consideration of the matter;
   (b) If an amicable solution to the matter on the basis of respect for human rights as recognized in the present Covenant is reached, the Commission shall confine its report to a brief statement of the facts and of the solution reached;
   (c) If a solution within the terms of sub-paragraph (b) is not reached, the Commission's report shall embody its findings on all questions of fact relevant ot the issues between the States Parties concerned, and its views on the possibilities of an amicable solution of the matter. This report shall also contain the written submissions and a record of the oral submissions made by the States parties concerned;
   (d) If the Commission's report is submitted under sub-paragraph (c), the States Parties concerned shall, within three months of the receipt of the report, notify the Chairman of the Committee whether or not they accept the contents of the report of the

Commission.

8. The provisions of this article are without prejudice to the responsibilities of the Committee under article 41.
9. The States Parties concerned shall share equally all the expenses of the members of the Commission in accordance with estimates to be provided by the Secretary-General of the United Nations.
10. The Secretary-General of the United Nations shall be empowered to pay the expenses of the members of the Commission, if necessary, before reimbursement by the States Parties concerned, in accordance with paragraph 9 of this article.

Article 43

The members of the Committee, and of the *ad hoc* conciliation commissions which may be appointed under article 42, shall be entitled to the facilities, privileges and immunities of experts on mission for the United Nations as laid down in the relevant sections of the Convention on the Privileges and Immunities of the United Nations.

Article 44

The provisions for the implementation of the present Covenant shall apply without prejudice to the procedures prescribed in the field of human rights by or under the constituent instruments and the conventions of the United Nations and of the specialized agencies and shall not prevent the States Parties to the present Covenant from having recourse to other p4rocedures for settling a dispute in accordance with general or special international agreements in force between them.

Article 45

The Committee shall submit to the Genral Assembly of the United Nations, through the Economic and Social Council, an annual report in its activities.

PART V

Article 46

Nothing in the present Covenant shall be interpreted as impairing the provisions of the Charter of the United Nations and of the constitutions of the specialized agencies which define the respective responsibilities of the various organs of the United Nations and of the specialized agencies in regard to the matters dealt with in the present Covenant.

Article 47

Nothing in the present Covenant shall be interpreted as impairing the inherent right of all peoples to enjoy and utilize fully and freely their natural wealth and resources.

PART VI

Article 48

1. The present Covenant is open for signature by any State Member of the United Nations or member of any of its specialized agencies, by any State Party to the Statute of the International Court of Justice, and by any other State which has been invited by the General Assembly of the United Nations to become a party to the present Covenant.
2. The present Covenant is subject to ratification. Instruments of ratification shall be deposited with the Secretary-General of the United Nations.
3. The present Covenant shall be open to accession by any State referred to in paragraph 1 of this article.
4. Accession shall be effected by the deposit of an instrument of accession with, the Secretary-General of United Nations.
5. The Secretary-General of the United Nations shall inform all States which have signed this Covenant or acceded to it of the deposit of each instrument of ratification or accession.

Article 49

1. The present Covenant shall enter in to force three months after the date of the deposit with the Secretary-General of the United Nations of the thirty-fifth instrument of ratification or instrument of accession.
2. For each State ratifying the present Covenant or acceding to it after the deposit of the thirty-fifth instrument of ratification or instrument of accession, the present Covenant shall enter into force three months after the date of the deposit of its own instrument of ratification or instrument of accession.

Article 50

The provision of the present Covenant shall extend to all parts of federal States without any limitations or exceptions.

Article 51

1. Any State Party to the present Covenant may propose an amendment and file it with the Secretary-General of the United Nations. The Secretary-General of the United Nations shall thereupon com-

municate any proposed amendments to the States Parties to the present Covenant with a request that they notify him whether they favour a conference of States Parties for the purpose of considering and voting upon the proposals. In the event that at least one third of the States Parties favours such a conference, the Secretary-General shall convene the conference under the auspices of the United Nations. Any amendment adopted by a majority of the States Parties present and voting at the conference shall be submitted to the General Assembly of the United Nations for approval.

2. Amendments hall come into force when they have been approved by the General Assembly of the United Nations and accepted by a two-thirds majority of the States Parties to the present Covenant in accordance with their respective constitutional processes.
3. When amendments come into force, they shall be binding on those States Parties which have accepted them, other States Parties still being bound by the provisions of the present Covenant and any earlier amendment which they have accepted.

Article 52

Irrespective of the notifications made under article 48, paragraph 5 the Secretary-General of the United Nations shall inform all States referred to in paragraph 1 of the same article of the folowoing particulars:

(a) Signatures, ratifications and accessions under article 48;
(b) The date of the entry into force of the present Covenant under article 49 and the date of the entry into force of any amendments under article 51.

Article 53

1. The present Covenant, of which the Chinese, English, French, Russian and Spanish texts are equally authentic, shall be deposited in the archives of the United Nations.
2. The Secretary-General of the United Nations shall transmit certified copies of the present Covenant to all States referred to in article 48.

OPTIONAL PROTOCOL TO THE INTERNATIONAL COVENANT ON CIVIL AND POLITICAL RIGHTS

The States Parties to The Present Protocol.,

Considering that in order further to achieve the purposes of the Covenant on Civil and Political Rights (hereinafter referred to as the Covenant) and the implementation of its provision it would be appropriate to enable the Human Rights Committee set up in part IV of the Covenant(hereinafter referred to as the Committee) to receive and consider, as provided in the present Protocol, communications from individuals claiming to be victims of violations of any of the rights set forth in the Covenant,

Have agreed as follows:

Article 1

A State Party to the Covenant that becomes a party to the present Protocol recognizes the competence of the Committee to receive and consider communications from individuals subject to its jurisdiation who claim to be victims of a violation by that State Party of any of the rights set forth in the Covenant. No communication shall be received by the Committee if it concerns a State Party to the Covenant which is not a party to the present Protocol.

Article 2

Subject to the provisions of article1, individuals who claim that any of thier rights enumerated in the Covenant have been violated and who have exhausted all available domestic remedies may submit a written communication to the Committee for consideration.

Artilce 3

The Committee shall consider inadmissible any communication under the present Protocol which is anonymous, or which it considers to be an abuse of the rights of submission of such communications or to be incompatible with the provisions of the Covenant.

Article 4

1. Subject to the provisions of article 3, the Committee shall bring any communications submitted to it under the present Protocol to the attention of the State Party to the present Protocol alleged to be violating any provisions of the Covenant.
2. Within six months, the receiving State shall submit to the Committee written explanations or statements clarifying the matter and the remedy, if any, that may have been taken by that State.

Article 5

1. The Committee shall consider communications received under the present Protocol in the light of all written information made available to it by the individual and by the State Party concerned.
2. The Committee shall not consider any communication from an individual unless it has ascertained that:

(a) The same matter is not being examined under another procedure of international investigation or settlement;

(b) The individual has exhausted all available domestic remedies, This shall not be the rule where the application of the remedies is unreasonably prolonged.

3. The Committee shall hold closed meetings when examining communications under the present Protocol.
4. The Committee shall forward its views to the State Party concerned and to the individual.

Article 6

The Committee shall include in its annual report under article 45 of the Covenant a summary of its activities under the present Protocol.

Article 7

Pending the achievement of the objectives of resolution 151 (1514,5) adopted by the General Assembly of the United Nations on 14 December 1960 concerning the Declaration on the Granting of Independence to Colonial Countries and Peoples, the provisions of the present Protocol shall in no way limit the right of petition granted to these peoples by the Charter of the United Nations and other international conventions and instruments under the United Nations and its specialized agencies.

Article 8

1. the present Protocol is open for signature by any State which has signed the Covenant.
2. The present Protocol is subject to ratification by any State which has ratified or acceded to the Covenant. Instruments of ratification shall be deposited with the Secretary-General of the United Nations.
3. The present Protocol shall be open to accession by any State which has ratified or acceded to the Covenant.
4. Accession shall be effected by the deposit of an instrument of accession with the Secretary-General of the United Nations.
5. The Secretary-General of the United Nations shall inform all States which have signed the present Protocol or acceded to it of the deposit of each instrument of ratification or accession.

Article 9

1. Subject to the entry into force of the Covenant, the present Protocol shall enter in to force three months after the date of the deposit with the Secretary-General of the United Nations of they tenth instrument of ratification or instrument of accession.

2. For each State ratifying the present Protocol or acceding to it after the deposit of the tenth instrument of ratification or instrument of accession, the present Protocol shall enter into force three months after the date of the deposit of its own instrument of ratification or instrument of accession.

Article 10

The provisions of the present Protocol shall extent to all parts of federal States without any limitations or exceptions.

Article 11

1. Any State Party to the present Protocol may propose an amendment and file it with the Secretary-General of the United Nations. The Secretary-General shall thereupon communicate any proposed amendments to the States Parties to the present Protocol with a request that they notify him whether they favour a conference of States Parties for the purpose of considering and voting upon the proposal. In the event that at least one third of the States Parties favours such a conference, the Secretary-General shall convene the conference under the auspices of the United Nations. Any amendment adopted by a majority of the State Parties present and voting at the conference shall be submitted to the General Assembly of the United Nations for approval.
2. Amendments shall come into force when they have been approved by the General Assembly of the United Nations and accepted by a two-thirds majority of the States Parties to the present Protocol in accordance with their respective constitutional processes.
3. When amendments come into force, they shall be binding on those States Parties which have accepted them, other States Parties still being bound by the provisions of the present Protocol and any earlier amendment which they have accepted.

Article 12

1. Any State Party may denounce the present Protocol at any time by written notification addressed to the Secretary-General of the United Nations. Denunciation shall take effect three months after the date of receipt of the notification by the Secretary-General.
2. Denunciation shall be without prejudice to the continued application of the provisions of the present Protocol to any communication submitted under article 2 before the effective date of denunciation.

Article 13

Irrespective of the Notifications made under article 8, paragraph 5, of the present Protocol, the Secretary-General of the United Nations shall inform all States referred to in article 48, paragraph 1, of the Covenant of the following particulars:

(a) Signatures, ratifications and accessions under article 8;

(b) The date of the entry into force of any amendments under article 11;

(c) Denunciation under article 12.

Article 14

1. The present Protocol,of which the Chinese, English, French, Russian and Spanish texts are equally authentic, shall be deposited in the archives of the United Nations.
2. The Secretary-General of the United Nations shall transmit certified copies of the present Protocol to all States referred to in article 48 of the Covenant.

SECOND OPTIONAL PROTOCOL TO THE INTERNATIONAL COVENANT ON CIVIL AND POLITICAL RIGHTS AIMING AT THE ABOLITION OF THE DEATH PENANLTY

Believing that abolition of the death penalty contributes to enhancement of human dignity and progressive development of human rights,

Recalling article 3 of the Universal Declaration of Human Rights adopted on 10 December 1948 and article 6 of the International Covenant on Civil and Political Rights adopted on 16 December 1966,

Noting that article 6 of the International Covenant on Civil and political Rights refers to abolition of the death penalty in terms that strongly suggest that abolition is desirable,

Convinced that all measures of abolition of the death penalty should be considered as progress in the enjoyment of the right to life,

Desirous to undertake hereby an international commitment to abolish the death penalty,

Have agreed as follows:

Article 1

1. No one within the jurisdiction of the State Party to the present Protocol shall be executed.
2. Each State Party shall take all necessary measures to abolish the death penalty within its jurisdiction.

Article 2

1. No reservation is admissible to the present Protocol, except for a reservation made at the time of ratification or accession that provides for the applications of the death penalty in time of war pursuant to a conviction for a most serious crime of a military nature committed during wartime.
2. The State Party making such a reservation shall at the time of ratification or accession communicate to the Secretary-General of the United Nations the relevant provisions of its national legislation applicable during wartime.
3. The State Party having made such a reservation shall notify the Secretary-General of the United Nations of any beginning or ending of a state of war applicable to its territory.

Article 3

The States Parties to the present Protocol shall include in the reports they submit to the Human Rights Committee, in accordance with article 40 of the Covenant, information on the measures that they have adopted to give effect to the present Protocol.

Article 4

With respect to the States Parties to the Covenant that have made a declaration under article 41, the competence of the Human Rights committee to receive and consider communications when a State Party claims that another State Party is not fulfilling its obligations shall extend to the provisions of the present Protocol, unless the State Party concerned has made a statement to the contrary at the moment of ratification or accession.

Article 5

With respect to the States Parties to the first Optional Protocol to the International Covenant on Civil and Political Rights adopted on 16 December 1966, the competence of the Human Rights Committee to receive and consider communications from individuals subject to its jurisdiction shall extend to the provisions of the present Protocol, unless the State Party concerned has made a statement to the contrary at the moment of ratification or accession.

Article 6

1. The provisions of the present Protocol shall apply as additional provisions to the Covenant.
2. Without prejudice to the possibility of a reservation under article 2

of the present Protocol, the right guaranteed in article 1, paragraph 1, of the present Protocol shall not be subject to any derogation under article 4 of the Covenant.

Article 7

1. The present Protocol is open for signature by any State that has signed the Covenant.
2. The present Protocol is subject to ratification by any State that has ratified the Covenant or acceded to it. Instruments of ratification shall be deposited with the Secretary-General of the United Nations.
3. The present Protocol shall be open to accession by any State that has ratified the Covenant or acceded to it.
4. Accession shall be effected by the deposit of an instrument of accession with the Secretary-General of the United Nations.
5. The Secretary-General of the United Nations shall inform all States that have signed the present Protocol or acceded to it of the deposit of each instrument of ratification or accession.

Article 8

1. The present Protocol shall enter into force three months after the date of the deposit with the Secretary-General of the United Nations of the tenth instrument of ratification or accession.
2. For each State ratifying the present Protocol or acceding to it after the deposit of the tenth instrument of ratification or accession, the present Protocol shall enter into force three months after the date of the deposit of its own instrument of ratification or accession.

Article 9

The provision of the present Protocol shall extend to all parts of federal States without any limitations or exceptions.

Article 10

The Secretary-General of the United Nations shall inform all States referred to in article 48, paragraph 1, of the Covenant of the following particulars:

(a) Reservations, communications and notifications under article 2 of the present protocol;
(b) Statements made under articles 4 or 5 of the present Protocol;
(c) Signatures, ratifications and accessions under article 7 of the present Protocol;
(d) The date of the entry into force of the present Protocol under article 8 thereof.

Article 11

1. The present Protocol, of which the Arabic, Chinese, English, French, Russian and Spanish texts are equally authentic, shall be deposited in the archives of the United Nations.
2. The Secretary-General of the United Nations shall transmit certified copies of the present Protocol to all States referred to in article 48 of the Covenant.

3

Discrimination Against Women

Introduction

Equality is the cornerstone of every democratic society which aspires to social justice and human rights. In virtually all societies and spheres of activity women are subject to inequalities in law and in fact. This situation is both caused and exacerbated by the existence of discrimination in the family, in the community and in the workplace. While causes and consequences may vary from country to country, discrimination against women is widespread. It is perpetuated by the survival of stereotypes and of traditional cultural and religious practices and beliefs detrimental to women.

Recent efforts to document the real situation of women worldwide have produced some alarming statistics on the economic and social gaps between women and men. Women are the majority of the world's poor and the number of women living in rural poverty has increased by 50 per cent since 1975. Women are the majority of the world's illiterate; the number rose from 543 million to 597 million between 1970 and 1985. Women in Asia and Africa work 13 hours a week more than men and are mostly unpaid. Worldwide, women earn 30 to 40 per cent less than men for doing equal work. Women hold between 10 and 20 per cent of managerial and administrative jobs world wide and less than 20 per cent of jobs in manufacturing. Women make up less than 5 per cent of the world's heads of State. Women's unpaid housework and family labour, if counted as productive output in national accounts, would increase measures of global output by 25 to 30 per cent.[1]

The concept of equality means much more than treating all persons in the same way. Equal treatment of persons in unequal situations will operate to perpetuate rather than eradicate injustice. True equality can only emerge from efforts directed towards addressing and correcting these situational imbalances. It is this broader view of equality which has become the underlying principle and the final goal in the struggle for recognition and acceptance of the human rights of women.

In 1979, the General Assembly adopted the Convention on the Elimination of All Forms of Discrimination against Women (see annex 1). The Convention sets, out, in legally binding form, internationally accepted principles on the rights of women which are applicable to all women in all fields. The basic legal norm of the Convention is the prohibition of all forms of discrimination against women. This norm cannot be satisfied merely by the enactment of gender-neutral laws. In addition to demanding that women be accorded equal rights with men, the Convention goes further by prescribing the measures to be taken to ensure that women everywhere are able to enjoy the right to which they are entitled.

The Committee on the Elimination of Discrimination against Women was established under article 17 of the Covention. The Committee is entrusted with the task of overseeing the implementation of the Convention by States parties.

This Fact Sheet is divided into two main parts. Part I sets out and explains the substantive provisions of the Convention. Part II provides an overview of the structure and functioning of the Committee. Some background information on the Covention is provided below.

The United Nations and the Human Rights of Women

Equality of rights for women is a basic principle of the United Nations. The Preamble to the Charter of the United Nations sets as a basic goal "to reaffirm faith in fundamental human rights, in the dignity and worth of the human person, in the equal rights of men and women". Furthermore, Article 1 of the Charter proclaims that one of the purposes of the United Nations is to achieve international co-operation in promoting and encouraging respect for human rights and fundamental freedoms for all people "without distinction as to race, sex, language or religion".

The International Bill of Human Rights strengthens and extends this emphasis on the equal rights of women. The International Bill of Human Rights is a term used to refer collectively to three instruments: the Universal Declaration of Human Rights, the International Covenant on Economic, Social and Cultural Rights, and the International Covenant on Civil and Political Rights and its two Optional Protocols. Taken to gether, these instruments form the ethical and legal basis for all of the human rights work of the United Nations and provide the foundation upon which the international system for the protection and promotion of human rights has been developed.

One of the first and most significant achievements of the Organization in the field of human rights was the Universal Declaration of Human Rights, which was adopted by the General Assembly in 19448. Based on the equal dignity and rights of every human being, the Declaration proclaims the entitlement of everyone to enjoy human rights and fundamental freedoms "without distinction of any kind, such as race, colour, sex, language, religion, political or other opinion, national or social origin, property, birth or other status" (art.2).

Immediately following the adoption of the Universal Declaration, work began on expanding upon the rights and freedoms proclaimed therein and codifying them in binding legal form. From this process emerged the two Covenants mentioned above, which were unanimously adopted by the General Assembly in 1966 and entered into force 10 years later. The Covenants are international legal instruments. When a State becomes a party to either Covenant, it undertakes to guarantee to all individuals in its territory or under its jurisdiction, without any discrimination, all the rights specified by that Covenant, and to provide for effective remedies in cases of violations.

The Covenants clearly state that the rights set forth therein are applicable to all persons without distinction of any kind, such as rice, colour, sex, language, religion, political or other opinion, national or social origin, property, birth or other status. In addition, States parties specifically undertake to ensure the equal right of men and women to the enjoyment of all rights set forth in each Covenant. The Committee on Economic, Social and Cultural Rights and the Human Rights Committee, set up to monitor the implementation of each of the two Covenants, are therefore competent to deal with issues of gender-based discrimination raised under the provisions of their respective instruments. The Human Rights Committee has been particularly active in the area of discrinination against women.

Despite the fact that there are two Covenants, each guaranteeing a separate set of human rights, the interdependence and indivisibility of all rights in a long-accepted and consistently reaffirmed principle. In practice, this means that respect for civil and political rights cannot be separated from the enjoyment of economic, social and cultural rights, and, on the other hand, that genuine economic and social development requires the political and civil freedoms to participate in this process.

Universality is another important principle which guides the vision of human rights and fundamental freedoms advocated by the United Nations. While historical, cultural and religious differences must be borne in mind, it is the duty of every State, regardless of its political, economic and cultural systems, to promote and protect all human rights, including the human rights of women.

The validity of these principles-interdependence, indivisibility and universality- was most recently affirmed in the Vienna Declaration and Programme of Aaction adopted by the World Conference on Human Rights 1993.

Why a Separaate Convention for Women?

The International Bill of Human Rights lays down a comprehensive set of rights to which all persons, including women, are entitled. Why then was it necessary to have a separate legal instrument for women?

Additional means for protecting the human rights of women were seen as necessary because the mere fact of their "humanity" has not been sufficient to guarantee women the protection of their rights.The preamble to the Convention on the Elimination of All Forms of Discrimination against Women explains that, despite the existence of other instruments, women still do not have equal rights with men. Discrimination against women continues to exist in every society.

The Convention was adopted by the General Assembly in 1979 to reinforce the provisions of existing international instruments designed to combat the continuing discrimination against women. It identifies many specific areas where there has been notorious discrimination against women, for example in regard to political rights, marriage and the family, and employment. In these and other areas the Convention spells out specific goals and measures that are to be taken to facilitate the creation of a global society in which women enjoy full equality with men and thus full realization of their guaranteed human rights.

To combat gender-based discrimination, the Convention requires States parties to recognize the important economic and social contribution of women to the family and to society as a whole. It emphasizes that discrimination will hamper economic growth and prosperity. It also expressly recognizes the need for a change in attitudes, through education of both men and women to accept equality of rights and responsibilities and to overcome prejudices and practices based on stereotyped roles. Another important feature of the Convention is its explicit recognition of the goal of actual, in addition to legal, equality, and of the need for temporary special measures to achieve that goal.

A Short History of the Convention

In November 1967, the General Assembly adopted the Declaration on the Elimination of Discrimination against Women. In 1972, the Secretary-General of the United Nations asked the Commission on the Status of Women [2] to request the views of Member States regarding the form and content of a possible international instrument on the human rights of women. The following year, a working group was appointed by the Economic and Social Council to consider the elaboration of such a convention. In 1974, the Commission on the Status of Women began drafting a convention on the elimination of discrimination against women. The work of the Commission was encouraged by the results of the World Conference of the International Women's Year, which was held in 1975. A Plan of Action adopted at that Conference called for a "convention on the elimination of discrimination against women, with effective procedures for its implementation".

For the next few years, the process of elaborating a convention continued within the Commission. In 1977, following submission to it of a draft instrument, the General Assembly appointed a special working group to finalize the draft.

The Convention on the Elimination of All Forms of Discrimination against Women was adopted by the General Assembly in 1979. In 1981, after receiving the necessary 20 ratifications, the Convention entered into force and the Committee on the Elimination of Discrimination against Women was formally established. The function of the Committee is to oversee the implementation of the Convention by States parties. Information on the practice of the Committee is contained in part II below.

I. SUBSTANTIVE PROVISIONS OF THE CONVENTION ON THE ELIMINATION OF ALL FORMS OF DISCRIMINATION AGAINST WOMEN

Defining Discrimination

Article 1

For the purposes of the present Convention, the term "discrimination against women" shall mean any distinction, exclusion or restriction made on the basis of sex which has the effect or purpose of impairing or nullifying the recognition, enjoyment or exercise by women, irrespective of their marital status, on a basis of equality of men and women, of human rights and fundamental freedoms in the political, economic,social, cultural,civil or any other field.

Article 1 Provides a comprehensive definition of discrimination which is then applicable to all provisions of the Convention. In contrast to the International Bill of Human Rights, which simply refers to "distinction" or "discrimination" on the basis of sex, article 1 gives a detailed explanation of the meaning of discrimination specifically against women. Such discrimination encompasses any difference in treatment on the grounds of gender which:

Intentionally or unintentionally disadvantage women:

Prevents society as a whole from recognizing women's rights in both the domestic and public spheres;

or which:

Prevents women from exercising the human rights and fundamental freedoms to which they are entitled.

In a number of countries throughout the world, women are denied their basic legal rights, including the right to vote and the right to own property. Such instances of legally entrenched differentiation will be easily identified as discrimination.

The definition set out above makes it clear that, in addition to establishing the criterion of differentiation (sex), it is also necessary to consider the outcome of the differentiation. If the result is a nullification or impairment of equal rights in any of the forms set out above then the differentiation is discriminatory and therefore prohibited under the Convention.

In 1992, the Committee on the Elimination of Discrimination against Women extended the general prohibition on sex discrimination in include gender-base violence. Further notes on this topic may be found at the end of part I.

Obligations of States Parties

Article 2

States Parties condemn discrimination against women in all its forms, agree to pursue by all appropriate means and without delay a policy of eliminating discrimination against women, and, to this end, undertake:

(a) To embody the principle of the equality of men and women in their national constitutions or other appropriate legislation if not yet incorporated therein and to ensure, through law and other appropriate means, the priactical realization of this principle;

(b) To adopt appropriate legislative and other measures, including sanctions where appropriate, prohibiting all discrimination against women:

(c) To establish legal protection of the rights of women on an equal basis with men and to ensure through cometent national tribunals and other public institutions the effective protection of women against any act of dicrimination;

(d) To refrain from engaging in any act or practice of discrimination against women and to ensure that public authorities and institutions shall act in conformity with this obligation;

(e) To take all appropriate measures to eliminate discrimination against women by any person, organization or enterprise;

(f) To take all appropriate measures, including legislation, to modify or abolish existing laws, regulations, customs and practices which constitute discrimination against women;

(g) To repeal all national penal provision which constitute discrimination against women.

Article 2 establishes, in a general way, the obligations of States under the Convention and the policy to be followed in eliminating discrimination against women. By becoming parties to the Covention, States accept the responsibility to take active steps to implement the principle of equality between men and women into their national constitutions and other relevant legislation. States should also eliminate the legal bases for discrimination by revising existing laws and vicil, penal and labour codes.

It is not enough merely to insert antidiscrimination clauses into legislation. The Convention also requires States parties to protect women's rights effectively and provide women with opportunities for recourse and protection against discrimination. They should incorporate sanctions into legislation that deter discrimination against women, and establish a system for filing complaints within national tribunals and courts.

States parties to the Convention must take steps to eleminate discrimination in both public and private spheres. It is not enough to strive for "vertical" gender equality of the individual women vis-a-vis public authorities; States must also work to secure non-discrimination at the "horizontal" level, even within the family.

Article 2 recognizes that legislative changes are most effective when made within a supportive frameowrk, i.e. when changes in the law are accompanied by a simultaneous change in the economic, social, political and cultural spheres.To this end, subparagraph (f) requires States not only to modify laws, but also to work towards the elimination of discriminatory customs and practices.

Appropriate Measures

Article 3

States Parties shall take in all fields, in particular in the political,Social, economic and cultural fields, all appropriate measures, including legislation, to ensure the full development and advancement of women, for the purpose of guaranteeing them the exercise and enjoyment of human rights and fundamental freedoms on a basis of equality with men.

Article 3 defines the appropriate measures in all fields which should be taken to implement the policies set out in article 2. It also serves to demonstrate the indivisibility and interdependence of the rights guaranteed by the Convention and the basic human rights to which all persons are entitled. Other United Nations instruments already guarantee equal dignity and rights for all human beings. Article 3 recognizes that, unless States take active steps to promote the advancement and development of women, they will not be able to enjoy fully the basic human rights guaranteed in the other instruments.

Temporary Special Measures to Combat Discrimination

Article 4

1. Adoption by States Parties of temporary speical measures aimed at accelerating *de facto* equality between men and women shall not be considered discrimination as defined in the present Convention, but shall in no way entail as a consequence the maintenance of unequal or separate standards; these measures shall be discountinued when the objectives of equality of opprotunity and treatment have been achieved.
2. Adoption by States Parties of special measures,including those measures contined in the present Convention, aimed at protecting maternity shall not be considered discriminatory.

Article 4 recognizes that, even if women are gicen legal (*de Jure*) equality, this does not automatically guarantee that they will in reality be treated equally (*de facto* equality). To accelerate women's actual equality in society and in the workplace, States are permitted to use special remedial measures for as long as inequalities continue to exist. The Convention thus reaches beyond the narrow concept of formal equality and sets its goals as equality of opportunity and equality of outcome. Positive measures are both lawful and necessary to achieve these goals.

At its seventh session, in 1988, the Committee on the Elimination of Discrimination against Women noted that significant progress had been made in guaranteeing women's legal equality, but that further steps needed to be taken to promote their *de facto* equality. In its general recommendation No.5 adopted at that session, the Committee recommended that

> States parties make more use of temporary special measures such as positive action, preferential treatment or quota systems to advance women's integration into education, the economy, politics and employment.

These special measures should be used simply to speed up the achievement of *de facto* equality for women, and should not create separate standards for women and men. In other words, the appropriateness of any special measures should be evaluated with regard to the actual existence of discriminatory paractices. Consequently, once the objectives of equality of opportunity and treatment are reached, these special measures are not longer needed and should be discountinued.

There will, however, always be exceptional cases where special treatment is the only way to guarantee true equality. The individual and community interests of children, for example, require continuous consideration of the health, income and earnings of mothers. Special measures to protect maternity are therefore always necessary and should never be abandoned.

Modifying Social and Cultural Patterns

Article 5

States Parties shall take all appropriate measures:

(a) To modify the social and cultural patterns of conduct of men and women, with a view to achieving the elimination of prejudices and customary and all other paractices which are based onthe idea of the the inferiority of the superiority of either of the sexes or on stereotyped roles for men and women;

(b) To ensure that family education includes a proper understanding of maternity as a social function and the recognition of the common responsibility of men and women in the upbringing and development of their children, it being understood that the interest of the children is the primordial consideration in all cases.

The importance of the Convention on the Elimination of All Forms of Discrimination against Women lies in the fact that it adds new, substantive provisions to the other instruments which also deal with equality and non-discrimination. Article 5 recognizes that, even if women's legal equality is guaranteed and special measures are taken to promote their *de facto* equality, another level of change is necessary for women's true equality. States should strive to remove the social, cultural and traditional patterns which perpetuate gender-role stereotypes and to create and overall framework in society that promotes the realization of women's full rights.

The prevalence of gender-role stereotypes is seen most particularly in the traditional concept of women's role in the domestic sphere. Many women are denied an education because their role is considered primarily as one of caring for the family. Moreover, this role is often viewed as unimportant and not,in itself, worthy of an education. Sub paragraph (b) of article 5 calls on States Parties to ensure that eudcation includes a proper understanding of the important role of maternity as a social function. It also requires that States recognize the raising of children asa responsibility that should be shared by women and men, and not as a task that is borne by women alone. This may well require the development of social infrastructures (e.g. paternal leave schemes) which would make possible a sharing of parental duties.

Suppressiing Exploitation of Women

Article 6

States Parties shall take all appropriate measures, including legislation, to suppress all forms of traffic in women and exploitation of prostitution of women.

Article 6 States to take all appropriate mesures to combat traffic in women and exploitative prostitution. In addressing these problems, it is essential for States to consider and act upon the conditions which are at the root of female prostituion: underdevelopment, poverty, drug abuse, illiteracy, and lack of training, education and employment opportunities. States Parties should also provide women with alternatives to prostitution by creating opportunities through rehabilitation, ob-raining and job-referral programmes.

States which tolerate the existence fo exploitative prostitution, girl-child prostitution and pornography (which are always exploitative), and other slave-like practices are in clear violation of their obligations under this article. It is not enough to enact laws against such injustices; in order adequately to discharge their responsibilities, States Parties must ensure that measures are taken to implement penal sanctions fully and effectively.

Equality in Political and Public Life at the National Level

Article 7

States Parties shall take all appropriate measures to eliminate discrimination against women in the political and public life of the country and, in particular,shall ensure to women,on equal terms with men, the right:

(a) To vote in all elections and public referenda and to be eligible for election to all publicly elected bodies:
(b) To participate in the formulation of government policy and the implementation thereof and to hold public office and perfom all public functions at all levels of government;
(c) To participate in non-governmental organizations and associations concerned with the public and political life of the country.

Article 7 requires States Parties to undertake two levels of action to create equality for women in political and public life. First, States must broaden the rights guaranteed in article 25 of the international Covenant on Civil and Political Rights and ensure to women the right to vote in all elections and public referenda. Of particular importance for women is the right to vote anonymously. Women who are not allowed to vote anonymously are often pressured to vote in the same way as their husbands and are thus prevented from expressing their own opinions.

Secondly, article 7 recognizes that, while it is essential, the right to vote is not in itself sufficient to guarantee the real and effective participation of women in the political process. The article therefore requires States to ensure to women the right to be elected to public office and to hold other government posts and positions in non-governmental organization. These obligations can be realized by including women on lists of governmental condidates, affirmative action and quotas,elimination gender restrictions for certain posts, increasing promotion rates for women into meaningful (as opposed to merely nominal) political leadership roles.

Equality in Political and Public Life at the International Level

Article 8

States Parties shall take all appropriate measures to ensure to women, on equal terms with men and without any discrimination, the opportunity to represent their Governments at the international level and to participate in the work of international organizations.

While many of the decisions which directly affect the lives of women are made within their own countires, important political,legal and social trends are both forged and reinforced at the international level. For this reason it is essential that women are adequately represented in international for a as members of government delegations and as employees of international organizations.

The goal of equal representation of women at the international level is still far from being realized. In general recommendation No.8 adopted at its seventh session, in 1988, the Committee on the Elimination of Discrimination against Women recommended that, in implementing article 8 of the Convention, States Parties make use of temporary special measures such as affirmative action and positive discrimination as envisaged by article 4.States should also use their influence in international organizations to ensure adequate and equal representation of women.

Equality in Nationality Laws

Article 9

1. States Parties shall grant women equal rights with men to acquire, change or retain their nationality. They shall ensure in particular that neither marriage to an alien nor change of nationality by the husband during marriage shall automatically change the nationality nationlity of the wife, render her stateless or force upon her the nationality of the husband.
2. States Parties shall grant women equal rights with men with respect to the nationality of their children.

In the context of article 9, nationality means citizenship.Many human rights, particularly political rights, derive directly from citizenship.

There are two obligations contained in article 9. First, it requires States parties to guarantee women the same rights as men to acquire, change or retain their nationality. For example, many countries discriminate against female nationals who marry foreigners. Foreign wives of male nationals may be permitted to acquire their husband's nationality, but foreign husbands of female nationals are not granted the same right. The result in such cases is that men who marry foreigners are allowed to remaining their country of origin, whereas women who marry foreigners may be forced to move to their husband's country of origin. Such a law would be considered discriminatory and should therefore be amended.

Secondly, article 9 requires States Parties to extend to women the same rights as men regarding the nationality of their children. In many countires, children automatically receive the nationality of the father. In implementing this article, States must establish formal legal equality between men and women wih regard to acquiring, changing or retaining nationality and conferring it upon their spouse or children.

Equality in Education

Article 10

States Paries shall take all appropriate measures to eliminate discrimination against women in order to ensure to them equal rights with men in the field of education and in particular to ensure, on a basis of equality of men and women:

(a) The same conditions for career and vocational guidance, for access to studies and for the achievement of diplomas in educational establishments of all categories in rural as well as in urban areas: this equality shall be ensured in pre-school, general, technical, professional and higher technical education, as well as in all types of vocational training;

(b) Access to the same curricula, the same examinations, teaching staff with qualifications of the same standard and school premises and equipment of the same quality;

(c) The elimination of any stereotyped concept of the roles of men and women at all levels and in all forms of education by encouraging coeducation and other types of education which will help to achieve this aim and, in particular,by the revision of textbooks and school programmes and the adaptation of teaching methods;

(d) The same opportunities to benefit from scholarships and other study grants;

(e) The same opportunities for access to programmes of continuing education, including adult and functional literacy programmes, particularly those aimed at reducing, at the earliest possible time, any gap in education existing between men and women;

(f) The reducation of female student drop-out rates and the organization of programmes for girls and women who have left school prematurely;

(g) The same opportunities to participate actively in sports and physical education;

(h) Access to specific educational information to help to ensure the health and well-being of families, including information and advice on family planning.

Article 10 recognizes that equality in education forms the foundation for women's empowerment in all spheres: in the workplace, in the family and in wider society. It is through education that traditions and beliefs which reinforce inequality between the sexes can be challenged, thereby helping to break down the legacy of discrimination handed from one generation to the next.

The obligations of States Parties under article 10 can be conveniently divided into three categoires.

The first obligation is equality of access. There are very few places in the world where women are denied a formal right to education. However, true equality in education requires the development of specific and effective guarantees to ensure that female students are provided with access to the same curricula and other educational and scholarship opportunities as male students. In many countires, parents do not expect their daughters to have careers out-side the home. Consequently, girl-children are encouraged to leave school after completing only a basic or elementary education. Evern at the elementary level, male students may be given a more rigorous and demanding curriculum than their female classmates. States parties shold reform the education system so that it no langer creates or permits the existence of separate standards and opportunities for females and males. In addition,States should, where necessary, create special programmes to encourage female students to further their education and to encourage parents to permit this. Such encouragement could take the form of scholarship funds designed for female students attending universities and technical and covational schools.

Secondly, States Parties have an obligation to eliminate gender -role stereotyping in and through the education system. Textbooks used in schools often reinforce traditional, unequal stereotypes, particularly as these apply to employment and domestic and parenting responsibilities. Teachers may promote this type of gender-role stereotyping by discouraging female students from engaging in mathematics, sciences, sports and other so-called "male" areas of study or activity. States should, where necessary, revise textbooks and offer special training courses for teachers in order to combat gender-based discrimination.

A third obligation of States Parties is to close existing gap in education levels between men and women. States should create programmes which give women the opportunity to return to school or attend special training courses. In this way, women who did not have the benefit of an equal education in the past will be offered the opportunity to "catch up" and thus to enjoy an equal role in the workplace and in society as a whole.

Equality in Employment and Labour Rights

Article 11

1. States Parties shall take all appropriate measures to eliminate discrimination against women in the field of employment in order to ensure,on basis of equality of men and owmen, the same rights, in particular:
   (a) The right to work as an inalienable right of all human beings;
   (b) The right to the same employment opportunities, including the application of the same criteria for selection in matters of employment;
   (c) The right to free choice of profession and employment, the right to promotion, job security and all benefits and conditions of service and the right to receive covational training and retraining, including apprenticeships, advanced vocational training and recurrent training; (d) the right to equal remuneration, including benefits, and to equal treatment in respect of work of equal value, as well as equality of treatment in the evaluation of the quality of work;
   (e) The right to social security, particularly in cases of retirement, unemployment, sickness, invalidity and old age and other incapacity to work, as well as the right to paid leave;
   (f) The right to protection of health and to safety in working conditions, including the safeguarding of the function of reproduction.
2. In order to prevent discrimination against women on the grounds of marriage or maternity and to ensure their effective right to work, States Parties shall take appropriate measures:
   (a) To prohibit,subject to the imposition of sanctions, dismissal on the grounds of pregnancy or of maternity leave and discrimination in dismissals on the basis of marital status;
   (b) To introduce maternity leave with pay or with comparable social benefits without loss of former employment, seniority of social allowances;
   (c) To encourage the provisions of the necessary supporting social services to enable parents to combine family obligations with work responsibilities and participation in public life, in particular through promoting the establishment and development of a network of child-care facilities;
   (d) To provide special protection to women during pregnancy in types of work proved to be harmful to them.

3. Protective legislation relating to matters covered in this article shall be reviewed periodically in the light of scientific and technological knowledge and shall be revised, repealed or extended as necessary.

Equality in employment and labour rights has long been recognized as an important element in the struggle for women's human rights. A large part of the battle at the international level has thus far been fought by the International Labour Organisation (ILO). Article 11 builds upon and consolidates many of the rights claimed for women by ILO.

Article 11 states clearly that women shall enjoy the basic human right to work. It then sets out a comprehensive list of obligations of States Parties on order to ensure that this right can be fully and effectively realized.

First, States Parties must guarantee women the same employment rights and opportunities as men. It is not sufficient for a State to outlaw discriminatory hiring practices. Equal employment opportunities, for example,presume equality in opportunities to prepare for employment through education and vocational training. In the recruitment process, women must be subject to the same hiring criteria as men.

Secondly, women must have the right to free choice in selecting a profession, and must not be automatically channelled into traditional "women's work". To discharge this obligation, States parties must grant women full equality in education and employment opportunities and must work towards the creation of social and cultural patterns which allow all members of society to accept and work towards the presence of women in many different types of career.

Thirdly, women in the workplace must have the right to equal remuneration and all work-related benefits. States parties must guarantee women equal pay for equal work, as well as equal treatment for work of equal value and equal treatment in evaluating the quality of work. Women are also to enjoy the protection of social security. Provision should be made for paid leave as well as retirement, unemployment, sickness and old-age benefits.

Fourthly, women in the workplace must be protected from discrimination based on marital status or maternity. The wording of this provision is very clear. State parties must prohibit employers from u4sing pregnancy or marital status as a criterion in the hiring or dismissal of women employees. States must also take measures that allow parents to combine family obligations with work responsibilities,by giving them benefits such as paid maternity leave, child-care subsidies and special health protection during pregnancy.

Finally, true equality in employment requires the implementation of measures to protect women from all forms of violence in the workplace. One of the most prevalent forms of violence against women in the workplace is sexual harassment of womenby male co-workers. In stead of being treated as equal co-workers, women are often treated as sexual objects. In response to this widespread problem, the Committee on the Elimination of Discrimination against Women, in general recommendation No 12 adopted at its eighth session, in 1989, called on States parties to include in their reports to the Committee information on legislation against sexual harassment in the workplace. In 1992, the Committee recommended that States Parties adopt effective legal measures, including penal sanctions, civil remedies and compensatory provisions, to protect women against all kinds of violence,including sexual assault and sexual harassment in the workplace (general recommendation No.19 (eleventh session), para. 24 (t)(i)).

It is important to note that the guarantees of equality and nondiscrimination contained in article 11 are applicable only to women in formal employment. This leaves vulnerable a vast number of women whose labour in the home,on the land or elsewhere goes unrecognized and whose rights therefore remain unprotected (see also, "Rural Women ", p. 68 below).

Equality in Access to Health Facilities

Article 12

1. States Parties shall take all appropriate measures to eliminate discrimination against women in the field of health care in order to ensure, on a basis of equality of men and women, access to health care services, including those related to family planning.
2. Not with standing the provisions of paragraph 1 of this article, States Parties shall ensure to women appropriate services in connection with pregnancy, confinement and the post-natal period, granting free services where necessary, as well as adequate nutrition during pregnancy and lactation.

Access to health care is a problem affecting women, men and children in many areas of the world. However, as recognized in article 12, women in particular, by virtue of their unequal status and their special vulnerabilities, encounter a great many obstacles in obtaining adequate health care.

Paragraph 1 of article 12 specifically requires States parties to ensure the equality of women and men in access to health care services. This requires the removal of any legal and social barriers which may operate to prevent of discourage women from making full use of available health care services. Steps should be taken to ensure access to health care services for all women, including those whose access may be impeded through poverty, illiteracy or physical isolation (see also "Rural Women" p. 68 below).

While not yet a universally recognized right in itself, the ability of a woman to control her own fertility is fundamental to her full enjoyment of the full range of human rights to which she is entitled, including the right to health. In recognition of this fact, article 12 makes specific reference to the area of family planning. Both women and men must have a voluntary choice in planning their families, and States must accordingly make available information and education about medically approved and appropriate methods of family planning. Any laws which operate to restrict a woman's access to family planning or any other medical services (e.g. by requiring prior permission of her husband or a near relative as a prerequisite for treatment or for the provision of information) would be contrary to this article and consequently should be amended. Where laws requiring the spouse's authorization for medical treatment or for the provision of family planning services have previously existed and subsequently been amended, States Parties should ensure that medical workers as well as the community are informed that such authorization is not required and that the practice is contrary to the rights of women.

Paragraph 2 of article 12 recognizes that women need extra care and attention during pregnancy and the post-natal period. States parties must recognize women's needs both as providers and receivers of health care during these timcs, and must ensure that they have access to adequate health care facilities and resources, including adequate nutrition during and after pregnancy.

It is estimated that, each year, at lest half a million women die from causes related to pregnancy and childbirth, most of these deaths occurring in the developing countries of Asia and Africa.[3] Implementation of the provisions of article 12 is an essential first step in reducing the high rate of maternal deaths.

In its examination of the scope and application of article 12, the Committee on the Elimination of Discrimination against Women has focused particularly on ending discrimination against women in national AIDS strategies. General recommendation No.15, adopted by the Committee at its ninth session, in 1990, calls on States parties to enhance women's role as care providers, health workers and educators in the prevention of infection with HIV, and to give special attention to the subordinate position of women in some societies which makes them especially vulnerable to HIV infection.

Together with the Sub-Commission on Prevention of Discrimination and Protection of Minorities, the Committee on the Elimination of Discrimination against Women has paid special attention to the area of traditional practices harmful to the health of women. Such practices include, but are not limited to, genital mutilation, dangerous birth practices and son preference. In its general recommendation No.14 (ninth session, 1990), the Committee called on States parties to take appropriate measures to eradicate the practice of female genital mutilation. Such measures could include the introduction of appropriate educational and training programmes and seminars, the development of national health policies aimed the eradicating female genital mutilation in public health facilities, and the provision of support to national organizations working for these goals.

Finance and Social Security

Article 13

States Parties shall take all appropriate measures to eliminate discrimination against women in other areas of economic and social life in order to ensure, on a basis of equality of men and women, the same rights, in particular:

(a) The right to family benefits:

(b) The right to bank loans, mortgages and other forms of financial credit;

(c) The right to participate in recreational activities, sports and all aspects of cultural life.

Article 13 recognizes that, unless States Parties guarantee Somen financial independence, they will not have true equality with men because they will not be able to head their own households, own their own homes,or start their own businesses. Many private businesses discriminate against women employees by not giving them the same access to family benefits and insurance as male employees; similarly, loan and mortgage companies often impose higher standards on women and require higher premiums or deposits for obtaining credit. Social security provisions may discriminate against single mothers by presuming dependence upon a man. States must take steps to ensure that women have equal access with men to credit and loans, and that they also have equal access to family benefits.

Equal rights of participation is sporting, recreational and other cultural activities presumes the existence of real equality of access. To achieve this, States should ensure that all legal or social obstacles to the full participation of women in these areas are removed and that funding, grants or other forms of support are implemented under a principle of equality of opportunity.

Rural Women

Article 14

1. States Parties shall take into account the particular problems faced by rural women and the significant roles which rural women play in the economic survival of their families, including their work in the non-monetized- sectors of the economy, and shall take all appropriate measures to ensure the application of the provisions of the present Convention to women in rural areas.
2. States Parties shall take all appropriate measures to eliminate discrimination against women in rural areas in order to ensure, on a basis of equality of men and women, that they participate in and benefit from rural development and, in particular, shall ensure to such women the right:
   (a) To participate in the elaboration and implementation of development planning at all levels;
   (b) To have access to adequate health care facilities, including information, counselling and services in family planning;
   (c) To benefit directly from social security programmes;
   (d) To obtain all types of training and education, formal and non-formal, including that relating to functional literacy, as well as, *inter alia*, the benefit of all community and extension services, in order to increase their technical proficiency;
   (e) To organize self-help groups and co-operatives in order to obtain equal access to economic opportunities through employment or self-employment;
   (f) To participate in all community activities;
   (g) To have access to agricultural credit and loans, marketing facilities, appropriate technology and equal treatment in land and agrarian reform as well as in land resettlement schemes;
   (h) To enjoy adequate living conditions, particularly in relation to housing, sanitation, electricity and water supply, transport and communications.

In many parts of the world, women living in rural areas bear a disproportionate amount of the burden of labour. Moreover, they often receive little or no recognition for their participation, nor are they allowed to enjoy the fruits of their work or share in the benefits of development. In addition, many of these women workers, by remaining "invisible" and unacknowledged, are not entitled to the protections and benefits afforded those in formal employment.

Article 14 recognizes that rural women are a group with special problems needing careful attention and consideration by States parties. In addition, by extending the Convention to women in rural areas, States parties are explicitly recognizing the importance of the work of rural women and their contribution to the well-being of their families and the economy of their countries. This emphasis on development is unique in human rights treaty and represents clear acknowledgement of the fundamental link between achieving equality and involving women in the development process.

Article 14 requires States Parties to eliminate discrimination against women in rural areas; to implement their right to adequate living conditions; and to take special measures to ensure them, in a basis of equality with; men, the same participation in and benefits of rural development. Special measures to achieve these goals could include:ensuring the participation of women, especially rural women, in the elaboration and implementation of development planning or order that they may work to create a better environment for themselves: encouraging and providing assistance for the establishment of self-help groups and co-operatives; and providing rural women with access to adequate health care, family planning facilities and social security programmes to give them greater financial and social control over their lives. States should also give women in rural areas the opportunity to break out of traditional roles and choose different lifestyles by ensuring them equal access to training and education programmes, as well as to agricultural credit, loans and marketing facilities.

Equality in Legal and Civil Matters

Article 15

1. States Parties shall accord to women equality with men before the law.
2. States Parties shall accord to women, in civil matters, a legal capacity identical to that of men and the same opportunities to exercise that capacity. In particular, they shall give women equal rights to conclude contracts and to administer property and shall treat them equally in all stages of procedure in courts and tribunals.
3. States Parties agree that all contracts and all other private instruments of any kind with a legal effect which is directed at restricting

the legal capacity of women shall be deemed null and void.

4. States Parties shall accord to men and women the same rights with regard to the law relating to the movement of persons and the freedom to choose their residence and domicile.

Article 15 confirms women's equality with men before the law, and additionally requires States Parties to guarantee women equality with men in areas of civil law where women have traditionally been discriminated against. For example, in many countries, women do not have the same property rights as men: traditional property law often discriminated against women in that only male children are able to inherit the family land, and that husbands have automatic ownership over all of their wife's property upon marriage. Similarly, legislation in a number of countries establishes that the administration of family property is to be undertaken by the male head of the family—thereby excluding women. Many legal systems do not allow a woman to enter into contracts in her own right but require the signature of her husband before a contract is considered legally binding, even in cases relating to her own property or earnings. Article 15 requires States Parties to take positive steps to ensure women full equality in civil law. States must therefore repeal or amend any laws or instruments which have the effect of restricting women's legal capacity.

Paragraph 4 of article 15 requires equality in the law regarding movement of persons and freedom to choose ones own residence and domicile. A law which makes a woman's domicile dependent upon her husband's would be considered discriminatory under this provision, as would a law which operated to restrict the right of a woman (including a married woman) to choose where she lives.

Equality in Family Law

Article 16

1. States Parties shall take all appropriate measures to eliminate discrimination against women in all matters relating to marriage and family relations and in particular shall ensure, on a basis of equality of men and women:
   (a) The same right to enter into marriage;
   (b) The same right freely to choose a spouse and to enter into marriage only with their free and full consent;
   (c) The same rights and responsibilities during marriage and at its dissolution;
   (d) The same rights and responsibilities as parents, irrespective of their marital status, in matters relating to their children; in all

cases the interests of the children shall be paramount;

(e) The same rights to decide freely and responsibly on the number and spacing of their children and to have access to the information, education and means to enable them to exercise these rights;

(f) The same rights and responsibilities with regard to guardianship, wardship, trusteeship and adoption of children, or similar institutions where these concepts exist in national legislation; in all cases the interests of the children shall be paramount;

(g) The same personal rights as husband and wife, including the right to choose a family name, a profession and an occupation;

(h) The same rights for both spouses in respect of the ownership, acquisition, management,administration, enjoyment and disposition of property, whether free of charge or for a valuable consideration.

2. The betrothal and the marriage of a child shall have no legal effect, and all necessary action, including legislation, shall be taken to specify a minimum age for marriage and to make the registration of marriages in an official registry compulsory.

Trticle 16 addresses the problem of discrimination against women in the private sphere, including discrimination in the area of family law discrimination against women takes place in their own homes by their husbands, their families and their communities. In some societies, young women or girls are forced into arranged marriages. In many areas of the world, married women are not permitted to participate equally in deciding how many children they will bear, how these children will be brought up, and when and whether or not they themselves should work. Even in countries where women enjoy a greater say in their family life, deeply ingrained stereotypes regarding the "proper" role of women as being that of housewife and homemaker may prevent them from pursuing outside careers or taking part in important decision-making with their husbands.

This area of discrimination is usually based on long-standing cultural or religious practices; it is thus one of the most difficult areas to penetrate and one of the most resistant to change. Yet the drafters of the Convention realized that change in this area is essential in order for women to attain full equality. To bring about this change, States parties must first take all appropriate measures to eliminate or amend existing laws or instruments relating to marriages to and the family which discriminate against women. Such laws would include, for example, those which do not give women the same legal rights to divorce and remarriage as men; laws which do not allow women full property-ownership rights; and laws which do not grant them equal rights regarding the care and custody of children, whether in marriage or following divorce. Secondly, State Parties must take steps actively to ensure that women are able to exercise the same right as men, including the right freely to enter into marriage and to choose a spouse. In keeping with the freedom of a woman to choose when and whom she should marry, a minimum age for marriage should be guaranteed by law.

Although domestic violence is not specifically addressed in article 16, the Committee on the Elimination of Discrimination against Women has made it clear that violence and abuse in the family is a human rights problem which must be addressed by States Parties. Additional information on gender-base violence is provided in the following commentary.

A Note on Gender-base Violence

The issue of gender-based violence is not specifically addressed in the Convention, although it is clearly fundamental to its most basic provisions. In general recommendation No.19 adopted at its eleventh session, in 1992, the Committee on the Elimination of Discrimination against Women took the important step of formally extending the general prohibition on gender-based discrimination to include gender based violence, which it defined (para.6) as

> violence that is directed at a woman because she is a woman or that affects women disproportionately .It includes acts that inflict physical, mental or sexual harm or suffering, threats of such acts, coercion and other deprivations of liberty.....

The Committee affirmed that violence against a woman constitutes a violation of her internationally recognized human rights—regardless of whether the perpetrator is a public official or a private person.

The responsibility of States Parties under the Convention extends to eliminating gender-based discrimination by any person, organization or enterprise. State responsibility may therefore be invoked not only when a government official is involved in an act of gender-based violence,but also when the State fails to act with due diligence to prevent violations of rights committed by private persons or to investigate and punish such acts of violence, and to provide compensation.

In the same general recommendation (para. 24 (t)), the Committee called on States Parties to take all measures necessary to prevent gender-based violence. Such measures would include not only legal sanctions, civil remedies and avenues for compensation, but also preventive measures such as public information and education programmes, as well as protective measures, including support services for victims of violence.

The work of the Committee in this area is being reinforced by other international developments. In 1993, the General Assembly adopted the Declaration on the Elimination of Violence against Women (resolution 48/104). The Declaration sets out the steps which States and the international community should take to ensure the elimination of all forms of violence against women, whether occurring in public or in private life.

Reservations to the Convention

Were a treaty permits -as is the case with the Convention on the Elimination of All Forms of Discrimination against Women-States parties may make a reservation,i.e. a formal declaration that they do not accept as binding on them a certain part or parts of the treaty.

Article 28 of the Convention states (para.2):

> A reservation incompatible with the object and purpose of the present Convention shall not be permitted.

This provision restates a fundamental rule of the international law of treaties: that a reservation to a convention which is contrary to its object and purpose cannot be permitted.

The Convention on the Elimination of All Forms of Discrimination against Women has been the subject of more reservations than any other major international human rights treaty. As of October 1993, 41 States parties had made and not subsequently withdrawn reservations to the Convention. Some of those reservations concern matters which are not fundamental to the object and purpose of the treaty. Others are to the dispute-settlement provisions of the Convention (art.29). Some reservations are so broad and vague that it is difficult to determine exactly what States are reserving. A relatively large number of States parties have made substantive reservations to basic articles, including those provisions relating to non-discrimination in family law, legal capacity and citizenship. Some States have even entered reservations to the very important article 2, which contains the central commitment of parties to eradicate all forms of discrimination against women, including gender-based discrimination. Many reservations are directed at those provisions which seek to eliminate discrimination in the "private" sphere of work,home and family.

Such substantive reservations have the potential to limit significantly the obligations undertaken by the reserving States and in this way they clearly undermine the object and purpose of the Convention.

In the course of its work, the Committee on the Elimination of Discrimination against Women regularly encourages States parties to review and withdraw their reservations. The Committee does not have the power to decide whether or not reservations are incompatible with the object and purpose of the Convention. The question of incompatibility can be answered by the International Court of Justice, but so far no State has sought an advisory opinion from the Court on the compatibility of reservations or on how specific they have to be, or challenged another State in this forum.

As recognized by the 1993 World Conference on Human Rights, the matter of reservations to the Convention on the Elimination of All Forms of Discrimination against Women is a serious one. The number and nature of reservations and the failure to invoke the formal procedure set out in the 1969 Vienna Convention on the Law of Treaties for deciding on the validity of reservations have provoked considerable controversy. Some States parties have expressed strong objection to many reservations on the ground that they are clearly incompatible with both the latter and the spirit of the Convention, while others have strongly defended their right to make reservations.

At its thirteenth session, in 1994, the Committee on the Elimination of Discrimination against Women voiced its agreement with the view of the World Conference that States should consider limiting the extent of any reservations they make to international human rights instruments, formulate any reservations as precisely and narrowly as possible, ensure that none is incompatible with the object and purpose of the treaty concerned and regularly review any reservations with a view to withdrawing them. At the same session, the Committee took a number of concrete steps to bring the issue of reservations to the attention of other United Nations bodies, including the Commission on the Status of Women and the Commission on Human Rights. The Committee also drafted specific guidelines for reporting by States parties on reservations which they have entered to the Convention on the Elimination of All Forms of Discrimination against Women.

II. IMPLEMENTING THE CONVENTION: THE COMMITTEE ON THE ELIMINATION OF DISCRIMINATION AGAINST WOMEN

Establishment and Composition of the Committee

Article 17 of the Convention on the Elimination of All Forms of Discrimination against Women establishes the Committee on the Elimination of Discrimination against Women to oversee the implementation of its provisions.

In accordance with the Convention, the Committee is composed of 23 experts who are elected by secret ballot from a list of persons "of high moral standing and competence in the field covered by the Convention" nominated by States Parties. In the election of persons to the Committee, consideration is given to equitable geographical distribution and to the representation of different civilization and legal systems. The members of the Committee serve four-year terms. Although nominated by their own Governments, members serve in their personal capacity and not as delegates or representatives of their countries of origin.

The composition of the Committee is noticeably different from that of other human rights treaty bodies. In the first place the Committee has, since its inception, and with only one exception, been composed entirely of women. Members have been and continue to be drawn from a wide variety of professional backgrounds. The breadth of experience in the Committee is reflected favourably in the process by which reports from States parties are examined and commented upon.

What does the Committee do?

The Committee acts as a monitoring system to oversee the implementation of the Convention by those States which have ratified or acceded to it. This is done principally by examining reports submitted by those States parties. The Committee considers these reports and makes suggestions and recommendations based on their consideration. It may also invite United Nations specialized agencies to submit reports for considerate and may receive information from non-governmental organizations. The Committee reports annually in its activities to the General Assembly through the Economic and Social Council, and the Council transmits these reports to the Commission on the Status of Women for information.

The Committee meets for two weeks each year. This is the shortest meeting time of any Committee established under a human rights treaty.

How Does a State Party Report to the Committee?

Under article 18 of the Convention, States parties are required to submit reports to the Secretary-General of the United Nations on legislative, judicial and other measures which they have taken in accordance with the provisions of the Convention. These reports are for consideration by the Committee.

A State party must submit its first report within one year after it has ratified or acceded to the Convention; subsequent reports must be submitted at least every four year or whenever the Committee so requests.

In ratifying or acceding to the Convention, States parties accept a legal obligation to submit timely and complete reports. Many States have failed to discharge this obligation. Whatever the reason for this failure,the end result is a large number of overdue reports and a significant proportion of incomplete or inadequate ones. As of October 1993, 72 States Parties to the Convention (almost two thirds of the total number of States Parties) had failed to submit reports by the due date.

The reporting process is a difficult one and the preparation of reports can be a time-consuming and complex task. Some problems in the process arise from a lack of personnel, experience and resources within the relevant ministry or department. The process of collecting information can be facilitated by ensuring collaboration between the reporting agency and those government department from which statistics or other information must be obtained. The ability of non-governmental organizations to assist in the preparation of reports should not be overlooked.

Unfortunately,, the Committee cannot effectively address all difficulties which may arise in the reporting process. It has, however, developed two sets of general guidelines for reporting in an effort to provide practical technical assistance to States parties. These guidelines suggest that initial reports could be usefully divided into two parts: the first on the country's political, legal and social framework and general measures used to implement the Convention, and the second part a detailed description of steps taken to comply with individual articles. Unfortunately, many States parties have not followed these guidelines, a fact which implies that the guidelines are too general to be especially helpful. It has been suggested that, in order to make the reporting process more effective, the Committee should develop detailed guidelines offering more concrete guidance to States parties.

How Does the Committee Work?

Procedural Aspects

Under article 20 of the Convention, the Committee meets once a year for "a period of not more than two weeks". It is serviced by the United Nations Division for the Advancement of Women, which moved from Vienna to New York in 1993.

In accordance with article 19 of the Convention, the Committee has adopted its own rules of procedure. These rules have established that the meetings of the Committee are generally held in public; that 12 members constitute a quorum; and that the presence of two thirds of the members is required for taking a decision. The rules of procedure further establish that the Committee shall endeavour to reach its decision by consensus.

The Committee elects a chairperson, three vice-chairpersons and a rapporteur from among its members. These persons hold office for a period of two years. To facilitate its work, the Committee has established the following working groups:

(a) Pre-sessional Working Group

In response to the problems encountered due to the lack of time and resources to consider adequately States parties' reports, the Committee established a pre-sessional working group to prepare the consideration of second and subsequent periodic reports. The pre-sessional working group is composed of five members of the Committee and its mandate is to prepare a list of issues and sets of questions to be sent in advance to the reporting States. This enables reporting States to prep4are replies for presentation at the session and thus contributes to a speedier consideration of second and subsequent reports.

(b) Two Standing Working Groups

In addition to the pre-sessional working group, the Committee has established two standing working group which meet during the regular session of the Committee. Working Group 1 considers and suggests ways and means of expediting the work of the Committee. Working group II considers ways and means of implementing article 21 of the Convention, which gives the Committee the power to issue suggestions and general recommendations on implementation of the Convention.

Consideration of Reports by the Committee

1. Submission of Reports

Individual States parties first submit a written report to the Committee. State representatives are then given the opportunity orally to introduce the report to the Committee. These introductions tend to provide a very general overview of the content of the report.

2. General Observation

After the introduction, the Committee makes general observations and comments regarding the report's form and content. In some cases, the Committee will also comment on any reservations to the Convention which have been made by the reporting State party and may also enquire as to whether such reservations could be reconsidered.

3. Consideration of Individual Articles

The committee members then ask questions relating to specific articles of the Convention. They focus on the actual position of women in society in an efforts to understand the true extent of the problem of discrimination. The Committee will accordingly request specific statistical information on he position of women in society, not only from the Government, but also from non-government, but also from non-governmental organizations and independent agencies.

The State party presenting its report may decide to answer some of these questions immediately, and usually will provide other answers a day or two later. At this point, the Committee may ask additional questions, or may request that further information be sent to the Secretariat before the next report is due.

4. Concluding Observations

The Committee will then prepare concluding comments on the reports of individual States parties so that these can be reflected in the report of the Committee. At its thirteenth session, in 1994, the Committee decided that these comments should deal with the most important points, covered in constructive dialogue, emphasizing both positive aspects of a State's report and matters on which the Committee had expressed concern, and clearly indicating what the Committee wished the State party to report on in its next report.

5. Encouraging a Constructive Dialogue between the Committee and States

The examination of States Parties' reports by the Committee is not meant to be an adversarial procedure, Instead, all efforts are made to develop a constructive dialogue between States parties and Committee members. Although some Committee members may criticize a State in a particular area, other members will go to great lengths to encourage the progress made by the State in other areas. The overall atmosphere of the Committee's sessions is one of a free exchange of ideas, information and suggestions.

One aspect of this cordial environment is that the Committee never formally pronounces a State to be in violation of the Convention, but instead points out the State's shortcomings through a series of questions and comments. However, this approach also means that the Committee does not put itself in a position to exert strong pressure on States who are in outright violation of the Convention to change their policies and legislation.

Interpreting and Applying the Convention

Article 21 of the Convention provides that the Committee may make suggestions and general recommendations based on its examination of the reports and information received from States parties. To date, the general recommendations issued by the Committee have not been addressed to individual States. Instead, the Committee had restricted itself to making recommendations to all States parties on specific steps which may be taken to fulfill their obligations under the Convention.

The general recommendations made by the Committee are limited in both range and effect. Because they are geared to all States parties rather than in individual States, the scope of these recommendations is often very broad-making compliance difficult to monitor. Such recommendations, along with any other suggestions made by the Committee to individual States Parties, are not legally binding.

Until recently, the Committee had not offered any substantive interpretation or analysis of the scope and meaning of the articles of the Convention. Indeed, the Convention does not specifically accord the Committee such interpretive authority. However, most of the other treaty-monitoring bodies (most notably the Committee on the Elimination of Racial Discrimination, the Human Rights Committee and the Committee on Economic, Social and Cultural Rights) have made substantive interpretations of their respective Conventions in the absence of an express authority to do so. These interpretations have made a major contribution to the development of substantive human rights law. They have proved to be very useful for States in compiling their reports, and for non-governmental organization working for change at the national level.

In general recommendation No. 19 adopted at its eleventh session, in 1992, the Committee on the Elimination of Discrimination against Women explored the coverage of gender-based violence in the various articles of the Convention. At its twelfth session, in 1993, the Committee undertook an analysis of article 16 and other articles relating to the family, which is expected to lead to a general recommendation. The Committee has established a work programme under which the various substantive articles of the Convention will be examined in turn during its annual sessions.

Improving the Work of the Committee

In fulfilling effectively its mandate of overseeing the implementation of the Convention by States parties, the Committee faces many challenges. It must strive to expand the information base available to it—not only for compiling but for reviewing reports; it must, where necessary, offer an interpretation of the norms embodied in the articles of the Convention; and it must endeavour to create a more effective monitoring system.

1. Expanding the Information Base of the Committee

At present, the Division for the Advancement of Women provides Committee members with analysis based upon statistical indicators relevant to specific articles of the Convention for each periodic report of States parties.

Article 22 of the Convention provides that the Committee may invite specialized agencies of the United Nations to submit reports for consideration by the Committee on the implementation of the Convention in areas falling within the scope of their activities. This is a useful opportunity for the Committee to receive detailed information on the implementation of the convention in specific areas. A number of specialized agencies and other United Nations bodies, including the Food and Agriculture Organization of the United Nations (FAO), the United Nations Development Programme (UNDP), the Office of the United Nations High Commissioner for Refugees (UNHCR) and the United Nations Children's Fund (UNICEF), are directly involved in issues which affect the human rights of women. To date, only the International Labour Organisation (ILO), the World Health Organization (WHO) and the United Nations Educational, Scientific and Cultural Organization (UNESCO) have submitted reports to the Committee.

In order to take full advantage of the vast store of relevant, country-specific information available within United Nations agencies, the Committee continues actively to seek their co-operation. Such information is, of course, most useful it relates to the situation in a country being discussed by the Committee at the session during which the information is submitted.

Another valuable source of information for the Committee is non-governmental human rights and women's organizations and independent agencies. Reports submitted by States parties do not always accurately reflect the human rights situation of women in the country concerned, nor do they always identify specific problem areas. Information and statistics from independent organizations are extremely useful to the Committee in assessing the actual situation of women in individual States. Submissions which are prepared in the context of the purposes of reporting, as outlined above, will be the most useful to Committee members in their task of scrutinizing States parties' reports. Submissions should, where possible identify the precise articles of the Convention which relate to the problems or issues being addressed. Non-governmental organizations and other groups may write to the Committee, care of the Division for the Advancement of Women, at the following address: Room DC2-1220,P.O. BOX 20,United Nations, New

York, NY 10017, United States of America. The Division for the Advancement of Women can also provide information on which States parties reports are to be considered at a particular session. It should be noted that accredited representatives of non-governmental organizations may attend sessions of the Committee as observers.

2. Clarification of Provisions of the Convention

The Convention on the Elimination of All Forms Discrimination against Women is a legal document and, for this reason, its provisions may require clarification and even elaboration in order that the obligations assumed by States will be perfectly clear. This process of developing a jurisprudence is an ongoing one because the Convention is a dynamic document. It must be flexible enough to take account of changing international attitudes and circumstances, while at the same time retaining its spirit and integrity.

Although in its general observations the Committee has made broad statements on the form and structure of States parties' reports, and has underscored the need to remedy discrimination against specific groups of women and in relation to specific traditional practices,it had not, until recently (see "Interpreting and applying the Convention", p.40 above), attempted formally to interpret the rights guaranteed in the Convention. The experience of the other treaty-monitoring bodies has shown that a proactive approach to monitoring can be extremely useful in assisting States parties in understand their obligations. Clarification of the norms contained in the Convention would also be extremely valuable for women in understanding the rights to which they are entitled. The process of interpreting substantive article of the Convention was begun by the Committee at its tenth session, in 1991, and has been given new impetus by the adoption of a programme of work under which substantive articles will be examined in turn.

3. Development of an Effective Monitoring System

By expanding its information base and by attempting to clarify norms contained in the Convention, the Committee has taken some important first steps in developing an effective monitoring system.

However, a number of challenges remain. One of these is to improve the timeliness and efficiency of the reporting process. To assist States which are overdue in reporting, the Committee has adopted procedures by which States are allowed to combine reports. Nevertheless, the fact that the Committee has the shortest meeting time of any treaty monitoring body (two weeks) had meant that a considerable backlog of reports has built up. There is now an average of three years between the time a State party submits a report and the consideration of that report by the Committee. This is itself a disincentive to report and leads to the need for the State to present additional information to update its report.

As a temporary measure,three-week sessions have been mandated until the backlog is removed. However, despite the best efforts of the Committee it has become clear that the temporary extension of sessions cannot be expected to eliminate the backlog. At its thirteenth session, in 1994, the Committee therefore recommended that States parties amend article 20 of the Convention in order to allow it to "meet annually" to consider reports (deleting the words "normally .... for a period of not more than two weeks"). It further recommended that, pending this amendment, the General Assembly authorize the Committee to meet for two sessions of three weeks' duration, starting in 1995 and continuing into the 1996-1998 biennium.

Outside the Committee, suggestions have been made that all treaty-monitoring bodies in the United Nations human rights system should work together to improve the timeliness and quality of States' reports by co-ordinating the different guidelines for reporting. If a standardized method for reporting under all conventions were in place, this would decrease the administrative burden on States. A uniform system of reporting would also increase the speed and efficiency with which the various committees could review and evaluate reports during their annual sessions.

The timeliness and quality of States parties' reports to the Committee on the Elimination of Discrimination against Women can also be improved through training of government officials responsible for their compilation. The Division for the Advancement of Women regularly conducts such training exercises. Training courses on reporting under all major human rights conventions are also organized by the United Nations Center for Human Rights as part of its technical assistance programme.

4. An Individual Complaints Procedure?

The possibility of introducing the right of petition through the preparation of an optional protocol to Convention on the Elimination of All Forms of Discrimination against Women (similar to the Optional Protocols to the International Covenant on Civil and Political Rights) was recommended in the Vienna Declaration and Programme of Action adopted by the World Conference on Human Rights in 1993. As part of the follow-up to that Conference, the Committee on the Elimination of

Discrimination against Women and the Commission on the Status of Women will study the possibility. Such a protocol would permit citizens of States parties to lodge complaints with the Committee alleging violation of their rights as set out in the Convention. It might also permit the lodging of complaints between States. It is apparent that such a development would considerably increase the strength of the Committee and its ability to have a direct impact on the problem of gender-based discrimination.

In the meantime, there are several avenues by which women may draw international attention to cases of discrimination. The Commission on the Status of Women is a United Nations body charged with, inter alia, developing recommendations and proposals for action on urgent problems in the field of women's rights. The Commission may receive communications from individuals and groups concerning discrimination against women. No action is taken on individual complaints. Instead, the procedure aims to discern emerging trends and patterns of discrimination against women in order to develop policy recommendations aimed at solving widespread problems. Communications may be sent to the Commission care of the United Nations Division for the Advancement of Women (address under 1, at p. 81 above).

In addition,the Human Rights Committee, which oversees implementation of the International Covenant on Civil and Political Rights,may receive complaints of violations of the sex equality provisions of the Covenant-in particular article 26. The prohibition of discrimination on the basis of sex has been extended to rights set out in other instruments, for example the right to social security guaranteed in the International Covenant on Economic, Social and Cultural Rights (art.9).[4]. The individual complaints procedure of the Human Rights Committee is available to individuals in 76 countries which have ratified the Optional Protocol to the Covenant on Civil and Political Rights. Women in these countries are thereby able to bring complaints about violations of their rights of equal entitlements protected by that Covenant as well as by the Covenant on Economic, Social and Cultural Rights and possibly other international human rights conventions, provided their country is also a party to those treaties.

III. CONVENTION ON THE ELIMINATION OF ALL FORMS OF DISCRIMINATION AGAINST WOMEN

Adopted and opened for signature, ratification and accession by General Assembly resolution 34/180 of 18 December 1979

ENTRY INTO FORCE; 3 September 1981, in Accordance with article 27(1)

The States Parties to the Present Convention,

Noting that the Charter of the United Nations reaffirms faith in fundamental human rights, in the dignity and worth of the human person and in the equal rights of men and women,

Noting that the Universal Declaration of Human Rights affirms the principle of the inadmissibility of discrimination and proclaims that all human beings are born free and equal in dignity and rights and that everyone is entitled to all the rights and freedoms set forth therein, without distinction of any kind, including distinction based on sex,

Noting that the States Parties to the International Covenants on Human Rights have the obligation to ensure the equal rights of men and women to enjoy all economic, social, cultural, civil and political rights,

Considering the international conventions concluded under the auspices of the United Nations and the specialized agencies promoting equality of rights of men and women,

Noting also the resolution, declarations and recommendations adopted by the United Nations and the specialized agencies promoting equality of rights of men and women,

Concerned, however, that despite these various instruments extensive discrimination against women continues to exist,

Recalling that discrimination against women violates the principles of equality of rights and respect for human dignity, is an obstacle to the participation of women, on equal terms with men, in the political, social, economic and cultural life of their countries, hampers the growth of the prosperity of society and the family and makes more difficult the full development of the potentialities of women in the service of their countries and of humanity,

Concerned that in situations of poverty women have the least access to food, health, education, training and opportunities for employment and other needs,

Convinced that the establishment of the new international economic order based on equity and justice will contribute significantly towards the promotion of equality between men and women,

Emphasizing that the eradication of apartheid, all forms of racism, racial discrimination, colonialism, neocolonialism, aggression, foreign occupation and domination and interference in the internal affairs of States is essential to the full enjoyment of the rights of men and women,

Affirming that the strengthening of international peace and security, the relaxation of international tension, mutual co-operation among all States irrespective of their social and economic systems, general and complete disarmament, in particular nuclear disarmament under strict and effective international control, the affirmation of the principles of justice, equality and mutual benefit in relations among countries and the realization of the right of peoples under alien and colonial domination and foreign occupation to self-determination and independence, as well as respect for national sovereignty and territorial integrity, will promote social progress and development and as a consequence will contribute to the attainment of full equality between men and women,

Convinced that the full and complete development of a country, the welfare of the world and the cause of peace require the maximum participation of women on equal terms with men in all fields,

Bearing in mind the great contribution of women to the welfare of the family and to the development of society, so far not fully recognized, the social significance of maternity and the role of both parents in the family and in the upbringing of children, and aware that the role of women in procreation should not be a basis for discrimination but that the upbringing of children requires a sharing of responsibility between men and women and society as a whole,

Aware that a change in the traditional role of men as well as the role of women in society and in the family is needed to achieve full equality between men and women,

Determined to implement the principles set forth in the Declaration on the Elimination of Discrimination against Women and, for that purpose, to adopt the measures required for the elimination of such discrimination in all its forms and manifestations,

Have agreed on the following:

PART I

Article 1

For the purposes of the present Convention, the term "discrimination against women" shall mean any distinction, exclusion or restriction made on the basis of sex which has the effect or purpose of impairing or nullifying the recognition, enjoyment or exercise by women, irrespective of their marital status, on a basis of equality of men and women, of human rights and fundamental freedoms in the political, economic, social, cultural, civil or any other field.

Article 2

States Parties condemn discrimination against women in all its forms, agree to pursue by all appropriate means and without delay a policy of eliminating discrimination against women and, to this end, undertake;

(a) To embody the principle of the equality of men and women in their national constitutions or other appropriate legislation if not yet incorporated therein and to ensure, through law and other appropriate means, the practical realization of this principle;

(b) To adopt appropriate legislative and other measures, including sanctions where appropriate, prohibiting all discrimination against women;

(c) To establish legal protection of the rights of women on an equal basis with men and to ensure through competent national tribunals and other public institutions the effective protection of women against any act of discrimination;

(d) To refrain from engaging in any act or practice of discrimination against women and to ensure that public authorities and institutions shall act in conformity with this obligation;

(e) To take all appropriate measures, to eliminate discrimination against omen by any person, organization or enterprise;

(f) To take all appropriate measures, including legislation, to modify or abolish existing laws, regulations, customs and practices which constitute discrimination against women;

(g) To repeal all national penal provisions which constitute discrimination against women.

Article 3

States Parties shall take in all fields, in particular in the political, social, economic and cultural fields, all appropriate measures, including legislation, to ensure the full development and advancement of women, for the purpose of guaranteeing them the exercise and enjoyment of human rights and fundamental freedoms on a basis of equality with men.

Article 4

1. Adoption by States Parties of temporary special measures aimed at accelerating *de facto* equality between men and women shall not be considered discrimination as defined in the present Convention, but shall in no way entail as a consequence the maintenance of unequal or separate standards; these measures shall be discontinued when the objectives of equality of opportunity and treatment have been achieved.

2. Adoption by States Parties of special measures, including those measures contained in the present Convention, aimed at protecting maternity shall not be considered discriminatory.

Article 5

States Parties shall take all appropriate measures:

(a) To modify the social and cultural pattern of conduct of men and women, with a view to achieving the elimination of prejudices and customary and all other practices which are based on the idea of the inferiority or the superiority of either of the sexes or on stereotyped roles for men and women;

(b) To ensure that family education includes a proper understanding of maternity as a social function and the recognition of the common responsibility of men and women in the upbringing and development of their children, it being understood that the interest of the children is the primordial consideration in all cases.

Article 6

States Parties shall take all appropriate measures, including legislation, to suppress all forms of traffic in women and exploitation of prostitution women.

PART II

Article7

States Parties shall take all appropriate measures to eliminated discrimination against women in the political and public life of the country and, in particular, shall ensure to women, on equal terms with men, the right:

(a) To vote in all elections and public referenda and to be eligible for election to all publicly elected bodies;

(b) To participate in the formulation of government policy and the implementation thereof and to hold public office and perform all public functions at all levels of government;

(c) To participate in non-governmental organizations and associations concerned with the public and political life of the country.

Article 8

States Parties shall take all appropriate measures to ensure to women,on equal terms with men and without any discrimination, the opportunity to Present their Governments at the international level and to participate in the work of international organizations.

Article 9

1. States Parties shall grant women equal rights with men to acquire, change or retain their nationality. They shall ensure in particular that neither marriage to an alien nor change of nationality by the husband during marriage shall automatically change the nationality of the wife, render her stateless or force upon her the nationality of the husband.
2. States Parties shall grant women equal rights with men with respect to the nationality of their children.

PART III

Article 10

States Parties shall take all appropriate measures to eliminate discrimination against women in order to ensure to them equal rights with men in the field of education and in particular to ensure, on a basis of equality of men and women;

(a) The same conditions for career and vocational guidance, for access to studies and for the achievement of diplomas in educational establishments of all categories in rural as well as in urban areas; this equality shall be ensured in preschool, general, technical, professional and higher technical education, as well as in all types of vocational training;

(b) Access to the same curricula, the same examinations, teaching staff with qualifications of the same standard and school premises and equipment of the same quality;

(c) The elimination of any stereotyped concept of the roles of men and women at all levels and in all forms of education by encouraging coeducation and other types of education which will help to achieve this aim and, in particular, by the revision of textbooks and school programmes and the adaptation of teaching methods;

(d) The same opportunities to benefit from scholarships and other study grants;

(e) The same opportunities for access to programmes of continuing education, including adult and functional literacy programmes, particularly those aimed at reducing, at the earliest possible time, any gap in education existing between men and women;

(f) The reduction of female student drop-out rates and the organization of programmes for girls and women who have left school prematurely;

(g) The same opportunities to participate actively in sports and physical education;

(h) Access to specific educational information to help to ensure that health and well-being of families, including information and advice on family planning.

Article 11

1. States Parties shall take all appropriate measures to eliminate discrimination against women in the field of employment in order to ensure, on a basis of equality of men and women, the same rights,in particular:

   (a) The right to work as an inalienable right of all human beings;

   (b) The right to the same employment opportunities, including the application of the same criteria for selection in matters of employment;

   (c) The right to free choice of profession and employment,the right to promotion, job security and all benefits and conditions of service and the right to receive vocational training and recurrent retraining, including apprenticeships, advanced vocational training and training;

   (d) The right to equal remuneration, including benefits, and to equal treatment in respect of work of equal value, as well as equality of treatment in the evaluation of the quality of work;

   (e) The right to social security, particularly in cases of retirement, unemployment, sickness, invalidity and old age and other incapacity to work, as well as the right to paid leave;

   (f) The right to protection of health and to safety in working conditions, including the safeguarding of the function of reproduction.

2. In order to prevent discrimination against women on the grounds of marriage or maternity and to ensure their effective right to work, States Parties shall take appropriate measures:

   (a) To prohibit, subject to the imposition of sanctions, dismissal on the grounds of pregnancy or of maternity leave and discrimination in dismissals on the basis of marital status;

   (b) To introduce maternity leave with pay or with comparable social benefits without loss of former employment, seniority or social allowances;

   (c) To encourage the provision of the necessary supporting social services to enable parents to combine family obligations with work responsibilities and participation in public life, in particular through promoting the establishment and development of a network of child care facilities.

(d) To provide special protection to women during pregnancy in types of work proved to be harmful to them.

3. Protective legislation relating to matters covered in this article shall be reviewed periodically in the light of scientific and technological knowledge and shall be revised, repealed or extended as necessary.

Article 12

1. States Parties shall take all appropriate measures to eliminate discrimination against women in the field of health care in order to ensure, on a basis of equality of men and women, access to health care services, including those related to family planning.
2. Notwithstanding the provisions of paragraph 1 of this article, States Parties shall ensure to women appropriate services in connection with pregnancy, confinement and the post-natal period granting free services where necessary, as well as adequate nutrition during pregnancy and lactation

Article 13

States Parties shall take all appropriate measures to eliminate discrimination against women in other areas of economic and social life in order to ensure, on a basis of equality of men and women, the same rights, in particular:

(a) The right to family benefits;

(b) The right to bank loans, mortgages and other forms of financial credit;

(c) The right to participate in recreational activities, sports and all aspects of cultural life.

Article 14

1. States Parties shall take into account the particular problems faced by rural women and the significant roles which rural women play in the economic survival of their families, including their work in the non-monetized sectors of the economy, and shall take all appropriate measures to ensure the application of the provisions of the present Convention to women in rural areas.
2. States Parties shall take all appropriate measures to eliminate discrimination against women in rural areas in order to ensure, on a basis of equality of men and women, that they participate in and benefit from rural development and, in particular,shall ensure to such women the right:

(a) To participate in the elaboration and implementation of development planning at al levels;
(b) To have access to adequate health-care facilities, including information, counselling and services in family planning;
(c) To benefit directly from social security programmes;
(d) To obtain all types of training and education, formal and non-formal, including that relating to functional literacy, as well as, *inter alia*, the benefit of all community and extension services, in order to increase their technical proficiency;
(e) To organize self-help groups and cooperatives in order to obtain equal access to economic opportunities through employment or self-employment;
(f) To participate in all community activities;
(g) To have access to agricultural credit and loans, marketing facilities, appropriate technology and equal treatment in land and agrarian reform as well as in land resettlement schemes;
(h) To enjoy adequate living conditions, particularly in relation to housing, sanitation, electricity and water supply, transport and communications.

PART IV

Article 15

1. States Parties shall accord to women equality with men before the law.
2. States Parties shall accord to women, in civil matters, a legal capacity identical to that of men and the same opportunities to exercise that capacity. In particular, they shall give women equal rights to conclude contracts and to administer property and shall treat them equally in all stages of procedure in courts and tribunals.
3. States Parties agree that all contracts and all other private instruments of any kind with a legal effect which is directed at restricting the legal capacity of women shall be deemed null and void.
4. States Parties shall accord to men and women the same rights with regard to the law relating to the movement of persons and the freedom to choose their residence and domicile.

Article 16

1. States Parties shall take all appropriate measures to eliminate discrimination against women in all matters relating to marriage and family relations and in particular shall ensure, on a basis of equality of men and women:

(a) The same right to enter into marriage;
(b) The same right freely to choose a spouse and to enter into marriage only with their free and full consent;
(c) The same rights and responsibilities during marriage and at its dissolution;
(d) The same rights and responsibilities as parents, irrespective of their marital status, in matters relating to their children; in all cases the interests of the children shall be paramount;
(e) The same rights to decide freely and responsibly on the number and spacing of their children and to have access to the information, education and means to enable them to exercise these rights;
(f) The same rights and responsibilities with regard to guardianship, warship, trusteeship and adoption of children, or similar institutions where these concepts exist in national legislation; in all cases the interests of the children shall be paramount;
(g) The same personal rights as husband and wide, including the right to choose a family name, a profession and an occupation;
(h) The same rights for both spouses in respect of the ownership, acquisition, management, administration, enjoyment and disposition of property, whether free of change or for a valuable consideration.

2. The betrothal and the marriage of a child shall have no legal effect, and all necessary action, including legislation, shall be taken to specify a minimum age for marriage and to make the registration of marriages in an official registry compulsory.

PART V

Article 17

1. For the purpose of considering the progress made in the implementation of the present Convention, there shall be established a Committee on the Elimination of Discrimination against Women (hereinafter referred to as the Committee) consisting, at the time of entry into force of the Convention of eighteen and, after ratification of or accession to the Convention by the thirty-fifth State Party, of twenty three experts of high moral standing and competence in the field covered by the Convention. The experts shall be elected by States Parties from among their nationals and shall serve in their personal capacity, consideration being given to equitable geographical distribution and to the reprepresentation of the different forms of civilization as well as the principal legal systems.

2. The members of the Committee shall be elected by secret ballot from a list of persons nominated by States Parties. Each State Party may nominate one person from among its own nationals.
3. The initial election shall be held six months after the date of the entry into force of the present Convention. At least three months before the date of each election and Secretary-General of the United Nations shall address a letter to the States Parties inviting them to submit their nominations within two months. The Secretary-General shall prepare a list in alphabetical order of all persons thus nominated, indicating the States Parties which have nominated them, and shall submit it to the State Parties.
4. Elections of the members of the Committee shall be held at a meeting of States Parties convened by the Secretary-General at United Nations Headquarters. At that meeting, for which two thirds of the States Parties shall constitute a quorum, the persons elected to the Committee shall be those nominees who obtain the largest number of votes and an absolute majority of the votes of the representatives of States Parties present and voting.
5. The members of the Committee shall be elected for a term of four years. However, the terms of nine of the members elected at the first election shall expire at the end of two years; immediately after the first election the names of these nine members shall be chosen by lot by the Chairman of the Committee.
6. The election of the five additional members of the Committee shall be held in accordance with the provisions of paragraphs 2, 3 and 4 of this article, following the thirty-fifth ratification or accession. The terms of two of the additional members elected on this occasion shall expire at the end of two years, the names of these two members having been chosen by lot by the Chairmen of the Committee.
7. For the filling of casual vacancies, the State Party whose expert has ceased to function as a member of the Committee shall appoint another expert from among its nationals, subject to the approval of the Committee.
8. The members of the Committee shall, with the approval of the General Assembly, receive emoluments from United Nations resources on such terms and conditions as the Assembly may decide, having regard to the importance of the Committee's responsibilities.
9. The Secretary-General of the United Nations shall provide the necessary staff and facilities for the effective performance of the functions of the Committee under the present Convention.

Article 18

1. States Parties undertake to submit to the Secretary-General of the United Nations, for consideration by the Committee, a report on the legislative, judicial, administrative or other measures which they have adopted to give effect to the provisions of the present Convention and on the progress made in this respect:
   (a) Within one year after the entry into force for the State concerned;
   (b) Thereafter at least every four years and further whenever the Committee so requests.
2. Reports may indicate factors and difficulties affecting the degree of fulfilment of obligations under the present Convention.

Article 19

1. The Committee shall adopt its own rules of procedure.
2. The Committee shall elect its officers for term of two years.

Article 20

1. The Committee shall normally meet for a period of not more that two weeks annually in order to consider the reports submitted in accordance with article 18 of the present Convention.
2. The meetings of the Committee shall normally be held at United Nations Headquarters or at any other convenient place as determined by the Committee.

Article 21

1. The Committee shall, through the Economic and Social Council, report annually to the General Assembly of the United Nations on its activities and may make suggestions and general recommendations based on the examination of reports and information received from the States Parties. Such suggestions and general recommendations shall be included in the report of the Committee together with comments, if any, from States Parties.
2. The Secretary-General of the United Nations shall transmit the reports of the Committee to the Commission on the Status of Women for its information.

Article 22

The specialized agencies shall be entitled to be represented at the consideration of the implementation of such provisions of the present Convention as fall within the scope of their activities. The Committee may invite the specialized agencies to submit reports on the implementation of the Convention in areas falling within the scope of their activities.

PART VI

Article 23

Noting in the present Convention shall affect any provisions that are more conducive to the achievement of equality between men and women which may be contained:

(a) In the legislation of a State Party or

(b) In any other international convention, treaty or agreement in force for that State.

Article 24

State Parties undertake to adopt all necessary measures at the national level aimed at achieving the full realization of the rights recognized in the present Convention.

Article 25

1. The present Convention shall be open for signature by all States.
2. The Secretary-General of the United Nations is designated as the depositary of the present Convention.
3. The present Convention is subject to ratification. Instruments of ratification shall be deposited with the Secretary-General of the United Nations.
4. The present Convention shall be open to accession by all States. Accession shall be effected by the deposit of an instrument of accession with the Secretary-General of the United Nations.

Article 26

1. A request for the revision of the present Convention may be made at any time by any State Party by means of a notification in writing addressed to the Secretary-General of the United Nations.
2. The General Assembly of the United Nations shall decide upon the steps, if any, to be taken in respect of such a request.

Article 27

1. The present Convention shall enter into force on the thirtieth day after the date of deposit with the Secretary-General of the United Nations of the twentieth instrument of ratification or accession.
2. For each State ratifying the present Convention or acceding to it after the deposit of the twentieth instrument of ratification or accession, the Convention shall enter into force on the thirtieth day after

the date of the deposit of its own instrument of ratification or accession.

Article 28

1. The Secretary-General of the United Nations shall receive and circulate to all States the text of reservations made by States at the time of ratification or accession.
2. A reservation incompatible with the object and purpose of the present Convention shall not be permitted.
3. Reservations may be withdrawn at any time by notification to this effect addressed to the Secretary-General of the United Nations, who shall then inform all States thereof. Such notification shall take effect on the date on which it is received.

Article 29

1. Any dispute between two or more States Parties concerning the interpretation or application of the present Convention which is not settled by negotiation shall, at the request of one of them be submitted to arbitration If within six months from the date of the request for arbitration the parties are unable to agree on the organization of the arbitration, any one of those parties may refer the dispute to the International Court of Justice by request in conformity with the Statute of the Court.
2. Each State Party may at the time of signature or ratification of the present Convention or accession thereto declare that is does not consider itself bound by paragraph 1 of this article. The other States Parties shall not be bound by that paragraph with respect to any State Party which had made such a reservation.
3. Any State Party which has made a reservation in accordance with paragraph 2 of this article may at any time withdraw that reservation by notification to the Secretary-General of the United Nations.

Article 30

The present Convention, the Arabic, Chinese,English, French, Russian and Spanish texts of which are equally authentic, shall be deposited with the Secretary-General of the United Nations.

IN WITNESS WHERE OF the undersigned, duly authorized, have signed the present Convention.

IV. RESERVATIONS TO THE CONVENTION ON THE ELIMINATION OF ALL FORMS OF DISCRIMINATION AGAINST WOMEN[a]

A. Declarations, Reservations, Objections and Withdrawals of Reservations by States Parties

State party	*Article for which declarations have been made*	*States parties which have raised objections*	*Article for which reservations have been withdrawn*
1	2	3	4
Argentina....	29, para.1		
Australia.....	11, para.2 (b)		
Austria.......	7, subpara. (b)		
	11, para.1 (f)		
Bangladesh...	2	Germany..	
		Mexico...	
		Netherlands	
		Sweden..	
	13,subpara(a)	Germany...	
		Mexico..	
		Netherlands	
		Sweden..	
	16, para.1 (c) and (f)	Germany..	
		Mexico..	
		Netherlands	
		Sweden..	
Belarus......	[29,para.1]		29, para 1
Belgium....	7, subparas. (a) and (b)		
	15, paras. 2 and 3		
Brazil...	15, para. 4	Germany	
		Netherlands	
		Sweden	
	16,para 1 (a), (c),(g) and (h)	Germany..	
		Netherlands	
		Sweden...	
	29, para, 1		
Bulgaria...	[29, para, 1]		29,para.1
Canada...	[11, para, 1(d)]		11,para,1(d)
China...	29, para, 1		
Cuba...	29, para. 1		
Cyprus...	9, para. 2	Mexico...	
Egypt...	2	Germany..	
		Netherlands	
		Sweden...	
	9, para. 2	Germany..	

{Cont.}......

1	2	3	4
		Mexico....	
		Netherlands	
		Sweden..	
	16	Germany	
		Mexico...	
		Netherlands	
		Sweden..	
	29, para. 1	Mexico...	
El Savador..	29, para. 1		
Ethiopia..	29, para. 1		
France...	[7]		7
	14,para.2 (c) and (h)		
	[15, paras.2and 3]		15, paras. 2 and 3
	[16, para.1(c), (d) and (h)]		16, para. 1(c) (d) and (h)
	16, para.1(g)		
	29, para.1		
Germany...	General declaration		
	7, subpara. (b)		
Hungary..	[29, para. 1]		29.para.1
Indonesia...	29, para. 1		
Iraq....	2, subparas. (f) and (g)	Germany..	
		Mexico...	
		Netherlands	
		Sweden..	
	9, para.1	Sweden..	
	9, paras.1and 2	Germany	
		Israel...	
		Mexico...	
		Netherlands	
		Sweden..	
	16	Germany	
		Mexico...	
		Netherlands	
		Sweden..	
	29, para.1	Sweden..	
Ireland..	[9, para.1]		9, para.1
	[11, para.1]		11, para.1
	[13, subpara.(a)]		13. subpara. (a)
	13, subparas. (b) and (c)		
	15, para. 3		
	[15, para. 4]		15, para. 4
	16, para. 1 (d) and (f)		
Israel...	7, subpara. (b)		

{Cont.}......

1	2	3	4
	16		
	29, para. 1		
Jamaica...	9, para. 2	Germany.. Mexico.. Netherlands Sweden..	
	29, para. 1		
Jordan...	9, para. 2		
	15, para. 2		
	15, para.4		
	16, para. 19c), (d) and (g)	Sweden..	
Libyan Arab Jamahiriya..	General	Denmark.. Finland... Germany.. Mexico.. Netherlands Norway.. Sweden...	
Luxembourg..	7		
	16, para.1(g)		
Malawi..	[5]	Germany.. 5 Mexico.. Netherlands Norway.. Sweden..	
	[29, para. 1]		29, para.1
Maldives...	2		
Malta...	11, para. 1		
	13		
	15		
	16, para. 1 (e)		
Mauritius..	11, para. 1 (b) and (d)	Germany.. Mexico.. Netherlands Sweden...	
	16, para. 1(g)	Germany.. Mexico.. Netherlands Sweden..	
	29, para. 1		
Mongolia..	[29, para. 1]		29, para. 1
Morocco..	2,		
	9, para. 2,		
	15, para. 4,		
	16		
	29, para. 1		

{Cont.}......

1	2	3	4
New Zealand (Cook Islands)	2, subpara. (f)	Mexico.. Sweden..	
	5, subpara. (a)	Mexico... Sweden..	
(Cook Islands and Niue)	11, para. 2 (b)		
Poland...	29, para. 1		
Republic of Korea..	9	Germany... Mexico.. Netherlands Sweden..	
	16, para. 1[(c), (d), (f)] and (g)	Germany.. Mexico... Netherlands' Sweden..	16,para.1(c) (d)and (f)
Romania.....		29,para.1	
Russian Federation..		[29, para. 1]	29, para.1
Spain....	7 (declaration)		
Thailand...	7	Germany...	
	9, para. 2	Germany.. Mexico.. Netherlands Sweden..	
	10	Germany.. Mexico...	
	[11, para. 1(b)]	Germany..11, para. 1(b)	
	[15, para. 3]	Germany.. 15, para. 3 Mexico.. Netherlands Sweden..	
	10	Germany... Mexico...	
	[11, para. 1 (b)]	Germany..	11, para. 1(b)
	[15, para. 3]	Germany.. Mexico.. Netherlands Sweden..	15, para. 3
	16	Germany... Mexico... Netherlands Sweden...	
	29, para. 1		
Trinidad and Tobago..	29, para. 1		
Tunisia..	9, para. 2	Germany.. Netherlands	

{Cont.}......

1	2	3	4
		Sweden...	
	15, para. 4	Germany..	
		Netherlands...	
		Sweden...	
	16, para. 1 (c), (d), (f), (g) and (h)	Germany.... Netherlands Sweden.....	
	29, para. 1		
Turkey..	9, para. 1 (declaration)		
	15, paras. 2 and 4	Germany.. Netherlands	
	16, para. 1(c), (d), (f) and (g)	Germany.. Mexico.. Netherlands	
	29, para. 1		
Ukraine...	[29, para. 1]		29, para. 1
United Kingdom of Great Britain and Northern Ireland..	(declarations)	Argentina.	
	1		
	2, subparas. (f) and (g)		
	9		
	10, subpara (c)		
	11, paras. 1 and 2		
	13		
	15, paras. 2 and 3		
	16, para. 1		
on behalf of:	(declarations)		
British Virgin Islands, Falkland Islands (malvinas), Isle of Man, South Georgia and South Sandwich Islands, and Turks and Caicos Islands	1, 2, 9, 11, 13, 15, 16		
Venezuela...	29, para. 1		
Viet Nam...	29, para. 1		
Yemen..	29, para. 1		

[a] Status as a October 1993.

B. Articles for which States Parties have not yet Withdrawn their Reservations

Article	State Party
1.	United Kingdom and on behalf of:British Virgin Islands, Falkland Islands (Malvinas), Isle of Man, South Georgia and South Sandwich Islands, and Turks and Caicos Islands
2.	Bangladesh Egypt Maldives Morocco United kingdom and on behalf of: British Virgin Island, Falkland Islands (Malvinas), isle of Man, South Georgia and South Sandwich Islands, and Turks and Caicos Islands
2.subpara. (f)	New Zealand (Cook Islands)
2.subpara. (f) and (g)	Iraq, United Kingdom
5, subpara. (a)	New Zealand (Cook Islands)
7	Luxembourg, Spain, Thailand
7. subpara. (a) and (b)	Belgium
7,subpara.(b)	Austria, Germany,Israel
9	Republic of Korea, United Kingdom and on behalf of : British Virgin Islands, Falkland Islands (Malvinas), Isle of Man, South Georgia and South Sandwich islands, and Turks and Caicos Islands
9,paras.1 and 2	Iraq
9,para.2	Cyprus, Egypt, Jamaica, Jordan, Morocco, Thailand, Tunisia
10	Thailand
10,subpara.(c)	United Kingdom
11	United Kingdom and on behalf of: British Virgin Islands, Falkland Islands (Malvinas,), Isle of Man, South Georgia and South Sandwich Islands, and Turks and Caicos islands Malta
11, para. 1	Mauritius
11, para. 1(b)and (d)	Austria
11, para. 1(f)	Australia, New Zealand (Cook Islands and Niue)
11. para. 2(b)	
13	Malta,United Kingdom and on behalf of:British Virgin Islands, Falkland Islands (Malvinas), Isle of Man, South Georgia and

{Cont.}.......

Article	*State Party*
	South Sandwich Islands, and Turks and Caicos Islands
13, subpara. (a)	Bangladesh
13, subparas. (b) and (c)	Ireland
14, para2 (c) and (h)	France
15	Malta
15, paras. 2 and 3	Belgium, United Kingdom and on behalf of: British Virgin, Islands, Falkland Islands (Malvinas), Isle of Man, South Georgia and South Sandwich Islands, and Turks and Caicos Islands
15, paras. 2and 4	Turkey
15, para. 3	Ireland
15, para. 4	Brazil, jordan, Morocco, Tunisia
16	Egypt, Iraq, Isral, Morocco, Thailand
16, para. 1(a).(c). (g) and (h)	Brazil
16, para. 1(c), (d), (f) and (g)	Turkey
16, para. 1(c). (d). (f) and (g)	Tunisia
16, para. 1(c). (d). and (g)	Jordan
16, para. 1(c) and (f)	Bangladesh
16, para. 1(d) and (f)	Ireland
16, para. 1(e)	Malta
16, para. 1(f)	United Kingdom and on behalf of: British Virgin Islands, Falkland Islands (Mavinas), Isle of Man, South Georgia at South Sandwich Islands, and Turks and Caicos Islands
16, para. 1(g)	France, Luxembourg, Mauritius, Republic of Korea
29, para. 1	Argentina, Brazil, China, Cuba, Egypt, El Salvador, Ethiopia, France, Indonesia, Iraq, Israel, Jamaica, Mauritius, Morocco, Poland, Romania, Thailand, Tnidad and Tobago, Tunisia, Turkey, Venezuela, Viet Nam, Yemen

[a]Status as of October 1993.

Notes

1 The World's Women 1970-1990: Trends and Statistics (United Nations publication, Sales No. E. 90. XVII.3).

2 The Commission on the Status of Women was established by the Economic and Social Council in 1946. Its functions is to prepare reports and recommendations to the Council on promoting women's rights in the political, economic, civil, social and educational fields and to develop recommendations and proposals for action on urgent problems in the field of women's right with the object of implementing the principle that men and women shall have equal rights. The Commission has been gicen the task of monitoring, reviewing and appraising the implementation of the Nairobi Forwardlooking Strategies for the Advancement of Women adopted by the 1985 World Conference of Women. The Commission may receive communications from individuals and groups concerning discrimination against women.

3 World Health Organization, Maternal Mortality: A Global Factbook (Geneva, 1991),p.3.

4 See, for example, S.W.M. Broeks V. the netherlands, Communication No.172/1984 (9 April 1987), Selected Decisions of the Human Rights Committee under the Optional Protocol, International Covenant on Civil and political Rights, Volume 2, Seventeenth to Thirty-second Sessions (october 1982-April 1988)(United Nations publication, Sales No.E.89.XIV.1),p.196.

4

Harmful Traditional Practices Affecting the Health of Women and Children

Introduction

The Charter of the United Nations includes among its basic principles the achievement of international co-operation in promoting and encouraging respect for human rights and fundamental freedoms for all without distinction as to race, sex, language or religion (Art.1.para.3).

In 1948, three years after the adoption of the Charter, the General Assembly adopted the Universal Declaration of Human Rights,[1] which has served as guiding principles on human rights and fundamental freedoms in the constitutions and laws of many of the Member States of the United Nations. The Universal Declaration prohibits all forms of discrimination based on sex and ensures the right to life, liberty and security of person; it recognizes equality before the law and equal protection against any discrimination in violation of the Declaration.

Many international legal instruments on human rights further reinforce individual rights, and also protect-and prohibit discrimination against-specific groups, in particular women. The Convention on the Elimination of All Forms of Discrimination against Women, for example, had been ratified by 136 States as of January 1995. The Convention obliges States parties, in general, to "pursue by all appropriate means and without delay a policy of eliminating discrimination against women" (art.2). It reaffirms the equality of human rights for women and men in society and in the family; it obliges States parties to take action against the social causes of women's inequality; and it calls for the elimination of laws, stereotypes, practices and prejudices that impair women's well-being.

Traditional cultural practices reflect values and beliefs held by members of a community for periods often spanning generations. Every social grouping in the world has specific traditional cultural practices and beliefs, some of which are beneficial to all members, while others are harmful to a specific group, such as women. These harmful traditional practices include female genital mutilation (FGM); forced feeding of women; early marriage;the various taboos or practices which prevent women from controlling their own fertility; nutritional taboos and traditional birth practices; son preference and its implications for the status of the girl child; female infanticide; early pregnancy; and dowry price. Despite their harmful nature and their violation of international human rights laws, such practices persist because they are not questioned and take on an aura of morality in the eyes of those practising them.

The International community has become aware of the need to achieve equality between the sexes and of the fact that an equitable society cannot be attained if fundamental human rights of half of human society, i.e. women, continue to be denied and violated. However, the bleak reality is that the harmful traditional practices focused on in this Fact Sheet have been performed for male benefit. Female sexual control by men, and the economic and political subordination of women, perpetuate the inferior status of women and inhibit structural and attitudinal changes necessary to eliminate gender inequality.

As early as the 1950s, United Nations specialized agencies and human rights bodies began considering the question of harmful traditional practices affecting the health of women, in particular female genital mutilation. But these issues have not received consistent broader consideration, and action to bring about any substantial change has been slow or superficial.

A number of reasons are given for the persistence of traditional practices detrimental to the health and status of women, including the fact that, in the past, neither the Governments concerned nor the international community challenged the sinister implications of such practices, which violate the rights to health, life, dignity and personal integrity. The international community remained wary about treating these issues as a deserving subject for international and national scrutiny and action. Harmful practices such as female genital mutilation were considered sensitive cultural issues falling within the spheres of women and the family . For a long time, Governments and the international community had not expressed sympathy and understanding for women who, due to ignorance or unawareness of their rights, endured pain, suffering and even death inflicted on themselves and their female children.

Despite the apparent slowness of action to challenge and eliminate harmful traditional practices, the activities of human rights bodies in this field have, in recent years, resulted in noticeable progress. Traditional practices have become a recognized issue concerning the status and human rights of women and female children. The slogan "Women's Rights are Human Rights", adopted at the World Conference on Human Rights in Vienna in 1993, as well as the Declaration on the Elimination of Violence against Women, adopted by the General Assembly the same year, captured the reality of the status accorded to women. These issues have been further emphasized in the reports of the Special Rapporteur on harmful traditional practices, Mrs. Halima Embarek Warzazi, appointed in 1988, and in the draft Platform for Action for the Fourth World Conference on Women, to be held in September 1995.

The Special Rapporteur on violence against women, its causes and consequences, Ms. Radhika Coomaraswamy, appointed by the Commission on Human Rights in 1994, has also examined all forms of traditional practives referred to in this Fact Sheet, as well as other practices, including virginity tests, foot binding, female infanticide and dowry deaths, all of which violate female dignity. In her preliminary report, the Special Rapporteur pointed out that

> blind adherence to these practives and State inaction with regard to these customs and traditions have made possible large-scale violence against women. States are enacting new laws and regulations with regard to the development of a modern economy and modern technology and to developing practives which suit a modern democracy, yet it seems that in the area of women's rights change in slow to be accepted. (E/CN.4/1995/42.para. 67.)

The harmful traditional practices identified in this Fact Sheet are categorized as separate issues; however, they are all consequences of the value placed on women and the girl child by society. They persist in an environment where women and the girl child have unequal access to education, wealth, health and employment.

In part i, the Fact Sheet identified and analyses the background to harmful traditional practives, their causes, and their consequences for the health of women and the girl child. Part II reviews the action taken by United Nations, organs and agencies, Governments and Non Governmental Organizations (NGOS). The Conclusions highlight the drawbacks in the implementation of the practical steps identified by the United Nations, NGOs and women's organizations.

1. AN APPRAISAL OF HARMFUL TRADITIONAL PRACTIVES AND THEIR EFFECTS ON WOMEN AND THE GIRL CHILD

A. Female Genital Mutilation[2]

Female Genital Mutilation (FGM,), or female circumcision as it is sometimes erroneously referred to, involves surgical removal of parts or all of the most sensitive female genital organs. It is an age-old practice which is perpetuated in many communities around the world simply because it is customary. FGM forms an important part of the rites of passage ceremony for some communities, marking the coming of age of the female child. It is believed that, by mutilating the female's genital organs, her sexuality will be controlled; but above all it is to ensure a woman's virginity before marriage and chastity thereafter. In fact, FGM imposes on women and the girl child a catalogue of health complications and untold psychological problems. The practice of FGM violates, among other international human rights laws, the right of the child to the "enjoyment of the highest attainable standard of health", as laid down in article 24 (paras. 1and 3) of the Convention on the Rights of the Child.

The origin of FGM has not yet been established, but records show that the practice predates Christianity and Islam in practicing communities of today. In ancient Rome, metal rings were passed through the labia minora of slaves to prevent procreation; in medieval England, metal chastity belts were worn by women to prevent promiscuity during their husbands' absence; evidence from mummified bodies reveals that, in ancient Egypt, both excision and infibulation were performed, hence Pharaonic circumcision; in tşarist Russia, as well as nineteenth-century England, France and America, records indicate the practice of clitoridectomy. In England and America, FGM was performed on women a "cure"for numerous psychological ailments.

The age at which mutilation is carried out varies from area to area. FGM is performed on infants as young as a few days old, on children from 7 to 10 years old, and on adolescents. Adult women also undergo the operation at the time of marriage. Since FGM is performed on infants as well as adults, it can no longer be seen as marking the rites of passage into adulthood, or as ensuring virginity.

Among the types of surgical operation on the female genital organs listed below, there are many variations, performed throughout Africa, Asia, the Middle East, the Arabian Peninsula, Australia and Latin America.

Types of Surgical Forms

(a) Circumcision or Sunna ("traditional") circumcision: This involves the removal of the prepuce and the tip of the clitoris. This is the only operation which, medically, can be likened to male circumcision.

(b) Excision or clitoridectomy: This involves the removal of the clitoris, and often also the labia minora. It is the most common operation and is practiced throughout Africa, Asia, the Middle East and the Arabian peninsula.

(c) Infibulation or Pharaonic circumcision: This is the most severe operation, involving excision plus the removal of the labia majora and the sealing of the two sides, through stitching or natural fusion of scar tissue. What is left is a very smooth surface, and a small opening to permit urination and the passing of menstrual blood. This artificial opening is sometimes no larger that the head of a match.

Another form of mutilation which has been reported is introcision, practised specifically by the Pitta-Patta aborigines of Australia. When a girl reaches puberty, the whole tribe-both sexes—assembles. The operator, an elderly man, enllarges the vaginal orifice by tearing it downward with three fingers bound with opossum string. In other districts, the perineum is split with a stone knife. This is usually followed by compulsory sexual intercourse with a number of young men.

It is reported that introcision has been practised in eastern Mexico and in Brazil. In Peru, in particular among the Conibos, a division of the Pano Indians in the north-east, an operation is performed in which, as soon as a girl reaches maturity, she is intoxicated and subjected to mutilation in front of her community. The operation is performed by an elderly woman, using a bamboo knife. She cuts around the hymen from the vaginal entrance and severs the hymen from the labia, at the same time exposing the clitoris. Medicinal herbs are applied, followed by the insertion into the vagina of a slightly moistened penis-shaped object made of clay.

Like all other harmful traditional practices, FGM is performed by women, with a few exceptions (in Egypt, men are known to perform the operation). In most rural settings throughout Africa, the operation is accompanied with celebrations and often takes place away from the community at a special hidden place. The operation is carried out by women (excisors) who have acquired their "skills" from their mothers or other female relatives; they are often also the community's traditional birth attendants.

The type of operation to be performed is decided by the girl's mother or grandmother beforehand and payment is made to the excisor before, during and after the operation, to ensure the best service. This payment, partly in kind and partly in cash, is a vital source of livelihood for the excisors.

The conditions under which these operations take place are often unhygienic and the instruments used are crude and unsterilized. A kitchen knife, a razor-blade, a piece of glass or even a sharp fingernail are the tools of the trade. These instruments are used repeatedly on numerous girls, thus increasing the risk of blood-transmitted diseases, in including HIV/AIDS.

The operation takes between 10 and 20 minutes, depending on its nature; in most cases, anaesthetic is not administered. The child is held down by three or four women while the operation is done. The wound is then treated by applying mixtures of local herbs, earth, cow-dung, ash or butter, depending on the skills of the excisor. If infibulation is performed, the child's legs are bound together to impair mobility for up to 40 days. If the child dies from complications, the excisor is not held responsible; rather, the death is attributed to evil spirits or fate. Throughout South-East Asia and urban African communities, FGM is becoming increasingly medicalized.

FGM is known to be practised in least 25 countries in Africa. Infibulation is practised in Djibouti, Egypt, some parts of Ethiopia, Mali, Somalia and the northern part of the Sudan. Excision and circumcision occur in parts of Benin, Burkina Faso, Cameroon, the Central African Republic, Chad, Cote d' Ivoire, the Gambia, the northern part of Ghana, Guinea, Guinea-Bissau, Kenya, Liberia, Mauritania, Nigeria, Senegal, Sierra Leone, Togo, Uganda and parts of the United Republic of Tanzania.

Outside Africa, a certain form of female genital mutilation exists in Indonesia, Malaysia and Yemen. Recent information has revealed that the practice also exists in some European countries and Australia among immigrant communities.

FGM is a custom or tradition synthesized over time from various values, especially religious and cultural values. The reasons for maintaining the practice include religion, custom, decreasing the sexual desire of women, hygiene, aesthetics, facility of sexual relations, fertility, etc. In general, it can be said that those who preserve the practice are largely women who live in traditional societies in rural areas. Most of these women follow tradition passively.

In the countries where the practice exists, most women believe that, as good Muslims, for example, they have to undergo the operation. In order to be clean and proper, fit for marriage, female circumcision is a precondition. Among the Bambara in Mali, it is believed that, if the clitoris touches the head of a baby being born, the child will die. The clitoris is seen as the male characteristic of the women; in order to enhance her femininity, this male part of her has to be removed Among women in Djibouti, Ethiopia, Somalia and the Sudan, circumcision is performed to reduce sexual desire and also to maintain virginity until marriage. A circumcised woman is considered to be clean.

Establishing identity and belongingness is another reason advanced for the perpetuation of the practice. For example,in Liberia and Sierra Leone, groups of girls of 12 and 13 of the indigenous population undergo an initiation rite, conducted by an older woman "Sowie". This involves education on how to be a good wife or co-wide, the use of herbal medicine and the "secrets" of female society. It also involves the ritual of circumcision.

Health and Psychological Implications

The effects of female genital mutilation have short-term and long-term implications. Haemorrhage, infection and acute pain are the immediate consequences. Keloid formation, infertility as a result of infection,obstructed labour and psychological complications are identified as later effects. In rural areas where untrained traditional birth attendants perform the operations, complications resulting from deep cuts and infected instruments can cause the death of the child.

Most physical complications result from infibulation, although cataclysmic haemorrhage can occur during circumcision with the removal of the clitoris: accidental cuts to other organs can also lead to heavy loss of blood. Acute infections are commonplace when operations are carried out in unhygienic surroundings and with unsterilized instruments. The application of traditional medicine can also lead to infection, resulting in tetanus and general septicaemia. Chronic infection can also lead to infertility and anaemia.

Haematocolpos, or the inability to pass menstrual blood (because the remaining opening is often too small), can lead to infection of other organs and also infertility.

Obstetric complications are the most frequent health problem, resulting from vicious scars in the clitoral zone after excision. These scars open during childbirth and cause the anterior perineum to tear,leading to haemorrhaging that is often difficult to stop. Infibulated women have to be opened, or deinfibulated,on delivery of their child and it is common for them to be reinfibulated after each delivery.

There has been little research in the area of the psychological implications of FGM, but evidence indicate that most children experience recurring nightmares.

In her recent book, *Cutting the Rose-Female Genital Mutilation: The practice and its Prevention,*[3] Efua Dorkenoo reports that some evidence of psychological effects is merging among the large immigrant communities now living in Europe, the Americas, Australia and New Zealand. Teenagers, in particular, are having to live in two very different cultures, where different values prevail. At school they move within the very liberal setting of the Western culture; at home they have to conform to values held by their parents. Some of these values often conflict. For some teenagers this is proving to be problematic. Girls who have been genitally mutilated have to come to terms with the fact that they are not like their classmates. Mood swings and irritability, a constant state of depression, and anxiety have all been noted among infibulated girls. A small number, upon reaching the age of consent, are being deinfibulated without their parents 'knowledge and engaging in premarital relationships, thus validating the reasoning behind their parents' wishes to have the operation performed.

There are also reports of psychological and health problems suffered by women seeking medical assistance in Western medical facilities due to lack of knowledge regarding genital mutilation. Excised and infibulated women have special needs which have been ignored or dealt with on a trial-and-error basis. In Western countries, severe forms of FGM present challenges to midwives and obstetricians in provinding antenatal and post-natal care. For example, professionals need training to know how to deliver infibuated women. The provision of health care for women and girls who have been genitally mutilated should be appropriate and sensitive to their needs. Health promotion work through women's health services can develop appropriate information materials and actively contribute to outreach work and awareness raising.

B. SON PREFERENCE AND ITS IMPLICATIONS FOR THE STATUS OF THE GIRL CHILD

One of the principal forms of discrimination and one which has far-reaching implications for women is the preference accorded to the boy child over the girl child. This practice denies the girl child good health, education, recreation, economic opportunity and the right to choose her partner, violating her rights under articles 2,6,12,19,24,27 and 28 of the Convention on the the Rights of the Child.

Son preference refers to a whole range of values and attitudes which are manifested in many different practives, the common feature of which is a preference for the male child, often with concomitant daughter neglect. It may mean that a female child is disadvantaged from birth; it may determine the quality and quantity of parental care and the extent of investment in her development; and it may lead to acute discrimination, particularly in settings where resources are scarce. Although neglect is the rule, in extreme cases son preference may lead to selective abortion or female infanticide.

In many societies, the family lineage is carried on by male children. The preservation of the family name is guaranteed through the son(s). Except in a few countries (e.g., Ethiopia), a girl takes her husband's family name, dropping that of her own parents. The fear of losing a name prompts families to wish to have a son. Some men marry a second or a third wife to be sure of having a male child. Among many communities in Asia and Africa, sons perform burial rites for parents. Parents with no male child do not expect to have an appropriate burial to "secure their peace in the next world". In almost all religions, ceremonies are performed by men. Priests, pastors, sheikhs and other religious leaders are men of great status to whom society attaches great importance, and this important role for men obliges parents to wish for a male child. Religious leaders have a major involvement in the perpetuation of son preference.

Son preference is universal and not unique to developing countries or rural areas. It is a practice enshrined in the value systems of most societies. It thus dictates the value judgments, expectations and behaviour of family members.

Son preference is a transcultural phenomenon, more marked in Asian Societies and historically rooted in the patriarchal system. In certain countries in the Asian region, the phenomenon is less prevalent that in others. Son preference is stronger in countries where patriarchy and patriliny are more firmly rooted. Tribal societies, which are matrilineal societies, tended to be more gender egalitarian until the advent of settled agriculture.

In almost all regions, the practice is rooted in culture and the economics of son preference, these factors playing a major role in the low valuation and neglect of female children. The practice of son preference emerged with the shift from subsistence agriculture, which was primarily controlled by women, to settled agriculture, which is primarily controlled by men. In the patrilineal landowning communities with settled agriculture which are prevalent in the Asian region, the economic obligations of sons towards parents are greater. The son is considered to be the family pillar, who ensures continuity and protection of the family property. Sons provide the workforce and have to bring in a bride-"an extra pair of hands". Sons are the source of family income and have to provide for parents in their old age. They are also the interpreters of religious teachings and the performers of rituals, especially on the death of parents, which include feeding a large number of people, sometimes several villages. As soldiers, sons protect the community and hold political power.

Son preference in the Asian region manifests itself either covertly or overtly. The birth of a son is welcomed with celebration as an asset, whereas that of a girl is seen as a liability, an impending economic drain. According to an Asian proverb, "bringing up girls is like watering the neighbour's garden".

Psychological and Health Consequences

The psychological effect of son preference on women and the girl child is the internalization of the low value accorded them by society. Scientific evidence of the deleterious effect of son preference on the health of female children is scarce,but abnormal sex ratios in infant and young child mortality rates,in nutritional status indicators and even in population figures show that discriminatory practives are widespread and have serious repercussions. Geographically, there is often a close correspondence between the areas of strong son preference and of health disadvantage for females.

The areas most affected by the problem seem to be South Asia (Bangladesh, India, Nepal, Pakistan), the Middle East (Algeria, Egypt, Jordan, the Libyan Arab Jamahiriya, Morocco, the Syrian Arab Republic, Tunisia, Turkey) and parts of Africa (Cameroon, Liberia, Madagascar, Senegal).In Latin America, there is evidence of abnormal sex ratios in mortality figures in Ecuador, Mexico, Peru and Uruguay.

Discrimination in the feeding and care of female infants and or higher rates of morbidity and malnutrition have been reported in most of the countries already listed and also in Bolivia, Colombia, the Islamic Republic of Iran, Nigeria, the Philippines and Saudi Arabia. More than two thirds of the world's population live in countries where registration of death does not occur and many more live in countries where death rates are not published by sex. Moreover, discrimination against girls has to be extreme to emerge in mortality rates. For every growing girls who dies, there are many whose health and potential for growth and development are permanently impaired. Countless reports the world over have demonstrated that, in societies where son preference is practised, the health of the female child is adversely affected.

In some communities in the Asian region where son preference highly marked, efforts to differentiate a female child from a male child through various socio-economic norms and practies start as early as the foetal stage and continue throughout the entire life cycle. In these communities, amniocentesis tests and sonography for sex determination have resulted in the abortion of female foetuses. The introduction and expansion of scientific methods of sex detection have led to a revival of female foeticide and infanticide.

Education

Access to education by itself is not enough to eliminate values held by society, for such values are in most countries transmitted into educational curricula and textbooks. Women are thus still depicted as passive and domestically oriented, while men are depicted as dominant and as breadwinners.

Education does, however, offer the female child an improved opportunity to be less dependent on men in later life. It increases her prospects of obtaining work outside the home. As laid down in articles 28 and 29 of the Convention on the Rights of the Child, all children have the right to education, and the content of such education should be directed to the development of the child's personality, talents and mental and physical abilities to their fullest potential.

According to the United Nations Children's Fund (UNICEF), the expansion of educational opportunities over the past several decades has clearly affected girls, although this has not been a result of deliberate policy to reduce gender disparities in educational access. Girls' education, measured by gross primary school enrolment rations, has improved substantially in the Middle East and North Africa region, for example. Nevertheless, in 1990, the region still had 44 million illiterate mothers, a large and increasing backlog left over from times of lower enrolment levels. Differences in primary school enrolment levels for boys and girls and competition between them are still very significant in a number of countries. In countries where overall enrolment is much lower than desired, girls are particularly disadvantaged.

Although in many countries school drop-out rates are steadily falling, they continue to be higher among girls than among boys. The reasons for the high drop-out rate among girls are poverty, early marriage, helping parents with housework and agricultural work, the distance of school from homes, the high costs of schooling, parents, illiteracy and indifference, and the lack of a positive educational climate. Girls begin school very late and withdraw with the onset of puberty. Parents do not see the benefits of girl's education because girls are given away in marriage to serve the husband's family. Sons are given priority. In certain countries. enrolment rates for girls have actually declined despite atttempts to increase them.

Recreation and Work Opportunities

According to article 31, paragraph 1, of the Convention on the Rights of the Child, States parties "recognize the right of the child to rest and leisure, to engage in play and recreational activities". However, from an early age, girls from rural and poor urban homes are burdened with domestic tasks and child care, which leaves them no time to play. Studies have shown that recreation plays a vital part in a child's emotional and mental development. When time for play is found by girls, it often takes place near the home. Young boys, however, have fewer demands made of them and are allowed to engage in activities outside the home. The status of girls is linked to that of women and their exploitation. A woman's work never ends, especially in rural areas and in poor urban households.

The Convention on the Elimination of All Forms of Discrimination against Women calls for the elimination of discrimination against women in the field of employment," in order to ensure, on basis of equality of men and women, the same rights"(art11, para. 1). It also calls upon States to ensure that women in rural areas have access to agricultural credit and loans, marketing facilities, appropriate technology and equal treatment in land and agrarian reform (art 14, para. 2 (g)).Evidence indicates,however, that as girls grow older they face discriminatory treatment in gaining access to economic opportunities. Major inequalities persist in employment, access to credit, inheritance rights, marriage laws and other socio-economic dispensations. Compared with men women have fewer opportunities for paid employment and less access to skill training that would make such employment possible. Women are usually restricted to low-paid and casual jobs, or to informal activities.

Landlessness has increased among women, and the number of women cultivators has declined in some regions, partly due to increased mechanization of agriculture. An increasing number of women in most developing countries are occupied in the informal, invisible sectors where national social and labour legislation on maternity benefits, equal wages and creche facilities does not apply.

C. Female Infanticide

Sex bias or son preference places the female child in a disadvantageous position from birth. In some communities, however, particularly in Asia, the practice of infanticide ensures that some female children have no life at all, violating the basic right to life laid down in article 6 of the Convention on the Rights of the Child. Selective abortion, foeticide and infanticide all occur because the female child is not valued by her culture, or because certain economic and legislative acts have ruled her life worthless.

In India,for example, infanticide was formally legislated against during British rule, after centuries of practice in some communities. However, recent reports have shown that there is a revival.

In certain parts of India and Pakistan, women are still considered unnecessary evils. In the past, when victorious armies took their revenge on defeated communities, women were raped as part of the spoils of war. Subsequently, these communities resorted to killing their daughters at birth or when the enemy was advancing, to spare the female population and community from shame.

Modern techniques such as amniocentesis and ultrasound tests have given women greater power to detect the sex of their babies in time to to abort. Illegal abortion, particularly of female foetuses, either self-inflicted or performed by unskilled birth attendants, under poor sanitary conditions has led to increased maternal mortality, particularly in South and South-East Asia.

Female foeticide is an emerging problem in some parts of India, and the Government has introduced a bill in Parliament to ban the use of amniocentesis for sex-determination purposes. Such misuse of amniocentesis is also prohibited in the States of Maharashtra, Punjab, Rajasthan and Haryana, where the problem is more prevalent.

D. Early Marriage and Dowry

Early marriage in another serious problem which some girls, as opposed to boys, must face. The practice of giving away girls for marriage at the age of 11,12 or 13, after which they must start producing children, is prevalent among certain ethnic groups in Asia and Africa. The principal reasons for this practice are the girls' virginity and the bride-price. Young girls are less likely to have had sexual contact and thus are believed to be virgins upon marriage; this condition raises the family status as well as the dowry to be paid by the husband. In some cases, virginity is verified by female relatives before the marriage.

Child marriage robs a girl of her childhood-time necessary to develop physically, emotionally and psychologically. In fact, early marriage inflicts great emotional stress as the young woman is removed from her parents' home to that of her husband and in-laws. Her husband, who will invariably be many years her senior, will have in common with a young teenager. It is with this strange man that she has to develop an intimate emotional and physical relationship. She is obliged to have intercourse, although physically she might not be fully developed.

Girls from communities where early marriages occur are also victims of son preferential treatment and will probably be malnourished and consequently have stunted physical growth.

Neglect of and discrimination against daughters, particularly in societies with strong son preference, also contribute to early marriage of girls. It has been generally recognized at United Nations seminars on traditional practives affecting women and children, and on the basis of research, that early marriage devalues women in some societies and that the practice continues as a result of son preference. In some countries, girls as young as a few months old are promised to male suitors for marriage. Girls are fattened up, groomed, adorned with jewels and kept in seclusion to make them attractive so that they can be married off to the highest bidder.

Health complications that result from early marriage in the Middle East and North Africa, for example, include the risk of operative delivery, low weight and malnutrition resulting from frequent pregnancies and lactation in the period of life when the young mothers are themselves growing.

Another economic reason which perpetuates the practice of female genital mutilation is related to dowries.

The dowry price of a woman is her exchange value in cash, kind or any other agreed form, such as a period of employment. This value is determined by the family of the bride-to-be and her future in-laws. Both families must gain from the exchange. The women's in-laws want an extra pair of hands and children; her family desire payment which will provide greater security for other relatives. The dowry price will be higher if the woman's virginity has been preserved, notably through genital mutilation.

In certain communities in South Asia, the low status of girls has to be compensated for by the payment of a dowry by the parents of the girl to the husband at the time of marriage. This has resulted in a number of dowry crimes, including mental and physical torture, starvation, rape, and even the burning alive of women by their husbands and or in laws in cases where dowry payments are not met.

It should be noted that the Committee on the Rights of the Child, in a number of recommendations in the light of article 2 of the Convention on the Rights of the Child, has called upon States to recognize the principle of equality before the law and forbid gender discrimination,including the adoption of legislation prohibiting harmful traditional practives such as genital mutilation, forced and early marriage of girl children, early pregnancy and related prejudicial health practices.

The work of the Committee has also permitted the identification of certain areas where law reform should be undertaken, in both civil and penal areas, such as the minimum age for marriage and establishment of the age of criminal responsibility as being the attainment of puberty. Some states have argued that girls attain their physical maturity earlier,but it is the view of the Committee that maturity cannot simply the identified with physical development when social and mental development are lacking and that, on the basis of such criteria, girls are considered adults before the law upon marriage, thus being deprived of the comprehensive protection ensured by the Convention on the Rights of the Child. The International Conference on Population and Development, held at Cairo in September 1994, encouraged Governments to raise the minimum age for marriage. In her preliminary report to the Commission on Human Rights, the Special Rapporteur on violence against women, its causes and consequences, Ms. Radhika Coomaraswamy, also recognized that the age of marriage was a factor contributing to the violation of women's rights (E/CN.4/1995/42,PARA.165).

E. Early Pregnancy, Nutritional Taboos and Practices Related to Child Delivery

Early pregnancy can have harmful consequences for both young mothers and their babies. According to UNICEF, no girl should become pregnant before the age of 18 because she is not yet physically ready to bear children. Babies of mothers younger than 18 tend to be born premature and have low body weight; such babies are more likely to die in the first year of life. The risk to the young mother's own health is also greater. Poor health is common among indigent pregnant and lactating women.

In many parts of the developing world, especially in rural areas, girls marry shortly after puberty and are expected to start having children immediately. Although the situation has improved since the early 1980s,in many areas the majority of girls under 20 years of age are already married and having children. Although many countries have raised the legal age for marriage, this has had little impact on traditional societies where marriage and child-bearing confer "status" on a woman.

Those who start having children early generally have more children, at shorter intervals, than those who embark on parenthood later. Fertility rates have been falling over the past decade, but they remain very high in Africa parts of Latin America and Asia. Once again, the link between delayed child-bearing and education is crucial.

An additional health risk to young mother is obstructed labour, which occurs when the baby's head is too big for the orifice of the mother. This provokes vesicovaginal fistulas, especially when an untrained traditional birth attendant forces the baby's head out unduly.

Generally throughout the developing world, the average food intake of pregnant and lactating mothers is far below that of the average male. Cultural practices, including nutritional taboos, ensure that pregnant women are deprived of essential nutriments, and as a result they tend to suffer from iron and protein deficiencies.

Poor health can be improved by a more balanced diet. The choice of food consumed is determined by a number of factors, including availability of natural resources, economics, religious beliefs, social status and traditional taboos. Because these factors place limits in one way or another on the intake of food, communities and individuals are deprived of essential nutriments and, as a result, physical and mental development is impaired. This is generally the case in most developing countries, but especially throughout Africa.

Although poor distribution of resources—whether due to harsh geographical or climatic conditions in a region, or to poverty resulting from a lack of purchasing power-contributes greatly to the severe imbalance of diets throughout Africa, taboos placed on food for religious or cultural reasons are an unnecessary practice which exacerbates the situation.

The reasons for such taboos are many, but all are steeped in superstition. Many taboos are upheld because it is believed that the consumption of a particular animal or plant will bring harm to the individual.

Permanent taboos are also placed on female members of most communities throughout Africa. From infancy, the female child is given a low-nutrition diet. She is weaned at a much earlier age than the male infant, and throughout her life she will be deprived of highprotein food such as animal meat, eggs, fish and milk. As a result,the intake of nutriments by the female population is lower that that of the male population.

Temporary taboos which are applicable only at certain times in the life of an individual also affect women disproportionately. Most communities throughout Africa have food taboos specially for pregnant women.

Often these taboos exclude the consumption of nutriments essential for the expectant mother and foetus.

These nutritional taboos are unnecessary impositions made on women, who are already malnourished. It is perhaps not surprising that maternal and infant mortality rates are so high and life expectancy low in the countries concerned. But nutritional taboos also have reaching implications for women in the field of work, where their levels of productivity can be affected.

Lack of basic knowledge of human bodily functions can lead to illogical conclusions when illness sets in, or especially when a mother or her infant dies. Surrounded by myths and superstition, what may be a simple mishap can be explained in much more sinister terms as the product of evil spirits or bad omens.

Most rural areas throughout the developing world have disproportionately fewer health centres and clinics, trained midwives, nurses and doctors than urban areas. For most rural dwellers, health treatment must be obtained from traditional birth attendants (TBAs). Most TBAs have no formal training in health practices but acquire their skills via apprenticeship. These are skills passed down through generations of women. By observing a given situation, the TBA learns which remedy to use for which illness, or how to perform different kinds of delivery. If the situation changes, they try to adapt their knowledge and remedies and hope that works. If things go wrong, however, supernatural explanations are given; blame is never attributed to the TBA.

According to the World Health Organization (WHO), more than half the births in developing nations are attended by TBAs and relatives. Although these women have every good intention to assist their patients, mortality rates are higher in the rural areas where they operate.

The use of herbal mixtures and magic is common during delivery throughout Africa. The chemical components of some of these mixtures are beneficial, but others are quite lethal, especially when taken in large dosage.

In the case of obstructed labour, the abdomen is at times massaged or pressed to force the baby out. Some TBAs perform surgical operations to extract the foetus, using a knife or razor-blade to cut the labia minora and vaginal opening. A similar operation, known as the "Gishiri cut", is performed in some parts of Africa, and the likely complications are known to be haemorrhaging and infection.

Among the most bizarre treatments for obstructed labour are the psychological ones. In many societies, difficulty in labour or delay in delivery is believed to be punishment for marital infidelity. The women is pressured to confess her misdeed so that labour may continue without complications. This practice, which inflicts great mental cruelty on a woman already in agony due to obstructed labour, is prevalent in several African countries. In addition to the psychological trauma suffered by the woman, the practice further delays her being taken to hospital.

Treatment of obstructed labour by ineffective and harmful traditional methods can also cause uterine rupture. Rupture of the uterus still constitutes one of the major causes of maternal death in obstetric practice in developing countries. Death rates as high as 37 per cent have been reported in studies of hospitalized women with ruptured uterus. Foetal mortality is also very high: it was 100 per cent in a study of 144 cases of uterine rupture in one African country and 96 per cent in an Indian review of 181 cases.

Even when obstructed labour does not result in maternal death,it leads to prolonged or even permanent ill health in the majority of cases. For example, vesicovaginal fistula is a condition that has traumatic physical as well as social consequences. Due to prolonged pressure on the bladder during obstructed labour, the lower genital tract is severely damaged, causing a false passage between the bladder and the vagina. The women suffers from incontinence of urine and sometimes of faeces as well, since 10 to 15 per cent of all vesicovaginal fistula cases have associated vectovaginal fistula.

In two African countries, a practice known as "Zur Zur" is performed on women between the 34th and 35th weeks of their first pregnancy. A deep cut is made in the anterior wall of the vagina, sometimes on the posterior wall. The wound is allowed to bleed, then the woman rests for a while before being sent home to nurse her wound. The purpose of this operation is to prepare the woman for an easy delivery. However, the consequences can be death through excessive bleeding, shock, infection of the birth canal, and vesicovaginal or vaginal fistula.

Misdiagnoses have been made by midwives and doctors who receive these women once complications set in. The bleeding is often mistaken for an ante-partum haemorrhage, and Caesarean sections have been performed; but invariably the bleeding continues. Midwives are fighting to get the practice stopped in the countries concerned.

Various forms of contraception and methods of tightening the vagina are practiced throughout the world. Many involve inserting herbal mixtures and foreign objects—for example, aluminium hydroxide, cloth, stone, soap and lime—into the vagina. Many of these inserts have an irritating or erosive effect on the vaginal mucosa, which is a natural defence against infections and disease, such as HIV.

F. Violence Against Women

Most of the practices reviewed so far constitute acts of violence against women or the girl child by the family and the community, and are often condoned by the State. In its resolution 1994/45 of 4 March 1994, the Commission on Human Rights recognized other forms of non-traditional practices, such as rape and domestic violence, as violence against women. In that resolution (paras. 6 and 8), the Commission decided to appoint, for a three-year period, a special rapporteur on violence against women,including its causes and consequences. Ms.Radhika Coomaraswamy of Sri Lanka was subsequently appointed Special Rapporteur on violence against women.

This appointment came after more than two decades of tireless campaigning by women worldwide. An important step marked by resolution 1994/45 was that, for the first time, Governments were held accountable for acts of violence against women committed by the private individual.

In the same resolution (para.7), the Commission invited the Special Rapporteur,in carrying out her mandate, and within the framework of the Universal Declaration of Human Rights and all other international human rights instruments, including the Convention on the Elimination of All Forms of Discrimination against Women and the Declaration on the Elimination of Violence against Women, *inter alia*, to recommend measures, at the national, regional and international levels, to eliminate violence against women and its causes, and to remedy its consequences.

The special Rapporteur's mandate includes carrying our field missions, either separately or jointly with other special rapporteurs and working groups, and consulting periodically with the Committee on the Elimination of Discrimination against Women. In addition, the Commission requested the Secretary-General to ensure that the reports of the Special Rapporteur are brought to the attention of the Commission on the Status of Women.

The Special Rapporteur submitted a preliminary report to the Commission on Human Rights at its fifty-first session, in 1995 (E/CN1995/42).

II. REVIEW OF ACTION AND ACTIVITIES BY UNITED NATIONS ORGANS AND AGENCIES, GOVERNMENTS AND NGOS

A. United Nations Organs and Agencies

Action on traditional practices affecting the health of women and children, in particular Female Genital Mutilation (FGM), was first taken in 1958 when the Economic and Social Council (ECOSOC) invited the World Health Organization (WHO) to undertake a study of the persistence of customs subjecting girls to ritual operations and to communicate the results of the study to the Commission on the Status of Women.

In 1960, the issue of FGM was debated at the Seminar on the Participation of Women in Public life, held at Addis Ababa for the African region. Concluding remarks included a call to WHO to make a statement condemning all forms of medicalization of FGM. In its resolution 821 II (XXXII), adopted in July 1961, ECOSOC again invited WHO to study the medical aspects of operations based on customs. A seminar convened in 1979 by the WHO Regional Office for the Eastern Mediterranean in Khartoum marked a milestone in the campaign against harmful traditional practices, setting the pace and direction for international and national plans of action. Additional forms of harmful traditional practives were identified and a recommendation was made for the formation of the Inter-African Committee on Traditional Practices Affecting the Health of Women and Children. In addition, the seminar reiterated the concluding remarks made at the 1960 seminar and urged Governments to collaborate with international bodies in a concerted effort to eliminate these practices.

Commission on Human Rights and Sub-Commission on Prevention of Discrimination and Protection of Minorities

For a number of years, many voices, both national and international, have been echoing the United Nations call for an end to the suffering of girls and women caused by harmful traditional practives. In the 1980s, the campaign against such practices became so widespread that , in 1983, the issue was taken up by the Sub-Commission on Prevention of Discrimination and Protection of Minorities. The Sub-Commission's recommendation that a working group be established to conduct a study of all aspects of the problem was endorsed by the Commission on Human Rights and the Economic and Social Council.

The working Group on Traditional Practices Affecting the Health of Women and Children, composed of experts designated by the Sub-Commission on Prevention of Discrimination and Protection of Minorities, UNICEF,UNESCO and WHO, and representatives of concerned NGOs, held three sessions in Geneva during 1985 and 1986. The report of the Working Group (E/CN.4/1986/42) was submitted to the Commission on Human Rights at its forty-second session, in 1986.

By its resolution 1988/57 of 9 March 1988, the Commission on Human Rights requested the Sub-Commission to consider measures to be taken at the national and international levels to eliminate the practices in question, and to report to the Commission on the subject. Pursuant to that request, the Sub-Commission appointed one of its members, Mrs. Halima Embareak Warzazi, as Special Rapporteur to study, on the basis of information to be gathered from Governments, specialized agencies, other intergovernmental organizations and concerned NGOs, recent developments relating to traditional practices affecting the health of women and children (Sub-Commission resolution 1988/34 of 1 September 1988).

The Special Rapporteur submitted a preliminary report (E/CN.4/Sub.2/1989/42 and Add.1) and a final report (E/CN.4/Sub.2/1991/6), containing information received from the above-mentioned sources, as well as information gathered during field missions to the Sudan and Djibouti. These field missions, to together with two regional seminars on the subject organized by the Centre for Human Rights in Africa and Asia (Burkina Faso, 1991; Sri Lanka, 1994), have contributed to a better understanding of the phenomenon of harmful traditional practices which violate the rights of women and children.

Finally, in its resolution 1994/30 of 26 August 1994, the Sub Commission adopted the Plan of Action for the Elimination of Harmful Traditional Practices Affecting the Health of Women and Children which was prepared by the Sri Lanka regional seminar (see annex). In the same resolution, the Sub-Commission recommended the extension of the Special Rapporteur's mandate for an additional two years, to enable her to carry out an in-depth analysis of the issue, taking into consideration the conclusions and recommendations of the two regional seminars and the effects of the implementation of the Plan of Action. The resolution also called upon the Secretary-General to transmit the Plan of Action to the International Conference on Population and Development, held at Cairo in September 1994, and to the Fourth World Conference on Women, to be held at Beijing in September 1995. The Special Rapporteur was requested to submit reports at the forty-seventh and forty-eighth sessions of the Sub-Commission, in 1995 and 1996, respectively. The Sub-Commission's recommendations were endorsed by the Commission on Human Rights in its decision 1995/112 of 3 March 1995.

Committee on the Elimination of Discrimination Against Women

At its ninth session, in 1990, the Committee on the Elimination of Discrimination against Women addressed the issue of harmful traditional practices, in particular FGM. In general recommendation No.14 adopted at that session, it indicated its recognition of work carried out by women's organizations in identifying and combating harmful traditional practices. The Committee recommended that Governments support those efforts and encourage politicians, professionals, and religious and community leaders at all levels, including the media and the arts, to co-operate in influencing attitudes towards the eradication of FGM. The Committee also called for the introduction of appropriate educational and training programmes and seminars based on research findings about the problems arising from FGM.

The same general recommendation urged Governments to:

(b) Include in their national health policies appropriate strategies aimed at eradicating [FGM] in public health care .... including the special responsibility of .... .traditional birth attendants...;

(c) Invite assistance, information and advice from the appropriate organizations of the United Nations systems to support and assist efforts being deployed to eliminate harmful traditional practices;

(d) Include in their reports to the Committee under articles 10 and 12 of the Convention on the Elimination of All Forms of Discrimination Against Women information about measures taken to eliminate [FGM].

United Nations Children's Fund

The United Nations Children's Fund (UNICEF) has supported a wide range of porgramme activities for the advancement of women and girls through advocacy, policy-oriented research and technical co-operation. There are many examples in the sectors of health, education, income generation and water supply and sanitation of projects successfully addressing the needs of women and girls and promoting their participation in community development.

Special attention is given to the girl child and to the need to reduce disparities in the treatment of boys and girls. The Convention on the Rights of the Child and related policy efforts have stimulated regional and country-level action for advocacy and mobilization in favour of girls and for the elimination of discriminatory social and cultural practices. Social mobilization has focused on changing attitudes, particularly those related to the preference for sons in most countries in Africa, Asia, the Caribbean and Latin American. UNICEF's national, regional and international advocacy of appropriate policies and its efforts to bring about attitudinal and behavioural change, especially in such critical areas as early marriage, female genital mutilation, teenage pregnancy and female infanticide, will be intensified through support to local and national groups and organizations concerned with these issues.

In May 1994, UNICEF's Executive Board requested the Executive Director to give high priority to a number of efforts to promote gender equality and gender-sensitive development programmes, taking into account the special needs of individual countries and, *inter alia*, the provisions of the Convention on the Rights of the Child and the Convention on the Elimination of All Forms of Discrimination against Women. The priorities for action include:

(a) Strengthening the integration of gender concerns in country programmes by eliminating the disparities which exist at each stage of the life cycle of girls and women;

(b) promotion of ratification and implementation of the Convention on the Elimination of All Forms of Discrimination against Women, as well as the Convention on the Rights of the Child;

(c) support for specific action and strategies which promote gender equality within the family, including the sharing of parental responsibilities.

UNICEF country offices are working closely with NGO partners and Governments, as well as with other groups,including women's organizations, religious leaders, health workers and teachers.

World Health Organization

The World Health Organization (WHO) has been concerned with the issue of harmful traditional practices since 1958, when ECOSOC requested a study of the health implications of FGM. At a seminar in 1979, organized by the WHO Regional Office for the Eastern Mediterranean in Khartoum (see p. 125. above), WHO condemned FGM as a serious health risk which should be abolished, and called upon medical personnel to refrain from performing FGM.

WHO promotes and supports traditional practices which enhance health—for example,breast-feeding—and discourages those which are harmful, particularly to the health of women and girls. Among the latter, female genital mutilation presents the most dramatic risk of ill health, affecting some 75 million women and girls in Africa alone. The organization also discourages nutritional taboos which prevent pregnant and lactating women from eating essential foods, WHO works closely with all concerned national authorities, and particularly with non-governmental organizations, on these issues.

In 1993, the Forty-sixth World Health Assembly adopted resolution WHA 46.18 on maternal and child health and family planning for health. The resolution expressed concern, *inter alia*, about the continuing inequities affecting women in general and the persistence of harmful traditional practices such as child marriages, dietary limitations during pregnancy, and FGM. It urged member States to continue to monitor and evaluate the effectiveness of their efforts to achieve the goal of health for all, in particular in eliminating traditional practices affecting the health of women, children and adolescents.

In 1994, the Forty-Seventh World Health Assembly adopted resolution WHA 47,10 dealing specifically with harmful traditional practices, in which it urged all member States (para.2):

(1) to assess the extend to which harmful traditional practices affecting the health of women and children constitute a social and public health problem in any local community or subgroup;

(2) to establish national policies and programmes that will effectively, and with legal instruments, abolish female genital mutilation, child-bearing before biological and social maturity, and other harmful practices affecting the health of women and children:

(3) to collaborate with national non-governmental groups active in this field, draw upon their experience and, expertise and where such groups do no exist, encourage their establishment;

In the same resolution, the Assembly requested the Director-General of WHO to strengthen technical support to member States in implementing the above measures; and to continue global and regional collaboration with non—governmental organizations, United Nations bodies, and other agencies and organizations concerned in order to establish national, regional and global strategies for the abolition of harmful traditional practices.

B. Governments

The preliminary report (E/CN.4/Sub.2/1989/42 and Add.1) and final report (E/CN.4/Sub.2/1991/6) of the Special Rapporteur on traditional practices affecting the health of women and children contain summaries of information on the topic received, in response to requests by the Secretary-General, from 28 Governments. However, many of these Governments stated that harmful traditional practices were unknown in their countries. Others recognized the existence of some such practices, namely Female Genital Mutilation (FGM), son preference and inferior social status of women, and practices related to marriage, pregnancy and nutrition.

A number of countries throughout the world have either taken or supported action to prevent traditional practices affecting the health of women and children, in particular FGM.

Banglasesh clearly upholds the principle of equality of men and women and prohibits discrimination against women. To protect the legal rights of women and to stop violence and repression against them, the Government has adopted the following legislation:

(a) *Dowry Prohibition Act, 1980* which provides for punishment for giving, taking or abetting the giving or taking of dowry;

(b) *Cruelty to Women (Deterrent Punishment) ordinance, 1983*, which provides for punishment for abduction of women for unlawful purposes, trafficking in women, or causing or attempting to cause death or grievous harm to a wife for dowry;

(c) *Child Marriage Restraint Act Amendment Ordinance, 1984*, which raises the marriageable age for women from 16 to 18 years, and for men from 18 to 21 years. It also provides for punishment for marrying of giving in marriage of a child;

(d) *Muslim Family Laws Ordinance, 1961 (as amended in 1982)*. which provides for increased punishment in cases of polygamy and divorce in violation of the statutory provisions.

In the *Sudan*, a law was passed in 1946, under the British Colonial Administration, to prohibit the practice of infibulation.

In *Sweden*, the *Act on Prohibition of Female Circumcision* was passed in 1982. It not only seeks to bring to justice those breaking Swedish laws, but also any person living in Sweden who assists in carrying out FGM in another country which also has prohibitive laws.

In the *United Kingdom*, the *Prohibition of Female Circumcision Act* was adopted in 1985. Measures against FGM have also been included in the child protection p4procedures at local authority levels.

In the *United States of America*, the *Federal Prohibition of Female Genital Mutilation* Act was under consideration by the House of Representatives in early 1995.

A number of countries which have not yet passed specific laws use existing national legislation to prohibit the practice of female genital mutilation.

In *France*, no specific law exists, but article 312-3 of the Penal Code is applied to prosecute persons exercising violence against or seriously assaulting a child under 15, "if the result has been mutilation, amputation or .....loss of an eye or other permanent disabilities, or death not intentionally caused by the perpetrator". The Criminal Division of the Cour de cassation decided, by a judgment of 20 August 1983, that ablation of the clitoris resulting from wilful violence constituted a mutilation under article 312-3 of the Penal Code. While the term "female genital mutilation" is not used in the Penal Code, this decision makes it quite clear that such practices fall within the purview of the enactment.

In Norway, all hospitals were alerted in 1985 to the practice of female genital mutilation.

All the above Governments have also acknowledged the importance of education and awareness raising among both the practising communities and service provides. Practical steps are being taken in Australia, Belgium Canada, Djibouti, Egypt, Finland, France,Germany, Italy, the Netherlands, Norway, Somalia, the Sudan, Sweden and the United Kingdom to ensure that relevant information is disseminated. Lack of information from Africa and Asia makes it difficult to ascertain what recent action has been taken at national and grass-roots levels.

Some African countries are in the process of formulating national legislation against FGM, including Burkina Faso, Djibouti, Egypt; Ghana and Nigeria. In Burkina Faso, Kenya and Senegal, statements have been made by heads of State expressing the need to eliminate FGM.

As regard Asia, the following countries reported on ongoing and planned action to eradicate harmful traditional practices at the second United Nations regional seminar on the subject, held in Sri Lanka in July 1994: China, India, Islamic Republic of Iran, Iraq, Malaysia, Nepal, Pakistan, Republic of Korea, Singapore, Sri Lanka and Thailand (E/CN.4/Sub 2/1994/10. paras. 75 ff.).

C. Non-governmental Organizations

Available information indicated that increasingly more grassroots activities in the area of harmful traditional practices are taking place in Africa and Asia, as well as in Western countries. In Australia, Canada, Europe, New Zealand and the United States of America, the work of dedicated women is raising awareness and providing training and advice to service provides such as midwives, health visitors, nurses, doctors, teachers and social workers.

Of the 29 countries in Africa identified as having communities paractising female genital mutilation, 24 have branches of the inter African Committee on Traditional Practices Affecting the Health of Women and Children, in addition to many women's NGOs. Many established national women's organizations have carried out research and surveys, and other have ventured into communities where FGM and other harmful traditional practices prevail, setting up training programmes for excisors, traditional birth attendants and community members.

Work at this level is vital, for it is through the activities of NGOs that positive changes are being realized. Although early results of work in these communities are encouraging, to change a community's attitude totally will take at lest a generation. The NGOs in question thus urgently need continuing financial support to ensure that their programmes are fully implemented.

Prominent Non-governmental Organizations

(a) Inter-African Committee on Traditional Practices Affecting the Health of Women and Children

The Inter-African Committee (IAC) was formed in pursuance of a recommendation made at the 1979 khartoum seminar organized by WHO (See P.123 above). The Committee was officially established in 1984, following a regional seminar on harmful traditional practices held that year at Dakar, Senegal. The Committee has been granted consultative status with ECOSOC.

The aims of IAC are to reduce the morbidity and mortality rates for women and children through the eradication of harmful traditional practices; to promote traditional practices which are beneficial to the health of women and children; to play an advocacy role by promoting the importance of action against harmful traditional practices at the international, regional and national levels; and to raise funds for and support local activities of national committees and other partners.

The main areas of focus of IAC are training in information campaigns, and training of local activists and traditional birth attendants.

Intensive health education workshops, enhanced by the use of visual aids, are provided for local activists throughout communities, the objective being to raise awareness of issues related to harmful traditional practices. After five months of training, these activists are ready to go back to their communities and train other community members. In this way, the information on harmful traditional practices reaches a wide audience.

Traditional birth attendants are also trained to become active in the campaign against harmful traditional practices. Educational materials are disseminated to community groups such as students, youth groups, teachers, and religious and community leaders.

IAC also organizes international and regional seminars and workshops and is in close collaboration with the organization of African Unity, the Economic Commission for Africa and other United Nations agencies, as well as with other intergovernmental organizations, NGOs, funding bodies and individuals. The objective is to appraise and share experience and ideas in methods of good practice. The last seminar took place in April 1994 at Addis Ababa, Ethiopia.

(b) FORWARD International

FORWARD International (Foundation for Women's Health Research and Development) has been operational since 1983. It emerged from the Minority Rights Group (United Kingdom), an international human rights organization, as a special project unit. FORWARD'S aim is to promote good health among African women and children internationally. Its main focus is information provision, advocacy. training of service providers,counselling and networking with other groups internationally.

FORWARD is a United Kingdom-based charity. It co-operates with community groups to develop educational materials on the health aspects of FGM, and it works very closely with local authorities in the area of child protection, by providing training to social workers and teachers. FORWARD also provides training for health professionals and gives advice on policy guidelines. The organization is co-founder of a specialized Well Women Clinic based in the United Kingdom, which provides services and advice to excised and infibulated women.

FORWARD was instrumental at the national level in the formulation of the United Kingdom's 1985 *Prohibition of Female Circumcision Act*, as well as legislation on child protection. At the international level, FORWARD has provided advice and guidelines to legislators in relation to the drafting of national laws on FGM in the United States of America and Australia. The organization has worked closely with and addressed meetings organized by WHO, Amnesty International UK and other international agencies. In Africa, FORWARD has extensive links with women's groups working in the areas of health and FGM.

(c) Babiker Badri Scientific Association for Women's Studies

This organization was established in the Sudan in 1979 by a group of volunteer women in order to enhance research and education on women's issues. It is linked to the Ahfad College for Women, which is also controlled by the Babiker Badri Association. The organization is one of the pioneers in the fight against female genital mutilation, organizing seminars, workshops and studies on the subject. It runs an income-generating project for mothers in which education on FGM is gradually introduced. The Ahfad College for Women, which has more than 3,000 female students, has integrated education on FGM into its curriculum.

(d) Sudan National Committee on Traditional Practices

The main objective of this national women's organization is to educate and raise awareness of harmful traditional practices at all levels of society. The Committee has recognition and support from United Nations agencies, such as UNICEF, and other international bodies concerned with the health of children.

The Committee's main target groups are individuals who play influential roles in communities where FGM prevails, e.g. policy makers, service providers, and religious and community leaders. The Committee disseminates information via seminars, workshops, discussion groups and training sessions.

(e) Women for the Abolition of Sexual Mutilation (CAMS)

CAMS (Commission International pour l'Abolition des Mutilations Sexuelles) was established in France in 1980; its head office is in Dakar, Senegal.

One prominent member of CAMS (France) has devoted her time to campaigning throughout practising communities in France. As a lawyer, she seeks to protect the girl child by implementing existing French law, which has involved prosecuting parents and excisors who have performed FGM in France. Like other NGO working in this field, CAMS has a focus on research and awareness raising. It has also hosted a number of successful international seminars.

(f) Radda Barnen

Radda Barnen is the Swedish Save the Children organization. It has worked tirelessly with numerous women's groups in Africa and throughout Europe, providing vital financial support and advice.

D. United Nations Seminars and Conferences

(a) Regional Seminars

Two regional seminars on traditional practices affecting the health of women and children have been organized in Africa and Asia by the United Nations under its programme of advisory services in the field of human rights. The first was held at Ouagadougou, Burkina Faso, from 29 April to 3 May 1991; the second was held at Colombo, Sri Lanka, from 4 to 8 July 1994.

The objectives of the seminars were to assess the human rights implications of harmful traditional practices, and togather information from participants on measures taken at the governmental and non-governmental levels to end those practices. Participants included representatives of national Governments, United Nations agencies, and intergovernmental and non-governmental organizations. Both seminars provided the opportunity for participants to exchange information and experience. Participants were also urged to implement the recommendations of the seminars.

The recommendations adopted by the Ouagadougou seminar (E/CN.4/Sub.2/1991/48.paras. 136-138) included the following:

(i) Governments should:

Ratify and implement international instruments, including those relating to the protection of women and children;

Adopt legislation prohibiting practices harmful to the health of women and children, particularly FGM, and create a governmental body to implement the official policy adopted;

Carry out a survey and review of school curricula and textbooks with a view to eliminating prejudices against women;

Establish a national committee to combat harmful traditional practices, particularly FGM;

Co-operate with religious institutions and their leaders and other traditional authorities in order to eliminate harmful traditional practices such as FGM;

(ii) At the international level, the recommendations addressed specific United Nations bodies and agencies, including:

The Commission on the Status of Women, which was encouraged to study the issues pertaining to harmful traditional practices, particularly FGM;

UNICEF, which was called upon to continue its contribution to the campaign against FGM;

UNESCO,which was requested to provide assistance to the States concerned in preparing teaching materials, and to include the question of traditional practices in functional literacy programmes.

In addition, a special recommendation was addressed to all United Nations specialized agencies to include in their government aid programmes activities relating to the campaign against FGM.

(iii) *NGOs* were encouraged to intensify their activities for the elimination of harmful traditional practices. In particular, international NGOs concerned with protecting the health of women and children were requested to extend their financial and material support to national NGOs; private donors were also encouraged to support such activities. Finally, NGOs and Governments were urged to co-operate with each other in developing programmes for the retraining of FGM practitioners.

The recommendations of the Colombo seminar (E/CN.4/Sub.2/1994/10.paras. 89-90) were incorporated in the Plan of Action for the Elimination of Harmful Traditional Practices Affecting the Health of Women and Children, adopted by the seminar, the text of which is reproduced in the annex to this Fact Sheet.

The success of the two regional seminars has stimulated great interest among researchers and women activists the world over, thus increasing the volume of work being done and the information available on harmful traditional practices. This is an important step in understanding the prevalence and cultural justifications of the practices in question.

(b) International Conference on Population and Development

The International Conference on Population and Development, convened by the United Nations, was held in Cairo from 5 to 13 September 1994. its main objective was to emphasize the direct links between reproductive health and human rights thus placing the concerns of women and the girl child at the center of the conference themes.

Concern over population explosion again prompted participants to examine the crucial causes of large families. Poverty, lack of family planning, poor health, limited access to education and lack of women's rights were identified as the main factors in that regard.

It was also pointed out that early marriage and pregnancy, leading to high fertility and poor sexual and reproductive health, prevented the girl child from pursuing fully her education and employment opportunities. The Conference reaffirmed that investment in the girl child's health, nutrition and education from infancy was crucial to development. The Conference further emphasized that there was a need to eliminate all forms of discrimination against the girl child-for example, son preference-which resulted in harmful and unethical practices such as prenatal sex selection and female infanticide.

The Conference urged Governments to increase public awareness of the value of girl children through public education, promoting equal treatment for girls and boys at all levels. It was emphasized that child marriages should be eliminated and arranged marriages discouraged. Respect for girls and women had to be instilled in boys from an early age. On the issue of FGM,Governments were urged to put a stop to the practice and to ensure that rehabilitation and counselling facilities were available for those concerned.

(c). Fourth World Conference on Women

The Fourth World Conference on Women will be held at Beijing from 4 to 15 September 1995. Convened by the United Nations, the Conference will adopt a Platform for Action—concentrating on "critical areas of concern" that have been identified as obstacles to the advancement of women in the world-and set an agenda for the advancement of women at national, regional and international levels into the next century. The themes that have been identified include poverty, education, health, violence against women, the effects of armed or other kinds of conflict on women, and human rights of women.

The issue of traditional practices affecting the health of women and children has been raised at various regional meetings held in preparation for the Conference. The draft Platform for Action for the Conference makes specific mention of harmful traditional practices (E/CN. 61995/2, annex, para, 88) and calls for increased public awareness about violence as a violation of women's human rights.

Conclusions

Most women in developing countries are unaware of their basic human rights. It is this state of ignorance which ensures their acceptance-and, consequently, the perpetuation—of harmful traditional practices affecting their well-being and that of their children. Even when women acquire a degree of economic and political awareness, they often feel powerless to bring about the change necessary to eliminate gender inequality. Empowering women is vital to any process of change and to the elimination of these harmful traditional practices.

Since the World Conference on Human Rights,held in Vienna in 1993, it is hoped that all States will recognize and accept the universality and indivisibility of the human rights of women. It is also expected that there will be more ratifications of the Convention on the Elimination of All Forms of Discrimination against Women. However, much remains to be done in the field of equality, taking into account the absence, in many countries, of real constitutional guarantees of fundamental human rights for all. The persistence of negative customary normas that conflict with and undermine implementation of both national legislation and international human rights standards must be addressed.

Although such national legislation and international standards are vital in tackling the issue of harmful traditional practices, there is an urgent need for a parallel programme that addresses the cultural environment from which these practices emerged, in order to eliminate the various justifications used to perpetuate them. It is the duty of States to modify the social and cultural attitudes of both men and women, with a view to eradicating customary practices based on the idea of the inferiority or superiority of either sex or on stereotyped roles of gender.

Comprehensive and intensive programmes of formal and informal education, awareness raising and training are the approach followed by some Governments, non-governmental organizations and women's groups. In part II.C above, reference was made to the various ways in which women's organizations are trying to empower women and service providers in an effort to change attitudes regarding harmful traditional practices. This approach needs to be supported by implementation of national and international human rights norms relating to the elimination of discrimination against women. The environment of discrimination, which denies women and the girl child equal access to health care, education, employment and wealth, must also be addressed and reformed.

In the international debate, the father's responsibility towards the girl child has never been challenged. However, the duties and responsibilities of men within the family have begun to receive special attention as instruments of change. The Programme of Action adopted by the International Conference on population and Development in September 1994 states:

> Changes in both men's and women's knowledge, attitudes and behaviour are necessary conditions for achieving the harmonious partnership of men and women......It is essential to improve communication between men and women on issues of sexuality and reproductive health, and the understanding of their joint responsibilities, so that men and women are equal partners in public and private life.
>
> ....
>
> Male responsibilities in family life must be included in the education of children from the earliest ages. Special emphasis should be placed on the prevention of violence against women and children[4]
>
> ....

One of the most noticeable achievements at the international level has been the lifting of the taboo against addressing the issue of female genital mutilation, which is now acknowledged as a violation of the human rights of women and the girl child. This has created new sociocultural forces in the countries concerned, particularly among women participating in the crusade against FGM. None the less, unprecedented efforts are needed at the national and international levels to eradicate all forms of harmful traditional practices.

Governments, the United Nations and its specialized agencies, and NGOs should now play a more important role in monitoring and implementing the Plan of Action for the Elimination of Harmful Traditional Practices Affecting the Health of Women and Children (see annex). Technical and financial support should be given to national and regional organizations which advocate gender equality and promote human rights for all.

III. PLAN OF ACTION FOR THE ELIMINATION OF HARMFUL TRADITIONAL PRACTICES AFFECTING THE HEALTH OF WOMEN AND CHILDREN[A]

A. National Action

(1) A clear expression of political will and an undertaking to put an end to traditional practices affecting the health of women and girl children, particularly female genital mutilation, are required on the part of the Governments of countries concerned.

(2) International instruments, including those relating to the protection of women and children, should be ratified and effectively implemented.

(3) Legislation prohibiting practices harmful to the health of women and children, particularly female genital mutilation, should be drafted.

(4) Governmental bodies should be created to implement the official policy adopted.

(5) Governmental agencies established to ensure the implementation of the Forward-looking Strategies for the Advancement of Women adopted at Nairobi in 1985 by the World Conference to Review and Appraise the Achievements of the United Nations Decade for Women: Equality, Development and Peace should be involved in activities undertaken to combat harmful traditional practices affecting the health of women and children.

(6) National committees should be established to combat traditional practices affecting the health of young girls and women, particularly female genital mutilation, and governmental financial assistance provided to those committees.

(7) A survey and review of school curricula and textbooks should be undertaken with a view to eliminating prejudices against women.

(8) Courses on the ill effects of female genital mutilation and other traditional practices should be included in training programmes for medical and paramedical personnel.

(9) Instruction on the harmful effects of such practices should be included in health and sex education programmes.

(10) Topics relating to traditional practices affecting the health of women and children should be introduced into functional literacy campaigns.

(11) Audiovisual programmes (sketches, plays, etc.)should be prepared and articles published in the press on traditional practices adversely affecting the health of young girls and children, particu-

larly female genital mutilation.

(12) Co-operation with religious institutions and their leaders and with traditional authorities is required in order to eliminate traditional practices such as female genital mutilation which are harmful to the health of women and children.

(13) All persons able to contribute directly or indirectly to the elimination of such practices should be mobilized.

Son Preference

(14) The family being the basic institution from where gender biases emanate, wide-ranging motivational campaigns should be launched to educate parents to value the worth of a girl child, so as to eliminate such biases.

(15) In view of the scientific fact that male chromosomes determine the sex of children, it is necessary to emphasize that the mother is not responsible for selection. Governments must, therefore, actively attempt to change the misconceptions regarding the responsibilities of the mother in determining the sex of the child.

(16) Non-discriminatory legislation on succession and inheritance should be introduced.

(17) In the light of the dominant role religion plays in shaping the image of women in each society, efforts should be made to remove misconceptions in religious teachings which reinforce the unequal status of women.

(18) Governments should mobilize all educational institutions and the media to change negative attitudes and values towards the female gender and project a positive image of women in general, and the girl child in p4articular.

(19) Immediate measures should be taken by Governments to introduce and implement compulsory primary education and free secondary education and to increase the access of girls to technical education. Affirmative action in this field should be adopted in favour of the promotion of girls' education to achieve gender equity. Parents should be motivated to ensure the education of their daughters.

(20) Considering the importance of promoting self-esteem as a prerequisite for the higher status of women in the family and the community, Governments should take effective measures to ensure that women have access to and have control over economic resources, including land, credit, employment and other institutional facilities.

(21) Measures must be taken to provide free health care and services to women and children (in particular, girls) and to promote health consciousness among women, with emphasis on their own basic health needs.

(22) Governments should regularly conduct nutritional surveys,identify nutritional gender disparities and undertake special nutritional programmes in areas where malnutrition in various forms is manifested.

(23) Governments should also undertake nutritional education programmes to address, *inter alia*, the special nutritional needs of women at various stages of their life cycle.

(24) As son preference is often associated with future security, Governments should take measures to introduce a social security system, especially for widows, women-headed families and the aged.

(25) Governments are urged to take measures to eliminate gender stereotyping in the educational system, including removing gender bias from the curricula and other teaching materials.

(26) Governments should encourage by all means the activities of non-governmental organizations concerned with this problem.

(27) Public opinion makers, national institutions, religious leaders, political parties, trade unions, legislators, educators, medical practitioners and all other organizations should be actively involved in combating all forms of discrimination against women and girls.

(28) Gender disaggregated data on morbidity, mortality, education, health, employment and political participation should be collected regularly, analysed and utilized for the formulation of policy and programmes for girls and women.

Early Marriage

(29) Governments are urged to adopt legislative measures fixing a minimum age for marriage for boys and girls. As recommended by the World Health Organization, the minimum age for girls should be 18 years. Such legislative measures should be reinforced with necessary mechanisms for their implementation.

(30) Registration of births and deaths, marriages and divorces should be made compulsory.

(31) Health issues relating to sex and family-life education should be included in school curricula to promote responsible and harmonious parenthood and to create awareness among young people about the harmful effects of early marriage, as well as the need for education about sexually transmitted diseases, especially AIDS.

(32) The media should be mobilized to raise public awareness on the consequences of child marriage and other such practices and the need to combat them. Governments and women's activist groups could monitor the role of the mass media in this regard. All Governments should adopt and work towards"safe motherhood"initiatives.

(33) Effective training programmes should be ensured for traditional birth attendants and paramedical personnel to equip them with the necessary skills and knowledge, including concerning the effects of harmful traditional practices, to provide care and services during the antenatal, child delivery and postnatal periods, especially for rural mothers.

(34) Governments should promote male contraception, as well female contraception.

(35) To discourage the early marriage of girls, Governments should make provision to increase vocational training, retraining and apprenticeship programmes for young women to empower them economically. A certain percentage of the places in existing training institutions should be reserved for women and girls.

(36) Governments should recognize and promote the reproductive rights of women, including their right to decide on the number and spacing of their children.

(37) Considering that non-governmental organizations have an effective role in urging Governments to enhance women's health status and in keeping international organizations informed about the trends relating to traditional practices affecting the health of women and children, they should continue to report on the progress made and obstacles encountered in this area.

Child Delivery Practices

(38) Contraception should be encouraged as a means of promoting the health of women and children rather than as a means of achieving demographic goals.

(39) Governments should eliminate, through educational and legislative measures and the creation of monitoring mechanisms, all forms of harmful traditional childbirth practices.

(40) Governments should expand and improve health services in introduce training programmes for traditional birth attendants to upgrade their positive traditional skills, as well as to give them new skills on a priority basis.

(41) Research and documentation are essential to assess the harmful

effects of certain traditional birth-related practices and to identify and continue some positive traditions like breast-feeding.

Violence Against Women and Girl Children

(42) Violence against women and girl children is a golbal phenomenon which cuts across geographical, cultural and political boundaries and varies only in its manifestations and severity. Gender violence has existed from time immemorial and continues up to the present day. It takes covert and overt forms, including physical and mental abuse. Violence against women, including female genital mutilation, wife burning, dowry-related violence, rape, incest, wife battering, female foeticide and female infanticide, trafficking and prostitution, is a human rights violation and not only a moral issue. It has serious negative implications for the economic and social development of women and society and is an expression of the societal gender subordination of women.

(43) Governments should openly condemn all forms of violence against women and children, in particular girls, and commit themselves to confronting and eliminating such violence.

(44) To stop all forms of violence against women, all available media should be mobilized to cultivate a social attitude and climate against such totally unacceptable human behaviour.

(45) Governments should set up monitoring mechanisms to control depiction of any form of violence against women in the media.

(46) Violence being a form of social aberration, Governments should advocate the cultivation of a social attitude so that victims of violence do not suffer any continuing disability, feelings of guilt, or low self-esteem.

(47) Governments should enact and regularly review legislation for effectively combating all forms of violence, including rape, against women and children. In this connection, more severe penalties for acts of rape and trafficking should be introduced and specialized courts should be established to process such cases speedily and to create a climate of deterrence.

(48) Female infanticide and female foeticide should be openly condemned by all Governments as a flagrant violation of the basic right to life of the girl child.

(49) The hearing of cases of rape should be in camera and the details not published, and legal assistance should be provided to the victims.

(50) Traditional practices of dowry and bride-price should be con-

demned by Governments and made illegal. Acts of bride burning should likewise be condemned and a heavy penalty inflicted on the guilty.

(51) Families, medical personnel and the public should be encouraged to report and have registered all forms of violence.

(52) More and more women should be inducted in law enforcement machinery as police officers, judiciary, medical personnel and counsellors.

(53) Gender-sensitization training should be organized for all law enforcement personnel and such training should be incorporated in all induction and refresher courses in police training institutions.

(54) Mechanisms for networking and exchanges of information on violence should be established and-strengthened.

(55) Governments should provide shelters, counselling an rehabilitation centres for victims of all forms of violence. They should also provide free legal assistance to victims.

(56) Governments must develop and implement a legal literacy campaign to improve the legal awareness of women, including dissemination of information through all available means, particularly NGO programmes, adult literacy courses and school curricula.

(57) Governments must promote research on violence against women and create and update databases on this subject.

(58) Community-based vigilance should be promoted regarding gender violence, including domestic violence.

(59) At the national level, Governments should promote and set up independent, autonomous and vigilant institutions to monitor and inquire into violations of women's rights, such as national 1f commissions for women consisting of individuals and experts from outside the Government.

(60) Governments which have not done so are urged to ratify the Convention on the Elimination of All Forms of Discrimination against Women and the Convention on the Rights of the Child, to ensure full gender equality in all spheres of life. The States Parties to these Conventions must comply with their provisions in order to achieve their ultimate objectives, including the eradication of all harmful traditional practices.

(61) NGOs should be active in bringing all available information on systematic and massive violence against women and children, in particular girls, to the attention of all relevant bodies of the United Nations, such as the Centre for Human Rights, the Commission

on the Status of Women and specialized agencies, for the necessary intervention. Such information should also be shared with the Governments concerned, women's commissions and human rights organizations.

(62) Women's organizations should mobilize all efforts, including action research, to eradicate prejudicial and internalized values which project a diminished image of women. They should take action towards raising awareness among women about their potential and self-esteem, the lack of which is one of the factors perpetuating discrimination

B.International Action

The Commission on Human Rights and the Sub-Commission on Prevention of Discrimination and Protection of Minorities

(63) The question of traditional practices affecting the health of women and girl children should be retained on the agenda of the Commission on Human Rights and the Sub-Commission, so as to keep it under constant review.

The Commission on the Status of Women

(64) The Commission should give more attention to the question of harmful traditional practices.

(65) All the organs of the United Nations working for the protection and the promotion of human rights, and in particular the mechanisms established by the Convention on the Elimination of All Forms of Discrimination against Women, the Convention on the Rights of the Child, the Covenants on Human Rights and the Convention against Torture, should include in their agenda the question of all harmful traditional practices which jeopardize the health of women and girls and discriminate against them.

(66) Intergovernmental organizations and specialized agencies and bodies of the United Nations system, such as the United Nations Children's Fund, the United Nations Development Programme, the United Nations Population Fund, the United Nations Development Fund for Women, the International Labour Organization, the United Nations Educational, Scientific and Cultural Organization and the World Health Organization, should integrate in their activities the issue of confronting harmful traditional practices and elaborate programmes to cope with this problem.

United Nations Specialized Agencies

(67) Close coordination should be established between the Inter -Afri-

can Committee on Traditional practices Affecting the health of Women and Children and the relevant United Nations bodies, specialized agencies and regional organizations for the effective implementation of the Plan of Action. All specialized agencies should include in their aid programmes activities relating to the campaign against female genital mutilation and other traditional practices affecting the health of women and girl children.

Non-governmental Organizations

(68) National and international non-governmental organizations concerned with protecting the health of women and children should include in their programmes activities relating to traditional practices affecting the health of women and girl children.

(69) International non-governmental organizations concerned with protecting the health of women and children should extend their financial and material support to national non-governmental organizations to ensure the success of their activities.

(70) Non-governmental organizations already positively engaged in activities for the elimination of traditional practices affecting the health of women and children should intensify those activities.

(71) Cooperation should also take place between non-governmental organizations and Governments in developing programmes for the retraining of female genital mutilation practitioners to enable then to achieve financial self-sufficiency through gainful activities.

(72) Non-governmental organizations should continue and reinforce their activities in favour of protecting the human rights of women and girl children, including the promotion of beneficial traditional practices.

Other Measures

(73) Health workers should be required to dissociate themselves completely from harmful traditional practices.

(74) All women aware of the problem should be called on to react against traditional practices affecting the health of women and children and to mobilize other women.

(75) Women engaged in combating traditional practices affecting the health of women and children should exchange their experience.

Notes

1 For the texts of the international human rights instruments cited in this Fact Sheet, see Human Rights: A Compilation of International Instruments, vol.1(2Parts), Universal Instruments (United Nations Publication, Sales No.E.94.XIV.1).

2 See, generally, Fran P.Hosken,The Hosken Report: Genital and Sexual Mutilation of Females, 4th rev.ed.(Lexington(Mass),Women's international Network News.1994).

3 London, Minority Rights publications, 1994. antenatal and post-natal care. For example, professionals need training to know how to deliver infibulated women. The provision of health care for women and girls how have been genitally mutilated should be appropriate and sensitive to their needs. Health promotion work through women's health services can develop appropriate information materials and actively contribute to outreach work and awareness raising.

4 A/CONF.171/13,chap.1.resolution 1,annex, paras.4.24 and 4.27. III. Plan of Action for the Elimination of Harmful Traditional practives Affecting the Health of Women and Children[a]

a Prepared by the Second United Nations REgional Seminar on Traditional Practices Affecting the Health and Children, held at Colombo,Sri Lanka, from 4to 8 July 1994 (E/CN.4/Sub.2/1994/10/Add.1 and Corr.1): adopted by the Sub.Commission on Prevention of Discrimination and Protection of Minorities in its resolution 1994/30 of 26 August 1994 (para.3).

Selected Bibliography

Abdalla, Raqiya Haji Dualeh, Sisters in affliction; circumcision and infibulation of women in Africa, London, Zed Press, 1982. 122. 122 p. Bibliography.

Dorkenoo, Efua, Cutting the rose; female genital mutilation the practice and its prevention. London, Minority Rights Publications, 1994, p. 196. Bibliography.

Hosken, Fran P. The Hosken report; genital and sexual mutilation of females.4th rev.ed.lexington (Mass.), Women's International Network News, 1994. p. 444. Bibliography.

Inter-African Committee on Traditional Practices Affecting the Health of Women and Children. Report on the regional seminar on traditional practices affecting the health of women and children in Africa,6-10 April 1987, Addis Ababa,Ethiopia. p. 182.

United Nations; Economic and Social Council. Preliminary report submitted by the Special Rapporteur on violence against women, its causes and consequences, Ms. Radhika Coomaraswamy, in accordance with Commission on Human Rights resolution 1994/45. 22 November 1994. 92p. 9E/CN. 4/1995/42).

------,Economic and Social Council. Report of the second United Nations regional seminar on traditional practices affecting the health of women and children, Colombo, Sri Lanka, 4-8 July 1994. (E/CN. 4/Sub. 2/1994/10 and Corr. 1 and Add. 1and Add. 21/Corr.1).

-----, Economic and Social Council, Report of the United Nations seminar on traditional practices affecting the health of women and children, Ouagadougou, Burkina Faso, 29 April-3 May 1991. 12 June 1991. 46 p. (E/CN. 4/Sub. 2/1991/48).

-----, Economic and Social Council. Report of the Working Group on traditional practices affecting the health of women and children. 4 February 1986.50 p.(E/CN. 4/1986/42).

-----, Economic and Social Council. Study on traditional practices affecting the health of women and children; final report by the Special Rapporteur, Mrs. Halima Embarek Warzazi. 5 July 1991. 39 p. (E/CN. 4/Sub. 2/1991/6).

-----, Economic and Social Council. Study on traditional practices affecting the health of women and children; preliminary report by the Special Rapporteur, Mrs. Halima Embarek Warzazi. 21-22 August 1989. 21 p. (E/CN. 4/Sub. 2/1989/42 and Add.1).

5

Declaration on the Participation of Women in Promoting International Peace and Co-operation

Initially, United nations efforts to promote the principle of the equal rights of men and women were directed towards securing equality of men and women before the law. When legal equality for women was achieved in many Member States, the United Nations shifted the emphasis of its efforts in this area to stress *de facto* equality, and the Commission on the Status of Women and other organs of the United Nations system sought to encourage and assist Governments to give women equal opportunity with men. In 1962, in connection with the First United Nations Development Decade (the 1960s), the General Assembly called for a unified, long-term United Nations programme for the advancement of women. In 1970, the Assembly adopted such a programme within the framework of the Second Development Decade (the 1970s). In 1972, the Assembly proclaimed 1975 as International Women's Year, and subsequently proclaimed 1976 to 1985 as the United Nations Decade for Women: Equality, Development and Peace. In addition, over the years, the United Nations has repeatedly gone on record as an advocate of the rights of women in dozens of resolutions, statements, declarations and appeals adopted by the General Assembly, as well as in the final documents of two major world conferences (Mexico City, 1975, and Copenhagen ,1980) and of numerous other conferences, seminars, round-tables and world congresses of women.

One of the most significant of the United Nations statements on women is the Declaration on the Participation of Women in Promoting International Peace and Co-operation. In this Declaration, the connection is made between women's vital interest in world peace and their right to participate on an equal footing with men in the economic, social, cultural, civil and political affairs of society as a whole.

Drafting of the Declaration was first called for by the General Assembly in 1977 as part of the preparations for the 1980 World Conference of the United Nations Decade for Women at Copenhagen. The Assembly, in asking for the Declaration, indicated that it should deal with "the participation of women in the struggle for the strengthening of international peace and security and against colonialism, racism, racial discrimination, foreign aggression and occupation and all forms of foreign domination".

Thereafter, the views of United Nations Member States on a draft Declaration were sought and received by the Secretary-General, and these views and various proposals were considered by the Assembly's Third (Social, Humanitarian and Cultural) Committee in 1980 and 1981.

On 3 December 1982, by resolution 37/63, the Declaration was solemnly proclaimed by the General Assembly.

The text of the Declaration follows.

DECLARATION ON THE PARTICIPATION OF WOMEN IN PROMOTING INTERNATIONAL PEACE AND CO-OPERATION

Part I

Article 1

Women and men have an equal and vital interest in contributing to international peace and co-operation. To this end, women must be enabled to exercise their right to participate in the economic, social,cultural, civil and political affairs of society on an equal footing with men.

Article 2

The full participation of women in the economic, social, cultural, civil and political affairs of society and in the endeavour to promote international peace and co-operation is dependent on a balanced and equitable distribution of roles between men and women in the family and in society as whole.

Article 3

The increasing participation of women in the economic, social, cultural, civil and political affairs of society will contribute to international peace and co-operation.

Article 4

The full enjoyment of the rights of women and men and the full participation of women in promoting international peace and co-operation will contribute to the eradication of apartheid, of all forms of racism, racial discrimination, colonialism, neo-colonialism, *aggression*, foreign occupation and domination and interference in the internal affairs of States.

PART II

Article 5

Special national and international measures are necessary to increase the level of women's participation in the sphere of international relations so that women can contribute, on an equal basis with men, to national and international efforts to secure world peace and economic and social progress and to promote international co-operation.

Article 6

All appropriate measures shall be taken to intensify national and international efforts in respect of the participation of women in promoting international peace and co-operation by ensuring the equal participation of women in the economic, social, cultural, civil and political affairs of society through a balanced and equitable distribution of roles between men and women in the domestic sphere and in society as a whole, as well as by providing an equal opportunity for women to participate in the decision-making process.

Article 7

All appropriate measures shall be taken to promote the exchange of experience at the national and international levels for the purpose of furthering the involvement of women in promoting international peace and co-operation and in solving other vital national and international problems.

Article 8

All appropriate measures shall be taken at the national and international levels to give effective publicity to the responsibility and active participation of women in promoting international peace and co-operation and insolving other vital national and international problems.

Article 9

All appropriate measures shall be taken to render solidarity and support to those women who are victims of mass and flagrant violations of human rights such as *apartheid*, all forms of racism, racial discrimination, colonialism, neo-colonialism, aggression, foreign occupation and domination and of all other violations of human rights.

Article 10

All appropriate measures shall be taken to pay a tribute to the participation of women in promoting international peace and co-operation.

Article 11

All appropriate measures shall be taken to encourage women to participate in non-governmental and intergovernmental organizations concerned with the strengthening of international peace and security, the development of friendly relations among nations and the promotion of co-operation among States and, to that end, freedom of thought, conscience, expression, assembly, association, communication and movement, without distinction as to race, political or religious belief, language or ethnic origin, shall be effectively guaranteed.

Article 12

All appropriate measures shall be taken to provide practical opportunities for the effective participation of women in promoting international peace and co-operation, economic development and social progress including, to that end:

(a) The promotion of an equitable representation of women in governmental and non-governmental functions;

(b) The promotion of equality of opportunities for women to enter diplomatic service;

(c) The appointment or nomination of women, on an equal basis with men, as members of delegations to national, regional or international meetings;

(d) Support for increased employment of women at all levels in the secretariats of the United Nations and the specialized agencies, in conformity with Article 101 of the Charter of the United Nations.

Article 13

All appropriate measures shall be taken to establish adequate legal protection of the rights of women on an equal basis with men in order to ensure effective participation of women in the activities referred to above.

Article 14

Governments non-governmental and international organizations, including the United Nations and the specialized agencies, as well as individuals, are urged to do all in their power to promote the implementation of the principles set forth in the present Declaration.

6

The Nairobi Forward-Looking Strategies for the Advancement of Women

INTRODUCTION

A. Historical Background

Paragraph 1

The founding of the United Nations after the victory in the Second World War and the emergence of independent States following decolonization were some of the important events in the political, economic and social liberation of women. The International Women's Year, the world Conferences held at Mexico City in 1975 and Copenhagen in 1980, and the United Nations Decade for women: Equality, Development and Peace contributed greatly to the process of eliminating obstacles to the improvement of the status of women at the national, regional and international levels. In the early 1970s, efforts to end discrimination against women and to ensure their equal participation in society provided the impetus for most initiatives taken at all of those levels. Those efforts were also inspired by the awareness that women's reproductive and productive roles were closely linked to the political, economic, social, cultural, legal, educational and religious conditions that constrained the advancement of women and that factors intensifying the economic exploitation, marginalization and oppression of women stemmed from chronic inequalities, injustices and exploitative conditions at the family, community, national, subregional, regional and international levels.

Paragraph 2

In 1972, the General Assembly, in its resolution 3010 (XXVII), proclaimed 1975 International Women's Year , to be devoted to intensified action to promote equality between men and women, to ensure the full integration of women in the total development effort and to increase women's contribution to the strengthening of world peace. The World Plan of Action for the Implementation of the Objectives of the International Women's Year adopted by the World Conference of the International Women's Year at Mexico City in 1975, was endorsed by the General Assembly in its resolution 3520 (XXX). The General Assembly, in that resolution, proclaimed 1976—1985 the United Nations Decade for Women: Equality, Development and peace. In its resolution 33/185, the General Assembly decided upon the sub-theme "Employment, Health and Education" for the World Conference of the United Nations Decade for Women: Equality, Development and Peace, to be held at Copenhagen to review and evaluate the progress made in the first half of the Decade.

Paragraph 3

In 1980, at the mid-point of the Decade, the copenhagen World Conference adopted the programme of Action for the Second Half of the United Nations Decade for Women: Equality, Development and Peace,[2] which further elaborated on the existing obstacles and on the existing international consensus on measures to be taken for the advancement of women. The programme of Action was endorsed by the General Assembly that year in its resolution 35/136.

Paragraph 4

Also in 1980, the General Assembly, in its resolution 35/56, adopted the International Development Strategy for the Third United Nations Development Decade and reaffirmed the recommendations of the Copenhagen World Conference (General Assembly resolution 35/56, annex, para. 51). In the Strategy, the importance of the participation of women in the development process, as both agents and beneficiaries, was stressed. Also, the Strategy called for appropriate measures to be taken in order to bring about profound social and economic changes and to eliminate the structural imbalances that compounded and perpetuated women's disadvantages in society.

Paragraph 5

The strategies contained in the World Plan of Action and in the Programme of Action were important contributions towards enlarging the perspective for the future of women. In most areas, however, further action is required. In this connection the General Assembly confirmed the goals and objectives of the Decade—equality development and peace—stressed their validity for the future and indicated the need for concrete measures to overcome the obstacles to their achievement during the period 1986-2000.

Paragraph 6

The Forward-looking Strategies for the Advancement of Women during the Period from 1986 to the Year 2000 set forth in the present document present concrete measures to overcome the obstacles to the Decade's goals and objectives for the advancement of women. Building on principles of equality also espoused in the Charter of the United Nations the Universal Declaration of Human Rights,[3] the International Covenant on Civil and Political Rights,[4] the International Covenant on Economic, Social and Cultural Rights, [5] the Convention on the Elimination of All Forms of Discrimination against Women, [6] and the Declaration on the Participation of Women in Promoting International Peace and Co-operation, [7] the Forward-looking Strategies reaffirm the international concern regarding the status of women and provide a framework for renewed commitment by the international community to the advancement of women and the elimination of gender-based discrimination. The efforts for the integration of women in the development process should be strengthened and should take into account the objectives of a new international economic order and the International Development Strategy for the Third United Nations Development Decade.

Paragraph 7

The Nairobi World Conference is taking place at a critical moment for the developing countries. Ten years ago, when the Decade was launched, there was hope that accelerated economic growth, sustained by growing international trade, financial flows and technological developments, would allow the increased participation of women in the economic and social development of those countries. These hopes have been belied owing to the persistence and, in some cases, the aggravation of an economic crisis in the developing countries, which has been an important obstacle that endangers not only the pursuance of new programmes in support of women but also the maintenance of those that were already under way.

Paragraph 8

The critical international economic situation since the end of the 1970s has particularly adversely affected developing countries and, most acutely, the women of those countries. The overall picture for the developing countries, particularly the least developed countries, the drought-stricken and famine-stricken areas of Africa, the debt-ridden countries and the low-income countries, has reached a critical point as a result of structural imbalances and the continuing international economic situation. The situation calls for an increased commitment to improving and promoting national policies and multilateral co-operation for development in support of national programmes, bearing in mind that each country is responsible for its own development policy. The gap between the developed and developing countries, particularly the least developed among them, instead of narrowing, is widening further. In order to stem such negative trends and mitigate the current difficulties of the developing countries, which affect women the most, one of the primary tasks of the international community is to purpose with all vigour the efforts directed towards the establishment of a New International Economic Order founded on equity, sovereign equality, interdependence and common interest.

B. Substantive Background of the Forward-looking Strategies

Paragraph 9

The three objectives of the Decade—equality, development and peace—are broad, interrelated and mutually reinforcing, so that the achievement of one contributes to the achievement of another.

Paragraph 10

The Copenhagen World Conference interpreted equality as meaning not only legal equality, the elimination of *de jure* discrimination, but also equality of rights, responsibilities and opportunities for the participation of women in development, both as beneficiaries and as active agents.

Paragraph 11

Equality is both a goal and a means whereby individuals are accorded equal treatment under the law and equal opportunities to enjoy their rights and to develop their potential talents and skills so that they can participate in national political, economic, social and cultural development and can benefit from its results. For women in particular, equality means the realization of rights that have been denied as a result of cultural, institutional, behavioural and attitudinal discrimination. Equality is important for development and peace because national and global inequities perpetuate themselves and increase tensions of all types.

Paragraph 12

The role of women in development is directly related to the goal of comprehensive social and economic development and is fundamental to the development of all societies. Development means total development, including development in the political, economic, social, cultural and other dimensions of human life, as well as the development of the economic and other material resources and the physical, moral, intellectual and cultural growth of human beings. It should be conducive to providing women, particularly those who are poor or destitute, with the necessary means for increasingly claiming, achieving, enjoying and utilizing equality of opportunity. More directly,the increasingly successful participation of each woman in societal activities as a legally independent agent will contribute it further recognition in practice of her right to equality. Development also requires a moral dimension to ensure that it is just and responsive to the needs and rights of the individual and that science and technology are applied within a social and economic framework that ensures environmental safety for all life forms on our planet.

Paragraph 13

The full and effective promotion of women's rights can best occur in conditions of international peace and security where relations among States are based on the respect for the legitimate rights of all nations, great and small, and peoples to self-determination, independence, sovereignty, territorial integrity and the right to live in peace within their national borders.

Peace depends on the prevention of the use or threat of the use of force, aggression, military occupation, interference in the internal affairs of others, the elimination of domination, discrimination, oppression and exploitation, as well as of gross and mass violation of human rights and fundamental freedoms.

Peace includes not only the absence of war, violence and hostilities at the national and international levels but also the enjoyment of economic and social justice, equality and the entire range of human rights and fundamental freedoms within society. It depends upon respect for the Charter of the United Nations and the Universal Declaration of Human Rights, as well as international covenants and the other relevant international instruments on human rights, upon mutual co-operation and understanding among all States irrespective of their social political and economic systems and upon the effective implementation by States of the fundamental human rights standards to which their citizens are entitled.

It also embraces the whole range of actions reflected in concerns for security and implicit assumptions of trust between nations, social groups and individuals. It represents goodwill toward others and promotes respect for life while protecting freedom, human rights and the dignity of peoples and of individuals. Peace cannot be realized under conditions of economic and sexual inequality, denial of basic human rights and fundamental freedoms, deliberate exploitation of large sectors of the population, unequal development of countries, and exploitative economic relations. Without peace and stability there can be no development. Peace and development are interrelated and mutually reinforcing.

In this respect special attention is drawn to the final document of the tenth special session of the General Assembly, the first special session devoted to disarmament encompassing all measures thought to be advisable in order to ensure that the goal of general and complete disarmament under effective international control is realized. This document describes a comprehensive programme of disarmament, including nuclear disarmament, which is important not only for peace but also for the promotion of the economic and social development of all, particularly in the developing countries, through the constructive use of the enormous amount of material and human resources otherwise expended on the arms race.

Peace is promoted by equality of the sexes, economic equality and the universal enjoyment of basic human rights and fundamental freedoms. Its enjoyment by all requires that women be enabled to exercise their right to participate on an equal footing with men in all spheres of the political, economic and social life of their respective countries, particularly in the decision-making process, while exercising their right to freedom of opinion, expression, information and association in the promotion of international peace and co-operation.

Paragraph 14

The effective participation of women in development and in the strengthening of peace, as well as the promotion of the equality of women and men, require concerted multi-dimensional strategies and measures that should be people-oriented. Such strategies and measures will require continual upgrading and the productive utilization of human resources wit a view to promoting equality and producing sustained, endogenous development of societies and groups of individuals.

Paragraph 15

The three goals of the Decade—equality, development and peace-are inextricably linked to the three sub-themes—employment, health and education. They constitute the concrete basis on which equality, development and peace rest. The enhancement of women's equal participation in development and peace requires the development of human reasources, recognition by society of the need to improve women's status, and the participation of all in the restructuring of society. It involves, in particular, building a participatory human infrastructure to permit the mobilization of women at all levels, within different spheres and sectors. To achieve optimum development of human and material resources, women's strengths and capabilities, including their great contribution to the welfare of families and to the development of society, must be fully acknowledged and valued. The attainment of the goals and objectives of the Decade requires that women play a central role as intellectuals, policy-makers, decision-makers, planners, and contributors and beneficiaries of development.

Paragraph 16

The need for women's perspective on human development is critical since it is in the interest of human enrichment an progress to introduce and weave into the social fabric women's concept of equality, their choices between alternative development strategies and their approach to peace, in accordance with their aspirations, interests and talents. These things are not only desirable in themselves but are also essential for the attainment of the goals and objectives of the Decade.

Paragraph 17

The review and appraisal of progress achieved and obstacles encountered at the national level in the realization of the goals and objectives of the United Nations Decade for women: Equality, Development and Peace (see A/CONF. 116/5 and Add.1-14) identifies various levels of experience. Despite the considerable progress achieved and the increasing participation of women in society, the Decade has only partially attained its goals and objectives. Although the earlier years of the Decade were characterized by relatively favourable economic conditions in both the developed and developing countries, deteriorating economic conditions have slowed efforts directed towards promoting the equal participation of women in society and have given rise to new problems. With regard to development, there are indications that in some cases, although the participation of women is increasing, their benefits are not increasing proportionately.

Paragraph 18

Many of the obstacles discussed in the Forward-looking Strategies were identified in the review and appraisal (see A/CONF.116/5 and Add.1-14). The overwhelming obstacles to the advancement of women are in practice caused by varying combinations of political and economic as well as social and cultural factors. Furthermore, the social and cultural obstacles are sometimes aggravated by political and economic factors such as the critical international economic situation and the consequent adjustment programmes, which in general entail a high social cost. In this context, the economic constraints due in part to the prevailing macro-economic factors have contributed to the aggravation of economic conditions at the national level. Moreover, the devaluation of women's productive and reproductive roles, as a result of which the status of women continued to be regarded as secondary to that of men, and the low priority assigned to promoting the participation of women in development in development are historical factors that limit women's access to employment, health and education, as well as to other sectoral resources and to the effective integration of women in the decision-making process. Regardless of gains, the structural constraints imposed by a socio-economic framework in which women are second-class persons still limit progress. Despite changes in some countries to promote equity in all spheres of life, the "double burden" for women of having the major responsibility for domestic tasks and of participating in the labour force remains. For example, several countries in both the developed and developing world identify as a major obstacle the lack of adequate supportive services for working women.

Paragraph 19

According to responses from the developing countries, particularly the least developed, to the United Nations questionnaire to Governments (see A/CONF.116/5 and Add.1-14), poverty is on the increase in some countries and constitutes another major obstacle to the advancement of women. The exigencies created by problems of mass poverty, compounded by scarce national resources, have compelled Governments to concentrate on alleviating the poverty of both women and men rather than on equality issues for women. At the same time, because women's secondary position increases their vulnerability to marginalization, those belonging to the lowest socio-economic strata are likely to be the poorest of the poor and should be given priority. Women are an essential productive force in all economies, therefore it particularly important in times of economic recession that programmes and measures designed to raise the status of women should not be relaxed but rather intensified.

Paragraph 20

To economic problems, with their attendant social and cultural implications, must be added the threat to international peace and security resulting from violations of the principles of the United Nations Charter. This situation, affecting *inter alia* the lives of women, constitutes a most serious obstacle to development and thus hinders the fulfillment of the Forward-looking Strategies.

Paragraph 21

What is now needed is the political will to promote development in such a way that the strategy for the advancement of women seeks first and foremost to alter the current unequal conditions and structures that continue to define women as secondary persons and give women's issues a low priority. Development should now move to another plane in which women's pivotal role in society is recognized and given its true value. That will allow women to assume their legitimate and core positions in the strategies for effecting the changes necessary to promote and sustain development.

C. Current Trends and Perspectives to the Year 2000

Paragraph 22

In the absence of major structural changes or technological breakthroughs, it can be predicted that up to the year 2000 recent trends will, for the most part, be extended and adjusted. The situation of women, as it evolves during the period 1986-2000, will also cause other changes, establishing a process of cause and effect of great complexity. Changes in women's material conditions, consciousness and aspirations, as well as societal attitudes towards women, are themselves social and cultural processes having major implications and a profound influence on institutions such as the family. Women's advancement has achieved a certain momentum that will be affected by the social and economic changes of the next 15 years, but it will also continue to exist as a force to be reckoned with. Internal processes will exercise a major influence in the economic sphere, but the state of the global economic system and of the political, social, cultural, demographic and communication processes directly affected by it will invariably have a more profound impact on the advancement of women.

Paragraph 23

At the beginning of the Decade there was an optimistic outlook for development, but during the early 1980s the world economy experienced a widespread recession due, *inter alia,* to sharp inflationary pressures that affected regions and some groups of countries, irrespective of their level of development or economic structure. During the same period, however, the countries with centrally planned economies as a group experienced stable economic growth. The developed market economy countries also experienced growth after the recession.

Despite the recovery in the developed market economy countries which is being felt in the world economy, the immediate outlook for recovery in developing countries, especially in the low-income and the least developed countries, remains bleak, particularly in view of their enormous public and private external debts and the cost of servicing that debt, which are an evident manifestation of this critical situation. This heavy burden has serious political, economic and social consequences for them. No lasting recovery can be achieved without rectifying the structural imbalances in the context of the critical international economic situation and without continued efforts towards the establishment of a new international economic order. The present situation clearly has serious repercussions for the status of women, particularly underprivileged women, and for human resource development.

Women, subject to compound discrimination on the basis of race, colour, ethnicity and national origin, in addition to sex, could be even more adversely affected by deteriorating economic conditions.

Paragraph 24

If current trends continue, the prospects for the developing world, particularly the low-income and least developed countries, will be sombre. The overall growth in the developing countries as currently projected will be lower in the period 1980-2000 than that experienced in the period 1960-1980. In order to redress this outlook and thereby promote the advancement of women, policies should be reoriented and reinforced to promote world trade, in particular so as to promote market access for the exports of developing countries. Similarly, policies should be pursued in other areas which would also promote growth and development in developing countries, for example, in respect of further lowering interest rates and pursuit of non-inflationary growth policies.

Paragraph 25

It is feared that, if there is slow growth in the world economy, there will inevitably be negative implications for women since, as a result of diminished resources, action to combat women's low position, in particular, their high rates of illiteracy, low levels of education, discrimination in employment, their unrecognized contribution to the economy and their special health needs, may be postponed. A pattern of development promoting just and equitable growth on the basis of justice and equality in international economic relations could make possible the attainment of the goals and objectives of the International Development Strategy, which could make a significant improvement in the status of women while enhancing women's effective contribution to development and peace. Such a pattern of development has its own internal dynamics that would facilitate an equitable distribution of resources and is conducive to promoting sustained, endogenous development, which will reduce dependence.

Paragraph 26

It is very important that the efforts to promote the economic and social status of women should rely in particular on the development strategies that stem from the goals and objectives of the International Development Strategy and the Principles of a new international economic order. These principles include, *inter alia,* self-reliance, collective self-reliance, the activation of indigenous human and material resources. The restructuring of the world economy, viewed on a long-term basis, is to the benefit of all people—women and men of all countries.

Paragraph 27

According to estimates and projections of the International Labour Office, women constitute 35 per cent of the world's labour force, and this figure is likely to increase steadily to the year 2000. Unless profound and extensive changes are made, the type of work available to the majority of women, as well as the rewards will continue to be low. Women's employment is likely to be concentrated in areas requiring lower skills and lower wages and minimum job security. While women's total input of labour in the formal and informal sector will surpass that of men by the year 2000 they will receive an unequal share of the world's assets and income. According to recent estimates, it seems that women have sole responsibility for the economic support of a large number of the world's children, approximately one third and higher in some countries, and the numbers seem to be rising. Forward-looking strategies must be progressive, equitable and designed to support effectively women's roles and responsibilities as they evolve up to the year 2000. It will continue to be necessary to take specific measures to prevent discrimination and exploitation of their economic contribution at national and international levels.

Paragraph 28

During the period from 1986 to the year 2000, changes in the natural environment will be critical for women. One area of change is that of the role of women as intermediaries between the natural environment and society with respect to agro-ecosystems, as well as the provision of safe water and fuel supplies and the associated question of sanitation. The problem will continue to be greatest where water resources are limited — in arid and semi-arid areas- and in areas experiencing increasing demographic pressure. In a general manner, an improvement in the situation of women could bring about a reduction in mortality and morbidity as well as better regulation of fertility and hence of population growth, which would be beneficial for the environment and, ultimately, for women, children and men.

*Paragraph 29**

The issues of fertility rates and population growth should be treated in a context that permits women to exercise effectively their rights in matters pertaining to population concerns, including the basic right to control their own fertility which forms an important basis for the enjoyment of other rights, as stated in the report of the International Population Conference held at Mexico City in 1984.[8]

Paragraph 30

It is expected that the ever-expanding communications network will be better attuned than before to the concerns of women and that planners in this filed will provide increasing information on the objectives of the Decade—equality, development and peace—on the Forward-looking Strategies, and on the issues included in the subtheme-employment, health and education. All channels, including computer, formal and non-formal education and the media, as well as traditional mechanisms of communication involving the cultural media of ritual, drama, dialogue, oral literature and music, should be used.

Paragraph 31

Political and governmental factors that are likely to affect prospects for the achievement of progress by women during the period 1986-2000 will depend in large measure upon the existence or absence of peace. If widespread international tensions continue, with threats not only of nuclear catastrophe but also of localized conventional warfare, then the

---

* The Holy See delegation reserved its position with respect to paragraph 29 because it had not joined in the consensus at the International Conference on population (Mexico City, 1984) and did not agree with the substance of paragraph 29.

attention of policy-makers will be diverted from tasks directly and indirectly relevant to the advancement of women and men, and vast resources will be further applied to military and related activities. This should be avoided and these resources should be directed to the improvement of humanity.

Paragraph 32

To promote their interests effectively, women must be able to enjoy their right to take part in national and international decision-making processes, including the right to dissent publicly and peacefully from their Government's policies, and to mobilize to increase their participation in the promotion of peace within and between nations.

Paragraph 33

There is no doubt that, unless major measures are taken, numerous obstacles will continue to exist which retard the participation of women in political life, in the formulation of policies that affect them and in the formulation of national women's policies. Success will depend in large measure upon whether or not women can unite to help each other to change their poor material circumstances and secondary status and to obtain the time, energy and experience required to participate in political life. At the same time, improvements in health and educational status, legal and constitutional provisions and networking will increase the effectiveness of the political action taken by women so that they can obtain a much greater share in political decision-making than before.

Paragraph 34

In some countries and in some areas, women have made significant advances, but overall progress has been modest during the Decade, as is evident from the review and appraisal. During this period, women's consciousness and expectations have been raised, and it is important that this momentum should not be lost, regardless of the poor performance of the world economy. The changes occurring in the family, in women's roles and in relationships between women and men may present new challenges requiring new perspectives, strategies and measures. At the same time, it will be necessary to build alliances and solidarity groups across sexual lines in an attempt to overcome structural obstacles to the advancement of women.

*Paragraph 35**

The World Plan of Action for the Implementation of the objectives of the International Women's Year,[1] the Declaration of Mexico on the Equality of Women and their Contribution to Development and Peace, 1975[9], regional plans of action, the programme of Action for the Second Half of the United Nations Decade for women: Equality, Development and Peace[2], and the sub-theme —employment, health and education— the Declaration on the Participation of Women in Promoting International Peace and Co-operation[7] and the convention on the Elimination of All Forms of Discrimination against Women[6] remain valid and therefore constitute the basis for the strategies and concrete measures to be pursued up to the year 2000. The continuing relevance of the goals of the United Nations Decade for Women: Equality, Development and peace— and of its sub-theme-health, education and employment— should be stressed, as should the implementation of the relevant recommendations of the 1975 Plan of Action and the 1980 Programme of Action, so as to ensure the complete integration of women in the development process and the effective realization of the objectives of the Decade. The challenge now is for the international community to ensure that the achievements of the Decade become strong building blocks for development and to promote equality and peace, especially for the sake of future generations of women. The obstacles of the next 15 years must be met through concerted global, regional and national efforts. By the year 2000 illiteracy should have been eliminated, life expectancy for all women increased to at least 65 years of good quality life and opportunities for self-supporting employment made available. Above all, laws guaranteeing equality for women in all spheres of life must by then be fully and comprehensively implemented to ensure a truly equitable socio-economic framework within which real development can take place. Forward-looking Strategies for the advancement of women at the regional level should be basaed on a clear assessment of demographic trends and development forecasts that provide a realistic context for their implementation.

Paragraph 36

The Forward-looking Strategies and multidimensional measures

---

* Reservations to paragraph 35 were formulated by Australia, Belgium, Canada, Denmark, Finland, Germany, Federal Republic of, Iceland, Ireland, Israel, Italy, Luxembourg, Netherlands, New Zealand, norway, Sweden, Switzerland and United States of America. The United States reserved its position on the reference in paragraph 35 to the Declaration of Mexico on the Equality of Women and their Contribution to Development and Peace, 1975.

must be pursued within the framework of a just international society in which equitable economic relations will allow the closing of the gap that separates the industrialized countries from the developing countries. In this regard, all countries are called upon to show their commitment as was decided in General Assembly resolution 34/138 and, therefore, to continue informal consultations on the launching of global negotiations, as decided by the General Assembly in decision 39/454.

D. Basic Approach to the Formulation of the Forward-looking Strategies

Paragraph 37

It is necessary to reiterate the unity, inseparability and interdependence of the objectives of the Decade- equality, development and peace-as regards the advancement of women and their full integration in economic, political, social and cultural development, for which purpose the objectives should remain in effect in the operational strategies for the advancement of women to the year 2000.

Paragraph 38

The Forward-looking Strategies are intended to provide a practical and effective guide for global action on a long-term basis and within the context of the broader goals and objectives of a new international economic order. Measures are designed for immediate action, with monitoring and evaluation occurring every five years, depending on the decision of the General Assembly. Since countries are at various stages of development, they should have the option to set their own priorities based on their own development policies and resource capabilities. What may be possible for immediate action in one country may require more long-range planning in another, and even more so in respect of countries which are still under colonialism, domination and foreign occupation. The exact methods and procedures of implementing measures will depend upon the nature of the political process and the administrative capabilities of each country.

Paragraph 39

Some measures are intended to affect women and others directly and are designed to make the societal context less obstructive and more supportive of their progress. These measures would include the elimination of sex-based stereotyping, which is at the root of continuing discrimination. Measures to improve the situation of women are bound to have a ripple effect in society, since the advancement of women is without doubt a pre-condition for the establishment of a humane and progressive society.

Paragraph 40

The feasibility of policies, programmes and projects concerning women will be affected not only by their numbers and socio-economic heterogeneity but also by the different life-styles of women and by the constant changes in their life cycle.

Paragraph 41

The Forward-looking Strategies not only suggest measures for overcoming obstacles that are fundamental and operational, but also identify those that are emerging. Thus, the strategies and measures presented are intended to serve as guidelines for a process of continuous adaptation to diverse and changing national situations at speeds and modes determined by overall national priorities, within which the integration of women in development should rank high. The Forward-looking Strategies, acknowledging existing and potential obstacles, include separate basic strategies for the achievement of equality, development and peace. In line with the recommendations of the Commission in the Status of Women, acting as the Preparatory Body for the Conference at its second session, particular attention is given to "especially vulnerable and underprivileged groups of women such as rural and urban poor women, women in areas affected by armed conflicts, foreign intervention and international threats to peace; elderly women; young women; abused women; destitute women; women victims of trafficking and women in involuntary prostitution, women deprived of their traditional means of livelihood; women who are sole supporters of families, physically and mentally disabled women; women in detention; refugee and displaced women; migrant women; minority women; and indigenous women" [10].

Paragraph 42

Although addressed primarily to Governments, international and regional organizations, and non-governmental organizations, an appeal is made to all women and men in a spirit of solidarity. In particular, it is addressed to those women and men who now enjoy certain imporvements in their material circumstances and who have achieved positions where they may influence policy-making, development priorities and public opinion to change the current inferior and exploited condition of the majority of women in order to serve the goals of equality for all women, their full participation in development, and the achievement and strengthening of peace.

I. EQUALITY

A. Obstacles

Paragraph 43

One of the objectives of the Decade entails the full observance of the equal rights of women and the elimination of *de jure* and *de facto* discrimination. This is a critical first step towards human resource development. In developing countries inequality is, to a great extent, the result of underdevelopment and its various manifestations, which in turn are aggravated by the unjust distribution of the benefits of the international economy. The United Nations system, particularly the Commission on the Status of Women, has worked for four decades to establish international standards and to identify and propose measures to prevent discrimination on the basis of sex. Although much progress has been made in legislation, measures are necessary for effective implementation and enforcement. Legislative enactment is only one element in the struggle for equality, but an essential one as it provides the legitimate basis for action and acts as a catalyst for societal change.

*Paragraph 44**

The inequality of women in most countries stems to a very large extent from mass poverty and the general backwardness of the majority of the world's population caused by underdevelopment, which is a product of imperialism, colonialism, neo-colonialism, *apartheid,* racism, racial discrimination and of unjust international economic relations. The unfavourable status of women is aggravated in many countries, developed and underdeveloped, by *de facto* discrimination on the grounds of sex.

Paragraph 45

One of the fundamental obstacles to women's equality is that *de facto* discrimination and inequality in the status of women and men derive from larger social, economic, political and cultural factors that have been justified on the basis of physiological differences. Although there is no physiological basis for regarding the household and family as essentially the domain of women, for the devaluation of domestic work and for regarding the capacites of women as inferior to those of men, the

---

* The United States reserved its position on paragraph 44 because it did not agree that the obstacles listed should be considered the main reasons for the inequality of women in most countries.

belief that such a basis exists perpetuates inequality and inhibits the structural and attitudinal changes necessary to eliminate such inequality.

Paragraph 46

Women, by virtue of their gender, experience discrimination in terms of denial of equal access to the power structure that controls society and determines development issues and peace initiatives. Additional differences, such as race, colour and ethnicity, may have been more serious implications in some countries, since such factors can be used as justification for compound discrimination.

Paragraph 47

Fundamental resistance creates obstacles, which have wide-ranging implication in terms of denial of equal access to the power structure that controls society and determines development issues and peace initiatives. Additional differences, such as race, colour and ethnicity, may have even more serious implications in some countries, since such factors can be used as justification for compound discrimination.

Paragraph 48

The sharp contrasts between legislative changes and effective implementation of these changes are a major obstacle to the full participation of women in society. *De facto* and indirect discrimination, particularly by reference to marital or family status, often persists despite legislative action. The law as a recourse does not automatically benefit all women equally, owing to the socio-economic inequalities determining women's knowledge of and access to the law, as well as their ability to exercise their full legal rights without fear of recrimination or intimidation. The lack of inadequacy of the dissemination on women's rights and the available recourse to justice has hampered, in many instances, the achievement of expected results.

Paragraph 49

Some legislative changes are made without a through understanding of the relationship between existing legal systems. In practice, however, certain aspects of the law —for instance, customary provisions - may be in operation in societies with multiple and conflicting legal systems. Emerging and potential obstacles resulting from possible contradictions should be anticipated so that preventive measures can be taken. When passing new legislation, whatever its subject-matter, all possible care should be taken to ensure that it implies no direct or indirect discrimination so that women's right to equality is fully respected in law.

Paragraph 50

In some countries, discriminatory legislative provisions in the social, economic and political spheres still exist, including civil, penal and commercial codes and certain administrative rules and regulations. Civil codes in some instances have not yet been adequately studied to determine action for repealing those laws that still discriminate against women and for determining, on the basis of equality, the legal capacity and status of women, married women in particular, in terms of nationality, inheritance, ownership and control of property, freedom of movement and the custody and nationality of children. Above all, there is still a deeply rooted resistance on the part of conservative elements in society to the change in attitude necessary for a total ban on discriminatory practices against women at the family, local, national and international levels.

B. Basic Strategies

Paragraph 51

The political commitment to establish, modify, expand or enforce a comprehensive legal base for the equality of women and men and on the basis of human dignity must be strengthened. Legislative changes are most effective when made within a supportive framework promoting simultaneous changes in the economic, social, political and cultural spheres, which can help bring about a social transformation. For true equality to become a reality for women, the sharing of power on equal terms with men must be a major strategy.

Paragraph 52

Governments should take the relevant steps to ensure that both men and women enjoy equal rights, opportunities and responsibilities so as to guarantee the development of their individual aptitudes and capacities and enable women to participate as beneficiaries and active agents in development.

Paragraph 53

Changes in social and economic structures should be promoted which would make possible the full equality of women and their free access to all types of development as active agents and beneficiaries, without discrimination of any kind and to all types of education, training and employment. Special attention should be paid to implementing this right to the maximum extent possible for young women.

Paragraph 54

In order to promote equality of women and men, Governments should ensure, for both women and men, equality before the law, the provision of facilities for equality of educational opportunities and training, health services, equality in conditions and opportunities of employment, including remuneration, and adequate social security. Governments should recognize and undertake measures to implement the right of men and women to employment on equal conditions, regardless of marital status, and their equal access to the whole range of economic activities.

Paragraph 55

Effective institutions and procedures must be established or strengthened to monitor the situation of women comprehensively and identify the causes, both traditional and new, of discrimination and to help formulate new policies and effectively carry out strategies and measures to end discrimination. These arrangements and procedures must be integrated within a coherent policy for development but cannot wait indefinitely for such a policy to e formulated and implemented.

Paragraph 56

The obstacles to the equality of women created by stereotypes, perceptions of and attitudes towards women should be totally removed. Elimination of these obstacles will require, in addition tc legislation, education of the population at large through formal and informal channels, including the media, non-governmental organizations, political party platforms and executive action.

Paragraph 57

Appropriatc governmental machinery for monitoring and improving the status of women should be established where it is lacking. To be effective, this machinery should be established at a high level of government and should be ensured adequate resources, commitment and authority to advise on the impact on women of all government policies. Such machinery can play a vital role in enhancing the status of women, *inter alia*, through the dissemination of information to women on their rights and entitlements, through collaborative action with various ministries and other government agencies and with non-governmental organizations and indigenous women's societies and groups.

Paragraph 58

Timely and reliable statistics on the situation of women have an important role to play in the elimination of stereotypes and the movement towards full equality. Governments should help collect statistics and make periodic assessment in identifying stereotypes and inequalities, in providing concrete evidence concerning many of the harmful consequences of unequal laws and practices and in measuring progress in the elimination of inequities.

Paragraph 59

The sharing of domestic responsibilities by all members of the family and equal recognition of women's informal and invisible economic contributions in the mainstream of society should be developed as complementary strategies for the elimination of women's secondary status, which has fostered discrimination.

C. Measures for the Implementation of the Basic Strategies at the National level

1. Constitutional and Legal

Paragraph 60

Governments that have not yet done so are urged to sign the Convention on the Elimination of All Forms of Discrimination against Women[6] and to take all the necessary steps to ensure its ratification, or their accession to it. They should consider the possibility of establishing appropriate bodies charged with reviewing the national legislation concerned and with drawing up recommendations thereon to ensure that the provisions of the Convention and of the other international instruments to which they are parties that are relevant to the role, status and material circumstances of women are complied with.

Paragraph 61

Governments that have not yet done so should establish appropriate institutional procedures whereby the application of a revised set of laws and administrative measures may be effectively enforced from the village level up and may be adequately monitored so that individual women may, without obstruction or cost to themselves, seek to have discriminatory treatment redressed. Legislation that concerns women as a group should also be effectively enforced and monitored so that areas of systemic or *de facto* discrimination against women can be redressed. To this end, positive action policy should be developed.

Paragraph 62

Agrarian reform measures have not always ensured women's rights even in countries where women predominate in the agricultural labour force. Such reforms should guarantee women's constitutional and legal rights in terms of access to land and other means of production and should ensure that women will control the products of their labor and their income, as well as benefits from agricultural inputs, research, training, credits and other infrastructural facilities.

Paragraph 63

National research institutions, both government and private, are urged to undertake investigations of he problems associated with relationship between the law and the role, status and material circumstances of women. These should be integrated into the curricula of relevant educational institutions in an attempt to promote general knowledge and awareness of the law.

Paragraph 64

In the past decade there have been significant advances in the development of statistical concepts and methods for measuring inequality between women and men. The capabilities of national institutions concerned with statistics and women's issues should be improved to implement these concepts and methods in the regular statistical programmes of countries and to make effective use of these statistics in the policy-planning process. Training for producers and users of statistics on women should play a key role in the process.

Paragraph 65

In-depth research should be undertaken to determine instances when customary law may be discriminatory or protective of women's rights and the extent to which the interfaces between customary and statutory law may retard progress in the implementation of new legislative measures. Particular attention should be paid to double standards in every aspect of life, with a view to abolishing them.

Paragraph 66

Law-reform committees with equal representation of women and men from Governments and from non-governmental organizations should be set up to review all laws, not only as a monitoring device but also with a view to determining research-related activities, amendments and new legislative measures.

Paragraph 67

Employment legislation should ensure equity and provide benefits for women not only in the conventional and formal labour force but also in the informal sector, particularly with regard to migrant and service workers, by providing minimum wage standards, insurance benefits, safe working conditions and the right to organize. Opportunities for similar guarantees and benefits should also be extended to women making vital economic contributions in activities involving food production and processing, fisheries and food distribution through trade. These benefits should also pertain to women working in family enterprises and, if possible, to other self-employed women in an effort to give due recognition to the vital contribution of all these informal and invisible economic activities to the development of human resources.

Paragraph 68

Civil codes, particularly those pertaining to family law, should be revised to eliminate discriminatory practices where these exist and wherever women are considered minors. The legal capacity of married women should be reviewed in order to grant them equal rights and duties.

*Paragraph 69**

Such social and economic development should be encouraged as would secure the participation of women as equal partners with men in all fields of work, equal access to all positions of employment, equal pay for work of equal value and equal opportunities for education and vocational training, and would co-ordinate the legislation on the protection of women at work with the need for women to work and be highly productive producers and managers of all political, economic and social affairs and would develop branches of the social services to make domestic duties easier for women and men.

Paragraph 70

Measures for the implementation of legislation relating to working conditions for women must be taken.

Paragraph 71

Legislative and/or other measures should be adopted and implemented to secure for men and women the same right to work and to unemployment benefits, as well as to prohibit, through, *inter alia,* the imposition of sanctions, dismissal on the grounds of pregnancy or of maternity leave and discrimination in dismissals on the grounds of marital

---

* The United States reserved its position on paragraphs 69,72 and 137 specifically because it did not agree with the concept of "equal pay for work of equal value" and maintained the principle of "equal pay for equal work".

status. Legislative and other measures should be adopted and implemented to facilitate the return to the labour market of women who have left it for family reasons and to guarantee the right of women to return to work after maternity leave.

Paragraph 72

Governments should continue to take special action to institute programmes that would inform women workers of their rights under legislation and other remedial measures. The importance of freedom of association and the protection of the right to organize should be emphasized, this being particularly relevant to the position of women in employment. Special measures should be taken to ratify and implement in national legislation and relevant conventions and recommendations of the International Labour Organisation concerning the rights of women as regards access to equal employment opportunities, equal pay for work of equal value, equal working conditions, job security and maternity protection.

Paragraph 73

Marriage agreements should be based on mutual understanding, respect and freedom of choice. Careful attention should be paid to the equal participation and valuation of both partners so that the value of housework is considered equivalent of financial contributions.

Paragraph 74

The right of all women, in particular married women, to own, administer, sell or buy property independently should be guaranteed as an aspect of their equality and freedom under the law. The right to divorce should be granted equally to both partners under the same conditions, and custody of children decided in a non-discriminatory manner with full awareness of the importance of the input from both parents in the maintenance, rearing and socialization of children. Women should not forfeit their right to custody of their children or to any other benefits and freedoms simply because they have initiated a divorce. Without prejudice to the religious and cultural traditions of countries, and taking into account the *de facto* situations, legal or other appropriate provisions should be made to eliminate discrimination against single mothers and their children.

Paragraph 75

Appropriate action is necessary to ensure that the judiciary and all paralegal personnel are fully aware of the importance of the achievement by women of rights set out in internationally agreed instruments, constitutions and the law. Appropriate forms of in-service training and retraining should be designed and carried out for this purpose, with special attention given to the recruitment and training of women.

Paragraph 76

Special attention should be given in criminology training to the particular situation of women as victims of violent crimes, including crimes that violate women's bodies and result in serious physical and psychological damage. Legislation should be passed and laws enforced in every country to end the degradation of women through sex-related crimes. Guidance should be given to law enforcement and other authorities on the need to deal sensibly and sensitively with the victims of such crimes.

2. *Equality in Social Participation*

Paragraph 77

A comprehensive and sustained public campaign should be launched by all Governments, in close collaboration with non-governmental organizations, women's pressure groups, where they exist, and research institutions, as well as the media, educational institutions and traditional institutions of communication, to challenge and abolish all discriminatory perceptions, attitudes and practices by the year 2000. Target groups should include policy-makers and decision-makers, legal technical advisers, bureaucrats, labour and business leaders, business persons, professionals and the general public.

Paragraph 78

By the year 2000, all Governments should have adequate comprehensive and coherent national women's policies to abolish all obstacles to the full and equal participation of women in all spheres of society.

Paragraph 79

Governments should take all appropriate measures to ensure to women, on equal terms with men and without discrimination, the opportunity to represent their Government at all levels on delegations to subregional, regional and international meetings. More women should be appointed as diplomats and to decision-making posts within the United Nations system,including posts in fields relating to peace and development activities. Support services, such as educational facilities and day care, for families of diplomats and other civil servants stationed abroad, of United Nations officials, as well as employment of spouses at the duty station, wherever possible, should be strongly encouraged.

Paragraph 80

As future parents, young people and children should be educated and mobilized to act as stimulators for and monitors of changes in attitudes towards women at all levels of society, particularly with regard to the need for greater flexibility in the assignment of roles between women and men.

Paragraph 81

Research activities should be promoted to identify discriminatory practices in education and training and to ensure quality at those two levels. One priority area for research should be the impact of sexual discrimination on the development of human resources.

Paragraph 82

Governments and private institutions are urged to include in the curricula of all schools, colleges and universities courses and seminars on women's history and roles in society and to incorporate women's issues in the general curriculum and to strengthen research institutions in the area of women's studies by promoting indigenous research activities and collaboration.

Paragraph 83

New teaching methods should be encouraged, especially audio-visual techniques, to demonstrate clearly the equality of the sexes. Programmes, curricula and standards of education and training should be the same for females and males. Textbooks and other teaching materials should be continuously evaluated, updated and, where necessary, redesigned, rewritten to ensure that they reflect positive, dynamic and participatory images of women and to present men actively involved in all aspects of family responsibilities.

Paragraph 84

Governments are urged to encourage the full participation of women in the whole range of occupations, especially in fields previously regarded as male preserves, in order to break down occupational barriers and taboos. Employment equity programmes should be developed to integrate women into all economic activities on an equal basis with men. Special measures designed to redress the imbalance imposed by centuries of discrimination against women should be promoted to accelerate *de facto* equality between men and women. Those measures should not be considered discriminatory or entail the maintenance of unequal or separate standards. They are to be discontinued when the objectives of equality of opportunity and treatment have been achieved. Governments should ensure that their public service is an exemplary equal opportunity employer.

Paragraph 85

High priority should be given to substantial and continuing improvement in the partrayal of whom in the mass media. Every effort should be made to develop attitudes and to produce materials that portray positive aspects of women's roles and status in intellectual and other activities as well as egalitarian relations of sexes. Steps also should be taken to control pornography, other obscene portrayals of women and the portrayal of women as sex objects. In this regard all measures should be taken to ensure that women participate effectively in relevant councils and review bodies regarding mass media, including advertisement, and in the implementation of decisions of these bodies.

3. *Equality in Political Participation and Decision-Making*

Paragraph 86

Governments and political parties should intensify efforts to stimulate and ensure equality of participation by women in all national and local legislative bodies and to achieve equity in the appointment, election and promotion of women to high posts in executive, legislative and judiciary branches in these bodies. At the local level, strategies to ensure equality of women in political participation should be pragmatic, should bear a close relationship to issues of concern to women in the locality and should take into account the suitability of the proposed measures to local needs and values.

Paragraph 87

Governments and other employers should devote special attention to the broader and more equitable access and inclusion of women in management in various forms of popular participation, which is significant factor in the development and realization of all human rights.

Paragraph 88

Governments should effectively secure participation of women in the decision-making processes at a national, state and local level through legislative and administrative measures. It is desirable that governmental departments establish a special office in each of them,headed preferably by a woman,to monitor periodically and accelerate the process of equitable representation of women. Special activities should be undertaken to increase the recruitment, nomination and promotion of women, especially to decision-making and policy-making positions, by publicizing posts more widely, increasing upward mobility and so on, until equitable representation of women is achieved. Reports should be compiled periodically on the numbers of women in public service and on their levels of responsibility in their areas of work.

Paragraph 89

With respect to the increase in the number of couples in which both partners are employed in the public service, especially the foreign service, Governments are urged to consider their special needs, in particular the couple's desire to be assigned to the same duty station, with a view to reconciling family and professional duties.

Paragraph 90

Awareness of women's political rights should be promoted through many channels, including formal and informal education, political education, non-governmental organizations, trade unions, the media and business organizations. Women should be encouraged and motivated and should help each other to exercise their right to vote and to be elected and to participate in the political process at all levels on equal terms with men.

Paragraph 91

Political parties and other organizations such as trade unions should make a deliberate effort to increase and improve women's participation within their ranks. They should institute measures to activate women's constitutional and legal guarantees of the right to be elected and appointed by selecting candidates. Equal access to the political machinery of the organizations and to resources and tools for developing skills in the art and tactics of practical politics, as well as effective leadership capabilities, should be given to women. Women in leadership positions also have a special responsibility to assist in this field.

Paragraph 92

Governments that have not already done so should establish institutional arrangements and procedures whereby individual women, as well as representatives of all types of women's interest groups, including those from the most vulnerable, least privileged and most oppressed groups, may participate actively in all aspects of the formulation, monitoring, review and appraisal of national and local policies, issues and activities.

II. DEVELOPMENT

A. Obstacles

Paragraph 93

The United Nations Decade for women has facilitated the identification and overcoming of obstacles encountered by Member States in integrating women into society effectively and in formulating and implementing solutions to current problems. The continuation of women's stereotyped reproductive and productive roles, justified primarily on physiological, social and cultural grounds, has subordinated them in the general as well as sectoral spheres of development, even where some progress has been achieved.

*Paragraph 94**

There are coercive measures of an economic, political and other nature that are promoted and adopted by certain developed States and are directed towards exerting pressure on developing countries, with the aim of preventing them from exercising their sovereign rights and of obtaining from them advantages of all kinds, and furthermore affect possibilities for dialogue and negotiation. Such measures, which include trade restrictions, blockades, embargoes and other economic sanctions incompatible with the principles of the United Nations Charter and in violation of multilateral or bilateral commitments, have adverse effects on the economic, political and social development of developing countries and therefore directly affect the integration of women in development, since that is directly related to the objective of general social, economic and political development.

*Paragraph 95***

One of the main obstacles to the effective integration of women in the process of development is the aggravation of the international situation, resulting in a continuing arms race, which now may spread also to outer space. As a result, immense material and human resources needed for development are wasted. Other major obstacles to the implementation of goals and objectives set by the United Nations in the field of the advancement of women include imperialism, colonialism

* The United States abstained in the vote on paragraph 94 because of unacceptable language relating to economic measures by developed countries against developing States.

** The United States reserved its position on paragraph 95 because it did not agree with the listing of those abstacles categorized as being major impediments to the advancement of women.

neo-colonialism, expansionism, *apartheid* and all other forms of racism and racial discrimination, exploitation, policies of force and all forms of manifestations of foreign occupation, domination and hegemony, and the growing gap between the levels of economic development of developed and developing countries.

Paragraph 96

The efforts of many countries to implement the objectives of the United Nations Decade for women were undermined by a series of grave economic crises that have had severe repercussions, especially for many developing countries because of their generally greater vulnerability to external economic factors as well as because the main burden of adjustment to the economic crises has been borne by the developing countries pushing the majority of them towards economic collapse.

Paragraph 97

The worsening of the social situation in many parts of the world, and particularly in Africa, as a result of the disruptive consequences of the economic crisis had a great negative impact on the process of effective and equal integration of women in development. This adverse social situation reflects the lack of implementation of relevant United Nations conventions, declarations and resolutions in the social and economic fields, and of the objectives and overall development goals adopted and reaffirmed in the International Development Strategy for the Third United Nations Development Decade.

*Paragraph 98**

The lack of political will of certain developed countries to eliminate obstacles to the practical realization of such fundamental documents adopted by the United Nations as the Declaration on Social Progress and Development (General Assembly resolution 2542 (XXIV) the Charter of Economic Rights and Duties of States (General Assembly resolution 3281 (XXIX), the Declaration and the Programme of Action on the Establishment of a New International Economic order (General Assembly resolutions 3201 (S-VI) and 3202 (S-VI) respectively), the International economic relations on a just and democratic basis, should be counted among the main reasons for the conservation of the unfavourable and unequal position of women from the point of view of development, especially in the developming countries.

---

* The United States requested a vote on paragraph 98 and voted against the paragraph.

Paragraph 99

The last years of the Decade have witnessed a deterioration of the general economic situation in the developing countries. The financial, economic and social crisis of the developing world has worsened the situation of large sectors of the population, especially women. In particular, the decline in economic activity is having a negative impact on an already unbalanced distribution of income, as well as on the high levels of unemployment, which affect women more than men.

*Paragraph 100***

Protectionism against developing counties' exports in all its forms, the deterioration in the terms of trade, monetary instability, including high interest rates and the inadequate flow of official development assistance have aggravated the development problems of the developing countries, and consequently have complicated the difficulties hampering the integration of women in the development process.

One of the principal obstacles now confronting the developing countries is their gigantic public and private external debt, which constitutes a palpable expression of the economic crisis and has serious political, economic and social consequences for these countries. The amount of the external debt obliges the developing countries to devote enormous sums of their already scarce export income to the servicing of the debt, which affects their peoples' lives and possibilities of development, with particular effects on women. In many developing countries there is a growing conviction that the conditions for the payment and servicing of the external debt cause those countries enormous difficulties and that the adjustment policies traditionally imposed are inadequate and lead to a disproportionate social cost.

The negative effects of the present international economic situation on the least developed countries have been particularly grave and have caused serious difficulties in the process of integrating women in development.

The growth prospects of the low-income countries have seriously deteriorated owing to the reduction in international economic co-operation, particularly the inadequate flow of official development assistance and the growing trade protectionism in the developed countries, which restricts the capacity of the low-income countries to attain the objectives of the United Nations Decade for Women.

** The United States reserved its position on paragraph 100 because it did not accept the underlying philosophy of the paragraph as it concerned the economic situation in debtor and developing countries.

This situation is even more grave in the developing countries that are afflicted by drought, famine and desertification.

Paragraph 101

Despite significant efforts in many countries to transfer tasks traditionally performed by women to men or to public services, traditional attitudes still continue to persist and in fact have contributed to the increased burden of work placed on women. The complexity and multidimensional aspects of changing sex roles and norms and the difficulty of determining the specific structural and organizational requirements of such a change have hindered the formulation of measures to alter sex roles and to develop appropriate perspectives on the image of women in society. Thus, despite gains made by a few women, for the majority subordination in the labour force and in society has continued, through the exploitative conditions under which women often work have become more visible.

Paragraph 102

The effective participation of women in development has also been impeded by the difficult international economic situation, the debt crisis, poverty continued population growth, rising divorce rates, increasing migration, and the growing incidence of female-headed households. Yet, neither the actual expansion of employment for women nor the recognition that women constitute a significant proportion of producers has been accompanied by social adjustments to ease women's burden of child and household care. The economic recession led to a reduction in investments, particularly in those services that allow greater societal sharing of the social and economic costs of child care and housework.

Paragraph 103

Insufficient awareness and understanding of the complex and multifaceted relationships between development and the advancement of women have continued to make policy, programme and project formulation difficult. While during the earlier part of the Decade the belief that economic growth would automatically benefit women was more widely shared, an evaluation of the experience of the Decade has shed considerable doubt on this over-simplified premise. Consequently, the need to understand better the relationship between development and the advancement of women and to gather, analyse and disseminate information for the more effective formulation of policies, programmes and projects has become greater.

Paragraph 104

Although throughout history and in many societies women have been sharing similar experiences, in the developing countries the problems of women particularly those pertaining to their integration in the development process, are different from the problems women face in the industrialized countries and are often a matter of survival. Failure to recognize these differences leads, *inter alia,* to neglect the adverse effect of the insufficient progress made towards improvement in national policies or programmes and the present international economic situation as well as the interrelationships that exist between the goals and objectives of the Interrelationships that exist between the goals and objectives of the International Development Strategy for the Third United Nations Development Decade and the objectives of equality, development and peace.

Paragraph 105

The lack of political will and commitment continued to retard action to promote effective participation by women in development. Exclusion of women from policy-making and decision-making made it difficult for women and women's organizations to include in their preferences and interests the largely male-dominated choices of progress and development. Furthermore, because the issue of women in development has often been perceived as a welfare problem, it has received low priority, viewed simply as a cost to society rather than as a contribution. Thus, the specific formulation of targets, programmes and projects concerning women and development has often received little attention, awaiting the attainment of development rather than being instrumental to it. This, in turn, caused a parallel weakness in the institutional, technical and material resources devoted to the promotion of activities for effective participation by women in development.

Paragraph 106

Appropriate national machinery for the effective integration of women in the development process has been either insufficient or lacking. Where the machinery exists, it often lacks the resources, focus, responsibility and authority to be effective.

B. Basic Strategies

Paragraph 107

The commitment to remove obstacles to the effective participation of all women in development as intellectuals, policy-makers and decision-makers, planners, contributors and beneficiaries should be strengthened according to the specific problems of women in different regions and countries and the needs of different categories of women in them. That commitment should guide the formulation and implementation of policies, plans, programmes and projects,with the awareness that development prospects will be improved and society advanced through the full and effective participation of women.

Paragraph 108

Different socio-economic and cultural conditions are to be taken into account when identifying the foremost obstacles to the advancement of women. The current economic situation and the imbalances within the world monetary and financial system need adjustment programmes to overcome the difficulties. These programmes should not adversely affect the most vulnerable segments of society among whom women are disproportionately represented.

Paragraph 109

Development, being conceived as a comprehensive process, must be characterized by the search for economic and social objectives and goals that guarantee the effective participation of the entire population, especially women,in the process of development. It is also necessary to work in favour of the structural changes needed for the fulfilment of these aspirations. In line with these concerns, one should endeavour to speed up social and economic development in developing countries, accelerate the development of the scientific and technological capabilities of those countries· promote an equitable distribution of national income, and eradicate absolute poverty, experienced disproportionately by women and children, with the shortest possible delay by applying an overall strategy that, on the one hand, eliminates hunger and malnutrition and, on the other, works towards the construction of more just societies, in which women may reach their full development.

Paragraph 110

As the primary objective of development is to bring about sustained improvement in the well-being of the individual and of society and to bestow benefits on all, development should be seen not only as a desirable goal in itself but also as an important means of furthering equality of the sexes and the maintenance of peace.

Paragraph 111

Women should be an integral part of the process of defining the objectives and modes of development, as well as of developing strategies and measures for their implementation. The need for women to participate fully in political processes and to have an equal share of power in guiding development efforts and in benefiting from the should be recognized. Organizational and other means of enabling women to bring their interests and preference in to the evaluation and choice of alternative development objectives and strategies should be identified and supported. This would include special measures designed to enhance women's autonomy, bringing women into the mainstream of the development process on an equal basis with men, or other measures designed to integrate women fully in the total development effort.

Paragraph 112

The actual and potential impact on women of macro-economic processes operating at the international and national levels, as well as of financial spatial and physical development policies, should be assessed and appropriate modifications made to ensure that women are not adversely affected. Initial emphasis should be placed on employment, health and education. Priority should be given to the development of human resources, bearing in mind the need to avoid further increases in the work-load of women, particularly when alternative policies are formulated to deal with the economic and debt crisis.

Paragraph 113

With due recognition of the difficulties involved, Governments, international and regional organizations, and non-governmental organizations should intensify their efforts to enhance the self-reliance of women in a viable and sustained fashion. Because economic independence is a necessary pre-condition for self-reliance, such efforts should above all be focused on increasing women's access to gainful activities. Grass-roots participatory processes and planning approaches using local talent, expertise and resources are vital and should be supported and encouraged.

Paragraph 114

The incorporation of women's issues in all areas and sectors and at the local, national,regional and international levels should be institutionalized. To this end, appropriate machinery should be established or strengthened, and further legislative action taken. Sectoral policies and plans should be developed, and the effective participation of women in development should be integrated both in those plans and in the formulation and implementation of mainstream programmes and projects and should not be confined solely to statements of intent within plans or to small-scale, transitory projects relating to women.

Paragraph 115

The gender bias evident in most development programmes should be eliminated and the prejudices hindering the solution of women's problems removed. Particular attention should be given to the restructuring of employment, health and education systems and to ensuring equal access to land, capital and other productive resoruces. Emphasis should be placed on strategies to assist women in generating and keeping income, including measures designed to improve women's access to credit. Such strategies must focus on the removal of legal, customary and other barriers and on strengthening women's capacity to use existing credit systems.

Paragraph 116

Governments should seek means to increase substantially the number of women who are decision-makers, policy-makers, managers, professionals and technicians in both traditional and non-traditional areas and sectors. Women should be proved with equal opportunities for access to resources, especially education and training, in order to facilitate their equal representation at higher managerial and professional levels.

Paragraph 117

The role of women as a factor of development is in many ways linked to their involvement in various forms and levels of decision-making and management in economic and social structures, such as worker participation in management, industrial democracy, worker self-management, trade unions and co-operatives. The development of these forms of participation, which have an impact on the development and promotion of working and living conditions, and the inclusion of women in these forms of participation on an equal footing with men is of crucial importance.

Paragraph 118

The relationships between development and the advancement of women under specific socio-cultural conditions should be studied locally to permit the effective formulation of policies, programmes and projects designed for stable and equitable growth. The findings should be used to develop social awareness of the need for effective participation of women in development and to create realistic images of women in society.

Paragraph 119

It is vital that the link between the advancement of women and socio-economic and political development be emphasized for the effective mobilization of resources for women.

Paragraph 120

The remunerated and, in particular, the unremunerated contributions of women to all aspects and sectors of development should be recognized, and appropriate efforts should be made to measure and reflect these contributions in national accounts and economic statistics and in the gross national product. Concrete steps should be taken to quantify the unremunerated contribution of women to agriculture, food production, reproduction and household activities.

Paragraph 121

Concerted action should be directed towards the establishment of a system of sharing parental responsibilities by women and men in the family and by society. To this end, priority should be given to the provision of a social infrastructure that will enable society to share these responsibilities with families and, simultaneously, to bring about changes in social attitudes so that new or modified gender roles will be accepted, promoted and become exercisable. Household tasks and parental responsibilities, including decision-making regarding family size and child spacing, should be re-examined with a view to a better sharing of responsibilities between men and women and therefore, be conducive to the attainment of women's and men's self-reliance and to the development of future human resources.

Paragraph 122

Monitoring and evaluation efforts should be strengthened and directed specifically towards women's issues and should be based on a thorough review and extensive development of improved statistics and indicators on the situation of women as compared with men, over time and in all fields.

Paragraph 123

Appropriate national machinery should be established and should be utilized to integrate women effectively in the development process. To be effective, this machinery should be provided with adequate resources, commitment and authority to encourage and enhance development efforts.

Paragraph 124

Regional and international co-operation, within the framework of technical co-operation among developing countries, should be strengthened and extended to promote the effective participation of women in development.

C. Measures for the Implementation of the Basic Strategies at the National Level

1. Overall

Paragraph 125

Appropriate machinery with sufficient resources and authority should be established at the highest level of government as a focal point to ensure that the full range of development policies and programmes in all sectors recognizes women's contribution to development and incorporates strategies to include women and to ensure that they receive an equitable share of the benefits of development.

Paragraph 126

To achieve the goal of development, which is inseparably linked to the goals of equality and peace, Governments should institutionalize women's issues by establishing or strengthening appropriate machinery in all areas and sectors of development. In addition, they should direct specific attention to effecting a positive change in the attitudes of male decision-makers. Governments should ensure the establishment and implementation of legislation and administrative policies and mobilize communications and information systems to create social awareness of the legal rights of women to participate in all aspects of development at all levels and at all stages- that is, planning, implementation and evaluation. Governments should stimulate the formation and growth of women's organizations and women's groups and give financial and organizational support to their activities when appropriate.

Paragraph 127

National resources should be directed so as to promote the participation of women at all levels and in all areas and sectors. Governments should establish national and sectoral plans and specific targets for women in development, equip the machinery in charge of women's issues with political, financial and technical resources, strengthen intersectoral co-ordination in promoting women's participation, and establish institutional mechanisms to address the needs of especially vulnerable groups of women.

Paragraph 128

Governments should recognize the importance of and the need for the full utilization of women's potential for self-reliance and for the attainment of national development goals and should enact legislation to ensure this. Programmes should be formulated and implemented to provide women's organizations, co-operatives, trade unions and professional associations with access to credit and other financial assistance and to training and extension services. Consultative mechanisms through which the views of women may be incorporated in governmental activities should be set up, and supportive ties with women's grass-roots organizations, such as self-help community development and mutual aid societies and non-governmental organizations committed to the cause of women should be created and maintained to facilitate the integration of women in mainstream development.

Paragraph 129

There should be close co-ordination between Governments, agencies and other bodies at the national and local level. The effectiveness of national machinery, including the relationship between Governments and non-governmental organizations, should be evaluated and strengthened with a view to improving co-operation. Positive experiences and good models should be widely publicized.

Paragraph 130

Governments should compile gender-specific statistics and information and should develop or reorganize an information system to take decisions and action on the advancement of women. They should also support local research activities and local experts to help identify mechanisms for the advancement of women, focusing on the self-reliant, self-sustaining and self-generating social, economic and political development of women.

Paragraph 131

Governmental mechanisms should be established for monitoring and evaluating the effectiveness of institutional and administrative arrangements and of delivery systems, plans, programmes and projects to promote an equitable participation of women in development.

2. Areas for Specific Action

Employment

Paragraph 132

Special measures aimed at the advancement of women in all types of employment should be consistent with the economic and social policies promoting full productive and freely chosen employment.

Paragraph 133

Policies should provide the means to mobilize public awareness, political support, and institutional and financial resources to enable women to obtain jobs involving more skills and responsibility, including those at the managerial level, in all sectors of the economy. These measures should include the promotion of women's occupational mobility, especially in the middle and lower levels of the work-force, where the majority of women work.

Paragraph 134

Governments that have not yet done so should ratify and implement the Convention on the Elimination of All Forms of Discrimination against women and other international instruments relating to the improvement of the condition of women workers.

Paragraph 135

Measures based on legislation and trade union action should be taken to ensure equity in all jobs and avoid exploitative trends in part-time work, as well as the tendency towards the feminization of part-time, temporary and seasonal work.

Paragraph 136

Flexible working hours for all are strongly recommended as a measure for encouraging the sharing of parental and domestic responsibilities by women and men, provided that such measures are not used against the interests of employees. Re-entry programmes, complete with training and stipends, should be provided for women who have been out of the labour force for some time. Tax structures should be revised so that the tax liability on the combined earnings of married couples does not constitute a disincentive to women's employment.

Paragraph 137

Elimination all forms of employment discrimination, *inter alia* through legislative measures, especially wage differentials between women and men carrying out work of equal value, is strongly recommended to all parties concerned. Additional programmes should help to overcome still existing disparities in wages between women and men.

Differences in the legal conditions of work of women and men should also be eliminated, where there are disadvantages to women, and privileges should be accorded to male and female parents. Occupational desegregation of women and men should be promoted.

Paragraph 138

The public and private sectors should make concerted efforts to diversify and create new employment opportunities for women in the traditional, non-traditional and high productivity areas and sectors in both rural and urban areas through the design and implementation of incentive schemes for both employers and women employees and through widespread dissemination of information. Gender stereotyping in all areas should be avoided and the occupational prospects of women should be enhanced.

Paragraph 139

The working conditions of women should be improved in all formal and informal areas by the public and private sectors. Occupational health and safety and job security should be enhanced and protective measures against work-related health hazards effectively implemented for women and men. Appropriate measures should be taken to prevent sexual harassment on the job or sexual exploitation in specific jobs, such as domestic service. Appropriate measures for regress should be provided by Governments and legislative measures guaranteeing these rights should be enforced. In addition, Governments and the private sector should put in place mechanisms to identify and correct harmful working conditions.

Paragraph 140

National planning should give urgent consideration to the development and strengthening of social security and health schemes and maternity protection schemes in keeping with the principles laid down in the ILO maternity protection convention an maternity protection recommendation and other relevant ILO convention and recommendations as a prerequiste to the hastening of women's effective participation in production, and all business and trade unions should seek to promote the rights and compensations of working women and to ensure that appropriate infrastructures are provided. Parental leave following the birth of a child should be available to both women and men and preferably shared between them. Provision should be made for accessible child-care facilities for working parents.

Paragraph 141

Governments and non-governmental organizations should recognize the contribution of older women and the importance of their input in those areas that directly affect their well-being. Urgent attention should be paid to the education and training of young women in all fields. Special retraining programmes including technical training should also be developed for young women in both urban and rural sectors, who lack qualifications and are ill-equipped to enter productive employment. Steps should be taken to eliminate exploitative treatment of young women at work, in line with ILO Convention No. 111 concerning discrimination in respect of employment and occupation, 1958 and ILO Convention No. 122 concerning employment policy, 1964.

Paragraph 142

National planning, programmes and projects should launch a two-fold attack on poverty and unemployment. To enable women to gain access to equal economic opportunities, Governments should seek to involve and integrate women in all phases of the planning, delivery and evaluation of multisectoral programmes that eliminate discrimination against women, provide required supportive services and emphasize income generation. An increased number of women should be hired in national planning mechanisms. Particular attention should be devoted to the informal sector since it will be the major employment outlet of a considerable number of underprivileged urban and rural women. The co-operative movement could play an indispensable role in this area.

Paragraph 143

Recognition and application should be given to the fact that women and men have equal rights to work and, on the same footing, to acquire a personal income on equal terms and conditions, regardless of the economic situation. They should be given opportunities in accordance with the protective legislation of each country and especially in the labour market, in the context of measures to stimulate economic development and to promote employment growth.

Paragraph 144

In view of the persistence of high unemployment levels in many countries, Governments should endeavour to strengthen the efforts to cope with this issue and provide more job opportunities for women. Given that in many cases women account for a disproportionate share of total unemployment, that their unemployment rates are higher than those of men and that, owing to lower qualifications, geographical mobility and other barriers, women's prospects for alternative jobs are mostly limited, more attention should be given to unemployment as it affects women. Measures should be taken to alleviate the consequences of unemployment for women in declining sectors and occupations. In particular, training measures must be instituted to facilitate the transition.

Paragraph 145

Although general policies designed to reduce unemployment or to create jobs may benefit both men and women, by their nature they are often of greater assistance to men than to women. For this reason, specific measures should be taken to permit women to benefit equally with men from national policies to create jobs.

Paragraph 146

As high unemployment among youth, wherever it exists, is a matter of serious concern, polices designed to deal with this problem should take into account that unemployment rates for young women are often much higher that those for young men. Moreover, measures aimed at mitigating unemployment among youth should not negatively affect the employment of women in other age groups-for example, by lowering minimum wages. Women should not face any impediment to employment opportunities and benefits in cases where their husbands are employed.

Paragraph 147

Governments should also give special attention to women in the peripheral or marginal labour market, such as those in unstable temporary work or unregulated part-time work, as well as to the increasing number if women working in the informal economy.

Health

Paragraph 148

The vital role of women as providers of health care both inside and outside the home should be recognized, taking into account the following, the creation and strengthening of basic services for the delivery of health care, with due regard to levels of fertility and infant and maternal mortality and the needs of the most vulnerable groups and the need to control locally prevalent endemic and epidemic diseases. Governments that have not already done so should undertake, in co-operation with the World Health Organization, the United Nations Children's Fund and the United Nations Fund for Population Activities, plans of action relating to women in health and development in order to identify and reduce risks to women's health and to promote the positive health of women at all stages of life, bearing in mind the productive role of women in society and their responsibilities for bearing and rearing children. Women's participation in the achievement of Health for All by the Year 2000 should be recognized, since their health knowledge is crucial in their multiple roles as health providers and health brokers for the family and community, and as informed consumers of adequate and appropriate health care.

Paragraph 149

The participation of women in higher professional and managerial positions in health institutions should be increased through appropriate legislation training and supportive action should be taken to increase women's enrolment at higher levels of medical training and training in health-related fields. For effective community involvement to ensure the attainment of the World Health Organization's goal of Health for All by the year 2000 and responsiveness to women's health needs,women should be represented in national and local health councils and committees. The employment and working conditions of women health personnel and health workers should be expanded and improved at all levels. Female traditional healers and birth attendants should be more fully and constructively integrated in national health planning.

Paragraph 150

Health education should be geared towards changing those attitudes and values and actions that are discriminatory and detrimental to women's and girls'heath. Steps should be taken to change the attitudes and health knowledge and composition of health personnel so that there can be an appropriate understanding of women's health needs. A greater sharing by men and women of family and health-care responsibilities should be encouraged. Women must be involved in the formulation and planning of their health education needs. Health education should be available to the entire family not only through the health care system, but also through all appropriate channels and in particular the educational system. To this end, Governments should ensure that information meant to be received by women is relevant to women's health priorities and is suitably presented.

Paragraph 151

Promotive, preventive and curative health measures should be strengthened through combined measures and a supportive health infrastructure which, in accordance with the International Code of Marketing of Breast Milk Substitutes, should be free of commercial pressure. To provide immediate access to water and sanitary facilities for women, Governments should ensure that women are consulted and involved in the planning and implementation of water and sanitation projects, trained in the maintenance of water-supply systems, and consulted with regard to technologies used in water and sanitation projects. In this regard, recommendations arising from the activities generated by the International Drinking Water Supply and Sanitation Decade and other public health programmes should be taken into account.

Paragraph 152

Governments should take measures to vaccine children and pregnant women against certain endemic local diseases as well as other diseases as recommended by the vaccination schedule of the World Health Organization and to eliminate any differences in coverage between boys and girls (cf. WHO report EB 75/22). In regions where rubella is prevalent, vaccinations should preferably be given to girls before puberty. Governments should ensure that adequate arrangements are made to preserve the quality of vaccines. Governments should ensure the quality of vaccines. Governments should also ensure the full and informed participation of women in programmes to control chronic and communicable diseases.

Paragraph 153

The international community should intensify efforts to eradicate the trafficking, marketing and distribution of unsafe and ineffective drugs and to disseminate information on their ill effects. Those efforts should include educational programmes to promote the proper prescription and informed use of drugs. Efforts should also be strengthened to eliminate all practices detrimental to the health of women and children. Efforts should be made to ensure that all women have access to essential drugs appropriate to their specific needs and as recommended in the WHO List of Essential Drugs as applied in 1978. It is imperative that information on the appropriate the use of such drugs is made widely available to all women. When drugs are imported or exported Governments should use the WHO Certification Scheme on the Quality of Pharmaceutical Products Moving in International Commerce.

Paragraph 154

Women should have access to and control over income to provide adequate nutrition for themselves and their children. Also, Governments should foster activities that will increase awareness of the special nutritional needs of women, provide support to ensure sufficient rest in the last trimester of pregnancy and while breast-feeding, and promote interventions to reduce the prevalence of nutritional diseases such as anaemia in women of all ages, particularly young women, and promote the development and use of locally produced weaning food.

Paragraph 155

Appropriate health facilities should be planned, designed, constructed and equipped to be readily accessible and acceptable. Services should be in harmony with the timing and patterns of women's work, as well as with women's needs and perspectives. Maternal and child-care facilities, including family planning services, should be within easy reach of all women. Governments should also ensure that women have the same access as men to affordable curative, preventive and rehabilitative treatment. Wherever possible, measures should be taken to conduct general screening and treatment of women's common diseases and cancer. In view of the unacceptably high levels of maternal mortality in many developing countries, the reduction of maternal mortality from now to the year 2000 to a minimum level should be a key target for Governments and non-governmental organizations, including professional organizations.

*Paragraph 156**

The ability of women to control their own fertility forms an important basis for the enjoyment of other rights. As recognized in the World Population Plan of Action[11] and reaffirmed at the International Conference on Population, 1984, all couples and individuals have the basic human right to decide freely and informedly the number and spacing of their children, maternal and child health and family-planning components of primary health care should be strengthened, and family-planning information should be produced and services created. Access to such services shouls encouraged by Governments irrespective of their population policies and should be carried out with the participation of women's organizations to ensure their success.

*Paragraph 157**

Governments should make available, as a matter of urgency, information, education and the means to assist women and men to take decisions about their desired number of children. To ensure a voluntary and

---

* The Holy See delegation reserved its position with respect to paragraphs 156 to 159 because it did not agree with the substabce of those paragraphs.

free choice, family-planning information, education and means should include all medically approved and appropriate methods of family planning. Education for responsible parenthood and family-life education should be widely available and should be directed towards both men and women. Non-governmental organizations, particularly women's organizations, should be involved in such programmes because they can be the most effective media of motivating people at that level.

*Paragraph 158**

Recognizing that pregnancy occurring in adolescent girls, whether married or unmarried, has adverse effects on the morbidity and mortality of both mother and child, Governments are urged to develop policies to encourage delay in the commencement of childbearing. Governments should make efforts to raise the age of entry into marriage in countries in which this age is still quite low. Attention should also be given to ensuring that adolescents, both girls and boys, receive adequate information and education.

*Paragraph 159**

All Governments should ensure that fertility-control methods and drugs conform to adequate standards of quality, efficiency and safety. This should also apply to organizations responsible for distributing and administering these methods. Information on contraceptives should be made available to women. Programmes of incentives and disincentives should be neither coercive nor discriminatory and should be consistent with internationally recognized human rights, as well as with changing individual and cultural values.

Paragraph 160

Governments should encourage local women's organizations to participate in primary health-care activities including traditional medicine, and should devise ways to support women, especially underprivileged women, in taking responsibility for self-care and in promoting community care, particularly in rural areas. More emphasis should be placed on preventive rather than curative measures.

Paragraph 161

The appropriate gender-specific indicators for monitoring women's health that have been or are being developed by the World health Organization should be widely applied and utilized by Governments and other

* The Holy See delegation reserved its position with respect to paragraphs 156 to 159 because it did not agree with the substance of those paragraphs.

interested organizations in order to develop and sustain measures for treating low-grade ill health and for reducing high morbidity rates among women, particularly when illnesses are psychosomatic or social and cultural in nature. Governments that have not yet done so should establish focal points to carry out such monitoring.

Paragraph 162

Occupational health and safety should be enhanced by the public and private sectors. Concern with the occupational health risks should cover female as well as male workers and focus among other things on risks endangering their reproductive capabilities and unborn children. Efforts should equally be directed at the health of pregnant and lactating women, the health impact of new technologies and the harmonization of work and family responsibilities.

Education

Paragraph 163

Education is the basis for the full promotion and improvement of the status of women. It is the basic tool that should be given to women in order to fulfill their role as full members of society. Governments should strengthen the participation of women at all levels of national educational policy and in formulating and implementing plans, programmes and projects. Special measures should be adopted to revise and adapt women's education to the realities of the developing world. Existing and new services should be directed to women as intellectuals,policy-makers, decision-makers, planners, contributors and beneficiaries, with particular attention to the UNESCO Convention against Discrimination in Education (1960). Special measures should also be adopted to increase equal access to scientific, technical and vocational education, particularly for young women, and evaluate progress made by the poorest women in urban and rural areas.

Paragraph 164

Special measures should be taken by Governments and the international organizations, especially UNESCO, to eliminate the high rate of illiteracy by the year 2000, with the support of the international community. Governments should establish targets and adopt appropriate measures for this purpose. While the elimination of illiteracy is important to all, priority programmes are still required to overcome the special emphasis on health, nutrition and viable economic skills and opportunities, in order to eradicate illiteracy among women and to produce additional material for the eradication of illiteracy. Programmes for legal literacy in low-income urban and rural areas should be initiated and intensified. Raising the level of education among women is important for the general welfare of society and because of its close link to child survival and child spacing.

Paragraph 165

The causes of high absenteeism and drop-out rates of girls in the educational system must be addressed. Measures must be developed, strengthened and implemented that will, *inter alia*, create the appropriate incentives to ensure that women have an equal opportunity to acquire education at all levels, as well as to apply their education in a work or career context. Such measures should include the strengthening of communication and information systems,the implementation of appropriate legislation and the reorientation of educational personnel. Moreover, Governments should encourage and finance adult education programmes for those women who have never completed their studies or were forced to interrupt their studies, owing to family responsibilities,lack of financial resources or early pregnancies.

Paragraph 166

Efforts should be made to ensure that available scholarships and other forms of support from governmental, non-governmental and private sources are expanded and equitably distributed to girls and boys and that boarding and lodging facilities are equally accessible to them.

Paragraph 167

The curricula of public and private schools should be examined, textbooks and other educational materials reviewed and educational personnel retrained in order to eliminate all discriminatory gender stereotyping in education. Educational institutions should be encouraged to expand their curricula to include studies on women's contribution to all aspects of development.

Paragraph 168

The Decade has witnessed the rise of centres and programmes of women's studies in response to social forces and to the need for developing a new scholarship and a body of knowledge on women's studies from the perspective of women. Women's studies should be developed to reformulate the current models influencing the constitution of knowledge and sustaining a value system that reinforces inequality. The promotion and application of women's studies inside and outside and conventional institutions of learning will help to create a just and equitable society in which men and women enjoy equal partnership.

Paragraph 169

Encouragement and incentives, as well as counselling services, should be provided for girls to study scientific, technical and managerial subjects at all levels, in order to develop and enhance the aptitudes of women for decision-making, management and leadership in these fields.

Paragraph 170

All educational and occupational training should be flexible and accessible to both women and men. It should aim to improve employment possibilities and promotion prospects for women including those areas where technologies are improving rapidly, and vocational training programmes, as well as workers educational schemes dealing with co-operatives, trade unions and work associations, should stress the importance of equal opportunity for women at all level of work and work-related activities.

Paragraph 171

Extensive measures should be taken to diversify women's vocational education and training in order to extend their opportunities for employment in occupations that are non-traditional or are new to women and that are important to development. The present educational system, which in many countries is sharply divided by sex,with girls receiving instruction in home economics and boys in technical subjects, should be altered. Existing vocational training centres should be opened to girls and women instead of continuing a segregated training system.

Paragraph 172

A fully integrated system of training, having direct linkages with employment needs, pertinent to future employment and development trends should be created and implemented in order to avoid wastage of human resources.

Paragraph 173

Educational programmes to enable men to assume as much responsibility as women in the upbringing of children and the maintenance of the household should be introduced at all levels of the educational system.

Food, Water and Agriculture

Paragraph 174

Women, as key food producers in many regions of the world, Play a central role in the development and production of food and agriculture, participating actively in all phases of the production cycle, including the conservation, storage, processing and marketing of food and agricultural products. Women therefore make a vital contribution to economic development, particularly in agriculturally based economies, which must be better recognized and reward. Development strategies and programmes, as well as incentive programmes and projects in the field of food and agriculture, need to be designed in a manner that fully integrates women at all levels of planning, implementation, monitoring evaluation in all stages of the development process of a project cycle, so as to facilitate and enhance this key role of women and to ensure that women receive proper benefits and remuneration commensurate with their important contribution in this field. Moreover, women should be fully integrated and involved in the technological research and energy aspects of food and agricultural development.

Paragraph 175

During the Decade, the significant contribution of women to agricultural development has been more widely recognized, particularly their contribution in working hours to agricultural,fishery and forestry production and conservation, and to various parts of the food system. There are indications, however, that poverty and landlessness among rural women will increase significantly by the year 2000. In order to stem this trend, Governments should implement, as a matter of priority, equitable and stable investment and growth policies for rural development to ensure that there is a reallocation of the country's resources which, in many cases, are largely derived from the rural areas but allocated to urban development.

Paragraph 176

Governments should establish multisectoral programmes to promote the productive capacity of rural poor women in food and animal production, create off-farm employment opportunities, reduce their work-load, *inter alia,* by supporting the establishment of adequate child-care facilities and that of their children, reverse their pauperization, improve their access to all sources of energy, and provide them with adequate water, health, education, effective extension services and transportation within their region. In this connection it should be noted that the World Conference on Agrarian Reform and Rural Development, held at Rome in 1979[12] recognized women's vital role in the socio-economic life in both agricultural and non-agricultural activities as a prerequisite for successful rural development policies, planning and programmes, and proposed specific measures for improving their condition, which are still valid. The Programme of Action for the Second Half of the United Nations Decade for Women also included specific measures to improve the situation of women in food and agriculture, which remain a valid guide for action.

Paragraph 177

The General Assembly, in resolution 39/165 on the critical situation of food production and agriculture in Africa, confirmed the growing concern of the international community at the dramatic deterioration in African food and agricultural production and the resulting alarming increase in the number of people, especially women and children, exposed to hunger,malnutrition and even starvation. Concrete measures and adequate resources for the benefit of African women should be a priority. The international community, particularly donor countries, should be urged to assist African women by continuing and, where possible, by increasing financial assistance to enhance the role of women as food producers, with an emphasis on providing training in food technologies, thereby alleviating the problems of the continent resulting from extended drought and a severe shortage of food. Donor countries should also contribute to the special funds that have been launched by various organizations —for example, the United Nations Development Fund for Women. Emergency assistance should be increased and accelerated to alleviate the suffering of starving and dying women and children under famine conditions in Africa. Furthermore, given the critical food situation in Africa, aggravated *inter alia* by demographic pressures, the international community is urged to give priority to and provide support for the efforts of the African countries to overcome this serious situation. These efforts include the Lagos Plan of Action and the Nairobi Programme of Action, as well as the consultation by African Governments on the role of women in food production and food security.

Paragraph 178

Governments should give priority to supporting effective participation by women in food production and in food security programmes and should develop specific plans of action for this purpose. This would ensure that resources are directed towards women's programmes, that women are integrated in all mainstream rural development projects and that projects are located within technical ministries as well as ministries of social affairs. Governments should promote integrated solutions, such as national food policies, which are diversified according to specific natural regions for the improvement of self-reliance in food production, instead of resorting to palliatives or fragmented remedies.

Paragraph 179

Mechanisms should also include monitoring and evaluation and, where necessary, should modify the allocation of resources between women and men in mixed projects, should restructure rural development schemes to respond to women's needs, should assess women's projects in terms of technical and economic viability, as well as on social grounds, and should develop gender -specific statistics and information that reflect accurately women's contribution to food staples. Women's participation in programmes and projects to promote food security should be enhanced by providing them with opportunities to hold official positions, to receive training in leadership, administration and financial management and to organize on a co-operative basis. Research and experimentation should be conducted on food production and storage techniques to improve traditional knowledge and introduce modern technology.

Paragraph 180

Animal husbandry, fishery and forestry programmes should given greater attention to the effective participation of women as contributors and beneficiaries. Similarly, all other off-farm rural production programmes, as well as rural settlement, health, educational and social service programmes, should secure the participation of women as planners, contributors and beneficiaries

Paragraph 181

Also important are the dissemination of information to rural women through national information campaigns, using all available media and established women's groups the exposure of local populations to innovation and creativity through open-air films, talks, visits to areas where needs are similar, and demonstrations of scientific and technological innovations, the participation of women farmer in research and information campaigns; and the involvement of women in technical co-operation among developing countries and the exchange of information.

Paragraph 182

Rural women's access to land, capital, technology, know-how and other productive resources should be secured. Women should be given full and effective rights to land ownership, registration of land titles and allocation of tenancies on irrigation or settlement schemes and should also benefit from land reform. Women's customary land and inheritance rights under conditions of land shortage, land improvement of shifts into cash-cropping should be protected. Implementation of inheritance laws should be modified so that women can inherit a fair share of livestock, agricultural machinery and other property. Women's access to investment finance to increase their productivity and income should be supported by removing legal and institutional restrictions and by promoting women's savings groups and co-operatives and intermediary institutions, as well as training in and assistance with financial management, savings and investment and reallocation of land resources, with priority placed on production, especially of staple foods.

Paragraph 183

Women should be integrated into modern technology programmes that introduce new crops and improved varieties, rotation of crops, mixed farming, mixed and intercropping systems, low-cost soil fertility techniques, soil and water conservation methods and other modern improvements. In this connection, women's involvement in the construction, management and maintenance of irrigation schemes should be promoted.

Paragraph 184

Appropriate food-processing technologies can free women from time-and energy-consuming tasks and thus effect improvements in their health. Appropriate technologies can also increase the productivity and income of women, either directly or by freeing them to engage in other activities. Such technologies should be designed and introduced, however, in a manner that ensures women's access to the new technology and to its benefits and does not displace women from means of livelihood when alternative opportunities are not available. Appropriate labour-saving technologies should utilize local human and material resources and inexpensive sources of energy. The design, testing and dissemination of the technology should be appropriate also to the women who will be the users. Non-governmental organizations can play a valuable role in this process. Appropriate and affordable food-processing technologies should be made widely available to rural women, along with appropriate and affordable storage, marketing and transportation facilities to reduce post-harvest and income losses. Information on improved method which have been ecologically confirmed of reducing post-harvest food loss and of preserving and conserving food products should be widely disseminated.

Paragraph 185

Financial, technical, advisory and institutional support should be provided to women's organizations and groups to enhance the self-reliance of rural women. Women's co-operatives should be promoted to operate on a larger scale by improving farm input provisions, primary processing and the wholesale marketing of women's production. Comprehensive support should be given to women's organizations to facilitate the acquisition of farm inputs and information and to facilitate the marketing of produce.

Paragraph 186

Governments should set targets for increased extension contracts with rural women, reorient the training of male extension workers and train adequate numbers of female extension workers. Women should be given access to training programmes at different levels that develop various types of skills to widen the range of methods and technologies used for agricultural production.

Paragraph 187

Governments should involve women in the mobilization and distribution of food aid in countries affected by the drought, as well as in the fight against desertification, through large-scale afforestation campaigns (planting of woodlots,collective farms and seedlings).

Paragraph 188

Governments should pay greater attention to the preservation and the maintenance free from pollution of any kind of sources of water supply for irrigation and domestic consumption, applying special remedial measures to relieve the burden placed on women by the task of fetching water. To this end, they should construct wells, bore-holes, dams and locally made water-catchment devices sufficient for all irrigation and domestic needs, including those of livestock. Women should be included by Governments and agencies in all policy planning, implementation and administration of water supply projects and trained to take responsibility for the management of hydraulic infrastructures and equipment and for its maintenance.

Industry

Paragraph 189

The problems related to the industrial development of the developing countries reflect the dependent nature of their economies and the need to promote transformation industries based on domestic agricultural production as a fundamental issue of development. Women are an important part of the agricultural work-force, therefore, there should be special interest in the promotion of the technical training of women in this particular field. In this respect, Governments should take into account the following recommendations:

(a) There should be a link between agriculture and industry;
(b) Steps should be taken to eliminate the particular obstacles to industrialization and to the participation of women in industry, such as energy, the limited markets of some developing countries, the rural exodus, poor infrastructure, a lack of technical know-how, the dependence of the inductries of some countries and a lack of financial resources;
(c) Steps should also be taken to promote women's equitable and increased participation in industry by enabling them to have equal access to and to participate in adult education and in-service programmes that teach not only literacy but also saleable income-generating skills, and by encouraging women to participate in collective organizations, including trade unions,
(d) Industrial co-operation among developing countries should be promoted by creating subregional industries.
(e) International organizations and developed countries should assist developing countries in their industrialization effort and the integration of women in that process.

Paragraph 190

Governments should ensure that, at all levels of the planning process, women participate both directly in decision-making and indirectly through effective consultation with the potential beneficiaries of programmes and projects. Too this end, resources should be allocated to prepare women, through training, vocational guidance and career counselling and through increased incentives and other support measures, for increased participation in policy-making and decision-making roles and to intergrate them by means of special measures at all levels.

Paragraph 191

Women should be viewed as users and agents of change in science and technology, and their technological and managerial skills should be enhanced in order to increase national self-reliance in industrial production and to promote innovations in productive design, product adaptation and production techniques. At the same time, industrial technologies should be applied appropriately to the needs and situations of women so as to free from time and energy-consuming tasks.

Paragraph 192

The introduction of advanced technologies in industry in particular, must allow women to enter into sectors from which they have been so far excluded.

Paragraph 193

Governments should direct their efforts to expanding women's employment opportunities in the modern, traditional and self-employed sectors of both the rural and urban economy and to avoiding the exploitation of female labour. Efforts to improve the absolute and relative levels of women's earnings and working conditions should be directed simultaneously to all three sectors.

Paragraph 194

In accordance with accepted international labour standards, particularly, though not exclusively, in the field of female employment, appropriate legislation should be adopted and fully implemented at the national level. Specific consideration should be given to the removal of discriminatory practices concerning employment conditions, health and safety, and to guaranteeing provisions for pregnant women and maternity benefits and child care. Social security benefits, including unemployment benefits, should be guaranteed to women on an equal footing with men. Recruitment of female workers in existing or new capital-intensive, high-productivity sectors should be encouraged.

Paragraph 195

Governments should recognize the importance of improving the conditions and structure of the informal sector for national industrial development and the role of women within it. Traditional craft and cottage industries, as well as the small industrial efforts of women, should be supported with credits, training facilities, marketing opportunities and technological guidance. To this end, producers' co-operatives should be supported and women should be encouraged to establish, manage and own small enterprises.

Paragraph 196

Governments should design and promote as well as encourage the design and promotion of programmes and should allocate resources to prepare women to take up traditional and non-traditional industrial activities in organized and small enterprises, as well as in the informal sector, through innovative approaches to training, and should prep are and disseminate training materials and provide training to the trainers. They should support self-employment initiatives and offer guidance and career counselling.

Trade and Commercial Services

Paragraph 197

Governments should recognize the potential impact of short-term economic adjustment policies on women in the areas of trade and commerce. Government policies should promote the full participation and integration of women in these areas. Alternative sources of finance and new markets should be sought to maintain and increase women's participation in these activities. Not only should appropriate measures be taken to ensure that legal and administrative impediments that prevent women from enjoying effective and equal access to finance and credit are removed but in addition positive measures such as loan guarantees, technical advice and marketing development services should be introduced.

Paragraph 198

Governments should also recognize the positive contribution of women traders to local and national economies and should adopt policies to assist and organize these women. The infrastructure and management of markets, transportation and social services should be improved to increase the efficiency, security and income of women traders and to reduce their work-load and the hazards to their health, as well as to avoid wastage of marketable produce. Training opportunities in book-keeping, finance, packaging, standardization and processing technology should be provided to women traders. Such training should also aim at opening up employment opportunities to these women in other marketing and credit institutions. Governments should design innovative mechanisms to provide women traders with access to credit and to encourage the establishment and reinforcement of women's trade associations.

Paragraph 199

Efforts should be made to encourage enterprises to train women in economic sectors that traditionally have been closed to them, to promote diversification women's employment and to eliminate gender bias from labour markets.

Science and Technology

Paragraph 200

The full and effective participation of women in the decision-making and implementation process related to science and technology, including planning and setting priorities for research and development, and the choice, acquisition, adaptation, innovation and application of science and technology for development should be enhanced. Governments should reassess their technological capabilities and monitor current processes of change so as to anticipate and ameliorate any adverse impact on women, particularly adverse effects upon the quality of job.

Paragraph 201

The involvement of women in all of the peaceful uses of outer space should be enhanced, and effective measures should be undertaken to integrate women into all levels of decision-making and the implementation of such activities. In all countries special efforts should be made by Governments and non-governmental organizations to provide women and women's organization with information on the peaceful uses of outer space. Special incentives should be provided to enable women to obtain advanced education and training in areas related to outer space in order to expand their participation in the application of outer space technology for peaceful uses, especially in the high-priority development areas of water, health, energy, food production and nutrition. To achieve these goals, increased opportunities and encouragement should be given to women to study science, mathematics and engineering at the university level and to girls to study mathematics and science at the pre-university level.

Paragraph 202

Women with appropriate skills should be employed at managerial and professional levels and not restricted to service-level jobs. Special measures should be taken to improve working conditions for women in the science and technology fields, to eliminate discriminatory classification of jobs and to protect the right of women to promotion. Efforts should be made to ensure that women obtain their fair share of jobs at all levels in new technology industries.

Paragraph 203

Major efforts should be undertaken and effective incentives created to increase the access of women to both scientific and technological education and training. To achieve these goals, efforts should be made by Governments and women themselves to enhance, where necessary, the change of attitudes towards women's performance in scientific fields.

Paragraph 204

The potential and actual impact of science and technology on the developments that affect women's integration into the various sectors of the economy, as well as on their health, income and status, should be assessed. Relevant findings should be integrated in policy formulation to ensure that women benefit fully from available technologies and that any adverse effects are minimized.

Paragraph 205

Efforts in the design and delivery of appropriate technology to women should be intensified, and attention should be given to the achievement of the best possible standard in such technologies. In particular, the implication of advances in medical technology for women should be carefully examined.

Communications

Paragraph 206

In view of the critical role of this sector in elimination stereotyped images of women and providing women with easier access to information, the participation of women at all levels of communications policy and decision-making and in programme design, implementation and monitoring should be given high priority. The media's portrayal of stereotyped images of women and also that of the advertising industry can have a profoundly adverse effect on attitudes towards and among women. Women should be made an integral part of the decision-making concerning the choice an development of alternative forms of communication and should have an equal saying the determination of the content of all public information efforts. The cultural media, involving ritual, drama, dialogue, oral literature and music, should be promoted and women should have equal access to financial support. In the field of communication, there is ample scope for international co-operation regarding information related to the sharing of experience by women an to projecting activities concerning the role of women in development and peace in order to enhance the awareness of both accomplishments and the tasks that remain to be fulfilled.

Paragraph 207

The enrolment of women in publicly operated mass communication networks and in education and training should be increased. The employment of women within the sector should be promoted and directed towards professional, advisory and decision-making positions.

Paragraph 208

Organizations aimed at promoting the role of women in development as contributors and beneficiaries should be assisted in their efforts to establish effective communications and information networks.

Housing, Settlement, Community Development and Transport

Paragraph 209

Governments should integrate women in the formulation of policies, programmes and projects for the provision of basic shelter and infrastructure. To this end, enrolment of women in architectural, engineering and related fields should be encouraged, and qualified women graduates in these fields should be assigned to professional and policy-making and decision-making positions. The shelter and infrastructural needs of women should be assessed and specifically incorporated in housing, community development, and slum and squatter projects.

Paragraph 210

Women and women's groups should be participants in and equal beneficiaries of housing and infrastructure construction projects. They should be consulted in the choice of design and technology of construction and should be involved in the management and maintenance of the facilities. To this end, women should be provided with construction, maintenance and management skills and should be participants in related training and educational programmes. Special attention must be given to the provision of adequate water to all communities, in consultation with women.

Paragraph 211

Housing credit schemes should be reviewed and women's direct access to housing construction and improvement credits secured. In this connection, programmes aimed at increasing the possibilities of sources on income for women should be promoted and existing legislation or administrative practices endangering women's ownership and tenancy rights should be revoked.

Paragraph 212

Government efforts for the International Year of shelter for the Homeless[13] should incorporate assessments of the shelter needs of women and encourage the design and implementation of innovative projects that will increase women's access to services and finance. In these efforts special attention should be paid to women who are the sole supporters of their families. Low-cost housing and facilities should be designed for such women.

Paragraph 213

All measures to increase the efficiency of land, water and air transportation should be formulated with due regard to women as producers and consumers. All national and local decisions concerning transportation policies, including subsidies, pricing, choice of technology for construction and maintenance, and means of transport, should consider women's needs and should be based on consideration of the possible impact on the employment, income and health of women.

Paragraph 214

Women's roles as operators and owners of means of transport should be promoted through greater access to credit for women and other appropriate means and equal consideration with regard to the allocation of contracts. This is particularly important for women's groups and collectives, especially in rural areas, that are usually well organized but are cut off from serviceable means of transport and communication.

Paragraph 215

Rural transportation planning in developing countries should aim at reducing the heavy burden on women who carry agricultural produce, water and fuelwood as head-loads. In exploring modes of transportation, efforts should be made to avoid loss of income and employment for women by introducing costs that may be too high for them.

Paragraph 216

In the choice of modes of transportation and the design of transport routes, the increasing ratio of women whose income is essential for family survival should be taken into account.

Paragraph 217

In the design and choice of both commercial and appropriate vehicular technology, the needs of women, especially those with young children, should be taken into consideration. Institutional support to give women access to appropriate vehicles should be provided.

Energy

Paragraph 218

Measures developed to rationalize energy consumption and to improve energy systems, especially of hydrocarbons, and to increase technical training should be formulated with a view to women as producers, users and managers of energy sources.

Paragraph 219

In conventional and non-conventional national energy programmes, women should be integrated as contributors and beneficiaries with a view to their needs, as determined by specific socio-cultural factors at local and national levels and in both rural and urban contexts. Assessment of new energy sources, energy technologies and energy-delivery systems should specifically consider the reduction of the drudgery that constitutes a large part of the work of poor urban and rural women.

Paragraph 220

The grass-roots participation of women in energy-needs assessment, technology and energy conservation, management and maintenance efforts should be supported.

Paragraph 221

Priority should be given to substituting energy for muscle in the performance of the industrial and domestic work of women without loss of their jobs and tasks to men. In view of the high percentage of domestic use in total energy consumption in low-income countries, the implications of increasing energy costs, and the current threats posed by inflation, immediate attention should be directed towards, action concerning adapted technologies, fuel conservation and improved or new sources of energy, such as biomass, solar and wind energy, geothermal and nuclear energy, as well as mini-hydroelectric power plants. Improved stoves should be designed and disseminated to reduce the drudgery involved in the collection of fuel by women.

Paragraph 222

In order to prevent depletion of the forest areas on which most rural women rely for much of their energy needs and income, innovative programmes, such as farm woodlot development, should be initiated with the involvement of both women and men. In the commercialization of fuelwood energy, measures should be taken to avoid the loss of women's income to middlemen and urban industries. Development of fuelwood plantations, diffusion of fast-growing varieties of trees and technologies for more efficient production of charcoal should be accelerated with a view to poor rural and urban women being the major beneficiaries. The use of solar energy and biogas should be promoted with due regard to affordability, as well as to use and management by women who are the principal consumers.

Paragraph 223

The involvement of women at all levels of decision-making and implementation of energy-related decisions including peaceful use of nuclear energy should be enhanced. Special efforts should be made by Governments and non-governmental organizations to provide women and women's organizations with information on all sources and uses of energy, including nuclear energy. Special incentives should be provided to enable women to obtain advanced levels of education and training in all energy-related areas in order to expand their participation in decision-making relating to the application of nuclear technology for peaceful uses especially in high priority development areas of water, health, energy, food production and nutrition. To achieve these goals, increased opportunities and encouragement should be given to women to study scoemce, mathematics and engineering at the university level and for girls to study mathematics and science at the pre-university level.

Environment

Paragraph 224

Deprivation of traditional means of livelihood is most often a result of environmental degradation resulting from such natural and man-made disasters as droughts, floods, hurricanes, erosion, desertification, deforestation and inappropriate land use. Such conditions have already pushed great numbers of poor women into marginal environments where critically low levels of water supplies, shortages of fuel, over-utilization of grazing and arable lands and population density have deprived them of their livelihood. Most seriously affected are women in drought-afflicted arid and semi-arid areas and in urban slums and squatter settlements. These women need options for alternative means of livelihood. Women must have the same opportunity as men to participate in the wage-earning labour force in such programmes as irrigation and tree planting and in other programmes needed to upgrade urban and rural environments. Urgent steps need to be taken to strengthen the machinery for international economic co-operation in the exploration of water resources and the control of desertification and other environmental disasters.

Paragraph 225

Efforts to improve sanitary conditions, including drinking water supplies, in all communities should be strengthened, especially in urban slums and squatter settlements and in rural areas, with due regard to relevant environmental factors. These efforts should be extended to include improvements of the home and the work environment and should be effected with the participation of women at all levels in the planning and implementation process.

Paragraph 226

Awareness by individual women and all types of women's organizations of environmental issues and the capacity of women and men to manage their environment and sustain productive resources should be enhanced. All sources of information dissemination should be mobilized to increase the self-help potential of women in conserving and improving their environment. National and international emphasis on ecosystem management and the control of environmental degradation should be strengthened and women should be recognized as active and equal participants in this process.

Paragraph 227

The environmental impact of policies, programmes and projects on women's health and activities, including their sources of employment and income, should be assessed and the negative effects eliminated.

Social Services

Paragraph 228

Governments are urged to give priority to the development of social infrastructure, such as adequate care and education for the children of working parents, whether such work is carried out at home,in the fields or in factories, to reduce the "double burden" of working women in both urban and rural areas. Likewise they are urged to offer incentives to employers to provide adequate child-care services which meet the requirements of parents regarding opening hours. Employers should allow either parent to work flexible hours in order to share the responsibilities of child care. Simultaneously, Governments and non-governmental organizations should mobilize the mass media and other means of communication to ensure public consensus on the need for men and society as a whole to share with women the responsibilities of producing and rearing children, who represent the human resource capabilities of the future.

Paragraph 229

Governments should further establish ways and means of assisting women consumers through the provision of information and the creation of legislation that will increase consumer consciousness and protect consumers from unsafe goods, dangerous drugs, unhealthy foods and unethical and exploitative marketing practices.* Non-governmental organizations should work towards establishing strong and active organizations for consumer protection.

Paragraph 230

Public expenditure directed towards health, education and training and towards providing health-care and child-care services for women should be increased.

Paragraph 231

Governments should undertake effective measures, including mobilizing community resources, to identify, prevent and eliminate all violence, including family violence, against women and children and to provide shelter, support and reorientation services for abused women and children. These measures should notably be aimed at making women conscious that maltreatment is not an incurable phenomenon, but a blow to their physical and moral integrity, against which they have the right (and the duty) to fight, whether they are themselves the victims or the witnesses. Beyond these urgent protective measures for maltreated women and children, as well as repressive measures for the authors of this maltreatment, it would be proper to set in motion long-term supportive machineries of aid and guidance for maltreated women and children, as well as the people, often men, who maltreat them.

III. PEACE

A. Obstacles

Paragraph 232

The threat to peace resulting from continuing international tension

---

* The General Assembly adopted guidelines for consumer protection in resolution 39/248 of 9 April 1985.

and violations of the United Nations Charter, resulting in he unabated arms race, in particular in the nuclear field, as well as wars, armed conflicts, external domination, foreign occupation, acquisition of land by force, aggression, imperialism, colonialism, neo-colonialism, racism, *apartheid,* gross violation of human rights, terrorism repression, the disappearance of persons and discrimination on the basis of sex are major obstacles to human progress, specifically to the advancement of women.

Paragraph 233

Such obstacles, some of which occur with increasing frequency, continually reinforce and are reinforced by historically established hostile attitudes, ignorance and bigotry between countries, ethnic groups, races, sexes, socio-economic groups and by lack of tolerance and respect for different cultures and traditions. Their negative effects are increased by poverty, tensions in international economic and political relations which are often aggravated, as well as by the arms race, both nuclear and conventional. The arms race in particular diverts resources which could be used for developmental and humanitarian purposes, hinders national and international development efforts and further handicaps the well-being of the poorest nations and the most disadvantaged segments of the population.

Paragraph 234

Despite the achievements of the Decade, women's involvement in governmental and non-governmental activities, decision-making processes related to peace, mobilization efforts for peace, education for peace and peace research remains limited. Their participation in the struggle to eradicate colonialism, neo-colonialism, imperialism, totalitarianism including fascism and similar ideologies, alien occupation, foreign domination, aggression, racism, racial discrimination, *apartheid* and other violations of human rights has often gone unnoticed.

Paragraph 235

Universal and durable peace cannot be attained without the full and equal participation of women in international relations, particularly in decision-making concerning peace, including the processes envisaged for the peaceful settlement of disputed under the Charter of the United Nations nor without overcoming the obstacles mentioned in paragraph 232.

Paragraph 236

Full equality between women and men is severely hampered by the threats to international peace and security, lack of satisfying progress in the field of disarmament, including the spread of the arms race to outer space, violation of the principle of the right of peoples under alien and colonial domination and foreign occupation to self-determination and independence and respect for the national sovereignty and territorial integrity of States as well as justice, equality and mutual benefit in international relations.

Paragraph 237

It is evident that women all over the world have manifested their love for peace and their wish to play a greater role in international co-operation, amity and peace among different nations. All obstacles at national and international levels in the way of women's participation in promoting international peace and co-operation should be removed as soon as possible.

Paragraph 238

It is equally important to increase women's understanding and awareness of constructive negotiations aimed at reaching positive results for international peace and security. Governments should take measures to encourage the full and effective participation of women in negotiations on international peace and security. The rejection of the use of force or of the threat of the use of force and foreign interference and intervention should become widespread.

B. Basic Strategies

Paragraph 239

The main principles and directions for women's activities aimed at strengthening peace and formulated in the Declaration in the participation of Women in Promoting International Peace and Co-operation[7] should be put into practice. The Declaration calls for Governments, the United Nations system, non-governmental organizations, relevant institutions and individuals to strengthen women's participation in this sphere and it provides the overall framework for such activities.

Paragraph 240

Women and men have an equal right and the same vital interest in contributing to international peace and co-operation. Women should participate fully in all efforts to strengthen and maintain international peace and security and to promoted international co-operation, diplomacy, the process of detente, disarmament in the nuclear field in particular and respect the for the principle of the Character of he the United Nations, including respect for the sovereign rights of States, quarantees of fundamental freedoms and human rights, such as recognition of the dignity of the individual and self-determination, and freedom of thought, conscience,expression, association,assembly, communication and movement without distinction as to race, sex, political and religious beliefs, language or ethnic origin. The commitment to remove the obstacles to women's participation in the promotion of peace should be strengthened.

Paragraph 241

In view of the fact that women are still very inadequately represented in national and international political processes dealing with peace and conflict settlement, it is essential that women support and encourage each other in their initiatives and action relating either to universal issues, such as disarmament and the development of confidence-building measures between nations and people, or to specific conflict situations between or within States.

Paragraph 242

There exist situations in several regions of the world where the violation of principles of non-use of force, non-intervention, non-interference, non-aggression and the right to self-determination endangers international peace and security and creates massive humanitarian problems which constitute an impediment to the advancement of women and hence to the full implementation of the Forward-looking Strategies. In regard to these situations strict adherence to and respect for the cardinal principles enshrined in the Charter of the United nations and implementation of relevant resolutions consistent with the principles of the Charter are an imperative requirement with a view to seeking solutions to such problems, thereby ensuring a secure and better future for the people affected, most of whom are invariably women and children.

Paragraph 243

Since women are one of the most vulnerable groups in the regions affected by armed conflicts, special attention has to be drawn to the need to eliminate obstacles to the fulfilment of the objectives of equality, development and peace and the principles of the Charter of the United Nations.

Paragraph 244

One of the important obstacles to achieving international peace is the persistent violation of the principles and objectives of the Charter of the United Nations and the lack of political will of Governments of some countries to promote constructive negotiations aimed at decreasing international tension on the issues that seriously threaten the maintenance of international peace and security. For this reason, the strategies in this field should include the mobilization of women in favour of all acts and actions that tend to promote peace, in particular, the elimination of wars and danger of nuclear war.

Paragraph 245

Immediate and special priority should be given to the promotion and the effective enjoyment of human rights and fundamental freedoms for all without distinction as to sex, the full application of the rights of peoples to self-determination and the elimination of colonialism, neo-colonialism, *apartheid*, of all forms of racism and racial discrimination, oppression and aggression, foreign occupation, as well as domestic violence and violence against women.

Paragraph 246

In South-West Asia women and children have endured serious suffering owing to the violation of the Charter of the United Nations, leading, among other things, to the vast problem of refugees in neighbouring countries.

Paragraph 247

The situation of violence and destabilization that exists in Central America constitutes the most serious obstacle to the achievement of peace in the region and thus hinders the fulfilment of the Forward-looking Strategies vital to the advancement of women. In this regard and to promote conditions favourable to the objectives of the Strategies, it is important to reiterate the principles of non-intervention and self-determination, as well as the non-use of force or rejection of the threat of use of force in the solution of conflicts in the region. Therefore, the validity of the United Nations resolutions that establish the right of all sovereign States in he area to live in peace, free from all interference in their internal affairs, should be reaffirmed. It is necessary to support the negotiated political solutions and the peace proposals that the central American States adopt under the auspices of the Contadora Group, as the most viable alternative for the solution of the crisis in Central America for the benefit of their people. In this sense it is important that the five Central American Governments speed up their consultations with the Contadora Group with the aim of bringing to a conclusion the negotiation process with the early signing of the Contadora Act on peace and Co-operation in Central America (see A/39/562-S/16775, annex).

Paragraph 248

Women have played and continue to play an important role in the self-determination of peoples, including through national liberation, in accordance with the United Nations Charter. Their efforts should be recognized and commended and used as one basis for their full participation in the construction of their countries, and in the creation of humane and just social and political systems. Women's contribution in this area should be ensured by their equal access to political power and their full participation in the decision-making process.

Paragraph 249

Strategies at the national, regional and the global levels should be based on a clear recognition that peace and security, self-determination and national independence are fundamental for the attainment of the three objectives of the Decade: equality, development and peace.

Paragraph 250

Safeguarding world peace and averting a nuclear catastrophe is one of the most important tasks today in which women have an essential role to play, especially by supporting actively the halting of the arms race followed by arms reduction and the attainment of a general and completed disarmament under effective international control, and thus contributing to the improvement of their economic position. Irrespective of their socio-economic system, the States should strive to avoid confrontation and to build friendly relations instead, which should be also supported by women.

Paragraph 251

Peace requires the participation of all members of society, women and men alike, in rejecting any type of intervention in the domestic affairs of States, whether it is openly or covertly carried out by other States or by transnational corporations. Peace also requires that women and men alike should promote respect for the sovereign right of a State to establish its own economic, social and political system without undergoing political and economic pressures or coercion of any type.

Paragraph 252

There exists a relationship between the world economic situation, development and the stengthening of international peace and security, disarmament and the relaxation of international tension. All efforts should be made to reduce global expenditures on armaments and to reach an agreement on the internationally agreed disarmament goals in order to prevent the waste of immense material and human resources, some part of which might otherwise be used for development, especially of the developing countries, as well as for the improvement of standards of living and well-being of people in each country. In this context, particular attention should be given to the advancement of women, including to the participation of women in the promotion of international peace and co-operation and the protection of mothers and children who represent a disproportionate share of the most vulnerable group, the poorest of the poor.

Paragraph 253

Women's equal role in decision-making with respect to peace and related issues should be seen as one of their basic human rights and as such should be enhanced and encouraged at the national, regional and international levels. In accordance with the Convention on the Elimination of All Forms of Discrimination against Women, all existing impediments to the achievement by women of equality with men should be removed. To this end, efforts should be intensified at all levels to overcome prejudices, stereotyped thinking, denial to women of career prospects and appropriate educational possibilities, and resistance by decision-makers to the changes that are necessary to enable equal participation of women with men in the international and diplomatic service.

Paragraph 254

Mankind is confronted with a choice: to halt the arms race and proceed to disarmament or face annihilation. The growing opposition of women to the danger of war, especially a nuclear war, which will lead to a nuclear holocaust, and their support for disarmament must be respected. States should be encouraged to ensure unhindered flow and access to information, including to women, with regard to various aspects of disarmament to avoid dissemination of false and tendentious information concerning armaments and to concentrate on the danger of the escalation of the arms race and on the need for general and complete disarmament under effective international control. The resources released as a result of disarmament measures should be used to help promote the well-being of all peoples and improve the economic and social conditions of the developing countries. Under such the conditions, States should pay increased attention to the urgent need to improve the situation of women.

Paragraph 255

Peace education should be established for all members of society, particularly children and young people. Values, such as tolerance, racial and sexual equality, respect for and understanding of others, and good-neighbourliness should be developed, promoted and strengthened.

Paragraph 256

Women of the world, together with men, should, as informal educators and socialization agents, play a special role in the process of bringing up younger generations in an atmosphere of compassion, tolerance, mutual concern and trust, with an awareness that all people belong to the same world community. Such education should be part of all formal and informal educational processes as well as of communications, information and mass-media systems.

Paragraph 257

Further action should be taken at family and neighbourhood levels, as well as at national and international levels, to achieve a peaceful social environment compatible with human dignity. The questions of women and peace and the meaning of peace for women cannot be separated from the broader question of relationships between women and men in all spheres of life and in the family. Discriminatory practices and negative attitudes towards women should be eliminated and traditional gender norms changed to enhance women's participation in peace.

Paragraph 258

Violence against women exists in various forms in everyday life in all societies. Women are beaten, mutilated, burned, sexually abused and raped. Such violence is a major obstacle to the achievement of peace and the other objectives of the Decade and should be given special attention. Women victims of violence should be given particular attention and comprehensive assistance. To this end, legal measures should be formulated to prevent violence and to assist women victims. National machinery should be established in order to deal with the question of violence against women within the family and society. Preventive policies should be elaborated, and institutionalized forms of assistance to women victims provided.

C. Women and Children Under Apartheid

*Paragraph 259**

Women and children under *apartheid* and other racist minority regimes suffer from direct inhumane practices such as massacres and detention, mass population removal, separation from families and immobilization in relegation. They are subjected to the detrimental implications of the labour migrant system pass laws and of relation to the homelands where they suffer disproportionately from poverty, poor health and illiteracy. The programme of Action of the World conference to Combat Racism and Racial Discrimination (1978)[14] provides an overall framework for action. Its objective is to eradicate *apartheid* and to enable black African people in South Africa to enjoy their full sovereign rights in their country. Governments that have not already done so are urged to sign and ratify the International Convention on the suppression and Punishment of the Crime of *Apartheid* of 30 November 1973.[15]

Full international assistance should be given to the most oppressed group under *apartheid* - women and children. The United Nations system, Governments and non-governmental organization should identify the basic needs of women and children under *apartheid* and other racist minority regimes, including women in refugee camps in southern Africa, and provide them with adequate legal, humanitarian, medical and material assistance as well as education, training and employment.

Assistance should be given to women's sections in national liberation movements in order to strengthen their work for women's equal opportunities, education and training so as to prepare them to play an important political role in the present struggle and in nation-building after liberation.

The Forward-looking Strategies should take into account the destabilizing effects of *apartheid* on the economic infrastructure of neighbouring independent African States, which impede the development of the subregion.

Institutionalized *apartheid* in South Africa and Namibia as realized in the day-to-day political, legal, social and cultural life remains an enormous obstacle and hindrance to advancement, equality and peace in the African region.

The Forward-looking Strategies should aim at the speedy and effective implementation of Security Council resolution 435 (1978) concerning the independence of Namibia. The total and unconditional libera-

* The United States voted against paragraph 259 becauase of its opposition to the references in the eight and ninth subparagraphs to the imposition of sanctions and aid to liberation movements.

tion of Namibia should be a major objective of the Forward-looking Strategies, which should also aim at the improvement of the condition of women and children.

The United Nations and the international community must strengthen their resolve to see the abhorrent *apartheid* system eradicated and Namibia freed from the forces of occupation. Owing to South Africa's position in the international political and economic structure, the international community has the greatest responsibility to ensure that peace and human dignity are restored to southern Africa.

In addition to measures already taken, further effective measures, including sanctions, should be taken to terminate all collaboration with the racist regime of South Africa in the political, military, diplomatic and economic fields with a view to eliminating untold misery and loss of life of the oppressed people, the majority of whom are black women and children.

The international community must insist upon the effective implementation of Security Council resolution 435 (1978) concerning the independence of Namibia and all the United Nations resolutions calling for sanctions against South Africa, its isolation and abandonment of its racist policies. All efforts should be made for the immediate and unconditional withdrawal of South African forces from Angola.

The international community must condemn the direct aggression committed by the armed forces of the racist regime of South Africa against the front —line countries as well as the recruitment, training and financing of mercenaries and of armed bandits who massacre women and children and who are used to overthrow the legitimate Governments of these countries by reason of their support for the people of South Africa and Namibia.

The international community should provide greater moral and material assistance to all the bodies struggling to remove *apartheid*, especially the national liberation movements-the African National Congress of South Africa, the Pan Africanist Congress of Azania and the South West Africa People's organization the African front-line States, the Organization of African Unity, the movement of Non-Aligned Countries and non-governmental organizations.

Women, together with their Governments, should strengthen their commitment to the eradication of *apartheid* and support to their struggling sisters in all possible ways. To this end, women and women's organizations should keep themselves constantly informed about the situation of women and children under *apartheid,* disseminate information widely and build up awareness in their countries about the situation by organizing national solidarity and support committees where these do not yet exist as a means to educate the public about the evils of *apartheid* and its brutal oppression of women and children in South Africa and Namibia.

D. Palestinian Women and Children

*Paragraph 260**

For more than three decades, Palestinian women have faced difficult living conditions in camps and outside, struggling for the survival of their families and the survival of the Palestinian people who were deprived of their ancestral lands and denied the inalienable rights to return to their homes and their property, their right to self-determination, national independence and sovereignty (see A/CONF.116/6). Palestinian women are vulnerable to imprisonment, torture, reprisals and other oppressive practices by Israel in the occupied Arab territories. The confiscation of land and the creation of further settlements has affected the lives of Palestinian women and children. Such Israeli measures and practices are a violation of the Geneva Convention.[16] The Palestinian women as part of her nation suffers from discrimination in employment, health care and education.

The situation of violence and destabilization which exists in southern Lebanon and the Golan Heights put Arab women and children who are living under Israeli occupation in severe situations. Lebanese women are also suffering from discrimination and detention. Therefore, all relevant United Nations resolutions, in particular Security Council resolutions 497 (1981), 508 (1982) and 509 (1982), should be implemented.

The implementation of the Programme of Action for the Achievement of Palestinian Rights [17] should be kept under review and co-ordinated between the United Nations units and agencies concerned, with emphasis on the role of palestinian women in preserving their national identity, traditions and heritage and in the struggle for sovereignty. Palestinian people must recover their rights to self-determination and the right to establish an independent State in accordance with all relevant United Nations resolutions. The special and immediate needs of palestinian women and children should be identified and appropriate provision made. United Nations projects should be initiated to help palestinian women in the fields of health, education, and vocational training. Their living con-

---

The United States voted against this paragraph because of its strong objection to the introduction of tendentious and unnecessary elements into the Forward-looking Strategies document which have only a nominal connection with the unique concerns of women.

ditions inside and outside the occupied territories should be studied by the appropriate United Nations units and agencies assisted, as appropriate, by specialized research institutes from various regions. The results of these studies should be given broad publicity to promote actions at all levels. The international community should exert all efforts to stop the establishment of new Israeli settlements in the West Bank and the Gaza strip.Palestinian women should be allowed to enjoy security in a liberated homeland also in accordance with United Nations resolutions.

E. Women in Areas Affect by Armed Conflicts, Foreign Intervention and Threats to Peace

Paragraph 261

Armed conflicts and emergency situations impose a serious threat to the lives of women and children, causing constant fear, danger of displacement, destruction, devastation, physical abuse, social and family disruption, and abandonment. Sometimes these result in complete denial of access to adequate health and educational services, loss of job opportunities and overall worsening of material conditions.

Paragraph 262

International instruments, ongoing negotiations and international discussions aimed at the limitation of armed conflicts, such as the Fourth Geneva Convention of 1949, and the First Additional Protocol to the Geneva Conventions of 1949, adopted in 1977, provide a general framework for the protection of civilians in times of hostilities and the basis of provisions of humanitarian assistance and protection to women and children. Measures proposed in the 1974 Declaration on the Protection of Women and Children in Emergency and Armed Conflict (General Assembly resolution 3318 (XXIX) should be taken into account by governments.

F. Measures for the Implementation of the Basic Strategies at the National Level

1. Women's Participation in Efforts for Peace

Paragraph 263

Governments should follow the overall framework of action for disarmament as provided by the Final Document of the tenth special session of the General Assembly, which was devoted to disarmament (resolution S-10/2). Women's participation in the World Disarmament campaign and their contribution to education for disarmament should be supported.

Paragraph 264

Publicity should be given by Governments and non-governmental organizations to the main treaties concluded in the field of arms control and disarmament, and to other relevant documents. More should be done to mobilize women to overcome social apathy and helplessness in relation to disarmament and to generate wide support for the implementation of these agreements. Publicity should also be given to the declaration by the General Assembly of 1986 as the International Year of Peace[18], and the participation of women in the programme for the Year should be encouraged.

Paragraph 265

Non-governmental organizations should be encouraged to play an active role in promoting the restoration of peace in areas of conflict, in accordance with United Nations resolutions.

Paragraph 266

Women should be able to participate actively in the decision-making process related to the promotion of international peace and co-operation. Governments should take the necessary measures to facilitate this participation by institutional, educational and organizational means. Emphasis should be given to the grass-roots participation and co-operation of women's organizations with other non-governmental organizations in this process.

Paragraph 267

Governments which have not done so should undertake all appropriate measures to eliminate existing discriminatory practices towards women and to provide them with equal opportunities to join, at all levels, the civil service, to enter the diplomatic service and to represent their countries as members of delegations to national, regional and international meetings, including conferences on peace, conflict resolution, disarmament, and meetings of the Security Council and other United Nations bodies.

Paragraph 268

Women should be encouraged and given financial support to take university courses in government, international relations and diplomacy in order to obtain the necessary professional qualifications for careers in fields relating to peace and international security.

Paragraph 269

Governments should encourage women's participation in the promotion of peace at decision-making levels by providing information on opportunities for such participation in public service and by promoting equitable representation of women in governmental and non-governmental bodies and activities.

Paragraph 270

Non-governmental organizations should provide opportunities for women to learn how to develop self-reliance and leadership capabilities in order to promote peace, disarmament, human rights and international co-operation more effectively. They should emphasize the participation of women from trade unions and organizations in rural areas that have not as yet received sufficient attention and should make periodic assessments of strategies for women's participation in the promotion of peace at all levels, including the highest decision-making levels.

Paragraph 271

National machinery should be established to deal with the question of domestic violence. Preventive policies should be elaborated and institutionalized economic and other forms of assistance and protection for women and child victims should be provided. Legislative measures should be strengthened and legal aid provided.

2. Education for Peace

Paragraph 272

Governments, non-governmental organizations, women's groups and the mass media should encourage women to engage in efforts to promote education for peace in the family, neighbourhood and community. Special attention should be given to the contribution of women's grass-roots organizations. The multiple skills and talents of women artists, journalists, writers, educators and civic leaders can contribute to promoting ideas of peace if encouraged, facilitated and supported.

Paragraph 273

Special attention should be given to the education of children for life in peace within an atmosphere of understanding, dialogue and respect for others. In this respect, suitable concrete action should be taken to discourage the provision of children and young persons with games and publications and other media promoting the nation of favouring war, aggression, cruelty, excessive desire for power and other forms of violence, within the broad processes of the reparation of society for life in peace.

Paragraph 274

Governments, educational institutions, professional associations and non-governmental organizations should co-operate to develop a high-quality content for and to achieve widespread dissemination of books and programmes on education for peace. Women should take an active part in the preparation of those materials, which should include case studies of peaceful settlements of disputes, non-violent movements and passive resistance and the recognition of peace-seeking individuals.

Paragraph 275

Governments should create the conditions that would enable women to increase their knowledge of the main problems in contemporary international relations. Information should be widely and freely disseminated among women, thereby;y contributing to their full understanding of those problems. All existing obstacles and discriminatory practices regarding women's civil and political education should be removed. Opportunities should be provided for women to organize and choose studies, training programmes and seminars related to peace, disarmament, education for peace and the peaceful settlement of disputes.

Paragraph 276

The participation of women in peace research, including research on women and peace, should be encouraged. Existing barriers to women researchers should be removed and appropriate resources provided for peace researchers. Co-operation amongst peace researchers, government officials, non-governmental organizations and activists should be encouraged and fostered.

IV. AREAS OF SPECIAL CONCERN

Paragraph 277

There is an increasing number of categories of women who, because of their special characteristics, are experiencing not only the common problems indicated under the separate themes but also specific difficulties due to their socio-economic and health condition, age, minority status or a combination of these factors. Moreover, in many countries increasing demographic pressure, deteriorating rural conditions, curtailment of subsistence agriculture and difficult political conditions have been exacerbated by the current economic recession, leading to the dislocation of large sections of populations. In this process women experience particular difficulties and are often the more vulnerable because of their traditional lack of access to development opportunities.

Paragraph 278

The special groups of women identified below are extremely diverse, and their problems vary tremendously from one country to another. No single strategy or set of measures can apply adequately to all cases, and the present document is therefore limited to highlighting their special circumstances and the need for each country, as well as the international community, to give these issues the necessary attention. The basic strategy must remain one of fundamentally changing the economic conditions that produce such deprivation and of upgrading women's low status in society, which accounts for their extreme vulnerability to such conditions, especially to poverty. This is aggravated by the increase in drug-dependence, which adversely affects all sectors of society, including women. Building an organizational base for such change is a crucial strategy that can provide a rallying point for solidarity among women. Measures needed to provide immediate emergency assistance should be supplemented by longer-term efforts to enable women to break out of these situations. In many cases, permanent solutions to these issues can only be found through the broader efforts directed towards the reallocation of resources and decision-making power and towards the elimination of inequality and injustice.

Paragraph 279

There is a need to recognize the survival mechanisms already developed by these women as basic strategies in their own right and to build on them. A first priority would be to strengthen their organization capabilities by providing physical, financial and human resources, as well as education and training. Also of extreme importance is the need to revitalize these women's aspirations in order to eliminate the chronic despair that characterizes their daily lives.

Paragraph 280

The economic, social, cultural and political conditions of those groups of women should be improved basically by the implementation of the measures proposed for the attainment of equality, development and peace for women in general. Additional efforts should be directed towards ensuring the gainful and productive inclusion of these women in mainstream development and in political activities. Priority emphasis should be placed upon income-generating opportunities and for the independent and sustained improvement of their condition and by the full integration and active participation of women as agents and beneficiaries of development.

Paragraph 281

Policies, programmes and projects aimed at or incorporating especially vulnerable and underprivileged groups of women should recognize the particular difficulties of removing the multiple obstacles facing such groups and should place equal emphasis on addressing the social, economic and human dimensions of their vulnerability and their under privileged positions. Measures needed to provide them with immediate assistance should be supplemented by comprehensive long-term plans to achieve lasting solutions to their problems. These will usually necessitate global efforts in resolving the special problems of vulnerable groups, of which women are a significant part.

Paragraph 282

Basic to all efforts to improve the condition of these women should be the identification of their needs and hence the gathering of gender-specific data and economic indicators sensitive to conditions of extreme poverty and oppression. Such data should contain spatial, socio-economic and longitudinal characteristics and should be designed specifically for use in policy, programme and project formulation and implementation. Monitoring efforts at national, subregional, regional and international levels should be intensified.

A. Women in Areas Affected by Drought

Paragraph 283

During the Decade, the phenomenon of drought and desertification grew and developed incessantly, no longer affecting merely some localities in a single country but several entire countries. The scale and persistence of drought constitutes a grave threat, particularly for the countries of the Sahel, in which famine and a far-reaching deterioration of the environment set in as a result of the desertification process. Hence, despite the considerable efforts of the international community, the living conditions of the people, particularly those of women and children, which were already precarious, have become particularly miserable.

In view of that situation steps should be taken to promote concerted programmes between the countries concerned for combating drought and desertification. Efforts should be intensified for the formulation and implementation of programmes aimed at food security and self-sufficiency, in particular by the optimum control and exploitation of hydro-geological resources.

A distinction should be made between emergency aid and productive activities. Emergency aid should be intensified when necessary and as far as ever possible directed towards development aid.

Measures should be adopted to take into account women's contribution to production, involve them more closely in the design, implementation and evaluation of the programmes envisaged and ensure ample access for them to the means of production and processing and preservation techniques.

B. Urban Poor Women

Paragraph 284

Urbanization has been one of the major socio-economic trends over the past few decades and is expected to continue at an accelerating rate. Although the situation varies considerably from one region to another, it can generally be expected that by the year 2000 close to half the number of women in the world will be living in urban areas. In developing countries, the number of urban women could nearly double by the year 2000, and it is envisaged that there could be a considerable increase in the number of poor women among them.

Paragraph 285

To deal effectively with the issue, Governments should organize multi-sectoral programmes with emphasis on economic activities, elimination of discrimination and the provision of supportive services and, *inter alia*, adequate child-care facilities and, where necessary, workplace canteens to enable women to gain access to economic, social and education opportunities on an equal basis with men. Particular attention should be devoted to the informal sector, which constitutes a major outlet for employment of a considerable number of urban poor women.

C. Elderly Women

Paragraph 286

The International Plan of Action on Aging adopted by the World Assembly on Aging in 1982[19] emphasized both the humanitarian and developmental aspects of aging. The recommendations of the Plan of Action are applicable to women and men with a view to providing them with protection and care, and ensuring their involvement and participation in social life and development. However, the Plan of Action recognizes a number of specific areas of concern for elderly women since their longer life expectancy freguently means an old age aggravated by economic need and isolation for both unmarried women and widows, possibly with little or no prospect of paid employment. This applies particularly to those women whose lifetimes were spent in unpaid and unrecognized work in the home with little or no access to a pension. If women have an income, it is generally lower than men's partly because their former employment status has in the majority of cases been broken by maternity and family responsibilities. For this reason, the Plan of Action also noted the need for long-term policies directed towards providing social insurance for women in their own right. Governments and non-governmental organizations should, in addition to the measures recommended, explore the possibilities of employing elderly women in productive and creative ways and encouraging their participation in social and recreational activities.

It is also recommended that the care of elderly persons, including women, should go beyond disease orientation and should include their total well-being. Further efforts, in particular primary health care, health services and suitable accommodation and housing as strategies should be directed at enabling elderly women to lead a meaningful life as long as possible, in their own home and family and in the community.

Women should be prepared early in life, both psychologically and socially, to face the consequences of longer life expectancy. Although, while getting older, professional and family roles of women are undergoing fundamental changes, aging, as a stage of development,is a challenge for women. In this period of life, women should be enabled to cope in a creative way with new opportunities. The social consequences arising from the stereotyping of elderly women should be recognized and eliminated. The media should assist by presenting positive images of women, particularly emphasizing the need for respect because of their past and continuing contributions to society.

Attention should be given to studying and treating the health problems of aging, particularly in women. Research should also be directed towards the investigation and slowing down of the process of premature aging due to a lifetime of stress, excessive work-load, malnutrition and repeated pregnancy.

D. Young Women

Paragraph 287

Initiatives begun for the 1985 International Youth Year should be extended and expanded so that young women are protected from abuse and exploitation and assisted to develop their full potential. Girls and boys must be provided with equal access to health, education and employment to equip them for adult life. Both girls and boys should be educated to accept equal responsibilities for parenthood.

Urgent attention should be paid to the educational and vocational training of young women in all fields of occupation, giving particular emphasis to those who are socially and economically disadvantaged. Self-employed young women and girls should be assisted to organize co-operatives and ongoing training programmes to improve their skills in production, marketing and management techniques. Special retraining programmes should also be developed for teenage mothers and girls who have dropped out of school and are ill equipped to enter productive employment.

Steps should be taken to eliminate exploitative treatment of young women at work in line with ILO Convention No. 11 concerning discrimination in respect of employment and occupation, 1958 and ILO Convention No. 122 concerning employment policy, 1964. Legislative measures guaranteeing young women their rights should be enforced.

Governments should recognize and enforce the rights of young women to be free from sexual violence, sexual harassment and sexual exploitation. In particular. Governments should recognize that many young women are victims of incest and sexual abuse in the family, and should take steps to assist the victims and to prevent such abuse by education, by improving the status of women and by appropriate action against offenders. Young women should be educated to assert their rights. Particular attention should also be given to sexual harassment and exploitation in employment, especially those areas of employment such as domestic service, where sexual harassment and exploitation are most prevalent.

Governments must also recognize their obligation to provide housing for young women who because of unemployment and low incomes suffer special problems in obtaining housing. Homeless young women are particularly vulnerable to sexual exploitation.

In the year 2000 women aged 15-24 will constitute over 8 per cent of both rural and urban populations in developing countries. The great majority of these women will be out of school and in search of jobs. For those employed, frequent exploitation, long working hours and stress have serious implications for their health. Low nutritional levels and unplanned and repeated pregnancies are also aggravating factors.

E. Abused Women

Paragraph 288

Gender-specific violence is increasing and Governments must affirm the dignity of women, as a priority action.

Governments should therefore intensify efforts to establish or strengthen forms of assistance to victims of such violence through the provision of shelter, support, legal and other services.

In addition to immediate assistance to victims of violence against women in the family and in society, Governments should undertake to increase public awareness of violence against women as a societal problem, establish policies and legislative measures to ascertain its causes and prevent and eliminate such violence, in particular by suppressing degrading images and representations of women in society, and finally encourage the development of educational and re-educational measures for offenders.

F. Destitute Women

Paragraph 289

Destitution is an extreme form of poverty. It is estimated that its effects on large segments of the population in developing and developed countries are on the increase. Forward-looking Strategies to promote the objectives of the United Nations Decade for Women: Equality, Development and Peace at the national and international levels are the basis for dealing with this problem. In addition strategies already specified for the implementation of the International Development Strategy for the Third United Nations Development Decade and the new international economic order are suggested in these recommendations. Governments should therefore ensure that the special needs and concerns of destitute women are given priority in the above-mentioned strategies. Moreover, efforts being undertaken for the International Year of Shelter for the Homeless (1987) should focus attention on the particular situation of women commensurate with their relative needs.

G. Women Victims of Trafficking and Involuntary Prostitution

Paragraph 290

Force prostitution is a form of slavery imposed on women by procurers. it is, *inter alia,* a result of economic degradation that alienates women's labour through processes of rapid urbanization and migration resulting in underemployment and unemployment. It also stems from women's dependence on men. Social and political pressures produce refugees and missing persons. Often these include vulnerable groups of women who are victimized by procurers. Sex tourism, forced prostitution and pornography reduce women to mere sex objects and marketable commodities.

Paragraph 291

States parties to the United Nations Convention for the Suppression of the Traffic in Persons and of the Exploitation of the prostitution of Others should implement the provisions dealing with the exploitation of women as prostitutes. Urgent consideration should also be given to the improvement of international measures to combat trafficking in women for the purposes of prostitution. Resources for the prevention of prostitution and assistance in the professional personal and social reintegration of prostitutes should be directed towards providing economic opportunities, including training, employment, self-employment and health facilities for women and children. Governments should also endeavour to co-operate with non-governmental organizations to create wider employment possibilities for women. Strict enforcement provisions must also be taken at all levels to stem the rising tide of violence, drug abuse and crime related to prostitution. The complex and serious problems of the exploitation of and violence against women associated with prostitution call for increased and co-ordinated efforts by police agencies internationally.

H. Women Deprived of their Traditional Means of Livelihood

Paragraph 292

The excessive and inappropriate exploitation of land by any party for any purpose, *inter alia*, by transnational corporations, as well as natural and man-made disasters are among the predominant causes of deprivation of traditional means of livelihood. Droughts, floods, hurricanes and other forms of environmental hazards, such as erosion, desertification and deforestation, have already pushed poor women into marginal environments. At present the pressures are greatest in drought-afflicted arid and semi-arid areas. Urban slums and squatter settlements are also seriously affected. Critically low levels of water supplies, shortage of fuel, over-utilization of grazing and arable lands, and population density are all factors that deprive women of their livelihood.

Paragraph 293

National and international emphasis on ecosystem management

should be strengthened, environmental degradation should be controlled and options provided for alternative means of livelihood. Measures should be established to draw up national conservation strategies aimed at incorporating women's development programmes, among which are irrigation and tree planting and also orientation in the area of agriculture, with women constitution a substantial part of the wage-earning labour force for those programmes.

1. Women who are the Sole Supporters of Families

Paragraph 294

Recent studies have shown that the number of families in which women are the sole supporters is on the increase. Owing to the particular difficulties (social, economic and legal) which they face, many such women are among the poorest people concentrated in urban informal labour markets and they constitute large numbers of the rural unemployed and marginally employed. Those with very little economic, social and moral support face serious difficulties in supporting themselves as well as in bringing up their children alone. This has serious repercussions for society in terms of the quality, character, productivity and human resource capabilities of its present and future citizenry.

Paragraph 295

The assumptions that underlie a large part of the relevant legislation, regulations and household surveys that confine the role of supporter and head of household to men hinder women's access to credit, loans and material and non-material resources. Changes are needed in these areas to secure for women equal access to resources. There is a need to eliminate terms such as "head of household" and introduce others that are comprehensive enough to reflect women's role appropriately in legal documents and household surveys to guarantee the rights of these women. In the provision of social services, special attention has to be given to the needs of these women. Governments are urged to ensure that women with sole responsibility;y for their families receive a level of income and social support sufficient to enable them to attain or maintain economic independence and to participate effectively in society. To this end, the assumptions that underlie policies, including research used in policy development, and legislation that confines the role of supporter or head of household to men should be identified and eliminated. Special attention, such as accessible, quality child care, should be given to assisting those women in discharging their domestic responsibilities and to enabling them to participate in and benefit from education, training programmes and employment. The putative father should be made to assist in the maintenance and education of those children born out of wedlock.

J. Women with Physical and Mental Disabilities

Paragraph 296

It is generally accepted that women constitute a significant number of the estimated 500 million people who are disabled as a consequence of mental, physical or sensory impairment. Many factors contribute to the rising umbers of disabled persons, including war and other forms of violence, poverty, hunger, nutritional deficiencies, epidemics and work-related accidents. The recognition of their human dignity and human rights and the full participation by disabled persons in society is still limited, and this presents additional problems for women who may have domestic and other responsibilities. It is recommended that Governments should adopt the Declaration on the Rights of Disabled persons (1975) and the World Programme of Action concerning Disabled persons (1982) which provide an overall framework for action and also refer to problems specific to women that have not been fully appreciated by society because they are still not well known or understood. Community-based occupational and social rehabilitation measures, support services to help them with their domestic responsibilities, as well as opportunities for the participation of such women in all aspects of life should be provided. The rights of intellectually disabled women to obtain health information and advice and to consent to or refuse medical treatment should be respected, similarly, the rights of intellectually disabled minors should be respected.

K. Women in Detention and Subject to Penal Law

Paragraph 297

One of the major areas of current concern in the field of crime prevention and criminal justice is the need for equal treatment of women by the criminal justice system. In the context of changing socio-economic and cultural conditions some improvements have taken place but more need to be made. The number of women in detention haas increased over the Decade and this trends is expected to continue. Women deprived of freedom are exposed to various forms of physical violence, sexual and moral harassment. The conditions of their detention are often below acceptable hygienic standards and their children are deprived of maternal care. The recommendations of the Sixth United Nations congress on the

Prevention of crime and the Treatment of offenders, held at Caracas, in 1980[20] , and the principles of the caracas Declaration with special reference to the "fair and equal treatment of women", should be taken into account in designing and implementing concrete measures at the national and international levels. The indigenous of indigenous women imprisoned in some countries is a matter of concern.

L. Refugee and Displaced Women and Children

Paragraph 298

The international community recognizes a humanitarian responsibility to protect and assist refugees and displaced persons. In many cases refugee and displaced women are exposed to a variety of difficult situations affecting their physical and legal protection as well as their psychological and material well-being. Problems of physical debility, physical safety, emotional stress and socio-psychological effects of separation or death in the family, as well as changes in women's roles, to together with limitations often found in the new environment including lack of adequate food, shelter, health care and social services call for specialized and enlarged assistance. Special attention has to be offered to women with special needs. Furthermore, the potential and capacities of refugee and displaced women should be recognized and enhanced.

Paragraph 299

It is recognized that a lasting solution to the problems of refugees and displaced women and children should be sought in the elimination of the root causes of the flow of refugees and durable solutions should be found leading to their full integration in the economic, social and cultural life of their country of origin in the immediate future. Until such solutions are achieved, the international community, in an expression of international solidarity and burden-sharing, should continue providing relief assistance and also launching special relief programmes taking into account the specific needs of refugee women and children in countries of first asylum. Similarly, relief assistance and special relief programmes should also continue to be provided to returnees and displaced women and children. Legal, educational, social, humanitarian and moral assistance should be offered as well as opportunities for their voluntary repatriation, return or resettlement. Steps should also be taken to promote accession by Governments to the 1951 Convention relating to the Status of Refugees and to to implement, on a basis of equity for all refugees, provisions contained in this Convention an its 1967 protocol.

M. Migrant Women

Paragraph 300

The Decade has witnessed the increasing involvement of women in all forms of migration, including rural-rural, rural-urban and international movements of a temporary, seasonal or permanent nature. In addition to their lack of adequate education, skills and resources, migrant women may also face severe adjustment problems due to differences in religion, language, nationality, and socialization as well as separation from their original families. Such problems are often accentuated for international migrants as a result of the openly-expressed prejudices and hostilities, including violation of human rights in host countries. Thus recommendations of the World Population Plan of Action and the Programme of Action for the Second Half of the United Nations Decade for Women Pertaining to migrant women should be implemented and expanded in view of the anticipated increase in the scope of the problem. It is also urgent to conclude the elaboration of the draft International Convention on the Protection of the Rights of All Migrant Workers and their Families, as agreed by the General Assembly in the relevant resolutions.

Paragraph 301

The situation of migrant women, who are subject to double discrimination as women and as migrants, should be given special attention by the Governments of host countries, particularly with respect to protection and maintenance of family unity, employment opportunities and equal pay, equal conditions of work, health care, benefits to be provided in accordance with the existing social security rights in the host country, and racial and other forms of discrimination. Particular attention should also be given to the second generation of migrant women, especially with regard to education and professional training, to allow them to integrate themselves in their countries of adoption and to work according to their education and skills. In this process, loss of cultural values of their countries of origin should be avoided.

N. Minority and "Indigenous" Women

Paragraph 302

Some women are oppressed as a result of belonging to minority groups or populations which have historically been subjected to domination and suffered dispossession and dispersal. These women suffer the full burden of discrimination based on race, colour, descent, ethnic and national origin and the majority experienced serious economic deprivation. As women, they are therefore doubly disadvantaged. Measures should be taken by Governments in countries in which there are minority and indigenous populations to respect, preserve and promote all of their human rights, their dignity, ethnic, religious cultural and linguistic identity and their full participation in societal change.

Paragraph 303

Governments should ensure that the fundamental human rights and freedoms as enshrined in relevant international instruments are fully guaranteed also to women belonging to minority groups and indigenous populations. Governments in countries in which there are indigenous and minority populations should ensure respect for the economic, social and cultural rights of these women and assist them in the fulfilment of their family and parental responsibilities. Specific measures should address dietary deficiencies, high levels of infant and maternal mortality and other health problems, lack of education, housing and child care. Vocational, technical, professional and other training should be provided to enable these women to secure employment or to participate in income-generating activities and projects, and to secure adequate wages, occupational health and safety and their other rights as workers. As far as possible, overnments should ensure that these women have access to all services in their own languages.

Paragraph 304

Women belonging to minority groups or indigenous populations should be fully consulted and should participate in the development and implementation of programmes affecting them. The Governments of countries where minorities and indigenous populations exist should take proper account of the work of bodies such as the Committee on the Elimination of Racial Discrimination and the Sub-Commission on Prevention of Discrimination and Protection of Minorities, in particular its Working Group which is developing a set of international standards to protect the rights of indigenous population. The General Assembly should consider the advisability of designating an international year of indigenous and traditional cultures in order to promote international understanding and to emphasize the distinctive role of women in sustaining the identity of their people.

V. INTERNATIONAL AND REGIONAL CO-OPERATION

A. Obstacles

Paragraph 305

Insufficient attention has been devoted during the Decade at the international level and in some regions to the need to advance the status of women in relation to the goals and objectives of the Decade—equality, development and peace. International tensions, arms race, threat of nuclear war, failure to respect human rights and fundamental freedoms and failure to observe the principles of the United Nations Charter as well as global economic recession and other critical situations combined with dissatisfaction due to inadequate progress in multilateral and international co-operation since the Copenhagen World Conference has substantially affected scope and ability for international and regional co-operation including the role of the United Nations. The progress in the developing world has slackened or in some cases turned negative under conditions of serious indebtedness, economic and monetary instability, resource constraints and unemployment. This has also affected prospects for economic and technical co-operation among developing countries, particularly with regard to women. Nevertheless some progress has been made in terms of achieving equality between women and men, and a greater appreciation of the role of women in development and peace which should also contribute toward effective international co-operation.

Paragraph 306

International and regional organizations have been called upon during the Decade to advance the position of their women staff and to extend hiring practices to include qualified women. The results have been highly uneven and in some cases the situation has actually worsened during the Decade in the face of resource constraints and other limiting criteria, such as geographical distribution and attitudinal barriers. In particular, women are absent from the senior management levels, which seriously limits their influence on decision-making.

Paragraph 307

In order to institutionalize interorganizational exchanges of information and co-operation relation to women's advancement, several United Nations agencies, non-governmental organizations and regional bodies have designated, in response to pressures applied during the Decade, focal points for women's activities. However,, in many cases, insufficient tenure and resources accompanied those actions, thus limiting their long-term effectiveness. Moreover, activities that promote the integration of women in development have often been confined to these focal points and have not been integrated into all organizational planning and programme activities. Progress has also been limited in this area by the inadequate training of many of the staff members of international agencies and organizations with respect to the centrality of women's role in development.

Paragraph 308

International and regional co-operation strategies must be formulated on the premise that effective development requires the full integration of women in the development process as both agents and beneficiaries. Development agencies should take full cognizance of women as a development resource. This requires that all international and regional development institutions adopt explicity policies in this regard and put in place the management systems necessary to ensure the effective implementation and evaluation of these policies in the full range of their programmes and activities. Such policies should incorporate the principles endorsed in the Forward-looking Strategies of Implementation for the Advancement of Women. Strong and visible commitment to and interest in integrating women in the development process should be demonstrated by the senior-level management of development agencies.

B. Basic Strategies

Paragraph 309

Effective consultative and reporting arrangements are required to collect information on action taken to implement the Forward-looking Strategies and on successful ways and means used to overcome obstacles. Monitoring and evaluation should, therefore, be carried out at international, regional and subregional levels based on national-level monitoring, including input from non-governmental organizations.

Paragraph 310

Technical co-operation, training and advisory services should promote endogenous development and self-reliance with greater emphasis on economic and technical co-operation among developing countries. The special needs of women should be periodically assessed and methods developed to integrate women's concerns into the planning and evaluation of development activities. The participation of women in the formulation of technical co-operation policies and programmes should be ensured.

Paragraph 311

International, regional and subregional institutional co-ordination should be strengthened, particularly in relation to the exchange of information on the advancement of women and the establishment of collaborative arrangements to undertake activities with interrelated components.

Paragraph 312

Research and policy analysis should focus greater attention on the economic role of women in society, including access to economic resources such as land and capital. Research and policy analysis related to women should be action-oriented without losing sight of key analytical considerations. Further investment in evolving adequate gender-specific data is also required.

Paragraph 313

Steps should be taken to increase the participation of women in international, regional and subregional level activities and decision-making, including those directly or indirectly concerned with the maintenance of peace and security, the role of women in development and the achievement of equality between women and men.

Paragraph 314

Information on progress in achieving the goals of the Decade and on implementing the Forward-looking Strategies should be widely disseminated in the period from 1985 to the year 2000 at international, regional, subregional and national levels, based on experience gained during the Decade. Greater reliance is needed on audio-visual communications and expansion of networks for disseminating information on programmes and activities for women. Discriminatory, stereotyped and degrading images of women must be eliminated in the media.

Paragraph 315

On the basis of the results of the review and appraisal in the United Nations system that indicated the need for continued efforts to ensure the recruitment, promotion and retention of women, all United Nations bodies, the regional commissions and the specialized agencies should take all measures necessary to achieve an equitable balance between women and men staff members at managerial and professional levels in all substantive area, as well as in field posts, with particular attention to promoting equitable regional representation of women. Women should be appointed to decision-making and management posts within the United Nations system in order to increase their participation in activities at the

international and regional levels, including such as equality, development and peace.

Paragraph 316

In view of the difficulties of spouses of United Nations officials in securing employment at the various duty stations, the United Nations is urged to make every possible effort to provide the establishment of educational facilities and day care centres for families of officials in order to facilitate the employment of spouses at these duty stations.

C. Measures for the Implementation of the Basic Strategies

1. Monitoring

Paragraph 317

The implementation of the goals and objectives of the Decade—equality, development and peace—and of the Forward-looking Strategies should be monitored during the period 1986 to the year 2000. Monitoring at the international level should be based on reviews, at the regional, subregional and national levels, of action taken, resources allocated and progress achieved. The national reviews should take the form of a response to a regular statistical reporting request from the United Nations Secretariat, which should include indicators of the situation of women. The statistical reporting basis should be developed by the Statistical Commission, in consultation with the Commission on the Status of Women. The United Nations Secretariat should compile the results of such monitoring in consultation with the appropriate bodies of Governments, including national machinery established to monitor and improve the status of women. The action taken and progress achieved at the national level should reflect consultation with non-governmental organizations and integration of their concerns at all levels of government planning, implementation and evaluation, as appropriate.

Paragraph 318

The specialized agencies and other United Nations organizations, including the regional commissions, should establish monitoring capabilities and procedures to analyse the situation of women in their sectoral or geographical areas, and submit their reports regularly to their respective governing bodies and to the Commission on the Status of Women, which is the main intergovernmental body within the United Nations system concerned with women.

Paragraph 319

The Commission on the Status of Women should consider on a regular basis reports on the progress made and concrete measures implemented at national, regional and international levels to advance the status of women in relation to the goals of the Decade—equality, development and peace-and the sub-theme-employment, health and education—and the strategies and measures to the year 2000. The United Nations system should continue to carry out a comprehensive and critical review of progress achieved in implementing the provisions of the World Plan of Action and of the Programme for the Second Half of the Decade. The central role in carrying out this review and appraisal should be played by the Commission on the Status of Women. The Commission should also monitor progress in the implementation of international standards, codes of conduct, strategies, conventions and convenants as they pertain to women. In view of the important function, high-level expertise and representation on the Commission should be given priority, including officials with substantive policy responsibilities for the advancement of women.

Paragraph 320

The preparation of new instruments and strategies such as the overall strategies for international development, should pay specific, appropriate attention to the advancement of women. Intergovernmental bodies of the United Nations system, particularly those concerned with the monitoring, review and appraisal of the existing instruments, strategies, plans and programmes that may be of direct or indirect relevance to women, are urged as a matter of priority to develop explicit polices and reviewable plans of action for the integration of women in their regular work programmes.

Paragraph 321

The methods and procedures employed for collecting information from Governments, regional commissions, non-governmental organizations and other international organizations and bodies should be streamlined and based on guidelines to be discussed by the Commission on the Status of Women.

2. Technical Co-operation, Training and Advisory Services

Paragraph 322

Measures of technical co-operation, training and advisory services directed towards improving women's status at the international, interregional and regional levels, including co-operation among developing countries, need some impetus. This would require the re-ordering of principles for the allocation of resources as well as targeted financial, material and human resource assistance. Notwithstanding resource constraints, the United Nations should continue the important role of reinforcing these increased benefits for women.

Paragraph 323

Technical co-operation should be approached with a new concept that will break the cycle of dependency, emphasize local needs, and use local materials and resources as well as local creativity and expertise and be based on the full integration of women as agents and beneficiaries in all technical co-operation activities. Local associations and mechanisms should be oriented to play a more active role in planning and policy-making. Emphasis should be given to broader access by women to capital for self-help projects, income-generating activities, enterprise development and projects designed to reduce the drudgery in work performed by women. Innovative demonstration projects, particularly with respect to the integration of women in non-traditional sector activities, should be an essential element in technical co-operation activities.

Paragraph 324

Agencies which do not have specific guidelines or project procedures relating to women in development interlinked with the other aims of the period up to the year 2000 should ensure that they are developed. Such guidelines and procedures should apply to all aspects of the project cycle. Existing guidelines and procedures have to be applied more vigorously and consistently, in particular, each project document should contain a strategy to ensure that the project has a positive impact on the situation of women.

Paragraph 325

Substantive staff training is needed to enhance the ability of staff to recognize and deal with the centrality of women's role in development, and adequate resources must be made available for this purpose. Implementation of policies concerning women is the responsibility of the particular organization as a whole. Responsibility is not merely a matter of personal persuasion. Systems should be developed which allocate responsibility and accountability.

Paragraph 326

Governments should strengthen and improve their institutional arrangements for technical co-operation so that policy is effectively linked to local-level implementing mechanisms, and should promote sustained, endogenous development. In these efforts Governments may wish to make use of the accumulated experience, activities and resources of the whole United Nations system.

Paragraph 327

While technical co-operation should be focused equally on women and men, the incorporation of women's needs and aspirations in the formulation and review of technical co-operation policies and programmes should be ensured and the potential negative effects on women of technical assistance should be minimized. Technical co-operation and women must be linked to overall national development objectives and priorities, and technical assistance plans and programmes should be managed so as to ensure the full integration of activities specific to women. As a standard component of technical co-operation policies, women should be full and equal participants in technical co-operation projects and activities. The needs of especially vulnerable and underprivileged groups of women should be addressed in the technical co-operation programmes.

Paragraph 328

Participation of non-governmental organizations as a means to enhance the relevance and impact of technical co-operation activities of benefit to women should be encouraged.

Paragraph 329

In allocating multilateral and bilateral assistance, agencies, in consultation with recipient Governments, should establish measurable and reviewable plans of action, with goals and time frames. They should also give adequate impetus to sustained and real increases in the flow of resources for technical co-operation activities of benefit to women, including greater mobilization of resources from non-governmental sources and the private sector. Bilateral and multilateral aid agencies should give special consideration to assisting the least developed countries in their efforts to integrate women in development. In this regard, particular attention should be given to projects in the fields of health, education and training, and the creation of employment opportunities for women, especially in rural areas.

Paragraph 330

Bilateral and multilateral aid agencies should take a corporate-wide response to the integration of women in development. Bilateral aid agencies' policies for women in development should involve all parts of donors organizations and programmes, including participation of multilateral and bilateral programmes, training, technical assistance and financial aid. Policies for women in development should be incorporated into all applicable aid and agency procedures relating to sectoral and project levels.

Paragraph 331

In order to enable women to define and defend their own interests and needs, the United Nations system and aid agencies should provide assistance for programmes and projects which strengthen women's autonomy, in particular in the integration process.

Paragraph 332

International non-governmental organizations, including such organizations as trade unions, should be encouraged to involve women in their day-to-day work and to increase their attention to women's issues. The capacity of non-governmental organizations at all levels to reach women and women 's groups should receive greater recognitions and support. The potential role of those non-governmental organizations could be fully utilized by international and governmental agencies involved in development co-operation.

Paragraph 333

Technical and advisory assistance should be provided by the United Nations system at the national level to improve systematically statistical and other forms of gender-specific indicators and information that can help redirect policy and programmes for the more effective integration of women in development as contributors and beneficiaries.

Paragraph 334

Technical co-operation among developing countries should be strengthened in the service of women at all levels and in all sectors of activity, focusing particularly on promoting the exchange of experience, expertise, technology and know-how, as well as on diffusing innovative organizational models suitable for strengthening the self-reliance of women. The urgent need for information flows to facilitte the process of integrating women in development, and the need for relevant, transferable and appropriate information should be a priority of regional co-operation with the framework of technical co-operation among developing countries. Regional co-operation to assist disadvantaged groups of women should also be promoted in this context.

Paragraph 335

Technical assistance should be given by the United Nations system and other international and non-governmental organizations to women involved in the promotion of international peace and co-operation.

Paragraph 336

The United Nations system should continue to strengthen training programmes for women, in particular in the least developed countries, through fellowships and other means of assistance, particularly in the fields of economic planning, public affairs and public administration, business management and accounting, and farming and labour relations, and in scientific, engineering and technical fields. It is necessary to support and expand technical and economic activities for women by means of collaboration with international development assistance agencies. In this respect, the United Nations Development Fund for Women is particularly recognized for its innovative contribution in the area of development and technical assistance for disadvanted women, and its continuation and expansion beyond the Decade is considered of vital importance to the development needs of women.

Paragraph 337

The participation of women in technical assistance monitoring, planning, programming, evaluation and follow-up missions should be promoted, and guidelines should be developed and applied to assess the relevance and impact of development assistance projects on women. The United Nations funding agencies, such as the United Nations Development Programme, the United Nations Fund for Population Activities, the United Nations Children's Fund and the World Food Programme, as well as the World Bank, should ensure that women benefit from and participate in all projects and programmes funded by them.

3. Institutional Co-ordination

Paragraph 338

System-wide co-ordination of work on issues relating to women needs to be strengthened. The Economic and Social Council should be encouraged to play a more forceful and dynamic role in reviewing and co-ordinating all relevant United Nations activities in the field of women's issues. Regular consultations between United Nations agencies and organizations should be institutionalized in conjunction with meetings of the Commission on the Status of Women in order to exchange information on programme activities and co-ordinate future planning and programming with a view to ensuring adequate resource-allocation that would facilitate action and limit the unnecessary duplication of activities.

Paragraph 339

Future medium-term plans of the United Nations and the specialized agencies should contain intersectoral presentations of the various programes dealing with issues of concern to women. In order to achieve greater coherence and efficiency of the policies and programmes of the United Nations system related to women and development, the Secretary-General, in his capacity as Chairman of the Administrative Committee on Co-ordination and in conformity with Economic and Social Council resolution 1985/46 of 31 May 1985, should take the initiative in formulating a system-wide medium term plan for women and development.

Paragraph 340

The Centre for Social Development and Humanitarian Affairs of the Department of International Economic and Social Affairs, in particular the Branch for the Advancement of Women, should continue to serve as the focal point for co-ordination of, consultation on, promotion of and advice on matters relevant to women in the United Nations system and to co-ordinate information on system-wide activities related to the future implementation of the goals and objectives of the Decade and the Forward-looking Strategies. In this context, the United Nations system should explore ways and means of developing further collaboration between its organizations, including the regional commissions, the International Research and Training Institute for the Advancement of Women and the United Nations Development Fund for Women, in particular in connection with the holding of United Nations world conferences on women on a regular basis, if necessary, for example every five years. It is recommended that at least one world conference be held during the period betweem 1985 and the year 2000, taking into account that the General Assembly will take the decision on the holding of the conference in each case within existing financial resources.

Paragraph 341

Existing sectoral inter-agency task forces in the United Nations system should always include issues related to the advancement of women in their agenda.

Paragraph 342

Inter-agency co-ordination should be complemented where possible by networking, particularly in the fields of information, research, training and programme development, in order to facilitate the availability of data and information in these fields and the exchange of experience with national machinery.

Paragraph 343

Resolutions of the United Nations General Assembly, of governing bodies of the specialized agencies and of other organizations which promote the improvement of the status of women should be implemented. All institutions within the United Nations system that have not yet established special internal arrangements and procedures with respect to women's policies are urged to take the necessary measures to do so.

Paragraph 344

International machineries that promote and support education for peace should co-ordinate their efforts and include the role of women in promoting peace in their curricula. Particular attention should be paid to the Declaration in the participation of women in promoting International Peace and Co-operation adopted by the General Assembly in 1982. The University for peace should play a leading role in this regard.

4. Research and Policy Analysis

Paragraph 345

Institutes of women's affairs at the regional level should be strengthened or, where they do not exist, their establishment should be considered for the promotion of regional collaboration in undertaking research and analyses on emerging women's issues in order to facilitate and promote regional and international co-operation and understanding in this field.

Paragraph 346

Measures should be taken by the United Nations system to strengthen the capabilities of the United Nations Secretariat to provide assistance to Governments and other international organizations and bodies concerned with integrating women in policy formulation and in assessing the impact of development policies on women. The Branch for the Advancement of Women should act as the focal point for co-ordinating the exchange of information, providing advice on matters related to the advancement of women and monitoring and evaluating the progress of other bodies in that connection. The United Nations should develop guidelines for this purpose based on comparative analyses of experience world wide.

Paragraph 347

Guidelines should also be developed by the United Nations for action to remove gender-specific discriminatory perceptions, attitudes and behaviour based on models of successful initiatives.

Paragraph 348

The United Nations system should undertake research and prepare guidelines, case studies and practical approaches on integrating women on an equal basis with men into political life. Training programmes for and consultations between women already engaged in political life should be organized.

Paragraph 349

Research should be carried out and a report prepared by the United Nations, in consultation with other organizations and specialized agencies and in co-operation with Governments, on establishing effective institutional arrangements at the national level for the formulation of policies on women, including guidelines and summaries of national case studies.

Paragraph 350

United Nations agencies and, in particular, the Centre for Social Development and Humanitarian Affairs of the United Nations Secretariat, as part of its regular programme of work, should undertake in-depth research on the positive and negative effects of legislative change, the persistence of *de facto* discrimination and conflicts between customary and statutory laws. In carrying out this research, full use should be made of the work of the Committee on the Elimination of All Forms of Discrimination Against Women.

Paragraph 351

In the context of the Third United Nations Development Decade and any subsequent decade, the implications for women international decisions especially pertaining to international trade and finance, agriculture and technology transfer should be assessed by the United Nations system in consultation with the appropriate international organizations, bodies and research institutes, including, the United Nations Research Institute for Social Development, the International Research and Training Institute for the Advancement of Women and any others established by the United Nations University. The lack of reliable date prevents the assessment of relative improvements in women's status in the various sectors. It is therefore essential that the Statistical Commission, the Commission on the Status of Women and the International Research and Training Institute for the Advancement of Women should co-operate at the institutional level in the collection, analysis, utilization and dissemination of statistical data on the question of women. The data base on women's role in national, regional and international economic activities should be further developed by the United Nations in co-operation with Governments, specialized agencies and the regional commissions of the United Nations system.

Paragraph 352

The United Nations regional commissions, with a view to integrating women's concerns at all levels in each commission's overall programme of work,should undertake further research on the status of women in their regions to the year 2000 by developing the necessary data base and indicators and by drawing upon inputs from the national and local levels, including perspectives on and by women at the grass-roots level. To this end, the regional commissions should include in their annual reports an analysis of changes in the situation of women in their regions.

Paragraph 353

It is also necessary to strengthen the activities of the International Research and Training Institute for the Advancement of Women which performs and important role in the field of research, training, information and communication, and to request States and appropriate organizations, in particular, the organizations of the United Nations system, to continue to collaborate with the Institute in its work for the improvement of the status of women. The Institute should continue its work in appraising and evaluating what has been done by Governments and the United Nations system in promoting the status of women and it should be given increased voluntary financial support.

Paragraph 354

The United Nations should incorporate within its activities related to the World Disarmament Campaign the preparation of a study on the specific consequences of the arms race and modern warfare for women in general, especially aged or pregnant women and young children. Such a study should be given wide publicity in order to mobilize researchers, politicians and non-governmental organizations, as well as women themselves, for the promotion of disarmament.

Paragraph 355

The United Nations system and other intergovernmental, governmental and non-governmental organizations should encourage women, women's organizations and all the appropriate governmental bodies from different countries to discuss and study various aspects of promoting peace and other related issues in order to increase knowledge, facilitate understanding and develop friendly relations between countries and peoples. Exchange visits among women from different countries, and meetings and seminars in which women participate fully should be organized at regional and international levels.

5. Participation of Women in Activities at the International and Regional Levels and in Decision-Making

Paragraph 356

The United Nations system should take all necessary measures to achieve an equitable balance between women and men staff members at managerial and professional levels in all substantive areas, as well as in fields posts. Regular reporting to the General Assembly, the governing bodies of the specialized agencies, the regional commissions and the Commission on the Status of Women on the establishment an implementation of targets for the equal representation of women in professional posts should be continued.

Paragraph 357

Women and women's organizations from different countries should be encouraged to discuss and study various aspects of promoting peace and development issues in order to increase knowledge, facilitate understanding and develop friendly relations between countries and peoples. Exchange visits of women from different countries and meetings with full participation by women should be encouraged.

Paragraph 358

In order to ensure that programmes an activities of concern to women are given the necessary attention and priority, it is essential that women should participate actively in the planning and formulation of policies and programmes and in decision-making and appraisal processes in the United Nations. To this end, international, regional and national organizations have been called upon during the Decade to advance the status of their female staff and to increase the number of women recruited. In the absence of overall targets and effective mechanisms for their achievement, however, greater efforts are needed to ensure the recruitment, promotion an career development of women. All bodies and organizations of the United Nations system should therefore take all possible measures to achieve the participation of women on equal terms with men at all levels by the year 2000. To achieve this goal, the secretariats of the United Nations and all the organizations and bodies within the system should take special measures, such as the preparation of a comprehensive affirmative action plan including provisions for setting intermediate targets and for establishing and supporting special mechanisms- for example, co-ordinators- to improve the status of women staff. Progress made to implement those measures should be reported to the General Assembly, the Economic and Social Council and the Commission on the Status of Women on a regular basis.

Paragraph 359

Women should be assured of the opportunity to participate in international, regional and subregional meetings and seminars, including those organized by the United Nations system, particularly those related to equality, development and peace, including peace education, and those directed to promoting the role of women in development through research activities, seminars and conferences to exchange experience and expertise. Similarly, women Parliamentarians should always be included in delegations to inter-parliamentary meetings organized by the Inter-parliamentary Union and regional inter-parliamentary organizations.

Paragraph 360

The participation of women in promoting peace and in the struggle against the obstacles to peace at the international level should be encouraged. Networking of women at high decision-making levels related to peace and disarmament, including women leaders, peace researchers and educators, should also be encouraged in connection with United Nations system activities such as the International Year of Peace (1986). " Women and Peace" should be a separate item in the programme for that year.

Paragraph 361

In order to provide a firm basis for the integration of issues of concern to women in the overall development process, a greater efforts is needed to define such issues and to develop useful models for action in socio-cultural, economic and political contexts. Work in this area can be undertaken in the national and regional research institutions, as well as in the united Nations and other international agencies. In this context, attention should also be given to increasing the planning capabilities of women.

Paragraph 362

Special efforts should be made at both the national and regional levels to ensure that women have equal access to all aspects of modern science and technology, particularly in educational systems. The use of science and technology can be a powerful instrument for the advancement of women. Special research to evolve appropriate technology for rural women should be carried out, and existing and new technology should be disseminated as widely as possible. The co-ordination of such activities in the regions should be the responsibility of the regional commissions, in co-operation with other intergovernmental bodies and agencies that deal with the status of women and technology.

Paragraph 363

Governments and non-governmental organizations should organize regular training programmes that are aimed at improving the status of women workers and widening women's access to and improving their performance in managerial positions in the sectors of employment or self-employment. In this connection, the United Nations is urged to support programmes on network and exchange of expertise in vocational training being carried out by regional and subregional organizations.

Paragraph 364

Regional and subregional groups have an important role to play in strengthening the roles of women in development. Existing regional and subregional information systems on women should be reinforced. A stronger data and resarch base on women should be developed in the developing countries and in the regional commissions, in collaboration with the appropriate specialized agencies, and the sharing of information and research data should be encouraged. Information systems at the national level should be strengthened or, where they do not exist, should be established.

Paragraph 365

International, regional, subregional and national organizations should be strengthened through the injection of additional human and financial resources and through the placement of more women at policy— and decision-making levels.

6. Information Dissemination

Paragraph 366

International programmes should be designed and resources allocated to support national campaigns to improve public consciousness of the need for equality between women and men and for eliminating discriminatory practices. Special attention should be given to information about the Convention on the Elimination of All Forms of Discrimination against Women.

Paragraph 367

Studies must be carried out by the United Nations system on sex stereotyping in advertising and in the mass media, especially degrading images of women in articles and programmes disseminated world wide. Steps should be taken to promote the elimination or reduction of sex stereotyping in the media.

Paragraph 368

In order to promote peace, social justice and the advancement of women, wide publicity should be given by the United Nations to legal instruments and the United Nations resolutions and reports relating to women and the objectives of the Decade, that is, equality, development and peace. The mass media, including United Nations radio and television, should disseminate information on the role of women in achieving these objectives, particularly in promoting co-operation and understanding among peoples and the maintenance of international peace and security. Cultural mechanisms of communication should also be used to disseminate the importance of the concepts of peace and international understanding for the advancement of women.

Paragraph 369

It is essential that women be trained in the use of audio-visual forms of information dissemination, including visual display units and computers, and participate more actively in developing programmes on the advancement of women and for women at the international, regional, subregional and national levels.

Paragraph 370

The present United Nations weekly radio programme and co-production of films on women should be continued with adequate provision for distributing them in different languages.

Paragraph 371

The joint United Nations Information Committee should continue to include women's issues in its programmes of social and economic information. Adequate resources should be made available for these activities.

Paragraph 372

Governments and the organizations of the United Nations system, including the regional commissions and the specialized agencies, are urged to give the Forward-looking Strategies the widest publicity possible and to ensure that their content is translated and disseminated in order to make authorities and the public in general, especially women's grass-root organizations, aware of the objectives of that document and of the recommendations contained therein.

Notes

1. *Report of the World Conference of the International Women's Year, Mexico City, 19 June-2 July 1975* (United Nations Publication, Sales No. E.76.IV.1), chap 1, sect. A.
2. *Report of the World Conference of the United Nations Decade for Women: Equality, Development and Peace, Copenhagen, 24-30 July 1980* (United Nations Publication, Sales No. E.80.IV.3)., chap 1, sect. A.
3. General Assembly resolution 227 A (III).
4. General Assembly resolution 2200 A (XXI), annex.
5. *Ibid.*
6. General Assembly resolution 34/180, annex.
7. General Assembly resolution 37/63, annex.
8. *Report of the International Conference on Population, 1984, Mexico City, 6-14 August 1984* (United Nations Publication, Sales No. E.84.XIII.8), chap.1, sect. A, para. 1.
9. *Report of the World Conference of the International Women's Year...,* chap. 1.
10. Report of the Commission on the Status of Women acting as the Preparatory Body for the World Conference to Review and Appraise the Achievements of the United Nations Decade for Women: Equality, Development and Peace on its second session (A/CONF.116/PC/19), chap. 1, draft decision 1, para. 2 (h).
11. *Report of the United Nations World Population Conference, 1974, Bucharest, 19-30 August 1974* (United Nations Publication, Sales NO. E.75.XIII.3), Chap. 1.
12. *Report of the World Conference on Agrarian Reform and Rural Development, Rome, 12-20 July 1979* (WCARRD/REP) (Rome, FAO, 1979), Programme of Action, sect. IV.
13. General Assembly resolution 36/71.
14. *Report of the World Conference to Compat Racism and Racial Discrimination, Geneva, 14-25 August 1978* (United Nations Publication, Sales NO. E. 79. XIV. 2), chap. II.
15. General Assembly resolution 3086 (XXVIII).
16. Geneva Convention relative to the Protection of Civilian Persons in Time of War, of 12 August 1949, (United Nations *Treaty Series,* vol. 75, No. 973, p. 287).
17. *Report of the International Conference on the Question of Palestine, Geneva, 29 August -7 September 1983* (United Nations Publication, Sales No. E. 83. I. 21),chap.I, sect. B.
18. General Assembly resolution 37/16.
19. *Report of the World Assembly on Aging, Vienna, 26 July-6 August 1982* (United Nations Publication, Sales No. E.82. I.16),chap. VI. sect. A.
20. See United Nations Publication, Sales NO. E.81.IV.4.

7

The Beijing Declaration and the Platform for Action

(Fourth World Conference on Women, Beijing, China, 4-15 September 1995)

A. TRANSLATING THE MOMENTUM OF BEIJING INTO ACTION

By Boutros Boutros-Ghali

United Nations Secretary-General

All of us owe a debt of gratitude to the People's Republic of China, which has hosted one of the largest global conferences ever held, with some 17,000 participants, including 6,000 delegates from 189 countries, over 4,000 representatives of accredited non-governmental organizations a host of international civil servants and about 4,000 media representatives. More than 30,000 people also participated in the NGO Forum.

My special thanks also go to the President of the Conference, Madame Chen Muhua, and to the Secretary-General of the Fourth World Conference on Women, Mrs. Gertrude Mongella.

Now the momentum of Beijing must be translated into concrete action. We must all ensure that the decisions reached in Beijing will change the world.

The commitments made in Beijing are not only the result of diplomatic negotiation. Behind them lies the strong and organized power of the women's movement. The entire continuum of global conferences and summits has been shaped by the growing influence, passion and

* From the statement of the Secretary-General read on the concluding day of the Fourth World Conference on Women, Beijing, 15 September 1995.

intellectual conviction of the women's movement.

At Rio, Vienna, Cairo and Copenhagen the importance os issues related to the improvement of the status of women was stressed. Form each of these global conferences emerged a more powerful recognition of the crucial role of women in sustainable development and protection the environment; of the human rights of women as an inalienable,integral and indivisible part of universal human rights; of violence against women as an intolerable violation of these rights; of health, maternal care and family planning facilities, and of access to education and information, as essential to the exercise by women of their fundamental rights.

In the United Nations, the women's movement has a staunch ally. Starting from the assertion in the Charter, calling for full equality of men and women, the United Nations has worked with the women's movement to realize this goal of our funders. The Commission on the Status of Women was one of the first bodies established by the United Nations after its foundation. Over the past 20 years, World Conferences on Women, held in Mexico City, Copenhagen and Nairobi, have contributed to the progressive strengthening of the legal, economic, social and political dimensions of the role of women. In 1979, the General Assembly adopted the landmark Convention for the Elimination of all Forms of Discrimination against Women.

The movement for gender equality the world over has been one of the defining developments of our time. I am proud and honoured that the United Nations has been part of this movement.

Despite the progress made, much, much more remains to be done. While women have made significant advances in many societies, women's concerns are still given second priority almost everywhere. Women face discrimination and marginalization in subtle as well as in flagrant ways. Women do not share equally in the fruits of production. Women constitute 70 per cent of the world's poor.

The sign at the entrance to the NGO Forum at Huairou calls on us to "Look at the world through women's eyes". For the past two weeks, the world has done just that. We have seen that, despite the progress made since the First World Conference on Women, 20 years ago, women and men still live in an unequal world. Gender disparities and unacceptable inequalities persist in all countries. In 1995 there is no country in the world where men and women enjoy complete equality.

The message of this Conference is that women's issues are global and universal. Deeply entrenched attitudes and paractices perpetuate inequality and discrimination against women, in public and private life, on a daily basis, in all parts of the world. At the same time, there has emerged a consensus that equality of opportunity for all people is essential to the construction of just and democratic societies for the twenty-first century. The fundamental linkages between the three objectives of the Conference- equality, development and peace-are now recognized by all.

The Platform for Action has emerged from a preparatory process more participatory and inclusive than any in history. Never before have so many women, representing both Governments and non-governmental organizations, gathered to share experiences and chart the way ahead. The United Nations has provided the venue and the framework to move issues of gender equality to the top of the global agenda. The women of the world have been the driving force to shape this agenda and move it forward.

The Platform for Action is a powerful agenda for the empowerment of women. It calls for the integration of gender perspectives in all policies and programmes. It focuses on concrete measures to address the critical areas of concern worldwide. The Platform for Action must be our guide and constant point of reference. I ask that it receive wide dissemination globally, regionally and locally.The implementation of its goals, objectives and measures must be actively monitored. And it must be further strengthened, as needed, to take account of new developments as they emerge.

As we set out on the road from Beijing, the Platform is a call for concrete action to make a difference:

- Action to protect and promoe the human rights of women and the girl child as an integral part of universal human rights;
- Action to eradicate the persistent and increasing burden of poverty on women;
- Action to remove the obstacles to women's full participation in public life and decisio-making, at all levels- including the family;
- Action to eliminate all forms of violence against women;
- Action to ensure equal access for girl children and women to education and health services;
- Action to promote economic autonomy for women, and ensure their access to productive resources; and

Action to encourage an equitable sharing of family responsibilities. The Platform for Action places heavy responsibilities on the United Nations system. It calls upon United Nations organizations to play a key role in follow-up, implementation and mnitoring. It poses a challenge to the capacity and commitment of the United Nations. As Secretary-General, I accept that challenge. I will ensure that the recommendations addressed to me are implemented swiftly and effectively. I am committed to placing the gender perspective into the mainstream of all aspects of the work of the Organization. I will work with my colleagues, the Executive Heads of the United Nations specialized agencies and the United Nations Programmes and Funds, to ensure a co-ordinated system-wide response,integrating the follow-up of this Conference with that of other global conferences. And I will keep Member States regularly informed of the progress that is made.

Executive Heads of the organization of the United Nations system have expressed their commitment to the advancment of women in the secretariats of the system as a policy priority. They have all committed themselves to developing specific policies and monitoring mechanisms to improve the status of women and, in particular, to increase the number of women in seniour and policy-making positions.

The United Nations system is already active on a number of fronts wich will prove critical to the implementation of the Platform. Reversing the trend towards the feminization of povery. Raising the educataional levels and health standards of women and girls. Expanding legal protection for women in the home. Establishing stronger protection for women in times of war. All these must be given priority.

I call on all Governments that have not yet done so to accede to and ratify United Nations human rights instruments and labour conventions-in particular the Convention on the Elimination of Discrimination Against Women and the Convention on the Rights of the Child.

In conclusion, let me emphasize the institutions of civil society which have played such an important role in preparing for this Conference. Since. I assumed the office of Secretary-General, I have spoken often of the evolution of civil society and its importance for economic, cultural and democratic advancement. More effective mechanisms to ensure partnership between Governments and civil society will contribute significantly to the implementation of the policies and measures that are called for in the Platform. The United Nations will intensify the close ties and working relationships that already exist with the NGO community at the global and national levels. The United Nations will be prepared to support Governments in their endeavours to foster and strengthen the institutions of civil society.

In a few weeks, the leaders of the world will meet at United Nations Headquarters in a Summit of Heads of State and Government. There they will mark the fiftieth anniversary of the founding of the United Nations.

As the world celebrates this anniversary, let us work together to ensure that the equal rights of men and women, enshrined in the Charter, become a reality.

Let us work together to implement the Platform for Action adopted here at Beijing. Let us tell the worl—and let us tell it with pride: the empowerment of women is the empowerment of all humanity!

B. BEIJING DECLARATION

1. We,the Governments participating in the Fourth World Conference on Women,
2. Gathered here in Beijing in September 1995, the year of the fiftieth anniversary of the founding of the United Nations,
3. Determined to advance the goals of eauality, development and peace for all women everywhere in the interest of all humanity,
4. Acknowledging the voices of all women everywhere and taking note of the diversity of women and their roles and circumstances, honouring the women who paved the way and inspred by the hope present in the world's youth,
5. Recognize that the status of women has advanced in some important respects in the past decade but that progress has been uneven, inequalities between women and men have persisted and major obstacles remian, with serious consequences for the well-being of all people,
6. Also recognize that this situation is exacerbated by the incrasing poverty that is affecting the lives of the majority of the world's people, in particular women and children, with origins in both the national and international domains,
7. Dedicate ourselves unreservedly to addressing these constraints and obstacles and thus enhancing further the advancement and empowerment of women all over the world, and agree that this requires urgent action in the spirit of determination, hope, co-operation and solidarity, now and to carry us forward into the next century.

We reaffirm our commitment to:

8. The equal rights and inherent human dignity of women and men and other purposes and principles enshrined in the Charter of the United Nations, to the Universal Declaration of Human Rights and other international human rights instruments, in particular the Convention on the Elimination of All Forms of Discrimination against Women and the Convention on the Rights of the Child, as well as the Declaration on the Elimination of Violence against Women and the Declaration on the Right to Development.
9. Ensure the full implementation of the human rights of women and of the girl child as an inalienable, integral and indivisible part of all

human rights and fundamental freedoms;

10. Build on consensus and progress made at previous United Nations conferences and summits—on women in Nairobi in 1985, on children in New York in 1990, on environment and development in Rio de Janeiro in 1992, on human rights in Vienna in 1993, on population and development in Cairo in 1994 and on social development in Copenhagen in 1995 with the objective of achieving equality, develop-ment and peace;
11. Achieve the full and effective implementation of the Nairobi Forward-looking Strategies for the Advancement of Women;
12. The empowerment and advancement of women, including the right to freedom of thought, conscience, religion and belief, thus contributing to the moral, ethical, spiritual and intellectual needs of women and men, individually or in community with others and thereby guaranteeing them the possibility of realizing their full potential in society and shaping their lives in accordance with their own aspirations.

We are Convinced that:

13. Women's empowerment and their full participation on the basis of equality in all spheres of society, including participation in the decision-making process and access to power, are fundamental for the achievement of equality, development and peace;
14. Women's rights are human rights;
15. Equal rights, opportunities and access to resources, equal sharing of responsibilities for the family by men and women, and a harmonious partnership between them are critical to their well-being and that of their families as well as to the consolidation of democracy;
16. Eradication of poverty based on sustained economic growth, social development, environmental protection and social justice requires the involvement of women in economic and social development, equal opportunities and the full and equal participation of women and men as agents and beneficiaries of people-centred sustainable development;
17. The explicit recognition and reaffirmation of the right of all women to control all aspects of their health, in particular their own fertility, is basic to their empowerment;
18. Local, national, regional and global peace is attainable and is inextricably linked with the advancement of women, who are a fundamental force for leadership, conflict resolution and the promotion of lasting peace at all levels;

19. It is essential to design, implement and monitor, with the full participation of women, effective, efficient and mutually reinforcing gender-sensitive policies and programmes, including development policies and programmes, at all levels that will foster the empowerment and advancement of women;
20. The participation and contribution of all actors of civil society, particu- larly women's groups and networks and other non-governmental organizations and community-based organizations, with full respect for their autonomy, in co-operation with Governments, are important to the effective implementation and follow-up of the Platform for Action;
21. The implementation of the Platform for Action requires commitment from Governments and the international community. By making national and international commitments for action, including those made at the Conference, Governments and the international community recognize the need to take priority action for the empowerment and advancement of women.

We are Determined to:

22. Intensify efforts and actions to achieve the goals of the Nairobi Forward-looking Strategies for the Advancement of Women by the end of this century;
23. Ensure the full enjoyment by women and the girl child of all human rights and fundamental freedoms and take effective action against violations of these rights and freedoms;
24. Take all necessary measures to eliminate all forms of discrimination against women and the girl child and remove all obstacles to gender equality and the advancement and empowerment of women;
25. Encourage men to participate fully in all actions towards equality;
26. Promote women's economic independence, including employment, and eradicate the persistent and increasing burden of poverty on women by addressing the structural causes of poverty through changes in economic structures, ensuring equal access for all women, including those in rural areas, as vital development agents, to productive resources, opportunities and public services;
27. Promote people-centred sustainable development, including sustained economic growth, through the provision of basic education, lifelong education, literacy and training, and primaly health care for girls and women;
28. Take positive steps to ensure peace for the advancement of women and, recognizing the leading role that women have played in the

peace movement, work actively towards general and complete disarmament under strict and effective international control, and support negotia- tions on the conclusion, without delay, of a universal and multilaterally and effectively verifiable comprehensive nuclear-test-ban treaty which contributes to nuclear disarmament and the prevention of the proliferation of nuclear weapons in all its aspects;

29. Prevent and eliminate all forms of violence against women and girls;
30. Ensure equal access to and equal treatment of women and men in education and health care and enhance women's sexual and reproductive health as well as education;
31. Promote and protect all human rights of women and girls;
32. Intensify efforts to ensure equal enjoyment of all human rights and fundamental freedoms for all women and girls who face multiple barriers to their empowerment and advancement because of such factors as their race, age, language, ethnicity, culture, religion, or disability, or because they are indigenous people;
33. Ensure respect for international law, including humanitarian law, in order to protect women and girls in particular;
34. Develop the fullest potential of girls and women of all ages, ensure their full and equal participation in building a better world for all and enhance their role in the development process.

We are Determined to:

35. Ensure women's equal access to economic resources, including land, credit, science and technology, vocational training, information, communication and markets, as a means to further the advancement and empowerment of women and girls, including through the enhancement of their capacities to enjoy the benefits of equal access to these resources, *inter alia,* by means of international co-operation;
36. Ensure the success of the Platform for Action, which will require a strong commitment on the part of Governments, international organizations and institutions at all levels. We are deeply convinced that economic development, social development and environmental protection are interdependent and mutually reinforcing components of sustainable development, which is the framework for our efforts to achieve a higher quality of life for all people. Equitable social development that recognizes empowering the poor, particularly women living in poverty, to utilize environmental resources sustainably is a necessary foundation for sustainable development. We also recognize that broad-based and sustained economic growth in the context of sustainable development is necessary to sustain social develop-

ment and social justice. The success of the Platform for Action will also require adequate mobilization of resources at the national and international levels as well as new and additional resources to the developing countries from all available funding mechanisms, including multilateral, bilateral and private sources for the advancement of women; financial resources to strengthen the capacity of national, subregional, regional and international institutions; a commitment to equal rights, equal responsibilities and equal opportunities and to the equal participation of women and men in all national, regional and international bodies and policymaking processes; and the establishment or strengthening of mechanisms at all levels for accountability to the world's women;

37. Ensure also the success of the Platform for Action in countries with economies in transition, which will require continued international co-operation and assistance;
38. We hereby adopt and commit ourselves as Governments to implement the following Platform for Action, ensuring that a gender perspective is reflected in all our policies and programmes. We Urge the United Nations system, regional and intemational financial institutions, other relevant regional and international institutions and all women and men, as well as non-governmental organizations, with full respect for their autonomy, and all sectors of civil society, in co-operation with Governments, to fully commit themselves and contribute to the implementation of this Platform for Action.

C. PLATFORM FOR ACTION

1. Mission Statement

1. The Platform for Action is an agenda for women's empowerment. It aims at accelerating the implementation of the Nairobi Fonvard-looking Strategies for the Advancement of Women[1] and at removing all the obstacles to women's active participation in all spheres of public and private life through a full and equal share in economic, social, cultural and political decision-making. This means that the principle of shared power and respon-sibility should be established between women and men at home, in the workplace and in the wider national and international communities. Equality between women and men is a matter of human rights and a condition for social justice and is also a necessary and fundamental prerequisite for equality, development and peace. A transformed partnership based on equality between women and men is a condition for people-

centred sus-tainable development. A sustained and long-term commitment is essential, so that women and men can work together for themselves, for their children and for society to meet the challenges of the twenty-first century.

2. The Platform for Action reaffirms the fundamental principle set forth in the Vienna Declaration and Programme ofAction,[2] adopted by the World Conference on Human Rights, that the human rights of women and of the girl child are an inalienable, integral and indivisible part of universal human rights. As an agenda for action, the Platform seeks to promote and protect the full enjoyment of all human rights and the fundamental freedoms of all women throughout their life cycle.
3. The Platform for Action emphasizes that women share common concerns that can be addressed only by working together and in partnership with men towards the common goal of gender* equality around the world. It respects and values the full diversity of women's situations and conditions and recognizes that some women face particular barriers to their empowerment.
4. The Platform for Action requires immediate and concerted action by all to create a peaceful, just and humane world based on human rights and fundamental freedoms, including the principle of equality for all people of all ages and from all walks of life, and to this end, recognizes that broad-based and sustained economic growth in the context of sustainable development is necessary to sustain social development and social justice.
5. The success of the Platform for Action will require a strong commit-ment on the part of Governments, international organizations and institu-tions at all levels. It will also require adequate mobilization of resources at the national and international levels as well as new and additional resources to the developing countries from all available funding mechanisms, including multilateral, bilateral and private sources for the advancement of women; financial resources to strengthen the capacity of national, subregional, regional and international institutions; a commitment to equal rights,equal responsibilities and equal opportunities and to the equal participation of women and men in all national, regional and international bodies and policy-making processes; and the establishment or strengthening of mechanisms at all levels for accountability to the world's women.

---

* For the commonly understood meaning of the term "gender", see annex IV to the present report.

2. Global Framework

6. The Fourth World Conference on Women is taking place as the world stands poised on the threshold of a new millennium.
7. The Platform for Action upholds the Convention on the Elimination of All Forms of Discrimination against Women[3] and builds upon the Nairobi Forward-looking Strategies for the Advancement of Women, as well as relevant resolutions adopted by the Economic and Social Council and the General Assembly. The formulation of the Platform for Action is aimed at establishing a basic group of priority actions that should be carried out during the next five years.
8. The Platform for Action recognizes the importance of the agreements reached at the World Summit for Children, the United Nations Conference on Environment and Development, the World Conference on Human Rights, the International Conference on Population and Development and the World Summit for Social Development, which set out specific approaches and commitments to fostering sustainable development and international co-operation and to strengthening the role of the United Nations to that end. Similarly, the Global Conference on the Sustainable Development of Small Island Developing States, the International Conference on Nutrition, the International Conference on Primary Health Care and the World Conference on Education for All have addressed the various facets of development and human rights, within their specific perspectives, paying significant attention to the role of women and girls. In addition, the International Year for the World's Indigenous People,[4] the International Year of the Family,j the United Nations Year for Tolerance,[6] the Geneva Declaration for Rural Women,[7] and the Declaration on the Elimination of Violence against Women[8] have also emphasized the issues of women's empowerment and equality.
9. The objective of the Platform for Action, which is in full conformity with the purposes and principles of the Charter of the United Nations and international law, is the empowerment of all women. The full realization of all human rights and fundamental freedoms of all women is essential for the empowerment of women. While the significance of national and regional particularities and various historical, cultural and religious backgrounds must be borne in mind, it is the duty of States, regardless of their political, economic and cultural systems, to promote and protect all human rights and fundamental freedoms.[9] The implementation of this Platform, including through national laws and the formulation ofstrategies, policies, programmes and development priorities, is the Sovereign re-

sponsibility of each State, in conformity with all human rights and fundamental freedoms, and the significance of and full respect for various religious and ethical values, cultural backgrounds and philosophical convictions of individuals and their commu nities should contribute to the full enjoyment by women of their human rights in order to achieve equality, development and peace.

10. Since the World Conference to Review and Appraise the Achievements of the United Nations Decade for Women: Equality, Development and Peace, held at Nairobi in 1985, and the adoption of the Nairobi Forward-looking Strategies for the Advancement of Women, the world has experienced profound political, economic, social and cultural changes, which have had both positive and negative effects on women. The World Conference on Human Rights recognized that the human rights of women and the girl-child are an inalienable, integral and indivisible part of universal human rights. The full and equal participation of women in political, civil, economic, social and cultural life at the national, regional and international levels, and the eradication of all forms of discrimination on the grounds of sex are priority objectives of the international community. The World Conference on Human Rights reaffirmed the solemn commitment of all States to fulfil their obligations to promote universal respect for, and observance and protection of, all human rights and fundamental free-doms for all in accordance with the Charter of the United Nations, other instruments related to human rights and international law. The universal nature of these rights and freedoms is beyond question.

11. The endof the cold war has resulted in international changes and diminished competition between the Super-Powers. The threat of a global armed conflict has diminished, while international relations have improved and prospects for peace among nations have increased. Although the threat of global conflict has been reduced, wars of aggression, armed conflicts, colonial or other forms of alien domination and foreign occupation, civil wars and terrorism continue to plague many parts of the world. Grave violations of the human rights of women occur, particularly in times of armed conflict, and include murder, torture, systematic rape, forced pregnancy and forced abortion, in particular under policies of ethnic cleansing.

12. The maintenance of peace and security at the global, regional and local levels, together with the prevention of policies of aggression

and ethnic cleansing and the resolution of armed conflict, is crucial for the protection of the human rights of women and girl-children, as well as for the elimination of all forms of violence against them and of their use as a weapon of war.

13. Excessive military expenditures, including global military expenditures and arms trade or trafficking, and investments for arms production and acquisition have reduced the resources available for social development. As a result of the debt burden and other economic difficulties, many developing countries have undertaken structural adjustment policies. Moreover, there are structural adjustment programmes that have been poorly designed and implemented, with resulting detrimental effects on social development. The number of people living in poverty has increased disproportionately in most developing countries, particularly the heavily indebted countries, during the past decade.

14. In this context, the social dimension of development should be emphasized. Accelerated economic growth, although necessary for social development, does not by itself improve the quality of life of the population. In some cases, conditions can arise which can aggravate social inequality and marginalization. Hence, it is indispensable to search for new alternatives that ensure that all members of society benefit from economic growth based on a holistic approach to all aspects of development: growth, equality between women and men, social justice, conservation and protection of the environment, sustainability, solidarity, participation, peace and respect for human rights.

15. A worldwide movement towards democratization has opened up the political process in many nations, but the popular participation of women in key decision-making as full and equal partners with men, particularly in politics, has not yet been achieved. South Africa's policy of institutionalized racism — apartheid — has been dismantled and a peaceful and democratic transfer of power has occurred. In Central and Eastern Europe the transition to parliamentary democracy has been rapid and has given rise to a variety of experiences, depending on the specific circumstances of each country. While the transition has been mostly peaceful, in some countries this process has been hindered by armed conflict that has resulted in grave violations of human rights.

16. Widespread economic recession, as well as political instability in some regions, has been responsible for setting back development goals in many countries. This has led to the expansion of unspeak-

able poverty. Of the more than 1 billion people living in abject poverty, women are an overwhelming majority. The rapid process of change and adjustment in all sectors has also led to increased unemployment and underemployment, with particular impact on women. In many cases, structural adjustment programmes have not been designed to minimize their negative effects on vulnerable and disadvantaged groups or on women, nor have they been designed to assure positive effects on those groups by preventing their marginalization in economic and social activities. The Final Act of the Uruguay Round of multilateral trade negotiations[10] underscored the increasing interdependence of national economies, as well as the importance of trade liberalization and access to open, dynamic markets. There has also been heavy military spending in some regions. Despite increases in official development assistance (ODA) by some countries, ODA has recently declined overall.

17. Absolute poverty and the feminization of poverty, unemployment, the increasing fragility of the environment, continued violence against women and the widespread exclusion of half of humanity from institutions of power and governance underscore the need to continue the search for development, peace and security and for ways of assuring people-centred sustainable development. The participation and leadership of the half of humanity that is female is essential to the success of that search. Therefore, only a new era of international co-operation among Governments and peoples based on a spirit of partnership, an equitable, international social and economic environment, and a radical transformation of the relationship between women and men to one of full and equal partnership will enable the world to meet the challenges of the twenty-first century.

18. Recent international economic developments have had in many cases a disproportionate impact on women and children, the majority of whom live in developing countries. For those States that have carried a large burden of foreign debt, structural adjustment programmes and measures, though beneficial in the long term, have led to a reduction in social expenditures, thereby adversely affecting women, particularly in Africa and the least developed countries. This is exacerbated when responsibilities for basic social services have shifted from Governments to women.

19. Economic recession in many developed and developing countries, as well as ongoing restructuring in countries with economies in transition, have had a disproportionately negative impact on women's

employment. Women often have no choice but to take employment that lacks long-term job security or involves dangerous working conditions, to work in unprotected home-based production or to be unemployed. Many women enter the labour market in under-remunerated and undervalued jobs, seeking to improve their household income; others decide to migrate for the same purpose. Without any reduction in their other responsibilities, this has increased the total bur-den of work for women.

20. Macro- and microeconomic policies and programmes, including structural adjustment, have not always been designed to take account of their impact on women and girl-children, especially those living in poverty. Poverty has increased in both absolute and relative terms, and the number of women living in poverty has increased in most regions. There are many urban women living in poverty; however, the plight of women living in rural and remote areas deserves special attention given the stagnation of development in such areas. In developing countries, even those in which national indicators have shown improvement, the majority of rural women continue to live in conditions of economic underdevelopment and social marginalization.
21. Women are key contributors to the economy and to combating poverty through both remunerated and unremunerated work at home, in the community and in the workplace. Growing numbers of women have achieved economic independence through gainful employment.
22. One fourth of all households worldwide are headed by women and many other households are dependent on female income even where men are present. Female-maintained households are very often among the poorest because of wage discrimination, occupational segregation patterns in the labour market and other gender-based barriers. Family disintegration, population movements between urban and rural areas within countries, international migration, war and internal displacements are factors contributing to the rise of female-headed households.
23. Recognizing that the achievement and maintenance of peace and security are a precondition for economic and social progress, women are increasingly establishing themselves as central actors in a variety of capacities in the movement of humanity for peace. Their full participation in decision-making, conflict prevention and resolution and all other peace initiatives is essential to the realization of lasting peace.
24. Religion, spirituality and belief play a central role in the lives of

millions of women and men, in the way they live and in the aspirations they have for the future. The right to freedom of thought, conscience and religion is inalienable and must be universally enjoyed. This right includes the freedom to have or to adopt the religion or belief of their choice either individually or in community with others, in public or in private, and to manifest their religion or belief in worship, observance, practice and teaching. In order to realize equality, development and peace, there is a need to respect these rights and freedoms fully. Religion, thought, conscience and belief may, and can, contribute to fulfilling women's and men's moral, ethical and spiritual needs and to realizing their full potential in society. However, it is acknowledged that any form of extremism may have a negative impact on women and can lead to violence and discrimination.

25. The Fourth World Conference on Women should accelerate the process that formally began in 1975, which was proclaimed International Women's Year by the United Nations General Assembly. The Year was a turning-point in that it put women's issues on the agenda. The United Nations Decade for Women (1976-1985) was a worldwide effort to examine the status and rights of women and to bring women into decision-making at all levels. In 1979, the General Assembly adopted the Convention on the Elimination of All Forms of Discrimination against Women, which entered into force in 1981 and set an international standard for what was meant by equality between women and men. In 1985, the World Conference to Review and Appraise the Achievements of the United Nations Decade for Women: Equality Development and Peace adopted the Nairobi Forward-looking Strategies for the Advancement of Women, to be implemented by the year 2000. There has been important progress in achieving equality between women and men. Many Governments have enacted legislation to promote equality between women and men and have established national machineries to ensure the mainstreaming of gender perspectives in all spheres of society. International agencies have focused greater atten-tion on women's status and roles.

26. The growing strength of the non-governmental sector, particularly women's organizations and feminist groups, has become a driving force for change. Non-governmental organizations have played an important advocacy role in advancing legislation or mechanisms to ensure the promotion of women. They have also become catalysts for new approaches to development. Many Governments have in-

creasingly recognized the important role that non-governmental organizations play and the importance of working with them for progress. Yet, in some countries, Governments continue to restrict the ability of non-governmental organizations to operate freely. Women, through non-governmental organizations, have participated in and strongly influenced community, national, regional and global forums and international debates.

27. Since 1975, knowledge of the status of women and men, respectively, has increased and is contributing to further actions aimed at promoting equality between women and men. In several countries, there have been important changes in the relationships between women and men, espe-cially where there have been major advances in education for women and significant increases in their participation in the paid labour force. The boundaries of the gender division of labour between productive and repro- ductive roles are gradually being crossed as women have started to enter formerly male-dominated areas of work and men have started to accept greater responsibility for domestic tasks, including child care. However, changes in women's roles have been greater and much more rapid than changes in men's roles. In many countries, the differences between women's and men's achievements and activities are still not recognized as the consequences of socially constructed gender roles rather than immutable biological differences.

28. Moreover, 10 years after the Nairobi Conference, equality between women and men has still not been achieved. On average, women represent a mere 10 per cent of all elected legislators worldwide and in most national and international administrative structures, both public and private, they remain underrepresented. The United Nations is no exception. Fifty years after its creation, the United Nations is continuing to deny itself the benefits of women's leadership by their underrepresentation at decision-making levels within the Secretariat and the specialized agencies.

29. Women play a critical role in the family. The family is the basic unit of society and as such should be strengthened. It is entitled to receive comprehensive protection and support. In different cultural, political and social systems, various forms of the family exist. The rights, capabilities and responsibilities of family members must be respected. Women make a great contribution to the welfare of the family and to the development of society, which is still not recognized or considered in its full importance. The social significance of maternity, motherhood and the role of parents in the family and in

the upbringing of children should be acknowledged. The upbringing of children requires shared responsibility of parents, women and men and society as a whole. Maternity, motherhood, parenting and the role of women in procreation must not be a basis for discrimination nor restrict the full participation of women in society. Recognition should also be given to the important role often played by women in many countries in caring for other members of their family.

30. While the rate of growth of world population is on the decline, world population is at an all-time high in absolute numbers, with current increments approaching 86 million persons annually. Two other major demographic trends have had profound repercussions on the dependency ratio within families. In many developing countries, 45 to 50 per cent of the pop-ulation is less than 15 years old, while in industrialized nations both the number and proportion of elderly people are increasing. According to United Nations projections, 72 per cent of the population over 60 years of age will be living in developing countries by the year 2025, and more than half of that population will be women. Care of children, the sick and the elderly is a responsibility that falls disproportionately on women, owing to lack of equality and the unbalanced distribution of remunerated and unremunerated work between women and men.

31. Many women face particular barriers because of various diverse factors in addition to their gender. Often these diverse factors isolate or marginalize such women. They are, *inter alia,* denied their human rights, they lack access or are denied access to education and vocational training, employment, housing and economic self-sufficiency and they are excluded from decision-making processes. Such women are often denied the opportunity to contribute to their communities as part of the mainstream.

32. The past decade has also witnessed a growing recognition of the distinct interests and concerns of indigenous women, whose identity, cultural traditions and forms of social organization enhance and strengthen the com-munities in which they live. Indigenous women often face barriers both as women and as members of indigenous communities.

33. In the past 20 years, the world has seen an explosion in the field of com-munications. With advances in computer technology and satellite and cable television, global access to information continues to increase and expand, creating new opportunities for the participation of women in communications and the mass media and for the

dissemination of information about women. However, global communication networks have been used to spread stereotyped and demeaning images of women for narrow commercial and consumerist purposes. Until women participate equally in both the technical and decision-making areas of communications and the mass media, including the arts, they will continue to be misrepresented and awareness of the reality of women's lives will continue to be lacking. The media have a great potential to promote the advancement of women and the equality of women and men by portraying women and men in a non-stereotypical, diverse and balanced manner, and by respecting the dignity and worth of the human person..

34. The continuing environmental degradation that affects all human lives often has a more direct impact on women. Women's health and their liveli-hood are threatened by pollution and toxic wastes, large-scale deforestation, desertification, drought and depletion of the soil and of coastal and marine resources, with a rising incidence of environmentally related health problems and even death reported among women and girls. Those most affected are rural and indigenous women, whose livelihood and daily subsistence depends directly on sustainable ecosystems.
35. Poverty and environmental degradation are closely interrelated. While poverty results in certain kinds of environmental stress, the major cause of the continued deterioration of the global environment is the unsustainable patterns of consumption and production, particularly in industrialized countries, which are a matter of grave concern and aggravate poverty and imbalances.
36. Global trends have brought profound changes in family survival strategies and structures. Rural to urban migration has increased substantially in all regions. The global urban population is projected to reach 47 per cent of the total population by the year 2000. An estimated 125 million people are migrants, refugees and displaced persons, half of whom live in developing countries. These massive movements of people have profound consequences for family structures and well-being and have unequal consequences for women and men, including in many cases the sexual exploitation of women.
37. According to World Health Organization (WHO) estimates, by the beginning of 1995 the number of cumulative cases of acquired immunodeficiency syndrome (AIDS) was 4.5 million. An estimated 19.5 million men, women and children have been infected with the human immunodeficiency virus (HIV) since it was first diagnosed and it is projected that another 20 million will be infected by the end

of the decade. Among new cases, women are twice as likely to be infected as men. In the early stage of the AIDS pandemic, women were not infected in large numbers; however, about 8 million women are now infected. Young women and adolescents are particularly vulnerable. It is estimated that by the year 2000 more than 13 million women will be infected and 4 million women will have died from AIDS-related conditions. In addition, about 250 million new cases of sexually transmitted diseases are estimated to occur every year. The rate of transmission of sexually transmitted diseases, including HIV/AIDS, is increasing at an alarming rate among women and girls, especially in developing countries.

38. Since 1975, significant knowledge and information have been generated about the status of women and the conditions in which they live. Throughout their entire life cycle, women's daily existence and long-term aspirations are restricted by discriminatory attitudes, unjust social and economic structures, and a lack of resources in most countries that prevent their full and equal participation. In a number of countries, the practice of prenatal sex selection, higher rates of mortality among very young girls and lower rates of school enrolment for girls as compared with boys suggest that son preference is curtailing the access of girl-children to food, education and health care and even life itself. Discrimination against women begins at the earliest stages of life and must therefore be addressed from then onwards.

39. The girl-child of today is the woman of tomorrow. The skills, ideas and energy of the girl-child are vital for full attainment of the goals of equality, development and peace. For the girl-child to develop her full potential she needs to be nurtured in an enabling environment, where her spiritual, intellectual and material needs for survival, protection and development are met and her equal rights safeguarded. If women are to be equal partners with men, in every aspect of life and development, now is the time to recognize the human dignity and worth of the girl-child and to ensure the full enjoyment of her human rights and fundamental freedoms, including the rights assured by the Convention on the Rights of the Child,[11] universal ratification of which is strongly urged. Yet there exists worldwide evidence that discrimination and violence against girls begin at the earliest stages of life and continue unabated throughout their lives. They often have less access to nutrition, physical and mental health care and education and enjoy fewer rights, opportunities and benefits of childhood and adolescence than do boys. They are often

subjected to various forms of sexual and economic exploitation, paedophilia, forced prostitution and possibly the sale of their organs and tissues, violence and harmful practices such as female infanticide and prenatal sex selection, incest, female genital mutilation and early marriage, including child marriage.

40. Half the world's population is under the age of 25 and most of the world's youth—more than 85 per cent—live in developing countries. Policy makers must recognize the implications of these demographic factors. Special measures must be taken to ensure that young women have the life skills necessary for active and effective participation in all levels of social, cultural, political and economic leadership. It will be critical for the international community to demonstrate a new commitment to the future—a commitment to inspiring a new generation of women and men to work together for a more just society. This new generation of leaders must accept and promote a world in which every child is free from injustice, oppression and inequality and free to develop her/his own potential. The principle of equality of women and men must therefore be integral to the socialization process.

3. Critical Areas of Concern

41. The advancement of women and the achievement of equality between women and men are a matter of human rights and a condition for social justice and should not be seen in isolation as a women's issue. They are the only way to build a sustainable, just and developed society. Empowerment of women and equality between women and men are prerequisites for achieving political, social, economic, cultural and environmental security among all peoples.

42. Most of the goals set out in the Nairobi Forward-looking Strategies for the Advancement of Women have not been achieved. Barriers to women's empowerment remain, despite the efforts of Governments, as well as non-governmental organizations and women and men everywhere. Vast political, economic and ecological crises persist in many parts of the world. Among them are wars of aggression, armed conflicts, colonial or other forms of alien domination or foreign occupation, civil wars and terrorism. These situations, combined with systematic or de facto discrimination, violations of and failure to protect all human rights and fundamental freedoms of all women, and their civil, cultural, economic, political and social rights, induding the right to development and ingrained prejudicial attitudes towards women and girls are but a few of the impediments

encountered since the World Conference to Review and Appraise the Achievements of the United Nations Decade for Women: Equality Development and Peace, in 1985.

43. A review of progress since the Nairobi Conference highlights special concerns—areas of particular urgency that stand out as priorities for action. All actors should focus action and resources on the strategic objectives relating to the critical areas of concern which are, necessarily, interre-lated, interdependent and of high priority. There is a need for these actors to develop and implement mechanisms of accountability for all the areas of concern.

44. To this end, Governments, the international community and civil society, including non-governmental organizations and the private sector, are called upon to take strategic action in the following critical areas of concern:

* The persistent and increasing burden of poverty on women
* Inequalities and inadequacies in and unequal access to education and training
* Inequalities and inadequacies in and unequal access to health care and related services
* Violence against women
* The effects of armed or other kinds of conflict on women, including those living under foreign occupation
* Inequality in economic structures and policies, in all forms of productive activities and in access to resources
* Inequality between men and women in the sharing of power and deci-sion-making at all levels
* Insufficient mechanisms at all levels to promote the advancement of women
* Lack of respect for and inadequate promotion and protection of the human rights of women
* Stereotyping of women and inequality in women's access to and participation in all communication systems, especially in the media
* Gender inequalities in the management of natural resources and in the safeguarding of the environment
* Persistent discrimination against and violation of the rights of the girl-child

4. Strategic Objectives and Actions

45. In each critical area of concern, the problem is diagnosed and strategic objectives are proposed with concrete actions to be taken by

various actors in order to achieve those objectives. The strategic objectives are derived from the critical areas of concern and specific actions to be taken to achieve them cut across the boundaries of equality, development and peace—the goals of the Nairobi Forward-looking Strategies for the Advancement of Women—and reflect their interdependence. The objectives and actions are interlinked, of high priority and mutually reinforcing. The Platform for Action is intended to improve the situation of all women, without exception, who often face similar barriers, while special attention should be given to groups that are the most disadvantaged.

46. The Platform for Action recognizes that women face barriers to full equality and advancement because of such factors as their race, race, age, language, ethnicity, culture, religion or disability, because they are indigenous women or because of other status. Many women encounter specific obstacles related to their family status, particularly as single parents; and to their socio-economic status, including their living conditions in rural, isolated or impoverished areas. Additional barriers also exist for refugee women, other displaced women, including internally displaced women as well asa for immigrant women and migrant women, including women migrant workers. Many women are also particularly affected by environmental disasters, serious and infectious diseases and various forms of violence against women.

A. Women and Poverty

47. More than 1 billion people in the world today, the great majority of whom are women, live in unacceptable conditions of poverty, mostly in the developing countries. Poverty has various causes, including structural ones. Poverty is a complex, multidimensional problem, with origins in both the national and international domains. The globalization of the world's economy and the deepening interdependence among nations present challenges and opportunities for sustained economic growth and development, as well as risks and uncertainties for the future of the world economy. The uncertain global economic climate has been accompanied by economic restructuring as well as, in a certain number of countries, persistent, unmanagr cable levels of external debt and structural adjustment programmes. Inaddition, all types of conflict, displacement of people and environmental degradation have undermined the capacity of Governments to meet the basic needs of their populations. Transformations in the world economy are profoundly changing the parameters of social development in all countries. One significant trend

has been the increased poverty of women, the extent of which varies from region to region. The gender disparities in economic power-sharing are also an important contributing factor to the poverty of women. Migration and consequent changes in family structures have placed additional burdens on women, especially those who provide for several dependents. Macroeconomic policies need rethinking and reformulation to address such trends. These policies focus almost exclusively on the formal sector. They also tend to impede the initiatives of women and fail to consider the differential impact on women and men. The application of gender analysis to a wide range of policies and programmes is therefore critical to poverty reduction strategies. In order to eradicate poverty and achieve sustainable development, women and men must participate fully and equally in the formulation of macroeconomic and social policies and strategies for the eradication of poverty. The eradication of poverty cannot be accomplished through anti-poverty programmes alone but will require democratic participation and changes in economic structures in order to ensure access for all women to resources, opportunitierand public services. Poverty has various manifestations, including lack of income and productive resources sufficient to ensure a sustainable livelihood; hunger and malnutrition; ill health; limited or lack of access to education and other basic services; increasing morbidity and mortality from illness; homelessness and inadequate housing; unsafe environments; and social discrimination and exclusion. It is also characterized by lack of participation in decision-making and in civil, social and cultural life. It occurs in all countries—as mass poverty in many developing countries and as pockets of poverty amidst wealth in developed countries. Poverty may be caused by an economic recession that results in loss of livelihood or by disaster or conflict. There is also the poverty of low-wage workers and the utter destitution of people who fall outside family support systems, social institutions and safety nets.

48. In the past decade the number of women living in poverty has increased disproportionately to the number of men, particularly in the developing countries. The feminization of poverty has also recently become a significant problem in the countries with economies in transition as a short-term consequence of the process of political, economic and social transformation. In addition to economic factors, the rigidity of socially ascribed gender roles and women's limited access to power, education, training and productive resources as well as other emerging factors that may lead to insecurity for

families are also responsible. The failure to adequately mainstream a gender perspective in all economic analysis and planning and to address the structural causes of poverty is also a contributing factor.

49. Women contribute to the economy and to combating poverty through both remunerated and unremunerated work at home, in the community and in the workplace. The empowerment of women is a critical factor in the eradication of poverty.

50. While poverty affects households as a whole, because of the gender division of labour and responsibilities for household welfare, women bear a disproportionate burden, attempting to manage household consumption and production under conditions of increasing scarcity. Poverty is particularly acute for women living in rural households.

51. Women's poverty is directly related to the absence of economic opportunities and autonomy, lack of access to economic resources, including credit, land ownership and inheritance, lack of access to education and support services and their minimal participation in the decision-making process. Poverty can also force women into situations in which they are vulnerable to sexual exploitation.

52. In too many countries, social welfare systems do not take sufficient account of the specific conditions of women living in poverty, and there is a tendency to scale back the services provided by such systems. The risk of falling into poverty is greater for women than for men, particularly in old age, where social security systems are based on the principle of continuous remunerated employment. In some cases, women do not fulfil this requirement because of interruptions in their work, due to the unbalanced distribution of remunerated and unremunerated work. Moreover, older women also face greater obstacles to labour-market re-entry.

53. In many developed countries, where the level of general education and professional training of women and men are similar and where systems of protection against discrimination are available, in some sectors the economic transformations of the past decade have strongly increased either the unemployment of women or the precarious nature of their employment. The proportion of women among the poor has consequently increased. In countries with a high level of school enrolment of girls, those who leave the educational system the earliest, without any qualification, are among the most vulnerable in the labour market.

54. In countries with economies in transition and in other countries undergoing fundamental political, economic and social transforma-

tions, these transformations have often led to a reduction in women's income or to women being deprived of income.

55. Particularly in developing countries, the productive capacity of women should be increased through access to capital, resources, credit, land, technology, information, technical assistance and training so as to raise their income and improve nutrition, education, health care and status within the household. The release of women's productive potential is pivotal to breaking the cycle of poverty so that women can share fully in the benefits of development and in the products of their own labour.

56. Sustainable development and economic growth that is both sustained and sustainable are possible only through improving the economic, social, political, legal and cultural status of women. Equitable social development that recognizes empowering the poor, particularly women, to utilize environmental resources sustainably is a necessary foundation for sustainable development.

57. The success of policies and measures aimed at supporting or strengthening the promotion of gender equality and the improvement of the status of women should be based on the integration of the gender perspective in general policies relating to all spheres of society as well as the implementation of positive measures with adequate institutional and financial support at all levels.

Strategic objective A.1.

Review adopt and maintain macroeconomic policies and development strategies that address the needs and efforts of women in poverty

Actions to be taken

58. By Governments:

(a) Review and modify, with the full and equal participation of women, macroeconomic and social policies with a view to achieving the objectives of the Platform for Action;

(b) Analyse, from a gender perspective, policies and programmes—including those related to macroeconomic stability, structural adjustment, external debt problems, taxation, investments, employment, markets and all relevant sectors of the economy—with respect to their impact on poverty, on inequality and particularly on women; assess their impact on family well-being and conditions and adjust them, as appropriate, to promote more equitable distribution of productive assets, wealth, opportunities,income and services;

(c) Pursue and implement sound and stable macroeconomic and sectoral policies that are designed and monitored with the full and equal participation of women, encourage broad-based sustained economic growth, address the structural causes of poverty and are geared towards eradicating poverty and reducing gender-based inequality within the overall framework of achieving people-centred sustainable development;

(d) Restructure and target the allocation of public expenditures to promote women's economic opportunities and equal access to pro-ductive resources and to address the basic social, educational and health needs of women, particularly those living in poverty;

(e) Develop agricultural and fishing sectors, where and as necessary, in order to ensure, as appropriate, household and national food secu-rity and food self-sufficiency, by allocating the necessary financial, technical and human resources;

(f) Develop policies and programmes to promote equitable distribution of food within the household;

(g) Provide adequate safety nets and strengthen State-based and com-munity-based support systems, as an integral part of social policy, in order to enable women living in poverty to withstand adverse economic environments and preserve their livelihood, assets and revenues in times of crisis;

(h) Generate economic policies that have a positive impact on the employment and income of women workers in both the formal and informal sectors and adopt specific measures to address women's unemployment, in particular their long-term unemployment;

(i) Formulate and implement, when necessary, specific economic, social, agricultural and related policies in support of female-headed households;

(j) Develop and implement anti-poverty programmes, including employment schemes, that improve access to food for women living in poverty, including through the use of appropriate pricing and distribution mechanisms;

(k) Ensure the full realization of the human rights of all women migrants, including women migrant workers, and their protection against violence and exploitation; introduce measures for the empowerment of documented women migrants, including women migrant workers; facilitate the productive employment of documented migrant women through greater recognition of their skills, foreign education and credentials, and facilitate their full integration into the labour force;

(l) Introduce measures to integrate or reintegrate women iving in poverty and socially marginalized women into productive employment and the economic mainstream; ensure that internally displaced women have full access to economic opportunities and that the qualifications and skills of immigrant and refugee women are recognized;

(m) Enable women to obtain affordable housing and access to land by, among other things, removing all obstacles to access, with special emphasis on meeting the needs of women, especially those living in poverty and female heads of household;

(n) Formulate and implement policies and programmes that enhance the access of women agricultural and fisheries producers (including subsistence farmers and producers, especially in rural areas) to financial, technical, extension and marketing services; provide access to and control of land, appropriate infrastructure and technology in order to increase women's incomes and promote household food security, especially in rural areas and, where appropriate, encourage the development of producer-owned, market-based co-operatives;

(o) Create social security systems wherever they do not exist, or review them with a view to placing individual women and men on an equal footing, at every stage of their lives;

(p) Ensure access to free or low-cost legal services, including legal literacy, especially designed to reach women living in poverty;

(q) Take particular measures to promote and strengthen policies and programmes for indigenous women with their full participation and respect for their cultural diversity, so that they have opportunities and the possibility of choice in the development process in order to eradicate the poverty that affects them.

59. By multilateral financial and development institutions, including the World Bank, the International Monetary Fund and regional development institutions, and through bilateral development co-operation:

(a) In accordance with the commitments made at the World Summit for Social Development, seek to mobilize new and additional financial resources that are both adequate and predictable and mobilized in a way that maximizes the availability of such resources and uses all available funding sources and mechanisms with a view to contributing towards the goal of poverty eradication and targeting women living in poverty;

(b) Strengthen analytical capacity in order to more systematically strengthen gender perspectives and integrate them into the design and implementation of lending programmes, including structural adjustment and economic recovery programmes;

(c) Find effective development-oriented and durable solutions to external debt problems in order to help them to finance programmes and projects targeted at development, including the advancement of women, *inter alia,* through the immediate implementation of the terms of debt forgiveness agreed upon in the Paris Club in December 1994, which encompassed debt reduction, including cancellation or other debt relief measures and develop techniques of debt conversion applied to social development programmes and projects in conformity with the priorities of the Platform for Action;

(d) Invite the international financial institutions to examine innovative approaches to assisting low-income countries with a high propertion of multilateral debt, with a view to alleviating their debt burthat

(e) Ensure that structural adjustment programmes are designed to minimize their negative effects on vulnerable and disadvantaged groups and communities and to assure their positive effects on such groups and communities by preventing their marginalization in economic and social activities and devising measures to ensure that they gain access to and control over economic resources and economic and social activities; take actions to reduce inequality and economic disparity;

(f) Review the impad of structural adjustment programmes on social development by means of gender-sensitive social impact assessments and other relevant methods, in order to develop policies to reduce their negative effects and improve their positive impact ensuring that women do not bear a disproportionate burden of transition costs; complement adjustment lending with enhanced, targeted social development lending;

(g) Create an enabling environment that allows women to build and maintain sustainable livelihoods.

60. By national and international non-governmental organizations and women's groups:

(a) Mobilize all parties involved in the development process, including academic institutions, non-governmental organizations and grass-roots and women's groups, to improve the effectiveness of anti-poverty programmes directed towards the poorest and most disadvantaged groups of women, such as rural and indigenous women, female heads of household, young women and older women, refugees and migrant women and women with disabilities, recognizing that social development is primarily the responsibility of Governments;

(b) Engage in lobbying and establish monitoring mechanisms, as appropriate, and other relevant activities to ensure implementation of the recommendations on poverty eradication outlined in the Platform for Action and aimed at ensuring accountability and transparency from the State and private sectors;

(c) Include in their activities womenwith diverse needs and recognize that youth organizations are increasingly becoming effective partners in development programmes;

(d) In cooperation with the government and private sectors, participate in the development of a comprehensive national strategy for improving health, education and social services so that girls and women of all ages living in poverty have full access to such services; seek funding to secure access to services with a gender perspective and to extend those services in order to reach the rural and remote areas that are not covered by government institutions;

(e) In co-operation with Governments, employers, other social partners and relevant parties, contribute to the development of education and training and retraining policies to ensure that women can acquire a wide range of skills to meet new demands;

(f) Mobilize to protect women's right to full and equal access to eco-nomic resources, including the right to inheritance and to owner-ship of land and other property, credit, natural resources and appropriate technologies.

Strategic objective A.2.

Revise laws and administrative pradices to ensure women's equal rights and access to economic resources

Actions to be taken

61. By Governments:

(a) Ensure access to free or low-cost legal services, including legal literacy, especially designed to reach women living in poverty;

(b) Undertake legislative and administrative reforms to give women full and equal access to economic resources, including the right to inheritance and to ownership of land and other property, credit, natural resources and appropriate technologies;

(c) Consider ratification of Convention No 169 of the International Labour Organization (ILO) as part of their efforts to promote and protect the rights of indigenous people.

Strategic objective A.3.
Provide women with access to savings and credit mechanisms and institutions

Actions to be taken

62. By Governments:

(a) Enhance the access of disadvantaged women, including women entrepreneurs, in rural, remote and urban areas to financial services through strengthening links between the formal banks and intermediary lending organizations, including legislative support, training for women and institutional strengthening for intermediary institutions with a view to mobilizing capital for those institutions and increasing the availability of credit;

(b) Encourage links between financial institutions and non-governmental organizations and support innovative lending practices, including those that integrate credit with women's services and training and provide credit facilities to rural women.

63. By commercial banks, specialized financial institutions and the private sector in examining their policies:

(a) Use credit and savings methodologies that are effective in reaching women in poverty and innovative in reducing transaction costs and redefining risk;

(b) Open special windows for lending to women, including young women, who lack access to traditional sources of collateral;

(c) Simplify banking practices, for example by reducing the minimum deposit and other requirements for opening bank accounts;

(d) Ensure the participation and joint ownership, where possible, of women clients in the decision-making of institutions providing credit and financial services.

64. By multilateral and bilateral development co-operation organizations:

Support, through the provision of capital and/or resources, financial institutions that serve low-income, small-scale and micro-scale women entrepreneurs and producers, in both the formal and informal sec-tors.

65. By Governments and multilateral financial institutions, as appropriate:

Support institutions that meet performance standards in reaching large numbers of low-income women and men through capitalization, refinancing and institutional development support in forms that foster self-sufficency.

66. By international organizations:

Increase funding for programmes and projects designed to promote sustainable and productive entrepreneurial activities for income-generation among disadvantaged women and women living in poverty.

Strategic objective A.4.

Develop gender-based methodologies and conduct research to address the feminization of poverty

Actions to be taken

67. By Governments, intergovernmental organizations, academic and research institutions and the private sector:
    (a) Develop conceptual and practical methodologies for incorporating gender perspectives into all aspects of economic policy-making, including structural adjustment planning and programmes;
    (b) Apply these methodologies in conducting gender-impact analyses of all policies and programmes, including structural adjustment programmes, and disseminate the research findings.
68. Bynational and international statistical organizations:
    (a) Collect gender and age-disaggregated data on poverty and all aspects of economic activity and develop qualitative and quantitative statistical indicators to facilitate the assessment of economic performance from a gender perspective;
    (b) Devise suitable statistical means to recognize and make visible the full extent of the work of women and all their contributions to the national economy, including their contribution in the unremunerated and domestic sectors, and examine the relationship of women's unremunerated work to the incidence of and their vulnerability to poverty.

B. Education and Training of Women

69. Education is a human right and an essential tool for achieving the goals of equality, development and peace. Non-discriminatory education benefits both girls and boys and thus ultimately contributes to more equal relationships between women and men. Equality of

access to and attainment of educational qualifications is necessary if more women are to become agents of change. Literacy of women is an important key to improving health, nutrition and education in the family and to empowering women to participate in decision-making in society. Investing in formal and non-formal education and training for girls and women, with its exceptionally high social and economic return, has proved to be one of the best means of achieving sustainable development and economic growth that is both sustained and sustainable.

70. On a regional level, gjds and boys have achieved equal access to primary education, except in some parts of Africa, in particular sub-Saharan Africa, and Central Asia, where access to education facilities is still inadequate. Progress has been made in secondary education, where equal access of girls and boys has been achieved in some countries. Enrolment of girls and women in tertiary education has increased considerably. In many countries, private schools have also played an important complementary role in improving access to education at all levels. Yet, more than five years after the World Conference on Education for All (Jomtien, Thailand, 1990) adopted the World Declaration on Education for All and the Framework for Action to Meet Basic Learning Needs,[12] approximately 100 million children, including at least 60 million girls, are without access to primary schooling and more than two thirds of the world's 960 million illiterate adults are women. The high rate of illiteracy prevailing in most developing countries, in particular in sub-Saharan Africa and some Arab States, remains a severe impediment to the advancement of women and to development.

71. Discrimination in girls' access to educatiōn persists in many areas, owing to customary attitudes, early marriages and pregnancies, inadequate and gender-biased teaching and educational materials, sexual harassment and lack of adequate and physically and otherwise accessible schooling facil-ities. Girls undertake heavy domestic work at a very early age. Girls and young women are expected to manage both educational and domestic responsibilities, often resulting in poor scholastic performance and early drop-out from the educational system. This has long-lasting consequences for all aspects of women's lives.

72. Creation of an educational and social environment, in which women and men, girls and boys, are treated equal and encouraged to achieve their full potential, respecting their freedom of thought, conscience, religion and belief, and where educational resources promote non-

stereotyped images of women and men, would be effective in the elimination of the causes of discrimination against women and inequalities between women and men.

73. Women should be enabled to benefit from an ongoing acquisition of knowledge and skills beyond those acquired during youth. This concept of lifelong learning includes knowledge and skills gained in formal education and training, as well as learning that occurs in inform always, including volunteer activity, unremunerated work and traditional knowledge.

74. Curricula and teaching materials remain gender-biased to a large degree, and are rarely sensitive to the specific needs of girls and women. This reinforces traditional female and male roles that deny women oppor-tunities for full and equal partnership in society. Lack of gender awareness by educators at all Levels strengthens existing inequities between males and females by reinforcing discriminatory tendencies and undermining girls' self esteem. The lack of sexual and reproductive health education has a profound impact on women and men.

75. Science curricula in particular are gender-biased. Science textbooks do not relate to women's and girls' daily experience and fail to give recognistion to women scientists. Girls are often deprived of basic education in mathematics and science and technical training, which provide knowledge they could apply to improve their daily lives and enhance their employment pportunities· Advanced study in science and technology prepares women to take an active role in the technological and industrial development of their countries, thus necessitating a diverse approach to vocational and technical training. Technology is rapidly changing the world and has also affected the developing countries. It is essential that women not only benefit from technology, but also participate in the process from the design to the application, monitoring and evaluation stages.

76. Access for and retention of girls and women at all levels of education, including the higher level, and all academic areas is one of the factors of their continued progress in professional activities. Nevertheless, it can be noted that girls are still concentrated in a limited number of fields of study.

77. The mass media are a powerful means of education. As an educational tool the mass media can be an instrument for educators and governmental and non-governmental institutions for, the advancement of women and for development. Computerized education and information systems are increasingly becoming an important ele-

ment in learning and the dissemination of knowledge. Television especially has the greatest impact on young people and, as such, has the ability to shape values, attitudes and perceptions of women and girls in both positive and negative ways. It is therefore essential that educators teach critical judgment and analytical skills.

78. Resources allocated to education, particularly for girls and women, are in many countries insufficient and in some cases have been further diminished, including in the context of adjustment policies and programmes. Such insufficient resource allocations have a long-term adverse effect on human development, particularly on the development of women.

79. In addressing unequal access to and inadequate educational opportunities, Governments and other actors should promote an active and visible policy of mainstreaming a gender perspective into all policies and pro-grammes, so that, before decisions are taken, an analysis is made of the effects on women and men, respectively.

Strategic objective B.1.
Ensure equal access to education

Adions to be taken

80. By Governments:

(a) Advance the goal of equal access to education by taking measures to eliminate discrimination in education at all levels on the basis of gender, race, language, religion, national origin, age or disability, or any other form of discrimination and, as appropriate, consider establishing procedures to address grievances;

(b) By the year 2000, provide universal access to basic education and ensure completion of primary education by at least 80 per cent of primaly school-age children; close the gender gap in primaly and secondary school education by the year 2005; provide universal primary education in all countries before the year 2015;

(c) Eliminate gender disparities in access to all areas of tertiary education by ensuring that women have equal access to career development, training, scholarships and fellowships, and by adopting positive action when appropriate;

(d) Create a gender-sensitive educational system in order to ensure equal educational and training opportunities and full and equal participation of women in educational administration and policy-

and decision-making;

(e) Provide—in collaboration with parents, non-governmental organi zations, including youth organizations, communities and the private sector—young women with academic and technical training, career planning, leadership and social skills and work experience to prepare them to participate fully in society;

(f) Increase enrolment and retention rates of girls by allocating appropriate budgetary resources; by enlisting the support of parents and the community, as well as through campaigns, flexible school schedules, incentives, scholarships and other means to minimize the costs of girls' education to their families and to facilitate parents' ability to choose education for the girl-child; and by ensuring that the rights of women and girls to freedom of conscience and religion are respected in educational institutions through repealing any discriminatory laws or legislation based on religion, race or culture;

(g) Promote an educational setting that eliminates all barriers that impeded the schooling of pregnant adolescents and young mothers, including, as appropriate, affordable and physically accessible child-care facilities and parental education to encourage those who are responsible for the care of their children and siblings during their school years, to return to or continue with and complete schooling;

(h) Improve the quality of education and equal opportunities for women and men in terms of access in order to ensure that women of all ages can acquire the knowledge, capacities, aptitudes, skills and ethical values needed to develop and to participate fully under equal conditions in the process of social, economic and political development;

(i) Make available non-discriminately and gender-sensitive professional school counselling and career education programmes to encourage girls to pursue academic and technical curricula in order to widen their future career opportunities;

(j) Encourage ratification of the International Covenant on Economic, Social and Cultural Rights[13] where they have not already done so.

Strategic objective 8.2.
Eradicate illiteracy among women

Actions to be taken

81. By Governments, national, regional and international bodies, bilat-

eral and multilateral donors and non-governmental organizations:

(a) Reduce the female illiteracy rate to at least half its 1990 level, with emphasis on rural women, migrant, refugee and internally displaced women and women with disabilities;

(b) Provide universal access to, and seek to ensure gender equality in the completion of, primary education for girls by the year 2000;

(c) Eliminate the gender gap in basic and functional literacy, as recommended in the World Declaration on Education for All (Jomtien);

(d) Narrow the disparities between developed and developing countries;

(e) Encourage adult and family engagement in learning to promote total literacy for all people;

(f) Promote, together with literacy, life skills and scientific and technological knowledge and work towards an expansion of the definition of literacy, taking into account current targets and benchmarks.

Strategic objective B.3.
Improve women's access to vocational training, science and technology, and continuing education

Actions to be taken

82. By Governments, in co-operation with employers, workers and trade unions, international and non-governmental organizations, including women's and youth organizations, and educational institutions:

(a) Develop and implement education, training and retraining policies for women, especially young women and women re-entering the labour market, to provide skills to meet the needs of a changing socio-economic context for improving their employment opportunities;

(b) Provide recognition to non-formal educational opportunities for girls and women in the educational system;

(c) Provide information to women and girls on the availability and benefits of vocational training, training programmes in science and technology and programmes of continuing education;

(d) Design educational and training programmes for women who are unemployed in order to provide them with new knowledge and skills that will enhance and broaden their employment opportunities, including self-employment, and development of their entrepreneurial skills;

(e) Diversify vocational and technical training and improve access for and retention of girls and women in education and vocational training in such fields as science, mathematics, engineering, environmental sciences and technology, information technology and high technology, as well as management training;

(f) Promote women's central role in food and agricultural research, extension and education programmes;

(g) Encourage the adaptation of curricula and teaching materials, encourage a supportive training environment and take positive measures to promote training for the full range of occupational choices of non-traditional careers for women and men, including the development of multidisciplinary courses for science and mathematics teachers to sensitize them to the relevance of science and technology to women's lives;

(h) Develop curricula and teaching materials and formulate and take positive measures to ensure women better access to and participa-tion in technical and scientific areas, especially areas where they are not represented or are under represented;

(i) Develop policies and programmes to encourage women to participate in all apprenticeship programmes;

(j) Increase training in technical, managerial, agricultural extension and marketing areas for women in agriculture, fisheries, industry and business, arts and crafts, to increase income-generating opportunities, women's participation in, economic decision-making, in particular through women's organizations at the grass-roots level, and their contribution to production, marketing, business, and science technology;

(k) Ensure access to quality education and training at all appropriate levels for adult women with little or no education, for women with disabilities and for documented migrant, refugee and displaced women to improve their work opportunities.

Strategic objective B.4.
Develop non-discriminatory education and training

Action to be taken

83. By Governments, educational authorities and other educational and academic institutions:

(a) Elaborate 'ecommendations and develop curricula, textbooks and teaching aids free of gender-based stereotypes for all levels of educa-tion, including teacher training, in association with all concerned—publishers, teachers, public authorities a"d parents' associations;

(b) Development training programmesand materials fo' teachers and educators that raise awareness about the status, role and contribution of women and men in the family, as defined in paragraph 29 above, and society; in this context, promote equality, co-operation, mutual respect and shared responsibilities between girls and boys from pre-school level onward and develop, in particular, educational modules to ensure that boys have the skills necessary to take care of their own domestic needs and to share responsibility for their household and for the care of dependents;

(c) Develop training programmes and materials for teachers and educators that raise awareness of their own role in the educational process. with a view to providing them with effective strategies for gender-sensitive teaching;

(d) Take actions to ensure that female teachers and professor have the same opportunities as and equal status with male teachers and professors; in view of the importance of having female teachers at all levels and in order to attract girls to school and retain them in school;

(e) Introduce and promote training in peaceful conflid resolution;

(f) Take positive measures to increase the proportion of women gaining access to educational policy- and decision-making, particularly women teachers at all levels of education and in academic disciplines that are traditionally male-dominated, such as the scientific and technological fields;

(g) Support and develop gender studies and research at all levels of education, especially at the postgraduate level of academic institutions, and apply them in the development of curricula, including university curricula, textbooks and teaching aids, and in teacher training;

(h) Develop leadership training and opportunities for all women to encourage them to take leadership roles both as students and as adults in civil society;

(i) Develop appropriate education and information programmes with due respect for multilingualism, particularly in conjunction with the mass media, that make the public, particularly parents, aware of the importance of non-discriminatory education for children and the equal sharing of family responsibilities by girls and boys;

(j) Develop human rights education programmes that incorporate the gender dimension at all levels of education, in particular by encouraging higher education institutions, especially in their graduate and postgraduate juridical, social and political science curricula, to include the study of the human rights of women as they appear in United Nations conventions;

(k) Remove legal, regulatory and social barriers, where appropriate, to sexual and reproductive health education within formal education programmes regarding women's health issues;

(l) Encourage, with the guidance and support of their parents and in co-operation with educational staff and institutions, the elaboration of educational programmes for girls and boys and the creation of integrated services in order to raise awareness of their responsibilities and to help them to assume those responsibilities, taking into account the importance of such education and services to personal development and self-esteem, as well as the urgent need to avoid unwanted pregnancy, the spread of sexually transmitted diseases, especially HIV/AIDS, and such phenomena as sexual violence and abuse;

(m) Provide accessible recreational and sports facilities and establish and strengthen gender-sensitive programmes for girls and women of all ages in education and community institutions and support the advancement of women in all areas of athletics and physical activity, including coaching, training and administration, and as participants at the national, regional and international levels;

(n) Recognize and support the right of indigenous women and girls to education and promote a multicultural approach to education that is responsive to the needs, aspirations and cultures of indigenous women, including by developing appropriate education programmes, curricula and teaching aids, to the extent possible in the languages of indigenous people, and by providing for the participation of indigenous women in these processes;

(o) Acknowledge and respect the artistic, spiritual and cultural activities of indigenous women;

(p) Ensure that gender equality and cultural, religious and other diversity are respected in educational institutions;

(q) Promote education, training and relevant information programmes for rural and farming women through the use of affordable and appropriate technologies and the mass media—

for example, radio programmes, cassettes and mobile units;

(r) Provide non-formal education, especially for rural women, in order to realize their potential with regard to health, micro-enterprise, agriculture and legal rights;

(s) Remove all barriers to access to formal education for pregnant adolescents and young mothers, and support the provision of child care and other support services where necessary.

Strategic objective B. 5.
Allocate sufficient resources for and monitor the implementation of educational reforms

Actions to be taken

84. By Governments:

(a) Provide the required budgetary resources to the educational sector with reallocation within the educational sector to ensure increased funds for basic education, as appropriate;

(b) Establish a mechanism at appropriate levels to monitor the implementation of educational reforms and measures in relevant ministries, and establish technical assistance programmes, as appropriate, to address issues raised by the monitoring efforts.

85. By Governments and, as appropriate, private and public institutions, foundations, research institutes and non-governmental organizations:

(a) When necessary, mobilize additional funds from private and public institutions, foundations, research institutes and non-governmental organizations to enable girls and women, as well as boys and men on an equal basis, to complete their education, with particular emphasis on under-served populations;

(b) Provide funding for special programmes, such as programmes in mathematics, science and computer technology, to advance opportunities for all girls and women.

86. By multilateral development institutions, including the World Bank, regional development banks, bilateral donors and foundations:

(a) Consider increasing funding for the education and training needs of girls and women as a priority in development assistance programmes;

(b) Consider working with recipient Governments to ensure that fund-ing for women's education is maintained or increased in structural adjustment and economic recovery programmes, including lend-ing and stabilization programmes.

87. By international and intergovenmental organizations, especially the

United Nations Educational, Scientific and Cultural Organization, at the global level:

(a) Contribute to the evaluation of progress achieved, using educational indicators generated by national, regional and international bodies, and urge Governments, in implementing measures, to eliminate differences between women and men and boys and girls with regard to opportunities in education and training and the levels achieved in all fields, particularly in primary and literacy programmes;

(b) Provide technical assistance upon request to developing countries to strengthen the capacity to monitor progress in closing the gap between women and men in education, training and research, and in levels of achievement in all fields, particularly basic education and the elimination of illiteracy;

(c) Conduct an international campaign promoting the right of women and girls to education;

(d) Allocate a substantial percentage of their resources to basic education for women and girls.

Strategic objective B. 6.
Promote lifelong education and training for girls and women

Actions to be taken

88. By Governments. educational institutions and communities:

(a) Ensure the availability of a broad range of educational and training programmes that lead to ongoing acquisition by women and girls of the knowledge and skills required for living in, contributing to and benefiting from their communities and nations;

(b) Provide support for child care and other services to enable mothers to continue their schooling;

(c) Create flexible education, training and retraining programmes for lifelong learning that facilitate transitions between women's activities at all stages of their lives.

C. Women and health*

89. Women have the right to the enjoyment of the highest attainable standard of physical and mental health. The enjoyment of this right is vital to their life and well-being and their ability to participate in all areas of public and private life. Health is a state of complete physical, mental and social well-being and not merely the absence of disease or infirmity. Women's health involves their emotional,

social and physical well-being and is determined by the social, political and economic context of their lives, as well as by biology. However, health and well-being elude the majority of women. A major barrier for women to the achievement of the highest attainable standard of health is inequality, both between men and women and among women in different geographical regions, social classes and indigenous and ethnic groups. In national and international forums, women have emphasized that to attain optimal health throughout the life cycle, equality, including the sharing of family responsibilities, development and peace are necessary conditions.

90. Women have different and unequal access to and use of basic health resources, including primary health services for the prevention and treatment of childhood diseases, malnutrition, anaemia, diarrhoeal diseases, communicable diseases, malaria and other tropical diseases and tuberculosis, among others. Women also have different and unequal opportunities for the protection, promotion and maintenance of their health. In many developing countries, the lack of emergency obstetric services is also of particular concern. Health policies and programmes often perpetuate gender stereotypes and fail to consider socio-economic disparities and other differences among women and may not fully take account of the lack of autonomy of women regarding their health. Women's health is also affected by gender bias in the health system and by the provision of inadequate and inappropriate medical services to women.

91. In many countries, especially developing countries, in particular the least developed countries, a decrease in public health spending and, in some cases, structural adjustment, contribute to the deterioration of public health systems. In addition, privatization of health care systems without appropriate guarantees of universal access to affordable health care further reduces health-care availability. This situation not only directly affects the health of girls and women, but also places disproportionate responsibilities on women, whose multiple roles, including their roles within the family and the community, are often not acknowledged; hence they do not receive the necessary social, psychological and economic support.

92. Women's right to the enjoyment of the highest standard of health must be secured throughout the whole life cycle in equality with

---

* The Holy See expressed a general reservation on this section. The reservation is to be interpreted in terms of the statement made by the representative of the Holy Set at the 4th meeting of the Main Committee, on 14 September 1995 (see chap. V d the present report. para. 11).

men. Women are affected by many of the same health conditions as men, but women experience them differently. The prevalence among women of poverty and economic dependence, their experience of violence, negative attitudes towards women and girls, racial and other forms of discrimination, the limited power many women have over their sexual and reproductive lives and lack of influence in decision-making are social realities which have an adverse impact on their health. Lack of food and inequitable distribution of food for girls and women in the household, inadequate access to safe water, sanitation facilities and fuel supplies, particularly in rural and poor urban areas, and deficient housing conditions, all overburden women and their families and have a negative effect on their health. Good health is essential to leading a productive and fulfilling life, and the right of all women to control all aspects of their health, in particular their own fertility, is basic to their empowerment.

93. Discrimination against girls, often resulting from son preference, in access to nutrition and health-care services endangers their current and future health and well-being. Conditions that force girls into early marriage, pregnancy and child-bearing and subject them to harmful practices, such as female genital mutilation, pose grave health risks. Adolescent girls need, but too often do not have, access to necessary health and nutrition services as they mature. Counselling and access to sexual and reproductive health information and services for adolescents are still inadequate or lacking completely, and a young woman's right to privacy, confidentiality, respect and informed consent is often not considered Adolescent girls are both biologically and psychosociall: more vulnerable than boys to sexual abuse, violence and prostitution, and to the consequences of unprotected and premature sexual relations· The trend towards early sexual experience, combined with a lack of information and services, increases the risk of unwanted and too early pregnancy, HIV infection and other sexually transmitted disease, as well as unsafe abortions. Early child-bearing continues to be an impediment to improvements in the educational, economic and social status of women in all parts of the world. Overall, for young women early marriage and early motherhood can severely curtail educational and employment opportunities and are likely to have a long-term, adverse impact on the quality of their lives and the lives of their children Young men are often not edicated to respect women's self-determination and to share responsibility educated to respect women s with women in matters of sexuality and reproduction

94. Reproductive health is a state of complete physical, mental and social well-being and not merely the absence of disease or infirmity, in all matters, relating to the reproductive system and to its functions and processes. Reproductive health therefore implies that people are able to have a satisfying and safe sex life and that they have the capability to reproduce and the freedom to decide if, when and how often to do so. Implicit in this last condition are the right of men and women to be informed and to have access to safe, effective, affordable and acceptable methods of family planing of their choice, as well as other methods of their choice for regulation of fertility which are not against the law, and the right of access to appropriate health-care services that will enable women to go safely through pregnancy and childbirth and provide couples with the best chance of having a healthy infant. In line with the above definition of reproductive health, reproductive health care is defined as the constellation of methods, techniques and services that contribute to reproductive health and well-being by preventing and solving reproductive health problems. It also includes sexual health, the purpose of which is the enhancement of life and personal relations, and not merely counselling and care related to reproduction and sexually transmitted diseases·

95. Bearing in mind the above definition, reproductive rights embrace certain human rights that are already recognized in national laws, international human rights documents and other consensus documents These rights rest on the recognition of the basic right of all couples and individual to decide freely and responsibly the number, spacing and timing of their children and to have the information and means to do so, and the right to attain the highest standard of sexual and reproductive health. It also includes their right to make decisions concerning reproduction free of discrimination, coercion and violence, as expressed in human rights documents. In the exercise of this right, they should take into account the needs of their living and future children and their responsibilities towards the community. The promotion of the responsible exercise of these rights for all people should be the fundamental basis for government- and community-supported policies and programmes in the area of reproductive health, including family planning. As part of their commitment, full attention should be given to the promotion of mutually respectful and equitable gender relations and particularly to meeting the educational and service needs of adolescents to enable them to deal in a positive and responsible way with their sexuality.

reproductive health eludes many of the world's people because of such factors as: inadequate levels of knowledge about human sexuality and inappropriate or poor-quality reproductive health information and services; the prevalence of high-risk sexual behaviour; discriminatory social practices; negative attitudes towards women and girls; and the limited power many women and girls have over their sexual and reproductive lives. Adolescents are particularly vulnerable because of their lack of information and access to relevant services in most countries. Older women and men have distind reproductive and sexual health issues which are often inadequately addressed.

96. The human rights of women include their right to have control over and decide freely and responsibly on matters related to their sexuality, including sexual and reproductive health, free of coercion, discrimination and violence. Equal relationships between women and men in matters of sexual relations and reproduction, including full respect for the integrity of the person, require mutual respect, consent and shared responsibility for sexual behaviour and its consequences.

97. Further, women are subject to particular health risks due to inadequate responsiveness and lack of services to meet health needs related to sexuality and reproduction. Complications related to pregnancy and childbirth are among the leading causes of mortality and morbidity of women of reproductive age in many parts of the developing world. Similar problems exist to a certain degree in some countries with economies in transition. Unsafe abortions threaten the lives of a large number of women, representing a grave public health problem as it is primarily the poorest and youngest who take the highest risk. Most of these deaths, health problems and injuries are preventable through improved access to adequate health-care services, including safe and effective family planning methods and emer-gency obstetric care, recognizing the right of women and men to be informed and to have access to safe, effective, affordable and acceptable methods of family planning of their choice, as well as other methods of their choice for regulation of fertility which are not against the law, and the right of access to appropriate health-care services that will enable women to go safely through pregnancy and childbirth and provide couples with the best chance of having a healthy infant. These problems and means should be addressed on the basis of the report of the International Conference on Population and Development, with particular reference to relevant paragraphs

of the Programme of Action of the Conference.[14] In most countries, the neglect of women's reproductive rights severely limits their opportunities in public and private life, including opportunities for education and eco-nomic and political empowerment. The ability of women to control their own fertility forms an important basis for the enjoyment of other rights. Shared responsibility between women and men in matters related to sexual and reproductive behaviour is also essential to improving women's health.

98. HIV/AIDS and other sexually transmitted diseases, the transmission of which is sometimes a consequence of sexual violence, are having a devastating effect on women's health, particularly the health of adolescent girls and young women. They often do not have the power to insist on safe and responsible sex practices and have little access to information and services for prevention and treatment. Women, who represent half of all adults newly infected with HIV/ AIDS and other sexually transmitted diseases, have emphasized that social vulnerability and the unequal power relationships between women and men are obstacles to safe sex, in their efforts to control the spread of sexually transmitted diseases. The consequences of HIV/ AIDS reach beyond women's health to their role as mothers and caregivers and their contribution to the economic support of their families. The social, developmental and health consequences of HIV/AIDS and other sexually transmitted diseases need to be seen from a gender perspective.

99. Sexual and gender-based violence, including physical and psychological abuse, trafficking in women and girls, and other forms of abuse and sexual exploitation place girls and women at high risk of physical and mental trauma, disease and unwanted pregnancy. Such situations often deter women from using health and other services.

100. Mental disorders related to marginalization, powerlessness a poverty, along with overwork and stress and the growing incidence domestic violence as well as substance abuse, are among other health issues of growing concern to women. Women throughout the world, especially young women, are increasing their use of tobacco with serious effects on their health and that of their children. Occupational health issues are also growing in importance, as a large number of women work in low-paid jobs in either the formal or the informal labour market under tedious ; and unhealthy conditions, and the number is rising. Cancers of the breast and cervix and other cancers of the reproductive system, as well as infertility, affect growing numbers of women and may be preventable, or curable, if detected early.

101. With the increase in life expectancy and the growing number of older women, their health concerns require particular attention. The long-term health prospects of women are influenced by changes at menopause, which, in combination with lifelong conditions and other factors, such as poor nutrition and lack of physical activity, may increase the risk of cardiovascular disease and osteoporosis. Other diseases of ageing and the interrelationships of ageing and disability among women also need particular attention.

102. Women, like men, particularly in rural areas and poor urban areas, are increasingly exposed to environmental health hazards owing to environmental catastrophes and degradation. Women have a different susceptibility to various environmental hazards, contaminants and substances and they suffer different consequences from exposure to them.

103. The quality of women's health care is often deficient in various ways, depending on local circumstances. Women are frequently not treated with respect, nor are they guaranteed privacy and confidentiality, nor do they always receive full information about the options and services available. Furthermore, in some countries, women's life events are often treated as medical problems, leading to unnecessary surgical intervention and inappropriate medication.

104. Statistical data on health are often not systematically collected, disaggregated and analysed by age, sex and socio-economic status and by established demographic criteria used to serve the interests and solve the problems of subgroups, with particular emphasis on the vulnerable and marginalized and other relevant variables. Recent and reliable data on the mortality and morbidity of women and conditions and diseases particularly affecting women are not available in many countries. Relatively little is known about how social and economic factors affect the health of girls and women of all ages, about the provision of health services to girls and women and the patterns of their use of such services, and about the value of disease prevention and health promotion programmes for women. Subjects of importance to women's health have not been adequately researched and women's health research often lacks funding. Medical research, on heart disease, for example, and epidemiological studies in many countries are often based solely on men; they are not gender specific. Clinical trials involving women to establish basic information about dosage, side-effects and effectiveness of drugs, including contraceptives, are noticeably absent and do not always conform to ethical standards for research and testing. Many drug therapy protocols

and other medical treatments and interventions administered to women are based on research on men without any investigation and adjustment for gender differences.

105. In addressing inequalities in health status and unequal access to and inadequate health-care services between women and men, Governments and other actors should promote an active and visible policy of mainstreaming a gender perspective in all policies and programmes, so that, before decisions are taken, an analysis is made of the effects for women and men, respectively

Strategic objective C.1.
Increase women's access throughout the life cycle to appropriate, affordable and quality health rare, information and related services

Actions to be taken

106. By Governments, in collaboration with non-governmental organizations and employers' and workers' organizations and with the support of international institutions:

(a) Support and implement the commitments made in the Programme of Action of the International Conference on Population and Development, as established in the report of that Conference and the Copenhagen Declaration on Social Development and Programme of Action of the World Summit for Social Development[15] and the obligations of States parties under the Convention on the Elimination of All Forms of Discrimination against Women and other relevant international agreements, to meet the health needs of girls and women of all ages;

(b) Reaffirm the right to the enjoyment of the highest attainable standards of physical and mental health, protect and promote the attainment of this right for women and girls and incorporate it in national legislation, for example; review existing legislation, including health legislation, as well as policies, where necessary, to reflect a commitment to women's health and to ensure that they meet the changing roles and responsibilities of women wherever they reside;

(c) Design and implement, in cooperation with women and community-based organizations, gender-sensitive health programmes including decentralized health services, that address the needs women throughout their lives and take into account their multipleroles and responsibilities, the demands on their time, the special needs of rural women and womenwith disabilities and the diversi. women's needs arisingfrom age and socio-economic and cultural differences, among others; include women, especially local and indigenous women, in the identification and planning of health-care priorities and programmes; remove all barriers to women's health services and provide a broad range of health-care services;

(d) Allow women access to social security systems in equality with men throughout the whole life cycle;

(e) Provide more accessible, available and affordable primary health-care services of high quality, including sexual and reproductive health care, which includes family planning information and services, and giving particular attention to maternal and emergency obstetric care, as agreed to in the Programme of Action of the International Conference on Population and Development;

(f) Redesign health information, services and training for health workers so that they are gender-sensitive and reflect the user's perspectives with regard to interpersonal and communications skills and the user's right to privacy and confidentiality; these services, information and training should be based on a holistic approach;

(g) Ensure that all health services and workers conform to human rights and to ethical, professional and gender-sensitive standards in the delivery of women's health services aimed at ensuring responsible, voluntary and informed consent; encourage the development, implementation and dissemination of codes of ethics guided by existing international codes of medical ethics as well as ethical principles that govern other health professionals;

(h) Take all appropriate measures to eliminate harmful, medically unnecessary or coercive medical interventions, as well as inappropriate medication and over-medication of women, and ensure that all women are fully informed of their options, including likely benefits and potential side-effects, by properly trained personnel;

(i) Strengthen and reorient health services, particularly primary health care, in order to ensureuniversal access to quality health services for women and girls; reduce ill health and maternal morbidity and achieve worldwide the agreed-upon goal of reducing maternal mortality by at least 50 per cent of the 1990 levels by the year 2000 and a further one half by the year 2015; ensure that the necessary services are available at each level of the health system and make reproductive health care accessible, through the primary health care system, to all individuals of appropriate ages as soon as possible and no later than the year 2015;

(j) Recognize and deal with the health impact of unsafe abortion as a major public health concern, as agreed in paragraph 8.25 of the Programme of Action of the International Conference on Population and Development; [14]

(k) In the light of paragraph 8.25 of the Programme of Action of the International Conferenceon Population and Development, which states: "In no case should abortion be promoted as a method of family planning. All Govemments and relevant intergovemmental and non-governmental organizations am urged to strengthen their commitment to women's health, to deal with the health impact of unsafe abortion[16] as a major public health concern and to reduce the recourse to abortion through expanded improved family-planning services, Prevention of unwanted pregnancies must always be given the highest priority and every attempt should be made to eliminate the need for abortion. Women who have unwanted pregnancies should have ready access to reliable information and compassionate counselling. Any measures or changes related to abortion within the health system can only be determined at the national or local level according to the national legisiative process. In circumstances where abortion is not against the law, such abortion should be safe. In all cases, women should have access to quality services for the management of complications arising from abortion. Post-abortion counselling, education and family-planning services should be offered promptly, which will also help to avoid 'repeat abortions', consider reviewing laws containing containing punitive measures against women who have undergone illegal abortions;

(l) Give particular attention tothe needs of girls, especially the promotion of healthy behaviour, including physical activities; take specific measures for closing the gender gaps in morbidity and mortality where girls are disadvantaged, while achieving internationally approved goals for the reduction of infant and child mortality specifically, by the year 2000 the reduction of mortality rates of ınfants and children under five years of age by one third of the 1990 level, or 50 to 70 per 1,000 live births, whichever is less; by the year 2015 an infant mortality rate below 35 per 1,000 live births and an under-five mortality rate below 45 per 1,000;

(m) Ensure that girls have continuing access to necessary health and nutrition information and services as they mature, to facilitate a healthful transition from childhood to adulthood;

(n) Develop information, programmes and services to assist women to understand and adapt to changes associated with ageing and to address and treat the health needs of older women, paying particular attention to those who are physically or psychologically dependent;

(o) Ensure that girls and women of all ages with any form of disability receive supportive services;

(p) Formulate special policies, design programmes and enact the legislation necessary to alleviate and eliminate environmental and occupational health hazards associated with work in the home, in the workplace and elsewhere with attention to pregnant and lactating women;

(q) Integrate mental health services into primary health-care systems or other appropriate levels, develop supportive programmes and train primary health workers to recognize and care for girls and women of all ages who have experienced any form of violence especially domestic violence, sexual abuse or other abuse resulting from armed and non-armed conflict;

(r) Promote public information on the benefits of breast-feeding; examine ways and means of implementing fully the WHO/UNICEF International Code of Marketing of Breast-milk Substitutes, and enable mothers to breast-feed their infants by providing legal, economic, practical and emotional support;

(s) Establish mechanisms to support and involve non-governmental organizations, particularly women's organizations, professional groups and other bodies working to improve the health of girls and women, in government policy-making, programme design, as appropriate, and implementation within the health sector and related sectors at all levels;

(t) Support non-governmental organizations working on women's health and help develop networks aimed at improving co-ordination and collaboration between all sectors that affect health;

(u) Rationalize drug procurement and ensure a reliable, continuous supply of high-quality pharmaceutical, contraceptive and other supplies and equipment, using the WHO Model List of Essential Drugs as a guide, and ensure the safety of drugs and devices through national regulatory drug approval processes;

(v) Provide improved access to appropriate treatment and rehabilitation services for women substance abusers and their families;

(w) Promote and ensure household and national food security, as appropriate, and implement programmes aimed at improving the nutritional status of all girls and women by implementing the commitments made in the Plan of Action on Nutrition of the International Conference on Nutrition,[17] including a reduction worldwide of severe and moderate malnutrition among children under the age of five by one half of 1990 levels by the year 2000, giving special attention to the gender gap in nutrition, and a reduction in iron deficiency anaemia in girls and women by one third of the 1990 levels by the year 2000;

(x) Ensure the availability of and universal access to safe drinking-water and sanitation and put in place effective public distribution systems as soon as possible;

(y) Ensure full and equal access to health-care infrastructure and services for indigenous women.

Strategic Objective C.2.
Strengthen preventive programmes that promote women's health

Actions to be taken

107. By Governments, in co-operation with non-governmental organizations, the mass media, the private sector and relevant international organizations, including United Nations bodies, as appropriate:

(a) Give priority to both formal and informal educational programmes that support and enable women to develop self-esteem, acquire knowledge, make decisions on and take responsibility for their own health, achieve mutual respect in matters concerning sexuality and fertility and educate men regarding the importance of women's health and well-being, placing special focus on programmes for both men and women that emphasize the elimination of harmful attitudes and practices, including female genital mutilation, son preference (which results in female infanticide and prenatal sex selection), early marriage, including child marriage, violence against women, sexual exploitation, sexual abuse, which at times is conducive to infection with HIV/AIDS and other sexually transmitted diseases, drug abuse, discrimination against girls and women in food allocation and other harmful attitudes and practices related to the life, health and well-being of women, and recognizing that some of these practices can be violations of human rights and ethical medical principles;

(b) Pursue social, human development, education and employment policies to eliminate poverty among women in order to reduce their susceptibility to ill health and to improve their health;

(c) Encourage men to share equally in child care and household work and to provide their share of financial support for their families, even if they do not live with them;

(d) Reinforce laws, reform institutions and promote norms and practices that eliminate discrimination against women and encourage both women and men to take responsibility for their sexual and reproductive behaviour; ensure full respect for the integrity of the person, take action to ensure the conditions necessary for women to exercise their reproductive rights and eliminate coercive laws and practices;

(e) Prepare and disseminate accessible information, through public health campaigns, the media, reliable counselling and the education system, designed to ensure that women and men, particularly young people, can acquire knowledge about their health, especially information on sexuality and reproduction, taking into account the rights of the child to access to information, privacy, confidentiality, respect and informed consent, as well as the responsibilities, rights and duties of parents and legal guardians to provide, in a manner consistent with the evolving capacities of the child, appropriate direction and guidance in the exercise by the child of the rights recognized in the Convention on the Rights of the Child, and in conformity with the Convention on the Elimination of All Forms of Discrimination against Women; ensure that in all actions concerning children, the best interests of the child are a primary consideration;

(f) Create and support programmes in the educational system, in the workplace and in the community to make opportunities to participate in sport, physical activity and recreation available to girls and women of all ages on the same basis as they are made available to men and boys;

(g) Recognize the specific needs of adolescents and implement specific appropriate programmes, such as education and information on sexual and reproductive health issues and on sexually transmitted diseases, including HIV/AIDS, taking into account the rights of the child and the responsibilities, rights and duties of parents as stated in paragraph 107 (e) above;

(h) Develop policies that reduce the disproportionate and increasing burden on women who have multiple roles within the family and the community by providing them with adequate support and programmes from health and social services;

(i) Adopt regulations to ensure that the working conditions, including remuneration and promotion of women at all levels of the health system, are non-discriminatory and meet fair and professional standards to enable them to work effectively;

(j) Ensure that health and nutritional information and training form an integral part of all adult literacy programmes and school curricula from the primary level;

(k) Develop and undertake media campaigns and information and educational programmes that inform women and girls of the health and related risks of substance abuse and addiction and pursue strategies and programmes that discourage substance abuse and addiction and promote rehabilitation and recovery;

(l) Devise and implement comprehensive and coherent programmes for the prevention, diagnosis and treatment of osteoporosis, a condition that predominantly affects women;

(m) Establish and/or strengthen programmes and services, including media campaigns, that address the prevention, early detection and treatment of breast, cervical and other cancers of the reproductive system;

(n) Reduce environmental hazards that pose a growing threat to health, especially in poor regions and communities; apply a precautionary approach, as agreed to in the Rio Declaration on Environment and Development, adopted by the United Nations Conference on Environment and Development,[18] and include reporting on women's health risks related to the environment in monitoring the implementation of Agenda 21;[19]

(o) Create awareness among women, health professionals, policy mak- ers and the general public about the serious but preventable health hazards stemming from tobacco consumption and the need for regulatory and education measures to reduce smoking as important health promotion and disease prevention activities;

(p) Ensure that medical school curricula and other health-care training include gender-sensitive, comprehensive and mandatory courses on women's health;

(q) Adopt specific preventive measures to protect women, youth and children from any abuse—sexual abuse, exploitation, trafficking and violence, for example— including the formulation and enforcement of laws, and provide legal protection and medical and other assistance.

Strategic objective C. 3.
Undertake gender-sensitive initiatives that address sexually transmitted diseases, HIV/AIDS and sexual and reproductive health issues

Adions to be taken

108. By Governments, international bodies including relevant United Nations organizations, bilateral and multilateral donors and non-governmental organizations:

(a) Ensure the involvement of women, especially those infected with HIV/AIDS or other sexually transmitted diseases or affected by the HIV/AIDS pandemic, in all decision-making relating to the development, implementation, monitoring and evaluation of policies and programmes on HIV/AIDS and other sexually transmitted diseases;

(b) Review and amend laws and combat practices, as appropriate, that may contribute to women's susceptibility to HIV infection and other sexually transmitted diseases, including enacting legislation against those socio-cultural practices that contribute to it, and implement legislation, policies and practices to protect women, adolescents and young girls from discrimination related to HIV/AIDS;

(c) Encourage all sectors of society, including the public sector, as well as international organizations, to develop compassionate and supportive, non-discriminatory HIV/AIDS-related policies and practices that protect the rights of infected individuals;

(d) Recognize the extent of the HIV/AIDS pandemic in their countries, taking particularly into account its impact on women, with a view to ensuring that infected women do not suffer stigmatization and discrimination, including during travel;

(e) Develop gender-sensitive multisectoral programmes and strategies to end social subordination of women and girls and to ensure their social and economic empowerment and equality; facilitate promotion of programmes to educate and enable men to assume their responsibilities to prevent HIV/AIDS and other sexually transmitted diseases;

(f) Facilitate the development of community strategies that will protect women of all ages from HIV and other sexually transmitted diseases; provide care and support to infected girls, women and their families and mobilize all parts of the community in response to the HIV/AIDS pandemic to exert pressure on all responsible authorities to respond in a timely, effective, sustainable and gendersensitive manner;

(g) Support and strengthen national capacity to create and improve gender-sensitive policies and programmes on HIV/AIDS and other sexually transmitted diseases, including the provision of resources and facilities to women who find themselves the principal caregivers or economic support for those infected with HIV/AIDS or affected by the pandemic, and the survivors, particularly children and older persons;

(h) Provide workshops and specialized education and training to parents, decision makers and opinion leaders at all levels of the community, including religious and traditional authorities, on prevention of HIV/AIDS and other sexually transmitted diseases and on their repercussions on both women and men of all ages;

(i) Give all women and health workers all relevant information and education about sexually transmitted diseases including HIV/AIDS and pregnancy and the implications for the baby, including breast-feeding;

(j) Assist women and their formal and informal organizations to establish and expand effective peer education and outreach programmes and to participate in the design, implementation and monitoring of these programmes;

(k) Give full attention to the promotion of mutually respectful and equitable gender relations and, in particular, to meeting the educational and service needs of adolescents to enable them to deal in a positive and responsible way with their sexuality;

(l) Design specific programmes for men of all ages and male adolescents, recognizing the parental roles referred to in paragraph 107 (e) above, aimed at providing complete and accurate information on safe and responsible sexual and reproductive behaviour, including voluntary, appropriate and effective male methods for the prevention of HIV/AIDS and other sexually trans-mitted diseases through, *inter alia,* abstinence and condom use;

(m) Ensure the provision, through the primary health-care system, of universal access of couples and individuals to appropriate and affordable preventive services with respect to sexually transmitted diseases, including HIV/AIDS, and expand the provision of counselling and voluntary and confidential diagnostic and treatment services for women; ensure that high-quality condoms as well as drugs for the treatment of sexually transmitted diseases are, where possible, supplied and distributed to health services;

(n) Support programmes which acknowledge that the higher risk among women of contracting HIV is linked to high-risk behaviour, including intravenous substance use and substance-influenced unprotected and irresponsible sexual behaviour, and take appropriate preventive measures;

(o) Support and expedite action-oriented research on affordable methods, controlled by women, to prevent HIV and other sexually transmitted diseases, on strategies empowering women to protect themselves from sexually transmitted diseases, including HIV/AIDS, and on methods of care, support and treatment of women, ensuring their involvement in all aspects of such research;

(p) Support and initiate research which addresses women's needs and situations, including research on HIV infection and other sexually transmitted diseases in women, on women-controlled methods of protection, such as nonspermicidal microbicides, and on male and female risk-taking attitudes and practices.

Strategic Objective C. 4.
Promote research and disseminate information on women's health

Actions to be taken

109. By Governments, the United Nations system, health professions, research institutions, non-governmental organizations, donors, pharmaceutical industries and the mass media, as appropriate:

(a) Train researchers and introduce systems that allow for the use of data collected, analysed and disaggregated by, among other factors, sex and age, other established demographic criteria and socio-economic variables, in policy-making, as appropriate, planning, monitoring and evaluation;

(b) Promote gender-sensitive and women-centred health research, treatment and technology and link traditional and indigenous knowledge with modern medicine, making information available to women to enable them to make informedand responsible decisions;

(c) Increase the numbei of women in leadership positions in the health professions, including researchers and scientists, to achieve equality at the earliest possible date;

(d) Increase financial and other support from all sources for preventive, appropriate biomedical, behavioural, epidemiological and health service research on women's health issues and for research on the social, economic and political causes of women's health problems, and their consequences, including the impact of gender and age inequalities, especially with respect to chronic and noncommunicable diseases, particularly cardiovascular diseases and conditions, cancers, reproductive tract infections and injuries, HIV /AIDS and other sexually transmitted diseases, domestic violence, occupational health, disabilities, environmentally related health problems, tropical diseases and health aspects of ageing;

(e) Inform women about the factors which increase the risks of devel-oping cancers and infections of the reproductive tract, so that they can make informed decisions about their health;

(f) Support and fund social, economic, political and cultural research on how gender-based inequalities affect women's health, including etiology, epidemiology, provision and utilization of services and eventual outcome of treatment;

(g) Support health senrice systems and operations research to strengthen access and improve the quality of service delivery, to ensure appropriate support for women as health-care providers and to examine patterns with respect to the provision of health services to women and use of such services by women;

(h) Provide financial and institutional support for research on safe, effective, affordable and acceptable methods and technologies for the reproductive and sexual health of women and men, including more safe, effective, affordable and acceptable methods for the regulation of fertility, including natural family planning for both sexes, methods to protect against HIV/AIDS and other sexually transmitted diseases and simple and inexpensive methods of diagnosing such diseases, among others; this research needs to be guided at all stages by users and from the perspective of gender, particularly the perspective of women, and should be carried out in strict conformity with internationally accepted legal, ethical, medical and scientific standards for biomedical research;

(i) Since unsafe abortion[16] is a major threat to the health and life of women, research to understand and better address the determinants and consequences of induced abortion, including its effects on subsequent fertility, reproductive and mental health and contraceptive practice, should be promoted, as well as research on treatment of complications of abortions and post-abortion care;

(j) Acknowledge and encourage beneficial traditional health care, especially that practised by indigenous women. with a view to preserving and incorporating the value of traditional health care in the provision of health services, and support research directed towards achieving this aim;

(k) Develop mechanisms to evaluate and disseminate available data and research findings to researchers, policy makers, health professionals and women's groups, among others;

(l) Monitor human genome and related genetic research from the perspective of women's health and disseminate information and results of studies conducted in accordance with accepted ethical standards.

Strategic objective C. 5.
Increase resources and monitor follow-up for women's health

Actions to be taken

110. By Governments at all levels and, where appropriate, in cooperation with non-governmental organizations, especially women's and youth organizations:

(a) Increase budgetary allocations for primary health care and social services, with adequate support for secondary and tertiary levels, and give special attention to the reproductive and sexual health of girls and women and give priority to health programmes in rural and poor urban areas;

(b) Develop innovative approaches to funding health services through promoting community participation and local financing; increase, where necessary, budgetary allocations for community health centres and community-based programmes and services that address women's specific health needs;

(c) Develop local health services, promoting the incorporation of gender-sensitive community-based participation and self-care and specially designed preventive health programmes;

(d) Develop goals and time-frames, where appropriate, for improving women's health and for planning, implementing, monitoring and evaluating programmes, based on gender-impact assessments using qualitative and quantitative data disaggregated by sex, age. other established demographic criteria and socio-economic variables;

(e) Establish, as appropriate, ministerial and inter-ministerial mechanisms for monitoring the implementation of women's health policy and programme reforms and establish (as appropriate, high-level focal points in national planning authorities responsible for monitoring to ensure that women's health concerns are mainstreamed in all relevant government agencies and programmes.

111. By Governments, the United Nations and its specialized agencies, international financial institutions, bilateral donors and the private sector, as appropriate:

(a) Formulate policies favourable to investment in women's health and, where appropriate, increase allocations for such investment;

(b) Provide appropriate material, financial and logistical assistance to youth non-governmental organizations in order to strengthen them to address youth concerns in the area of health, including sexual and reproductive health;

(c) Give higher priority to women's health and develop mechanisms for co-ordinating and implementing the health objectives of the Platform for Action and relevant international agreements to ensure progress.

D. Violence Against Women

112. Violence against women is an obstacle to the achievement of the objectives of equality, development and peace. Violence against women both violates and impairs or nullifies the enjoyment by women of their human rights and fundamental freedoms. The long-standing failure to protect and promote those rights and freedoms in the case of violence against women is a matter of concern to all States and should be addressed. Knowledge about its causes and consequences, as well as its incidence and measures to combat it, have been greatly expanded since the Nairobi Conference. In all societies, to a greater or lesser degree, women and girls are subjected to physical, sexual and psychological abuse that cuts across lines of income, class and culture. The low social and economic status of

women can be both a cause and a consequence of violence against women.

113. The term "violence against women means any act of gender-based violence that results in, or is likely to result in, physical, sexual or psychological harm or suffering to women, including threats of such acts, coercion or arbitrary deprivation of liberty, whether occurring in public or private life. Accordingly, violence against women encompasses but is not limited to the following:
   (a) Physical, sexual and psychological violence occurring in the family, including battering, sexual abuse of female children in the house-hold, dowry-related violence, marital rape, female genital mutilation and other traditional practices harmful to women, non-spousal violence and violence related to exploitation;
   (b) Physical, sexual and psychological violence occurring within the general community, including rape, sexual abuse, sexual harass- ment and intimidation at work, in educational institutions and elsewhere, trafficking in women and forced prostitution;
   (c) Physical, sexual and psychological violence perpetrated or condoned by the State, wherever it occurs.

114. Other acts of violence against women include violation of the human rights of women in situations of armed conflict, in particular murder, systematic rape, sexual slavery and forced pregnancy.

115. Acts of violence against women also include forced sterilization and forced abortion, coercive/forced use of contraceptives, female infanticide and prenatal sex selection.

116. Some groups of women, such as women belonging to minority groups, indigenous women, refugee women, women migrants, including women migrant workers, women in poverty living in rural or remote communities, destitute women, women in institutions or in detention, female children, women with disabilities, elderly women, displaced women, repatriated women, women living in poverty and women in situations of armed conflict, foreign occupation, wars of aggression, civil wars, terrorism, including hostage-taking, are also particularly vulnerable to violence.

117. Acts or threats of violence, whether occurring within the home or in the community, or perpetrated or condoned by the State, instil fear and insecurity in women's lives and are obstacles to the achievement of equality and for development and peace. The fear of violence, including harassment, is a permanent constraint on the mo-

bility of women and limits their access to resources and basic activities. High social, health and economic costs to the individual and society are associated with violence against women. Violence against women is one of the crucial social mechanisms by which women are forced into a subordinate position compared with men. In many cases, violence against women and girls occurs in the family or within the home, where violence is often tolerated. The neglect, physical and sexual abuse, and rape of girl-children and women by family members and other members of the household, as well as incidences of spousal and non-spousal abuse, often go unreported and are thus difficult to detect. Even when such violence is reported, there is often a failure to protect victims or punish perpetrators.

118. Violence against women is a manifestation of the historically unequal power relations between men and women, which have led to domination over and discrimination against women by men and to the prevention of women's full advancement. Violence against women throughout the life cycle derives essentially from cultural patterns, in particular the harmful effects of certain traditional or customary practices and all acts of extremism linked to race, sex, language or religion that perpetuate the lower status accorded to women in the family, the workplace, the community and society. Violence against women is exacerbated by social pressures, notably the shame of denouncing certain acts that have been perpetrated against women; women's lack of access to legal information, aid or protection; the lack of laws that effectively prohibit violence against women; failure to reform existing laws; inadequate efforts on the part of public authorities to promote awareness of and enforce existing laws; and the absence of educational and other means to address the causes and consequences of violence. Images in the media of violence against women, in particular those that depict rape or sexual slavery as well as the use of women and girls as sex objects, including pornography, are factors contributing to the continued prevalence of such violence, adversely influencing the community at large, in particular children and young people.

119. Developing holistic and multidisciplinary approach to the challenging task of promoting families, communities and States that are free of violence against women is necessary and achievable. Equality, partnership between women and men and espect for human dignity must permeate all stages of the socialization process. Educational systems should promote Self-respect, mutual respect, and cooperation between women and men.

120. The absence of adequate gender disaggregated data and statistics on the incidence of violence makes the elaboration of programmes and monitoring of changes difficult. Lack of or inadequate documentation and research on domestic violence, sexual harassment and violence against women and girls in private and in public, including the workplace, impede efforts to design specific intervention strategies. Experience in a number of countries shows that women and men can be mobilized to overcome violence in all its forms and that effective public measures can be taken to address both the causes and the consequences of violence. Men's groups mobilizing against gender violence are necessary allies for change.

121. Women may be vulnerable to violence perpetrated by persons in positions of authority in both conflict and non-conflict situations. Training of all officials in humanitarian and human rights law and the punishment of perpetrators of violent acts against women would help to ensure that such violence does not take place at the hands of public officials in whom women should be able to place trust, including police and prison officials and security forces.

122. The effective suppression of trafficking in women and girls for the sex trade is a matter of pressing international concern. Implementation of the 1949 Convention for the Suppression of the Traffic in Persons and of the Exploitation of the Prostitution of Others,[20] as well as other relevant instruments, needs to be reviewed and strengthened. The use of women in international prostitution and trafficking networks has become a major focus of international organized crime. The Special Rapporteur of the Commission on Human Rights on violence against women, who has explored these acts as an additional cause of the violation of the human rights and fundamental freedoms of women and girls, is invited to address, within her mandate and as a matter of urgency, the issue of international trafficking for the purposes of the sex trade, as well as the issues of forced prostitution, rape, sexual abuse and sex tourism. Women and girls who are victims of this international trade are at an increased risk of further violence, as well as unwanted pregnancy and sexually transmitted infection, including infection with HIV/AIDS.

123. In addressing violence against women, Governments and other actors should promote an active and visible policy of mainstreaming a gender perspective in all policies and programmes so that before decisions are taken an analysis may be made of their effects on women and men, respectively.

Strategic objective D.1.
Take integrated measures to prevent and eliminate violence against women

Actions to be taken

124. By Governments:

(a) Condemn violence against women and refrain from invoking any custom, tradition or religious consideration to avoid their obligations with respect to its elimination as set out in the Declaration on the Elimination of Violence against Women;

(b) Refrain from engaging in violence against women and exercise due diligence to prevent, investigate and, in accordance with national legislation, punish acts of violence against women, whether those acts are perpetrated by the State or by private persons;

(c) Enact and/or reinforce penal, civil, labour and administrative sanctions in domestic legislation to punish and redress the wrongs done to women and girls who are subjected to any form of violence, whether in the home, the workplace, the community or society;

(d) Adopt and/or implement and periodically review and analyse legislation to ensure its effectiveness in eliminating violence against women, emphasizing the prevention of violence and the prosecution of offenders; take measures to ensure the protection of women subjected to violence, access to just and effective remedies, including compensationand indemnification and bealing of victims, and rehabilitation of perpetrators;

(e) Work actively to ratify and/or implement international human rights norms and instruments a, they relate to violence against women, including those contained in the Universal Declaration of Human Rights the International Covenant on Civil and Political Rights,[13] the International Covenant Economic, Social and Cultural Rights,[13] and the Convention against Torture and Other Cruel, Inhuman or Degrading Treatment or Punishment;[22]

(f) Implement the Convention on the Elimination of All Forms of Discrimination against Women, taking into account general recommendation 19, adopted by the Committee on the Elimination of Discrimination against Women at its eleventh session;

(g) Promote an active and visible policy of mainstreaming a gender perspective in all policies and programmes related to violence against women; actively encourage, support and implement measures and programmes aimed at increasing the knowledge and understanding of the causes, consequences and mechanisms of violence against women among those responsible for implementing these policies, such as law enforcement officers, police personnel and judicial, medical and Social workers, as well as those who deal with minority, migration and refugee issues, and develop strategies to ensure that the revictimization of women victims of violence does not occur because of gender-insensitive laws or judicial or enforcement practices;

(h) Provide women who are subjected to violence with access to the mechanisms of justice and, as provided for by national legislation, to just and effective remedies for the harm they have suffered and inform women of their rights in seeking redress through such mechanisms;

(i) Enact and enforce legislation against the perpetrators of practices and acts of violence against women, such as female genital mutilation: female infanticide, prenatal sex selection and dowry-related violence and give vigorous support to the efforts of non-governmental and community organizations to eliminate such practices;

(j) Formulate and implement, at all appropriate levels, plans of action to eliminate violence against women;

(k) Adopt all appropriate measures, especially in the field of education, to modify the social and cultural patterns of conduct of men and women, and to eliminate prejudices, customary practices and all other practices based on the idea of the inferiority or superiority of either of the sexes and on stereotyped roles for men and women;

(l) Create or strengthen institutional mechanisms so that women and girls can report acts of violence against them in a safe and confidential environment, free from the fear of penalties or retaliation, and file charges;

(m) Ensure that women with disabilities have access to information and services in the field of violence against women;

(n) Create, improve or develop, as appropriate, and fund the training programmes for judicial, legal, medical, social, educational and police and immigrant personnel, in order to avoid the abuse of power leading to violence against women and sensitize such personnel to the nature of gender-based acts and threats of violence so that fair treatment of female victims can be assured;

(o) Adopt laws, where necessary, and reinforce existing laws that punish police, security forces or any other agents of the State who engage in acts of violence against women in the course of the performance of their duties; review existing legislation and take effective measures against the perpetrators of such violence·

(p) Allocate adequate resources within the government budget and mobilize community resources for activities related to the elimination of violence against women, including resources for the implementation of plans of action at all appropriate levels;

(q) Include in reports submitted in accordance with the provisions of relevant United Nations human rights instruments, information pertaining to violence against women and measures taken to implement the Declaration on the Elimination of Violence against Women;

(r) Co-operate with and assist the Special Rapporteur of the Commission on Human Rights on violence against women in the performance of her mandate and furnish all information requested; co-operate also with other competent mechanisms, such as the Special Rapporteur of the Commission on Human Rights on torture and the Special Rapporteur of the Commission on Human Rights on summary, extrajudiciary and arbitrary executions, in relation to violence against women;

(s) Recommend that the Commission on Human Rights renew the mandate of the Special Rapporteur on violence against women when her term ends in 1997 and, if warranted, to update and strengthen it.

125. By Governments, including local governments, community organizations, non-governmental organizations, educational institutions, the public and private sectors, particularly enterprises, and the mass media, as appropriate:

(a) Provide well-funded shelters and relief support for girls and women subjected to violence, as well as medical, psychological and other counselling services and free or low-cost legal aid, where it is needed, as well as appropriate assistance to enable them to find a means of subsistence;

(b) Establish linguistically and culturally accessible services for migrant women and girls, including women migrant workers, who are victims of gender-based violence;

(c) Recognize the vulnerability to violence and other forms of abuse of women migrants, including women migrant workers, whose legal status in the host country depends on employers who may exploit their Situation;

(d) Support initiatives ofwomen's organizations and non-governmental organizations all over the world to raise awareness on the issue of violence against women and to contribute to its elimination;

(e) Organize, support and fund community-based education and training campaigns to raise awareness about violence against women as a violation of women's enjoyment of their human rights and mobilize local communities to use appropriate gendersensitive traditional and innovative methods of conflict resolution;

(f) Recognize, support and promote the fundamental role of intermediate institutions, such as primary health-care centres, family-planning centres, existing school health services, mother and baby protection services, centres for migrant families and so forth in the field of information and education related to abuse;

(g) Organize and fund information campaigns and educational and training programmes in order to sensitize girls and boys and women and men to the personal and social detrimental effects of violence in the family, community and society; teach them how to communicate without violence and promote training for victims and potential victims so that they can protect themselves and others against such violence;

(h) Disseminate information on the assistance available to women and fmilies who are victims of violence;

(i) Provide, fund and encourage counselling and rehabilitation programmes for the perpetrators of violence and promote research to further efforts concerning such counselling and rehabilitation so as to prevent the recurrence of such violence;

(j) Raise awareness of the responsibility of the media in promoting non-stereotyped images of women and men, as well as in eliminating patterns of media presentation that generate violence, and encourage those responsible for media content to establish professional guidelines and codes of conduct; also raise awareness of the important role of the media in informing and educating people about the causes and effects of violence against women and in stimulating public debate on the topic.

126. By Governments, employers, trade unions, community and youth organizations and non-governmental organizations, as appropriate:

(a) Develop programmes and procedures to eliminate sexual harassment and other forms of violence against women in all educational institutions, workplaces and elsewhere;

(b) Develop programmes and procedures to educate and raise awareness of acts of violence against women that constitute a crime and a violation of the human rights of women;

(c) Develop counselling, healing and support programmes for girls, adolescents and young women who have been or are involved in abusive relationships, particularly those who live in homes or institutions where abuse occurs;

(d) Take special measures to eliminate violence against women, particularly those in vulnerable situations, such as young women, refugee, displaced and internally displaced women, women with disabilities and women migrant workers, including enforcing any existing legislation and developing, as appropriate, new legislation for women migrant workers in both sending and receiving countries.

127. By the Secretary-General of the United Nations:

Provide the Special Rapporteur of the Commission on Human Rights on violence against women with all necessary assistance, in particular the staff and resources required to perform all mandated functions, especially in carrying out and following up on missions undertaken either separately or jointly with other special rapporteurs and working groups, and adequate assistance for periodic consultations with the Committee on the Elimination of Discrimination against Women and all treaty bodies.

128. By Governments, international organizations and non-governmental organizations:

Encourage the dissemination and implementation of the UNHCR Guidelines on the Protection of Refugee Women and the UNHCR Guidelines on the Prevention of and Response to Sexual Violence against Refugees.

Strategic Objective D. 2.

Study the causes and consequences of violence against women and the effectiveness of preventive measures

Actions to be taken

129. BY Governments, regional organizations, the United Nations, other international organizations, research institutions, women's and youth

organizations and non-governmental organizations, as appropriate:

(a) Promote research, collect data and compile statistics, especially concerning domestic violence relating to the prevalence of different forms of violence against women, and encourage research into the causes, nature, seriousness and consequences of violence against women and the effectiveness of measures implemented to prevent and redress violence against women;

(b) Disseminate findings of research and studies widely;

(c) Support and initiatere search on the impact of violence, such as rape, on women and girl-children, and make the resulting information and statistics available to the public;

(d) Encourage the media to examine the impact of gender role stereotypes, including those perpetuated by commercial advertisements which foster gender-based violence and inequalities, and how they are transmitted during the life cycle, and take measures to eliminate these negative images with a view to promoting a violence-free society.

Strategic objective D. 3.
Eliminate trafficking in women and assist victims of violence due to prostitution trafficking

Actions to be taken

130. By Governments of countries of origin, transit and destination, regional and international organizations, as appropriate:

(a) Consider the ratification and enforcement of international conventions on trafficking in persons and on slavery;

(b) Take appropriate measures to address the root factors, including external factors, that encourage trafficking in women and girls for prostitution and other forms of commercialized sex, forced marriages and forced labour in order to eliminate trafficking in women, including by strengthening existing legislation with a view to providing.better protection of the rights of women and girls and to punishing the perpetrators, through both criminal and civil measures;

(c) Step up co-operation and concerted action by all relevant law enforcement authorities and institutions with a view to dismantling national, regional and international networks in trafficking;

(d) Allocate resources to provide comprehensive programmes designed to heal and rehabilitate into society victims of trafficking, including through job training, legal assistance and confidential health care, through job training, legal assistance and confidential health care, and take measures to cooperate with non-governmental organizations to provide for the social, medical and psychological care of the victims of trafficking;

(e) Develop educational and training programmes and policies and consider enacting legislation aimed at preventing sex tourism and trafficking, giving special emphasis to the protection of young women and children.

E. Women and Armed Conflict

131. An environment that maintains world peace and promotes and protects human rights, democracy and the peaceful settlement of disputes, in accordance with the principles of non-threat or use of force against territorial integrity or political independence and of respect for sovereignty as set forth in the Charter of the United Nations, is an Important factor for the advancement of women. Peace is inextricably linked with equality between women and men and development. Armed and other types of connicts and terrorism and hostage taking still persist in many parts of the world. Aggression, foreign occupation, ethnic and other types of conflicts are an ongoing reality affecting women and men in nearly every region. Gross and Systematic violations and situations that constitute serious obstacles to the full enjoyment of human rights continue to occur in different parts of the world. Such violations and obstacles include, as well as torture and cruel, inhuman and degrading treatment or punishment, summary and arbitrary executions, disappearances, arbitrary detentions, all forms of racism and racial discrimination, foreign Occupation and alien domination, enophobia, poverty, hunger and other denials of economic, social and cultural rights, religious intolerance, terrorism, discrimination against women and lack of the rule of law. International humanitarian law, prohibiting attacks on civilian populations, as such, is at times systematically ignored and human rights are often violated in connection with situations of armed connict, affecting the civilian population, especially women, children, the elderly and the disabled. Violations of the human rights of women in situations of armed conflict are violations of the fundamental Principles of international human rights and humanitarian law. Massive violations of human rights, especially in the form of genocide, ethnic cleansing as a strategy of war and its consequences, and rape, including systematic rape of women

in war situations, creating a mass exodus of refugees and displaced persons, are abhorrent practices that are strongly condemned and must be stopped immediate while perpetrators of such crimes must be punished. Some of these situations of armed conflict have their origin in the conquest or colonialization of a country by another State and the perpetuation of that colonization through State and military repression.

132. 'The Geneva Convention relative to the Protection of Civilian Persons in Time of War, of 1949, and the Additional Protocols of 1977[24] provide that women shall especially be protected against any attack on their honour, in particular against humiliating and degrading treat ment, rape, enforced prostitution or any form of indecent assault. The Vienna Declaration and Programme of Action, adopted by the World Conference on Human Rights, states that "violations of the human rights of women in situations of armed conflict are violations of the fundamental principles of international human rights and humanitarian law"[25] All violations of this kind, including in particular murder, rape, including systematic rape, sexual slavery and forced pregnancy, require a particularly effective response. Gross and systematic violations and situations that constitute serious obstacles to the full enjoyment of human rights continue to occur in different parts of the world. Such violations and obstacles include, as well as torture and cruel, inhuman and degrading treatment or summary and arbitrary detention, all forms of racism, racial discrimination, xenophobia, denial of economic, social and cultural rights and religious intolerance.

133. Violations of human rights in situations of armed conflict and military occupation are violations of the fundamental principles of interna- tional human rights and humanitarian law as embodied in international human rights instruments and in the Geneva Conventions of 1949 and the Additional Protocols thereto. Gross human rights violations and policies of ethnic cleansing in war-torn and occupied areas continue to be carried out. These practices have created, *inter alia*, a mass flow of refugees and other displaced persons in need of international protection and internally displaced persons, the majority of whom are women, adolescent girls and children. Civilian victims, mostly women and children, often outnumber casualties among combatants. In addition, women often become caregivers for injured combatants and find themselves, as a result of conflict, unex pectedly cast as sole manager of household, sole parent, and caretaker of elderly relatives.

134. In a world of continuing instability and violence, the implementation of co-operative approaches to peace and security is urgently needed. The equal access and full participation of women in power structures and their full involvement in all efforts for the prevention and resolution of conflicts are essential for the maintenance and promotion of peace and security. Although women have begun to play an important role in conflict resolution, peace-keeping and defence and foreign affairs mechanisms, they are still underrepresented in decision-making positions. If women are to play an equal part in securing and maintaining peace, they must be empowered politically and economically and represented adequately at all levels of decision-making.

135. While entire communities suffer the consequences of armed conflict and terrorism, women and girls are particularly affected because of their status in society and their sex. Parties to conflict often rape women with impunity, sometimes using systematic rape as a tactic of war and terrorism. The impact of violence against women and violation of the human rights of women in such situations is experienced by women of all ages, who suffer displacement, loss of home and property, loss or involuntary disappearance of close relatives, poverty and family separation and disintegration, and who are victims of acts of murder, terrorism, torture, involuntary disappearance, sexual slavely, rape, sexual abuse and forced pregnancy in situations of armed conflict, especially as a result of policies of ethnic cleansing and other new and emerging forms of violence. This is compounded by the life-long social, economic and psychologically traumatic consequences of armed conflict and foreign occupation and alien domination.

136. Women and children constitute some 80 per cent of the world's millions of refugees and other displaced persons, including internally displaced persons. They are threatened by deprivation of property, goods and services and deprivation of their right to return to their homes of origin as well as by violence and insecurity. Particular attention should be paid to sexual violence against uprooted women and girls employed as a method of persecution in systematic campaigns of terror and intimidation and forcing members of a particular ethnic, cultural or religious group to flee their homes. Women may also be forced to flee as a result of a well-founded fear of persecution for reasons enumerated in the 1951 Convention relating to the Status of Refugees and the 1967 Protocol, including persecution through sexual violence or other gender-related persecution, and

they continue to be vulnerable to violence and exploitation while in flight, in countries of asylum and resettlement and during and after repatriation. Women often experience difficulty in some countries of asylum in being recognized as refugees when the claim is based on such persecution.

137. Refugee, displaced and migrant women in most cases display strength, endurance and resourcefulness and can contribute positively to countries of resettlement or to their country of origin on their return. They need to be appropriately involved in decisions that affect them.

138. Many women's non-governmental organizations have called for reductions in military expenditures worldwide, as well as in international trade and trafficking in, and the proliferation of weapons. Those affected most negatively by cbnflict and excessive military spending are people living in poverty, who are deprived because of the lack of investment in basic services. Women living in poverty, particularly rural women, also suffer because of the use of arms that are particularly injurious or have indiscriminate effects. There are more than 100 million anti-personnel land-mines scattered in 64 countries globally. The negative impact on development of excessive military expenditures, the arms trade, and investment for arms production and acquisition must be addressed. At the same time, maintenance of national security and peace is an important factor for development and the economic growth and impowerment of women.

139. During times of armed conflict and the collapse of communities, the role of women is crucial. They often work to preserve social order in the midst of armed and other conflicts. Women make an important but often unrecognized contribution as peace educators both in their families and in their societies.

140. Education to, foster a culture of peace that upholds justice and tolerance for all nations and peoples is essential to attaining lasting peace and Should be begun at an early age. It should include elements of conflict resolution, mediation, reduction of prejudice and respect for diversity.

141. In addressing armed or other conflict, and active and visible policy of mainstreaming a gender perspective into all policies and programmes should be promoted so that before decisions are taken an analysis is made of the effects of women and men, respectively.

Strategic objective E.1.

Increase the participation of women in conflict resolution at decision-making levels and protect women living in situations of armed and other conflicts or under foreign occupation

Actions to be taken

142. By Governments and international and regional intergovernmental

(a) Take action to promote equal participation of women and equal opportunities for women to participate in all forums and peace activities at all levels, particularly at the decision-making level, including in, the United Nations Secretariat with due regard to equitable: geographical distribution in accordance with Article 101of the Charter of the United Nations;

(b) Integrate a gender perspective in the resolution of armed or other conflicts and foreign occupation and aim for gender balance when nominating or promoting candidates for judicial and other positions in all relevant international bodies, such as the United Nations International Tribunals for the former Yugoslavia and for Rwanda and the International Court of Justice, as well as in other bodies related to the peaceful settlement of disputes;

(c) Ensure that these bodies are able to address gender issues properly by providing appropriate training to prosecutors, judges and other officials in handling cases involving rape, forced pregnancy in situations of armed conflict, indecent assault and other forms of violence against women in armed conflicts, including terrorism, and integrate a gender perspective into their work.

Strategic objective E.2.

Reduce excessive military expenditures and control the availability of armaments

Actions to be taken

143. By Governments:

(a) Increase and hasten, as appropriate, subject to national security considerations, the conversion of military resources and related industries to development and peaceful purposes;

(b) Undertake to explore new ways of generating new public and private financial resources, inter alia, through the appropriate reduction of excessive military expenditures, including global military expenditures, trade in arms and investment for arms production and acquisition, taking into consideration national security requirements, so as to permit the possible allocation of additional funds for social and economic development, in particular for the advancement of women;

(c) Take action to investigate and punish members of the police, security and armed forces and others who perpetrate acts of violence against women, violations of international humanitarian law and violations of the human rights of women in situations of armed conflict;

(d) While acknowledging legitimate national defence needs, recognize and address the dangers to society of armed conflict and the negative effect of excessive military expenditures, trade in arms, especially those arms that are particularly injurious or have indiscriminate effects, and excessive investment for arms production and acquisition; similarly, recognize the need to combat illicit arms trafficking, violence, crime, the production and use of and trafficking in illicit drugs, and trafficking in, women and children;

(e) Recognizing that women and children are particularly affected by the indiscriminate use of anti-personel land-mines:

(i) Undertake to, work actively towards ratification, if they have not already done so, of the 1981 Convention on Prohibitions "Restrictions on the Use of Certain Conventional Weapons Which May Be Deemed to be Excessively Injurious or to Have Indiscriminate Effects, Particularly the Protocol on Prohibitions or Restrictions on the Use of Mines, Booby Traps and Other Devices (Protocol II), 26/ with a view to universal ratification by the year 2000;

(ii) Undertake to, Strongly consider strengthening the Convention to promote a reduction in the casualties and intense suffering caused to the civilian population by the indiscriminate use of

(iii) Undertake to promote assistance in mine clearance, notably by facilitating, in respect of the means of mine-clearing, the exchange of information, the transfer of technology and the promotion of scientific research;

(iv) Within the United Nations context, undertake to support efforts to coordinate a common response programme of assistance in de-mining without unnecessary discrimination;

(v) Adopt, to the earliest possible date, if they have not already done so, a moratorium on the export of anti-personnel landmines, including to non-govemmental entities, noting with satisfaction that many States have already declared moratoriums on the export, transfer or sale of such mines;

(vi) Undertake to encourage further international efforts to seek solutions to the Problems caused by antipersonnel landmines, with a view to their eventual elimination, recognizing that States can move most effectively towards this goal as viable and humane alternatives are developed;

(f) Recognizing the leading role that women have played in the peace movement;

(i) Work actively towards general and complete, disarmament under strict and effective international control;

(ii) Support negotiations on the conclusion, without delay, of a universal and multilaterally and effectively verifiable comprehensive nuclear test-ban treaty that contributes to nuclear disarmament and the prevention of the proliferation of nuclear weapons in all its aspects;

(iii) Pending the entry into force of a comprehensive nuclear-test-ban treaty, exercise the utmost restraint in respect of nuclear testing.

Strategic objective E. 3.

Promote non-violent forms of conflict resolution and reduce the incidence of human rights abuse in conflict situations

Actions to be taken

144. By Governments:

(a) Consider the ratification of or accession to international instruments containing provisions relative to the protection of women and children in armed conflicts, including the Geneva Convention relative to the Protection of Civilian Persons in Time of War, of 1949, the Protocols Additional to the Geneva Conventions of 1949 relating to the Protection of Victims of International Armed Conflicts (Protocol I) and to the Protection of Victims of Non-Iinternational Armed Conflicts (Protocol II); 24/;

(b) Respect fully the norms of international humanitarian law in armed conflicts and take all measures required for the protection of women and children, in particular against rape, forced prostitution and any other form of indecent assault;

(c) Strengthen the role of women and ensure equal representation of women at all decision-making levels in national and international institutions which may make or influence policy with regard to matters related to peace-keeping, preventive diplomacy and related activities and in all stages of peace mediation and negotiations, taking note of the specific recommendations of the Secretary-General in his strategic plan of action for the improvement of the status of women in the Secretariat (1995-2000) (A/49/587, sect. IV);

145. By Governments and international and regional organizations:

(a) Reaffirm the right of self-determination of all peoples, in particular of peoples under colonial or other forms of alien domination or foreign occupation, and the importance of the effective realization of this right, as enunciated, *inter alia,* in the Vienna Declaration and Programme of Action,[2] adopted by the World Conference on Human Rights;

(b) Encourage diplomacy, negotiation and peaceful settlement of disputes in accordance with the Charter of the United Nations, in particular Article 2, paragraphs 3 and 4, thereof;

(c) Urge the identification and condemnation of the systematic practice of rape and other forms of inhuman and degrading treatment of women as a deliberate instrument of war and ethnic cleansing and take steps to ensure that full assistance is provided to the victims of such abuse for their physical and mental rehabilitation;

(d) Reaffirm that rape in the conduct of armed conflict constitutes a war crime and under certain circumstances it constitutes a crime against humanity and an act of genocide as defined in the Convention on the Prevention and Punishment of the Crime of Genocide;[27] take all measures required for the protection of women and children from such acts and strengthen mechanisms to investigate and punish all those responsible and bring the perpetrators to justice;

(e) Uphold and reinforce standards set out in international humanitarian law and international human rights instruments to prevent all acts of violence against women in situations of armed and other conflicts; undertake a full investigation of all acts of violence against women committed during war, including rape, in particular systematic rape, forced prostitution and other forms of indecent assault and sexual slavery; prosecute all criminals responsible for war crimes against women and provide full redress to women victims;

(f) Call upon the international community to condemn and act against all forms and manifestations of terrorism;

(g) Take into account gender-sensitive concerns in developing training programmes for all relevant personnel on international humanitarian law and human rights awareness and recommend such training for those involved in United Nations peace-keeping and humanitarian aid with a view to preventing violence against women, in particular;

(h) Discourage the adoption of and refrain from any unilateral measure, not in accordance with international law and the Charter of the United Nations, that impedes the full achievement of economic and social development by the population of the affected countries, in particular women and children, that hinders their well-being and that creates obstacles to the full enjoyment of their human rights, including the right of everyone to a standard of living adequate for their health and well-being and their right to food, medical care and the necessary social services. This Conference reaffirms that food and medicine must not be used as a tool for political pressure;

(i) Take measures in accordance with international law with a view to alleviating the negative impact of economic sanctions on women and children.

Strategic objective E.4.
Promote women's contribution to fostering a culture of peace

Actions to be taken

146. By Governments, international and regional intergovernmental institutions and non-governmental organizations:

(a) Promote peaceful conflict resolution and peace, reconciliation and tolerance through education, training, community actions and youth exchange programmes, in particular for young women;

(b) Encourage the further development of peace research, involving the participation of women, to examine the impact of armed conflict on women and children and the nature and contribution of women's participation in national, regional and international peace movements; engage in research and identify innovative mechanisms for containing violence and for conflict resolution for public dissemination and for use by women and men;

(c) Develop and disseminate research on the physical, psychological, economic and social effects of armed conflicts on women, particularry young women and girls, with a view to developing policies and programmes to address the consequences of conflicts;

(d) Consider establishing educational programmes for girls and boys to foster a culture of peace, focusing on conflict resolution by non-violent means and the promotion of tolerance.

Strategic objective E. 5.

Provide protection, assistance and training to refugee women, other displaced women in need of international protection and internally displaced women

Actions to be taken

147. By Governments, intergovernmental and non-governmental organizations and other institutions involved in providing protection, assistance and training to refugee women, other displaced women in need of international protection and internally displaced women, including the office of the United Nations High Commissioner for Refugees and the World Food Programme, as appropriate:

(a) Take steps to ensure that women are fully involved in the planning, design, implementation, monitoring and evaluation of all short-term and long-term projects and programmes providing assistance to refugee women, other displaced women in need of international protection and internally displaced women, including the management of refugee camps and resources; ensure that refugee and displaced women and girls have direct access to the services provided;

(b) Offer adequate protection and assistance to women and children displaced within their country and find solutions to the root causes of their displacement with a view to preventing it and, when appropriate, facilitate their return or resettlement;

(c) Take steps to protect the safety and physical integrity of refugee women, other displaced women in need of international protection and internally displaced women during their displacement and upon their return to their communities of origin, including programmes of rehabilitation; take effective measures to protect from violence women who are refugees or displaced; hold an impartial and thorough investigation of any such violations and bring those responsible to justice;

(d) While fully respecting and strictly observing the principle of *non-refoulement* of refugees, take all the necessary steps to ensure the right of refugee and displaced women to return voluntarily to their place of origin in safety and with dignity, and their right to protection after their return;

(e) Take measures, at the national level with international co-operation, as appropriate, in accordance with the Charter of the United Nations, to find lasting solutions to questions related to internally displaced women, including their right to voluntary and safe return to their home of origin;

(f) Ensure that the international community and its international organizations provide financial and other resources for emergency relief and other longer-term assistance that takes into account the specific needs, resources and potentials of refugee women, other displaced women in need of international protection and internally displaced women; in the provision of protection and assistance, take all appropriate measures to eliminate discrimination against women and girls in order to ensure equal access to appropriate and adequate food, water and shelter, education, and social and health services, including reproductive health care and maternity care and services to combat tropical diseases;

(g) Facilitate the availability of educational materials in the appropriate language—in emergency situations also—in order to minimize disruption of schooling among refugee and displaced children;

(h) Apply international norms to ensure equal access and equal treat-ment of women and men in refugee determination procedures and the granting of asylum, including full respect and strict observation of the principle of *non-refoulement* through, *inter alia*, bringing national immigration regulations into conformity with relevant international instruments, and consider recognizing as refugees those women whose claim to refugee status is based upon the wellfounded fear of persecution for reasons enumerated in the 1951 Convention[28] and the 1967 Protocol[29] relating to the Status of Refugees, including persecution through sexual violence or other gender-related persecution, and provide access to specially trained officers, including female officers to interview women regarding sensitive or painful experiences, such as sexual assault;

(i) Support and promote efforts by States towards the development of criteria and guidelines on responses to persecution specifically aimed at women, by sharing information on States' initiatives to develop such criteria and guidelines and by monitoring to ensure their fair and consistent application;

(j) Promote the self-reliant capacities of refugee women, other displaced women in need of international protection and internally displaced women and provide programmes for women, particularly young women, in leadership and decision-making within refugee and returnee communities;

(k) Ensure that the human rights of refugee and displaced women are protected and that refugee and displaced women are made aware of these rights; ensure that the vital importance of family reunification is recognized;

(l) Provide, as appropriate, women who have been determined refugees with access to vocational/professional training programmes, including language training, small-scale enterprise development training and planning and counselling on all forms of violence against women, which should include rehabilitation programmes for victims of torture and trauma; Governments and other donors should contribute adequately to assistance programmes for refugee women, other displaced women in need of international protection and internally displaced women, taking into account in particular the effects on the host countries of the Increasing requirements of large refugee populations and the need to widen the donor base and to achieve greater burden- sharing;

(m) Raise public awareness of the contribution made by refugee women to their countries of resettlement, promote understanding of their human rights and of their needs and abilities and encourage mutual understanding and acceptance through educational programmes promoting cross-cultural and interracial harmony;

(n) Provide basic and support services to women who are displaced from their place of origin as a result of terrorism, violence, drug trafficking or other reasons linked to violence situations;

(n) Develop awareness of the human rights of women and provide, as appropriate, human rights education and training to military and police personnel operating in areas of armed conflict and areas where there are refugees.

148. BY Governments:

(a) Disseminate and implement the UNHCR Guidelines on the Protection of Refugee Women and the UNHCR Guidelines on Evaluation and Care of Victims of Trauma and Violence, or provide similar guidance, in close co-operation with refugee women and in all sectors of refugee programmes;

(b) Protect women and children who migrate as family members from abuse or denial of their human rights by sponsors and consider extending their stay, should the family relationship dissolve, within the limits of national legislation.

Strategic objective E. 6.

Provide assistance to the territories women of the colonies and non-self-governing

Actions to be taken

149. By Governments and non-governmental and intergovernmental organizations:

(a) Support and promote the implementation of the right of self-deter. mination of all peoples as enunciated, inter alia, in the Vienna Declaration and Programme of Action by providing special programmes in leadership and in training for decision-making;

(b) Raise public awareness, as appropriate, through the mass media, education at all levels and special programmes to create a better understanding of the situation of women of the colonies and non-self-governing territories.

F. Women and the Economy

150. There are considerable differences in women's and men's access to and opportunities to exert power over economic structures in their societies. In most parts of the world, women are virtually absent from or are poorly represented in.economic decision-making, including the formulation of financial, monetary, commercial and other economic policies, as well as tax Systems and rules governing pay. Since it is often within the framework of such policies that individual men and women make their decisions, inter alia, on how to divide their time between remunerated and unremunerated work, on how to divide their time between women's and men's access to the actual development of these economic structures and policies has a direct impact on women's and men's access to economic resources, their economic power and consequently the extent of equality between them at the individual and family levels as well as in society as a whole.

151. In many regions, women's participation in remunerated work in the formal and non-formal labour market has increased significantly and has changed during the past decade. While women continue to

work in agriculture and fisheries, they have also become increasingly involved in micro, small and medium-sized enterprises and, in some cases, have become more dominant in the expanding informal sector. Due to, inter alia, difficult economic situations and a lack of bargaining power resulting from gender inequality, many women have been forced to accept low pay and poor working conditions and thus have often become preferred workers. On the other hand, women have entered the workforce increasingly by choice when they have become aware of and demanded their rights. Some have succeeded in entering and advancing in the workplace and improving their pay and working conditions. However, women have been particularly affected by the economic situation and restructuring processes, which have changed the nature of employment and, in some cases, have led to a loss of jobs, even for professional and skilled women. In addition, many women have entered the informal sector owing to the lack of other opportunities. Women's participation and gender concerns are still largely absent from and should be integrated in the policy formulation process of the multilateral institutions that define the terms and, in co-operation with Governments, set the goals of structural adjustment programmes, loans and grants.

152. Discrimination in education and training, hiring and remuneration, promotion and horizontal mobility practices, as well as inflexible working conditions, lack of access to productive resources and inadequate sharing of family responsibilities, combined with a lack of or insufficient services such as child care, continue to restrict employment, economic, professional and other opportunities and mobility for women and make their involvement stressful. Moreover, attitudinal obstacles inhibit women's participation in developing economic policy and in some regions restrict the access of women and girls to education and training for economic management.

153. Women's share in the labour force continues to rise and almost every where women are working more outside the household, although there has not been a parallel lightening of responsibility for unremunerated work in the household and community. Women's income is becoming increasingly necessary to households of all types. In some regions, there has been a growth in women's entrepreneurship and other self-reliant activities, particularly in the informal sector. In many countries, women are the majority of workers in non-standard work, such as temporary, casual, multiple part-time, contract and home-based employment.

154. Women migrant workers, including domestic workers, contribute to the economy of the sending country through their remittances and also to the economy of the receiving country through their participation in the labour force. However, in many receiving countries, migrant women experience higher levels of unemployment compared with both non-migrant workers and male migrant workers.

155. Insufficient attention to gender analysis has meant that women's contributions and concerns remain too often ignored in economic structures, such as financial markets and institutions, labour markets, economics as an academic discipline, economic and social infrastructure, taxation and social security systems, as well as in families and households. As a result, many policies and programmes may continue to contribute to inequalities between women and men. Where progress has been made in integrating gender perspectives, programme and policy effectiveness has also been enhanced.

156. Although many women have advanced in economic structures, for the majority of women, particularly those who face additional barriers, continuing obstacles have hindered their ability to achieve economic autonomy and to ensure sustainable livelihoods for themselves and their dependents. Women are active in a variety of economic areas, which they often combine, ranging from wage labour and subsistence farming and fishing to the informal sector. However, legal and customary barriers to ownership of or access to land, natural resources, capital, credit, technology and other means of production, as well as wage differentials, contribute to impeding the economic progress of women. Women contribute to development not only through remunerated work but also through a great deal of unremu-nerated work. On the one hand, women participate in the production of goods and services for the market and household consumption, in agriculture, food production or family enterprises. Though included in the United Nations System of National Accounts and therefore in international standards for labour statistics, this unremunerated workparticularly that related to agriculture—is often undervalued and under-recorded. On the other hand, women still also perform the great majority of unremunerated domestic work and community work, such as caring for children and older persons, preparing food for the family, protecting the environment and providing voluntary assistance to vulnerable and disadvantaged individuals and groups. This work is often not measured in quantitative terms and is not valued in national accounts. Women's contribution to development is seriously underestimated, and thus its so-

cial recognition is limited. The full visibility of the type, extent and distribution of this unremunerated work will also contribute to a better sharing of responsibilities.

157. Although some new employment opportunities have been created for women as a result of the globalization of the economy, there are also trends that have exacerbated inequalities between women and men. At the same time, globalization, including economic integration, can create pressures on the employment situation of women to adjust to new circumstances and to find new sources of employment as patterns of trade change. More analysis needs to be done of the impact of globalization on women's economic status.

158. These trends have been characterized by low wages, little or no labour standards protection, poor working conditions, particularly with regard to women's occupational health and safety, low skill levels, and a lack of job security and social security, in both the formal and informal sectors. Women's unemployment is a serious and increasing problem in many countries and sectors. Young workers in the informal and rural sectors and migrant female workers remain the least protected by labour and immigration laws. Women, particularly those who are heads of households with young children, are limited in their employment opportunities for reasons that include inflexible working conditions and inadequate sharing, by men and by society, of family responsibilities.

159. In countries that are undergoing fundamental political, economic and social transformation, the skills of women, if better utilized, could constitute a major contribution to the economic life of their respective countries. Their input should continue to be developed and supported and their poten-tial further realized.

160. Lack of employment in the private sector and reductions in public services and public service jobs have affected women disproportionat by some countries, women take on more unpaid work, such as the care of children and those who are ill or elderly, compensating for lost household income, particularly when public services are not available. In many cases, employment creation strategies have not paid sufficient attention to occupations and sectors where women predominate; nor have they adequately promoted the access of women to those occupations and sectors that are traditionally male.

161. For those women in paid work, many experience obstacles that prevent them from achieving their potential. While some are increasingly found in lower levels of management, attitudinal discrimination often prevents them from being promoted further. The

experience of sexual harassment is an affront to a worker's dignity and prevents women from making a contribution commensurate with their abilities. The lack of a family-friendly work environment, including a lack of appropriate and affordable child care, and inflexible working hours further prevent women from achieving their full potential.

162. In the private sector, including transnational and national enterprises, women are largely absent from management and policy levels, denoting discriminatory hiring and promotion policies and practices. The unfavourable work environment as well as the limited number of employment opportunities available have led many women to seek alternatives. Women have increasingly become self-employed and owners and managers of micro-, small- and medium-scale enterprises. The expansion of the informal sector, in many countries, and of self-organized and independent enterprises is in large part due to women, whose collaborative, self-help and traditional practices and initiatives in production and trade represent a vital economic resource. When they gain access to and control over capital, credit and other resources, technology and training, women can increase production, marketing and income for sustainable development.

163. Taking into account the fact that continuing inequalities and noticeable progress coexist, rethinking employment policies is necessary in order to integrate the gender perspective and to draw attention to a wider range of opportunities as well as to address any negative gender implications of current patterns of work and employment. To realize fully equality between women and men in their contribution to the economy, active efforts are required for equal recognition and appreciation of the influence that the work, experience, knowledge and values of both women and men have in society.

164. In addressing the economic potential and independence of women, Governments and other actors should promote an active and visible policy of mainstreaming a gender perspective in all policies and programmes so that before decisions are taken, an analysis is made of the effects on women and men, respectively.

Strategic objective F. 1.

Promote women's economic rights and independence, including access to employment, appropriate working conditions and control over economic resources

Actions to be taken

165. By Governments:

(a) Enact and enforce legislation to guarantee the rights of women and men to equal pay for equal work or work of equal value;

(b) Adopt and implement laws against discrimination based on sex in the labour market, especially considering older women workers, hiring and promotion, the extension of employment benefits and social security, and working conditions;

(c) Eliminate discriminatory practices by employers and take appropriate measures in consideration of women's reproductive role and functions, such as the denial of employment and dismissal due to pregnancy or breast-feeding, or requiring proof of contraceptive use, and take effective measures to ensure that pregnant women, women on maternity leave or women re-entering the labour market after childbearing are not discriminated against;

(d) Devise mechanisms and take positive action to enable women to gain access to full and equal participation in the formulation of policies and definition of structures through such bodies as ministries of finance and trade, national economic commissions, economic research institutes and other key agencies, as well as through their participation in appropriate international bodies;

(e) Undertake legislation and administrative reforms to give women equal rights with men to economic resources, including access to ownership and control over land and other forms of property, credit, inheritance, natural resources and appropriate new technology;

(f) Conduct reviews of national income and inheritance tax and social security systems to eliminate any existing bias against women;

(g) Seek to develop a more comprehensive knowledge of work and employment through, *inter alia,* efforts to measure and better understand the type, extent and distribution of unremunerated work, particularly work in caring for dependents and unremunerated work done for family farms or businesses, and encourage the sharing and dissemination of information on studies and experience in this field, including the development of methods for assessing its value in quantitative terms, for possible reflection in accounts that may be produced separately from, but consistent with, core national accounts;

(h) Review and amend laws governing the operation of financial institutions to ensure that they provide services to women and men on an equal basis;

(i) Facilitate, at appropriate levels, more open and transparent budget processes;

(j) Revise and implement national policies that support the traditional savings, credit and lending mechanisms for women;

(k) Seek to ensure that national policies related to international and regional trade agreements do not have an adverse impact on women's new and traditional economic activities;

(l) Ensure that all corporations, including transnational corporations, comply with national laws and codes, social security regulations, applicable international agreements, instruments and conventions, including those related to the environment, and other relevant laws;

(m) Adjust employment policies to facilitate the restructuring of work patterns in order to promote the sharing of family responsibilities;

(n) Establish mechanisms and other forums to enable women entrepreneurs and women workers to contribute to the formulation of policies and programmes being developed by economic ministries and financial institutions;

(o) Enact and enforce equal opportunity laws, take positive action and ensure compliance by the public and private sectors through various means;

(p) Use gender-impact analyses in the development of macro- and micro-economic and social policies in order to monitor such impact and restructure policies in cases where harmful impact occurs;

(q) Promote gender-sensitive policies and measures to empower women as equal partners with men in technical, managerial and entrepreneurial fields;

(r) Reform laws or enact national policies that support the establishment of labour laws to ensure the protection of all women workers, including safe work practices, the right to organize and access to justice.

Strategic objctive F. 2.
Facilitate women's equal access to resources, employment, markets and trade

Actions to be taken

166. By Governments:

(a) Promote and support women's self-employment and the development of small enterprises, and strengthen women's access to credit and capital on appropriate terms equal to those of men through the scaling-up of institutions dedicated to promoting women's entrepreneurship, including, as appropriate, non-traditional and mutual credit schemes, as well as innovative linkages with financial institutions;

(b) Strengthen the incentive role of the State as employer to develop a policy of equal opportunities for women and men;

(c) Enhance, at the national and local levels, rural women's incomegenerating potential by facilitating their equal access to and control over productive resources, land, credit, capital, property rights, development programmes and co-operative structures;

(d) Promote and strengthen micro-enterprises, new small businesses, co-operative enterprises, expanded markets and other employment opportunities and, where appropriate, facilitate the transition from the informal to the formal sector, especially in rural areas;

(e) Create and modify programmes and policies that recognize and strengthen women's vital role in food security and provide paid and unpaid women producers, especially those involved in food production, such as farming, fishing and aquaculture, as well as urban enterprises, with equal access to appropriate technologies, transportation, extension services, marketing and credit facilities at the local and community levels;

(f) Establish appropriate mechanisms and encourage intersectoral institutions that enable women's co-operatives to optimize access to necessary services;

(g) Increase the proportion of women extension workers and other government personnel who provide technical assistance or administer economic programmes;

(h) Review, reformulate, if necessary, and implement policies, includ-ing business, commercial and contract law and government regu-lations, to ensure that they do not discriminate against micro-,small- and medium-scale enterprises owned by women in rural and urban areas;

(i) Analyse, advise on, coordinate and implement policies that integrate the needs and interests of employed, self-employed and entrepreneurial women into sectoral and inter-ministerial policies, programmes and budgets;

(j) Ensure equal access for women to effective job training, retraining, counselling and placement services that are not limited to traditional employment areas;

(k) Remove policy and regulatory obstacles faced by women in social and development programmes that discourage private and individual initiative;

(l) Safeguard and promote respect for basic workers' rights, including: the prohibition of forced labour and child labour, freedom of association and the right to organize and bargain collectively, equal remuneration for men and women for work of equal value and non-discrimination in employment, fully implementing the conventions of the International Labour Organization in the case of States parties to those conventions and, taking into account the principles embodied in the case of those countries that are not parties to those conventions in order to achieve truly sustained economic growth and sustainable development.

167. By Governments, central banks and national development banks, and private banking institutions, as appropriate:

(a) Increase the participation of women, including women entrepreneurs, in advisory boards and other forums to enable women entrepreneurs from all sectors and their organizations to contribute to the formulation and review of policies and programmes being developed by economic ministries and banking institutions;

(b) Mobilize the banking sector to increase lending and refinancing through incentives and the development of intermediaries that serve the needs of women entrepreneurs and producers in both rural and urban areas, and include women in their leadership, planning and decision-making;

(c) Structure services to reach rural and urban women involved in micro-, small- and medium-scale enterprises, with special attention to young women, low-income women, those belonging to ethnic and racial minorities, and indigenous women who lack access to capital and assets; and expand women's access to financial markets by identifying and encouraging financial supervisory and regulatory reforms that support financial institutions' direct and indirect efforts to better meet the credit and other financial needs of the micro-, small- and medium-scale enterprises of women;

(d) Ensure that women's priorities are included in public investment programmes for economic infrastructure, such as water and sanitation, electrification and energy conservation, transport and road construction; promote greater involvement of women beneficiaries at the project planning and implementation stages to ensure access to jobs and contracts.

168. By Governments and non-governmental organizations:

(a) Pay special attention to women's needs when disseminating market, trade and resource information and provide appropriate training in these fields;

(b) Encourage community economic development strategies that build on partnerships ameng Governments, and encourage members of civil society to create jobs and address the social circumstances of individuals, families and communities.

169. By multilateral funders and regional development banks, as well as bilateral and private funding agencies, at the international, regional and subregional levels:

(a) Review, where necessary reformulate, and implement policies, programmes and projects, to ensure that a higher proportion of resources reach women in rural and remote areas;

(b) Develop flexible funding arrangements to finance intermediary institutions that target women's economic activities, and promote self-sufficiency and increased capacity in and profitability of women's economic enterprises;

(c) Develop strategies to consolidate and strengthen their assistance to the micro-, small- and medium-scale enterprise sector, in order to enhance the opportunities for women to participate fully and equally and work together to coordinate and enhance the effectiveness of this sector, drawing upon expertise and financial resources from within their own organizations as well as from bilateral agencies, Governments and non-governmental organizations.

170. By International, multilateral and bilateral development co-operation organizations:

Support, through the provision of capital and/or resources, financial institutions that serve low-income, small- and micro-scale women entrepreneurs and producers in both the formal and informal sectors.

171. By Governments and/or multilateral financial institutions:

Review rules and procedures of formal national and international financial institutions that obstruct replication of the Grameen Bank prototype, which provides credit facilities to rural women.

172. By international organizations:

Provide adequate support for programmes and projects designed to promote sustainable and productive entrepreneurial activities among women, in particular the disadvantaged.

Strategic objective F. 3.
Provide business services, training and access to markets, information and technology particularly to low-income women

Actions to be taken

173. By Governments in co-operation with non-governmental organizations and the private sector:

(a) Provide public infrastructure to ensure equal market access for women and men entrepreneurs;

(b) Develop programmes that provide training and retraining, particularlry in new technologies, and affordable services to women in business management, product development, finacing, production and quality control, marketing and the legal aspects of business;

(c) Provide outreach programmes to inform low-income and poor women, particularly in rural and remote areas, of opportunities for market and technology access, and provide assistance in taking advantage of such opportunities;

(d) Create non-discriminatory support services, including investment funds for women's businesses, and target women, particularly low-income women, in trade promotion programmes;

(e) Disseminate information about successful women entrepreneurs in both traditional and non-traditional economic activities and the skills necessary to achieve success, and facilitate networking and the exchange of information;

(f) Take measures to ensure equal access of women to ongoing training in the workplace, including unemployed women, single parents, women re-entering the labour market after an extended temporary exit from employment owing to family responsibilities and other causes, and women displaced by new forms of production or by retrenchment, and increase incentives to enterprises to expand the number of vocational and training centres that provide training for women in non-traditional areas;

(g) Provide affordable support services, such as high-quality, flexible and affordable child-care services, that take into account the needs of working men and women.

174 Bylocal, national, regional and international business organizations and'non-govemmental organizations concerned with women's issues:

Advocate, at all levels, for the promotion and support of women's businesses and enterprises, including those in the informal sector, and the equal access of women to productive resources.

Strategic objective F. 4.
Strategic women's economic capacity and commercial network

Actions to be taken

175. By Governments:

(a) Adopt policies that support business organizations, non-governmental organizations, co-operatives, revolving loan funds, credit unions, grass-roots organizations, women's self-help groups and other groups in order to provide services to women entrepreneurs, in rural and urban areas;

(b) Integrate a gender perspective into all economic restructuri"g and structural adjustment policies and design programmes for women who are affected by economic restructuring, including structural adjustment programmes and for women who work in the informal sector;

(c) Adopt policies that create an enabling environment for women's sector; self-help groups workers organizations and co-operatives through non-conventional forms of support and by recognizing the right to freedom of association and the right to organize;

(d) Support programmes that enhance the self-reliance of special groups of women, such as young women, women with disabilities, elderly women and women belonging to racial and ethnic minorities;

(e) Promote gender equality through the promotion of women's studies and through the use of the results of studies and gender research in all fields, including the economic, scientific and technological fields;

(f) Support the economic activities of indigenous women, taking into account their traditional knowledge. So as to improve their situation and development

(g) Adopt policies to extend or maintain the protection of labour laws and social security provisions for those who do paid work in the home;

(h) home; Recognize and encourage the contribution of research by women scientists and technologists;

(i) Ensure that policies and regulations do not discriminate against micro-, small- and medium-scale enterprises run by women.

176. By financial intermediaries, national training institutes, credit unions, non-governmental organizations, women's associations, professional organizations and the private sector, as appropriate:

(a) Provide, atthe national, regional and international levels, training in a variety of business-related and financial management and technical skills to enable women, especially young women, to participate in economic policy-making at those levels;

(b) Provide business services, including marketing and trade information, product design and innovation, technology transfer and equality, to women's business enterprises, including those in export sector of the economy

(c) Promote technical and commercial links and establish joint ventures among women entrepreneurs at the national, regional and international levels to support community-based initiatives;

(d) Strengthen the participation of women, including ma'ginalized taking into women, in production and marketing co-operatives by providing marketing and financial support, especially in rural and remote areas;

(e) Promote and strengthen women's micro-enterprises, new small businesses, co-operative enterprises, expanded markets and other employment opportunities and, where appropriate, facilitate the transition from the informal to the formal sector, in rural and urban

(f) Invest capital and develop investment portfolios to finance women's business enterprises;

(g) Give adequate attention to providing technical assistance, advisory services, training and retraining for women connected with the entry to the market economy;

(h) Support credit networks and innovative ventures, including traditional savings schemes;

(i) Provide networking arrangements for entrepreneurial women, including opportunities for the mentoring of inexperienced women by the more experienced;

(j) Encourage community organizations and public authorities to establish loan pools for women entrepreneurs, drawing on successful small-scale co-operative models.

177. By the private sector, including transnational and national corporations:

(a) Adopt policies and establish mechanisms to grant contracts on a non-discriminatory basis;

(b) Recruit women for leadership, decision-making and management and provide training programmes, all on an equal basis with men;

(c) Observe national labour, environment, consumer, health and safety laws, particularly those that affect women.

Strategic objective F. 5.
Eliminate occupational segregation and all forms of employment discrimination

Adions to be taken

178. By Governments, employers, employees, trade unions and women's organizations:

(a) Implement and enforce laws and regulations and encourage voluntary codes of conduct that ensure that international labour standards, such as International Labour Organization Convention No. 100 on equal pay and workers' rights, apply equally to female and male workers;

(b) Enact and enforce laws and introduce implementing measures, including means of redress and access to justice in cases of non-compliance, to prohibit direct and indirect discrimination on grounds of sex, including by reference to "marital or family status, in relation to access to employment, corditions of employment, including training, promotion, health and safety, as well as termination of employment and social security of workers, including legal protection against sexual and racial harassment;

(c) Enact and enforce laws and develop workplace policies against gender discrimination in the labour market, especially considering older women workers, in hiring and promotion, and in the extension of employment benefits and social security, as well as regarding discriminately working conditions and Sexual harassment; mechanisms should be developed for the regular review and monitoring of such laws;

(d) Eliminate discriminatory practices by employers on the basis of women reproductive roles and functions, including refusal of employment and dismissal of women due to pregancy and breast-feeding responsibilities;

(e) Develop and promote employment programme and services for women entering and/or re-entering the labour market, especially poor urban, rural and young women, the self-employed and those negatively affected by structural adjustment;

(f) Implement and monitor positive public-and private-sector employment, equity and positive action programmes to address systemic discrimination against women in the labour force, in palticular women with disabilities and women belonging to other disadvantaged groups, with respect to hiring, retention and promotion, and vocational training of women in all sectors;

(g) Eliminate occupational segregation, especially by promoting the equal participation of women in highly skilled jobs and senior management positions, and through other measures, such as counselling and placement, that stimulate their on-the-job career development and upward mobility in the labour market, and by stimulating the diversification of occupational choices by both women and men; encourage woment, take up non-traditional jobs, especially in science and technology, and encourage men to seek employment in the social sector;

(h) Recognize collective bargaining as a right and as an important mechanism for eliminating wage inequality for women and to improve working conditions;

(i) Promote the election of women trade union officials and ensure that trade union officials elected to represent women are given job protection and physical security in connection with the discharge of their functions;

(j) Ensure access to and develop special programmes to enable women with disabilities to obtain and retain employment, and ensure access to education and training at all proper levels, in accordance with the Standard Rules on the Equalization of Opportunities for Persons with Disabilities;[30] adjust working conditions, to the extent possible, in order to suit the needs of women with disabilities, who should be assured legal protection against unfounded job loss on account of their disabilities;

(k) Increase efforts to close the gap between women's and men's pay take steps to implement the principle of equal remuneration for equal work of equal value by strengthening legislation, including compliance with international labour laws and standards, and encourage job evaluation schemes with gender-neutral criteria;

(l) Establish and/or strengthen mechanisms to adjudicate matters relating to wage discrimination;

(m) Set specific target dates for eliminating all forms of child labour that are contrary to accepted international standards and ensure the full enforcement of relevant existingl laws and, where appropriate, enact the legislation necessary to implement the Convention on the, Rights of the Child and International Labour Organization standards, ensuring the protection of working children, in particular, street children, through the provision of appropriate health, education and other social services;

(n) Ensure that strategies to eliminate child labour also address the exessive demands made on some girls for unpaid work in their household and other households, where applicable;

(o) Review, analyse and, where appropriate, reformulate the wage structures in female-dominated professions, such as teaching, nursing and child care, with view to raising their low status and earnings;

(p) Facilitate the productive employment of documented migrant women (including women who have been determined refugees according to the 1951 Convention relating to the Status of Refugees) through greater recognition of foreign education and credentials and by adopting an integrated approach to labour market training that incorporates language training.

Strategic objective F. 6.

Promote harmonization of work and family responsibilities for women and men

Actions to be taken

179. By Governments:

(a) Adopt policies to ensure the appropriate protection of labour laws and social security benefits for part-time, temporary seasonal and home-based workers; promote career development based on Work conditions that harmonize work and family responsibilities;

(b) Ensure that full and part-time work can be freely chosen by women and men on an equal basis, and consider approppliate protection for atypical workers in terms, of access to employment, working conditions and social security;

(c) Ensure, through legislation, incentives and/or encouragement and social security; opportunities for women and men to take job-protected parental leave and to have parental benefits; promote the equal sharing of responsibilities for the family by men and women, including through appropriate legislation, incentives and/or encouragement, and also promote the facilitation of breast-feeding for working women;

(d) Development policies, *inter alia*, in education to change attitudes that reinforce the division of labour based on gender in order to promote the concept of shared family responsibility for work in the home, particularly in relation to children and elder care;

(e) Improve the development of and access to, technologies that facilitate occupational as well as domiestic work, encourage within the productive process and enable women to move out of low-paying jobs;

(c) Examine a range of policies and programmes, including social security legislation and taxation systems, in accordance with national priorities and policies, to determine how to promote gender equality and flexibility in the way people divide their time between and derive benefits from education and training, paid employment, family responsibilities, volunteer activity and other socially useful forms of work, rest and leisure·

180.By Govemments, the private sector and non-governmental organisations, trade unions and the United Nations,as appropriate:

(a) Adopt appropriate measures involving relevant governmental bodies and employer's and employees' associations so that women and men are able to take temporary leave from employment, have transferable employment and retirement benefits and make arrangements to modify work hours without sacrificing their prospects for development and advancement at work and in their careers;

(b) Design and provide educational programmes through innovative media campaigns and School and community education programmes to raise awareness on gender equality and non-stereotyped gender roles of women and men within the family; provide support services and facilities, such as on-site child care at workplaces and flexible working arrangements;

(c) Enact and enforce laws againstsexual and other forms of harassment in all workplaces.

G. Women in Power and Decision-Making

181. The Universal Declaration of Human Rights states that everyone has the right to take part in the Government of his/her country. The empower-ment and autonomy of women and the improvement of women's social, economic and political status is essential for the achievement of both transparent and accountable government and administration and sustainable development in all areas of life. The power relations that prevent women from leading fulfilling lives operate at many levels of society, from the most personal to the highly public. Achieving the goal of equal participation of women and men in decision-making will provide a balance that more accurately reflects the composition of society and is needed in order to strengthen democracy and promote it, proper functioning. Equality in political decision-making performs a leverage function without which it is highly unlikely that a real integration of the equality dimension in government policy-making is feasible. In this respect, women's equal participation in political life plays a pivotal role in the general process of the advancement of women Women's equal participation, in decision-making is not only a demand for simple justice or democracy but can also be seen as a necessary condition for women's interests to be taken into account Without the active participation of women and the incorporation of women's perspective at all levels of decision-making, the goals of equality, development and peace cannot be achieved·

182. Despite the widespread movement towards democratization in most countries women are largely underrepresented at most levels of government, especially in ministerial and other executive bodies, and have made little progr·ess in attaining political power' in legislative bodies or in achieving the target endorsed by the Economics and Social Council of having 30 per cent women in positions at decision-making levels by 1995. Globally, only 10 per cent of the members of legislative bodies and a lower percentage of ministerial positions are now held by women. Indeed, some countries, includ-ing those that are undergoing fundamental political, economic and social changes, have seen a significant decrease in the number of women repre- sented in legislative bodies. Although women make up at least half of the electorate in almost all countries and have attained the right to vote and hold office in almost all States Members of the United Nations, women continue to be seriously underrepresented as candidates for public office. The traditional working patterns of many political parties and government struc-

tures continue to be barriers to women's participation in public life. Women may be discouraged from seeking political office by discriminatory attitudes and practices, family and child-care responsibilities, and the high cost of seeking and holding public office. Women in politics and decision-making positions in Governments and legislative bodies contribute to redefining political priorities, placing new items on the political agenda that reflect and address women's gender-specific concerns, values and experiences, and providing new perspectives on mainstream political issues.

183. Women have demonstrated considerable leadership in community and informal organizations, as well as in public office. However, socialization and negative stereotyping of women and men, including stereotyping through the media, reinforces the tendency for political decision-making to, remain the domain ofmen. Likewise, the underrepresentation of women in decision-making positions in the areas of art, culture, sports, the media, education, religion and the law have prevented women from having a significant impact on many key institutions.

184. Owing to their limited access to the traditional avenues to power, such as the decision-making bodies of political parties, employer organizations and trade unions, women have gained access to power through alternative structures, particularly in the non-governmental organization sector. Through non-governmental organizations and grass-roots organizations, women have been able to articulate their interests and concerns and have placed women's issues on the national, regional and international agendas.

185. Inequality in the public arena can often start with discriminatory attitudes and practices and unequal power relations between women and men within the family, as defined in paragraph 29 above. The unequal division of labour and responsibilities within households based on unequal power relations also limits women's potential to find the time and develop the skills required for participation in decision-making in wider public forums. A more equal sharing of those responsibilities between women and men not only provides a better quality of life for women and their daughters but also enhances theiropportunities to shape and design public policy, practice and expenditure so that their interests may be recognized and addressed. Non-formal networks and patterns of decision-making at the local community level that reflect a dominant male ethos restrict women's ability to participate equally in political, economic and social life.

186. The low proportion of women among economic and political decision makers at the local, national, regional and international levels reflects structural and attitudinal barriers that need to be addressed through positive measures. Governments, transnational and national corporations, the mass media, banks, academicand scientific institutions, and regional and international organizations, including those in the United Nations system, donot make full use of women's talents as top-level managers, policy makers, diplomats and negotiators.

187. The equitable distribution of power and decision-making at all levels is dependent on Governments and other actors undertaking statistical gender analysis and mainstreaming a gender perspective in policy development and the implementation of programmes. Equality in decision-making is essential to the empowerment of women. In some countries, affirmative action has led to 33.3 per cent or larger representation in local and national Govemments.

188. National, regional and international statistical institutions still have insufficient knowledge of how to present the issues related to the equal treatment of women and men in the economic and social spheres. In particular, there is insufficient use of existing databases and methodologies in the important sphere of decision-making.

189. In addressing the inequality between men and women in the sharing of power and decision-making at all levels, Governments and other actors should promote an active and visible policy of mainstreaming a gender perspedive in all policies and progammes so that before decisions are taken, an analysis is made of the effects on women and men, respectively

Strategic objective G. 1.
Take measures to ensure women's equal access to and full participation in power structures and decision-making

Actions to be taken

190. By Governments:

(a) Commit themselves to establishing the goal of gender balance in governmental bodies and committees, as well as in public administrative entities, and in the judiciary, including, *inter alia,* setting specific targets and implementing measures to substantially increase the number of women with a view to achieving equal representation of women and men, if necessary through positive action, in all governmental and public administration positions;

(b) Take measures, including, where appropriate, in electoral systems that encourage political parties to integrate women in elective and non-elective public positions in the same proportion and at the same levels as men;

(c) Protect and promote the equal rights of women and men to engage in political activities and to freedom of association, including membership in political parties and trade unions;

(d) Review the differential impact of electoral systems on the political representation of women in elected bodies and consider, where appropriate, the adjustment or reform of those systems;

(e) Monitor and evaluate progress in the representation of women through the regular collection, analysis and dissemination of quantitative and qualitative data on women and men at all levels in various decision-making positions in the public and private sectors, and disseminate data on the number of women and men employed at various levels in Governments on a yearly basis; ensure that women and men have equal access to the full range of public appointments and set up mechanisms within governmental structures for monitoring progress in this field;

(f) Support non-governmental organizations and research institutes that conduct studies on women's participation in and impact on decision-making and the decision-making environment;

(g) Encourage greater involvement of indigenous women in decision making at all levels;

(h) Encourage and, where appropriate, ensure that government funded organizations adopt non-discriminatory policies and practices in order to increase the number and raise the position of women in their organizations;

(i) Recognize that shared work and parental responsibilities between women and men promote women's increased participation in public life, and take appropriate measures to achieve this, including measures to reconcile family and professional life;

(j) Aim at gender balance in the lists of national candidates nominated for election or appointment to United Nations bodies, specialized agencies and other autonomous organizations of the United Nations system, particularly for posts at the senior level.

191. By political parties:

(a) Consider examining party structures and procedures to remove all barriers that directly or indirectly discriminate against the participation of women;

(b) Consider developing initiatives that allow women to participate fully in all internal policy-making structures and appointive and electoral nominating processes;

(c) Consider incorporating gender issues in their political agenda, taking measures to ensure that women can participate in the leadership of political parties on an equal basis with men.

192. By Govemments, national bodies, the private sector, political parties, trade unions, employers' organizations, research and academic institutions, subregional and regional bodies and non-governmental and international organizations:

(a) Take positive action to build a critical mass of women leaders, executives and managers in strategic decision-making positions;

(b) Create or strengthen, as appropriate, mechanisms to monitor women's access to senior levels of decision-making;

(c) Review the criteria for recruitment and appointment to advisory and decision-making bodies and Promotion to senior positions to ensure that such criteria are relevant and do not discriminate against women;

(d) Encourage efforts by non-governmental organizations, trade unions and the private sector to achieve equality between women and men in their ranks, including equal participation in their decision-making bodies and in negotiations in all areas and at all levels;

(e) Develop communications Strategies to promote public debate on the new roles of men and women in society, and in the family as defined in paragraph 29 above;

(f) Restructure recruitment and career-development programmes to ensure that all women, especially young women, have equal access to managerial, entrepreneurial, technical and leadership training, including on-the-job training;

(g) Develop career advancement programmes for women of all ages that include career planning, tracking, mentoring, coaching, training and retraining;

(h) Encourage and support the participation of women's nongovernmental organizations in United Nations conferences and their preparatory processes;

(i) Aim at and support gender balance in the composition of delegations to the United Nations and other international forums.

193. By the United Nations:

(a) Implement existing and adopt new employment policies and measures in order to achieve overall gender equality, particularly at the Professional level and above, by the year 2000, with due regard to the importance of recruiting staff on as wide a geographical basis as possible, in conformity with Article 101, paragraph 3, of the Charter of the United Nations;

(b) Develop mechanisms to nominate women candidates for appoint- ment to senior posts in the United Nations, the specialized agencies and other organizations and bodies of the United Nations system;

(c) Continue to collect and disseminate quantitative and qualitative data on women and men in decision-making and analyse their differential impact on decision-making and monitor progress towards achieving the Secretary-General's target of having women hold 50 per cent of managerial and decision-making positions by the year 2000.

194. By women's organizations, non-governmental organizations, trade unions, social partners, producers, and industrial and professional organizations:

(a) Build and strengthen solidarity among women through information, education and sensitization activities;

(b) Advocate at all levels to enable women to influence political, economic and social decisions, processes and systems, and work towards seeking accountability from elected representatives on their commitment to gender concerns;

(c) Establish, consistent with data protection legislation, databases on women and their qualification for use in appointing women to senior decision-making and advisory positions, for dissemination to Governments, regional and international organizations and private enterprise, political parties and other relevant bodies.

Strategic objective G. 2.
Increase women's capacity to participate in decision-making and leadership

Actions to be taken

195. By Governments, national bodies, the private sector, political parties, trade unions, employers' organizations, subregional and regional bodies, non-governmental and international organizations and educational institutions:

(a) Provide leadership and self-esteem training to assist women and girls, particularly those with special needs, women with disabilities and women belonging to racial and ethnic minorities to strengthen their self-esteem and to encourage them to take decision-making positions;

(b) Have transparent criteria for decision-making positions and ensure that the selecting bodies have a gender-balanced composition;

(c) Create a system of mentoring for inexperienced women and, in particular, offer training, including training in leadership and decision-making, public speaking and self-assertion, as well as in political campaigning;

(d) Provide gender-sensitive training for women and men to promote non-discriminatory working relationships and respect for diversity in work and management styles;

(e) Develop mechanisms and training to encourage women to participate in the electoral process, political activities and other leadership areas.

H. Institutional Mechanisms for the Advancement of Women

196. National machineries for the advancement of women have been established in almost every Member State to, inter alia, design, promote the implementation of, execute, monitor, evaluate, advocate and mobilize support for policies that promote the advancement of women. National machineries are diverse in form and uneven in their effectiveness, and in some cases have declined. Often marginalized in national government structures, these mechanisms are frequently hampered by unclear mandates, lack of adequate staff, training, data and sufficient resources, and insufficient support from national political leadership.

197. At the regional and international levels, mechanisms and institutions to promote the advancement of women as an integral part of mainstream political, economic, social and cultural development, and of initiatives on development and human rights, encounter similar problems emanating from a lack of commitment at the highest levels.

198. Successive international conferences have underscored the need to take gender factors into account in policy and programme planning. However, in many instances this has not been done.

199. Regional bodies concerned with the advancement of women have been strengthened, together with international machinery, such as the Commission on the Status of Women and the Committee on the Elimination of Discrimination against Women. However, the limited resources available continue to impede full implementation of

their mandates.

200. Methodologies for conducting gender-based analysis in policies and programmes and for dealing with the differential effects of policies on women and men have been developed in many organizations and are available for application but are often not being applied or are not being applied consistently.

201. A national machinery for the advancement of women is the central policy-co-ordinating unit inside government. Its main task is to support government-wide mainstreaming of a gender-equality perspective in all policy areas. The necessary conditions for an effective functioning of such national machineries include:

(a) Location at the highest possible level in the government, falling under the responsibility of a Cabinet minister;

(b) Institutional mechanisms or processes that facilitate, as appropriate, decentralized planning, implementation and monitoring with a view to involving non-governmental organizations and community organizations from the grass roots upwards;

(c) Sufficient resources in terms of budget and professional capacity;

(d) Opportunity to influence development of all government policies.

202. In addressing the issue of mechanisms for promoting the advancement of women, Governments and other actors should promote an active and visible policy of mainstreaming a gender perspective in all policies and programmes so that, before decisions are taken, an analysis is made of the effects on women and men, respectively.

Strategic objective H. 1.
Create or strengthen national machineries and other governmental bodies

Actions to be taken

203. By Governments:

(a) Ensure that responsibility for the advancement of women is vested in the highest possible level of government; in many cases, this could be at the level of a Cabinet minister;

(b) Based on a strong political commitment, create a national machinery, where it does not exist, and strengthen, as appropriate, existing national machineries, for the advancement of women at the highest possible level of government; it should have clearly defined mandates and authority; critical elements would be adequate resources and the ability and competence to influence policy and formulate and review legislation; among other things, it should perform policy analysis, undertake advocacy, communication, co-ordination and monitoring of implementation;

(c) Provide staff training in designing and analysing data from a gender perspective;

(d) Establish procedures to allow the machinery to gather information on government-wide policy issues at an early stage and continuously use it in the policy development and review process within the Government;

(e) Report, on a regular basis, to legislative bodies on the progress of efforts, as appropriate, to mainstream gender concerns, taking into account the implementation of the platform for action;

(f) Encourage and promote the active involvement of the broad and diverse range of institutional actors in the public, private and voluntary sectors to work for equality between women and men.

Strategic objective H.2.
Integrate gender perspectives in legislation, public policies, programmes and projects

Actions to be taken

204. By Governments:

(a) Seek to ensure that before policy decisions are taken, an analysis of their impact on women and men, respectively, is carried out;

(b) Regularly review national policies, programmes and projects, as well as their implementation, evaluating the impact of employment and income policies in order to guarantee that women are direct beneficiaries of development and that their full contribution to development, both remunerated and unremunerated, is considered in economic policy and planning;

(c) Promote national strategies and aims on equality between women and men in order to eliminate obstacles to the exercise of women's rights and eradicate all forms of discrimination against women;

(d) Work with members of legislative bodies, as appropriate, to promote a gender perspective in all legislation and policies;

(e) Give all ministries the mandate to review policies and programmes from a gender perspective and in the light of the Platform for Action; locate the responsibility for the implementation of that mandate at the highest possible level; establish and/or strengthen an inter-ministerial co-ordination structure to carry out this mandate, to monitor progress and to network with relevant machineries.

205. By national machinery:

(a) Facilitate the formulation and implementation of government policies on equality between women and men, develop appropriate strategies and methodologies, and promote coordination and co-operation within the central Government in order to ensure main-streaming of a gender perspective in all policy-making processes;

(b) Promote and establish co-operative relationships with relevant branches of government, centres for women's studies and research, academic and educational institutions, the private sector, the media, nongovernmental organizations, especially women's organizations, and all other actors of civil society;

(c) Undertake activities focusing on legal reform with regard, inter alia, to the family, conditions of employment, social security, income tax, equal opportunity in education, positive measures to promote the advancement of women, and the perception of attitudes and a culture favourable to equality, as well as promote a gender perspective in legal Policy and programming reforms;

(d) promote the increased participation of women as both active agents and beneficiaries of the development process, which would result in an improvement in the quality of life for all;

(e) Establish direct links with national, regional and international bodies dealing with the advancement of women;

(f) Providetrainingand advisory assistance to government agencies in order to integrate a gender perspective in their policies and programmes.

Strategic objective H. 3.

Generate and disseminate gender-disaggregated data and information for planning and evaluation

Actions to be taken

206. Bynational, regional and intemational statistical services and relevant governmental and United Nations agencies, in co-operation with research and documentation organizations, in their respective areas of responsibility:

(a) Ensure that statistics related to individuals are collected, compiled, analysed and presented by sex and age and reflect problems, issues and questions related to women and men in society;
(b) Collect, compile, analyse and present on a regular basis data disaggregated by age, sex, socio-economic and other relevant indicators, including number of dependents, for utilization in policy and programme planning and implementation;
(c) Involve centres for women's studies and research organizations in developing and testing appropriate indicators and research methodologies to strengthen gender analysis, as well as in monitoring and evaluating the implementation of the goals of the platform for Action;
(d) Designate or appoint staff to strengthen gender-statistics programmes and ensure co-ordination, monitoring and linkage to all fields of statistical work, and prepare output that integrates statistics from the various subject areas;
(e) Improve data collection on the full contribution of women and men to the economy, including their participation in the informal sector(s);
(f) Develop a more comprehensive knowledge of all forms of work and employment by:
 (i) Improving data collection on the unremunerated work which is already included in the United Nations System of National Accounts, such as in agriculture, particularly subsistence agriculture, and other types of non-market production activities;
 (ii) Improving measurements that at present underestimate women's unemployment and underemployment in the labour market;
 (iii) Developing methods, in the appropriate forums, for assessing the value, in quantitative terms, of unremunerated work that is outside national accounts, such as caring for dependents and preparing food, for possible reflection in satellite or other official accounts that may be produced separately from but are consistent with core national accounts, with a view to recognizing the economic contribution of women and making visible the unequal distribution of remunerated and unremunerated work between women and men;
(g) Develop an international classification of activities for time-

use statistics that is sensitive to the differences between women and men in remunerated and unremunerated work, and collect data disaggregated by sex. At the national level, subject to national constraints:

(i) Conduct regular time-use studies to measure, in quantitative terms, unremunerated work, including recording those activities that are performed simultaneously with remunerated or other unremunerated activities;

(ii) Measure, in quantitative terms, unremunerated work that is outside national accounts and work to improve methods to assess and accurately reflect its value in satellite or other official accounts that are separate from but consistent with core national accounts;

(h) Improve concepts and methods of data collection on the measurement of poverty among women and men, including their access to resource;

(i) Strengthen vital statistical systems and incorporate gender analysis into publications and research; give priority to gender differences in, research design and in data'collection and analysis in, order to improve data on mobidity; and improve data collection on access to health services, including access to comprehensive sexual and reproductive health services, maternal care and family planning, with special priority for adolescentmothers and for elder care;

(j) Develop improved gender-disaggregated and age-specific data on the victims and perpetrators of all forms of violence against women, such as domestic violence, sexual harassment, rape, incest and sexual abuse, and trafficking in women and girls, as well as on violence by agents of the State;

(k) Improve concepts and methods of data collection on the participation of women and men with disabilities, including their access to resources.

207. BY Governments:

(c) Ensure the regular production of a statistical publication on gender that presents and interpretstopical data on women and men in a form suitable for a wide range of non-technical users;

(b) Ensure that producers and users of statistics in each country regularly review the adequacy of the official statistical system and its coverage of gender irssues, and prepare a plan for needed impliments, where necessary;

(c) Develop and encourage the development of quantitative and qual-itative studies by research or ganizations, trade unions, employers, the private sector and non-governmental organizations on the sharing of power and influence in society, including the number of women and men in senior decisionmaking positions in both the public and private sectors:

(d) Use more gender-sensitive data in the formulation of policy and implementation of programmes and projects.

208.By the United Nations:

(a) Promote the development of methods to find better ways to collect, collate and analyse data that may relate to the human rights of women, including violence against women, for use by all relevant United Nations bodies;

(b) Promote the further development of statistical methods to improve data that relate to women in economic, social, cultural and political development;

(c) Prepare a new issue of The World's Women at regular five-year intervals and distribute it widely;

(d) Assist countries, upon request, in the development of gender policies and programmes;

(e) Ensure that the relevant reports, data and publications of the Statistical Division of the United Nations Secretariat and the International Research and Training Institute for the Advancement of Women on progress at the national and international levels are transmitted to the Commission on the Status of Women in a regular and coordinated fashion.

209. By multilateral development institutions and bilateral donors:

Encourage and support the development of national capacity in developing countries and in countries with economies in transition by providing resources and technical assistance so that countries can fully measure the work done by women and men, including both remunerated and unremunerated work, and where appropriate, use satellite or other official accounts for unremunerated work.

I. Human Rights of Women

210.Human rights and fundamental freedoms are the birthright of all human beings; their protection and promotion is the first responsibility of governments.

211.The World Conference on Human Rights reaffirmed the solemn commitment of all States to fulfil their obligation to promote universal respect for, and observance and protection of, all human rights and fundamental freedoms for all, in accordance with the Charter of the United Nations, other instruments relating to human rights, and international law. The universal nature of these rights and freedoms is beyond question.

212. The promotion and protection of all human rights and fundamental freedoms must be considered as a priority objective of the United Nations, in accordance with its purposes and principles, in particular with the purpose of international co-operation. In the framework of these purposes and principles, the promotion and protection of all human rights is a legitimate concern of the international community. The international community must treat human rights globally, in a fair and equal manner, on the same footing, and with the same emphasis. The Platform for Action reaffirms the importance of ensuring the universality, objectivity and non-selectivity of the con-sideration of human rights issues.

213. The Platform for Action reaffirms that all human rightscivil, cultural, economic, political and social, including the right to development—are universal, indivisible, interdependent and interrelated, as expressed in the Vienna Declaration and Programme of Action adopted by the World Conference on Human Rights. The Conference reaffirmed that the human rights of women and the girl-child are an inalienable, integral and indivisible part of universal human rights. The full and equal enjoyment of all human rights and fundamental freedoms by women and girls is a priority for Governments and the United Nations and is essential for the advancement of women.

214. Equal rights of men and women are explicitly mentioned in the Preamble to the Charter of the United Nations. All the major international human rights instruments include sex as one of the grounds upon which States may not discriminate.

215. Governments must not only refrain from violating the human rights of all women, but must work actively to promote and protect these rights. Recognition of the importance of the human rights of women is reflected in the fact that three quarters of the States Members of the United Nations have become parties to the Convention on the Elimination of All Forms of Discrimination against Women.

216. The World Conference on Human Rights reaffirmed clearly that the human rights of women throughout the life cycle are an inalienable, integral and indivisible part of universal human rights. The International Conference on Population and Development reaffirmed

women's reproductive rights and the right to development. Both the Declaration of the Rights of the Child[36] and the Convention on the Rights of the Child[11] guarantee children's rights and uphold the principle of non-discrimination on the grounds of gender.

217. The gap between the existence of rights and their effective enjoyment derives from a lack of commitment by Governments to promoting and protecting those rights and the failure of Governments to inform women and men alike about them. The lack of appropriate recourse mechanisms at the national and international levels, and inadequate resources at both levels, compound the problem. In most countries, steps have been taken to reflect the rights guaranteed by the Convention on the Elimination of All Forms of Discrimination against Women in national law. A number of countries have established mechanisms to strengthen women's ability to exercise their rights.

218. In order to protect the human rights of women, it is necessary to avoid, as far as possible, resorting to reservations and to ensure that no reservation is incompatible with the object and purpose of the Convention or is otherwise incompatible with international treaty law. Unless the human rights of women, as defined by international human rights instruments, are fully recognized and effectively protected, applied, implemented and enforced in national law as well as in national practice in family, civil, penal, labour and commercial codes and administrative rules and regulations, they will exist in name only.

219. In those countries that have not yet become parties to the Convention on the Elimination of All Forms of Discrimination against Women and other international human rights instruments, or where reservations that are incompatible with the object or purpose of the Convention have been entered, or where national laws have not yet been revised to implement international norms and standards, women's *de jure* equality is not yet secured. Women's full enjoyment of equal rights is undermined by the discrepancies between some national legislation and international law and international instruments on human rights. Overly complex administrative procedures, lack of awareness within the judicial process and inadequate monitoring of the violation of the human rights of all women, coupled with the under representation of women in justice systems, insufficient information on existing rights and persistent attitudes and practices perpetuate women's *de facto* inequality. *De facto* inequality is also perpetuated by the lack of enforcement of, *inter alia,* family,

civil, penal, labour and commercial laws or codes, or administrative rules and regulations intended to ensure women's full enjoyment of human rights and fundamental freedoms.

220. Every person should be entitled to participate in, contribute to and enjoy cultural, economic, political and social development. In many cases women and girls suffer discrimination in the allocation of economic and social resources. This directly violates their economic, social and cultural rights.

221. The human rights of all women and the girl-child must form an integral part of United Nations human rights activities. Intensified efforts are needed to integrate the equal status and the human rights of all women and girls into the mainstream of United Nations system-wide activities and to address these issues regularly and systematically throughout relevant bodies and mechanisms. This requires, inter alia, improved cooperation and coordination between the Commission on the Status of Women, the United Nations High Commissioner for Human Rights, the Commission on Human Rights, including its special and thematic rapporteurs, independent experts, working groups and its Subcommission on Prevention of Discrimination and Protection of Minorities, the Commission on Sustainable Development, the Commission for Social Development, the Commission on Crime Prevention and Criminal Justice, and the Committee on the Elimination of Discrimination against Women and other human rights treaty bodies, and all relevant entities of the United Nations system, including the specialized agencies. Co-operation is also needed to strengthen, rationalize and streamline the United Nations human rights system and to promote its effectiveness and efficiency, taking into account the need to avoid unnecessary duplication and overlapping of mandates and tasks.

222. If the goal of full realization of human rights for all is to be achieved,international human rights instruments must be applied in such a way as to take more clearly into consideration the systematic and systemic nature of discrimination against women that gender analysis has dearly indicated.

223. Bearing in mind the Programme of Action of the International Conference on Population and Development[14] and the Vienna Declaration and Programme of Action[2] adopted by the World Conference on Human Rights, the FourthWorld Conference on Women reaffirms that reproductive rights rest on the recognition of the basic right of all couples and individuals to decide freely and responsibly the number, spacing and timing of their children and to have

the information and means to do so, and the right to attain the highest standard of sexual and reproductive health. It also includes their right to make decisions concerning reproduction free of discrimination, coercion and violence, as expressed in human rights documents.

224. Violence against women both violates and impairs or nullifies the enjoyment by women of human rights and fundamental freedoms. Taking into account the Dedaration on the Elimination of Violence against Women and the work of Special Rapporteurs, gender-based violence, such as battering and other domestic violence, sexual abuse, sexual slavely and exploitation, and international trafficking in women and children, forced prostitution and sexual harassment, as well as violence against women, resulting from cultural prejudice, racism and racial discrimination, xenophobia, pornography, ethnic cleansing, armed conflict, foreign occupation, religious and anti-religious extremism and terrorism are incompatible with the dignity and the worth of the human person and must be combated and eliminated. Any harmful aspect of certain traditional, customary or modern practices that violates the rights of women should be prohibited and eliminated, Governments should take urgent action to combat and eliminate all forms of violence against women in private and public life, whether perpetrated or tolerated by the State or private persons.

225. Many women face additional barriers to the enjoyment of their human rights because of such factors as their race, language, ethnicity, culture, religion, disability or socio-economic class or because they are indigenous people, migrants, including women migrant workers, displaced women or refugees. They may also be disadvantaged and marginalized by a general lack of knowledge and recognition of their human rights as well as by the obstacles they meet in gaining access to information and recourse mechanisms in cases of violation of their rights.

226. The factors that cause the flight of refugee women, other displaced women in need of international protection and internally displaced women may be different from those affecting men. These women continue to be vulnerable to abuses of their human rights during and after their flight.

227. While women are increasingly using the legal system to exercise their rights, in many countries lack of awareness of the existence of these rights is an obstacle that prevents women from fully enjoying their human rights and attaining equality. Experience in many coun-

tries has shown that women can be empowered and motivated to assert their rights, regardless of their level of education or socio-economic status. Legal literacy programmes and media strategies have been effective in helping women to understand the link between their rights and other aspects of their lives and in demonstrating that cost-effective initiatives can be undertaken to help women obtain those rights. Provision of human rights education is essential for promoting an understanding of the human rights of women, including knowledge of recourse mechanisms to redress violations of their rights. It is necessary for all individuals, especially women in vulnerable circumstances, to have full knowledge oftheir rights and access to legal recourse against violations of their rights.

228. Women engaged in the defence of human rights must be protected. Governments have a duty to guarantee the full enjoyment of all rights set out in the Universal Declaration of Human Rights, the International Covenant on Civil and Political Rights and the International Covenant on Economic, Social and Cultural Rights by women working peacefully in a personal or organizational capacity for the promotion and protection of human rights. Non-governmental organizations, women's organizations and feminist groups have played a catalytic role in the promotion of the human rights of women through grass-roots activities, networking and advocacy and need encouragement, support and access to information from Governments in order to carry out these activities.

229. In addressing the enjoyment of human rights, Governments and other actors should promote an active and visible policy of mainstreaming a gender perspective in all policies and programmes so that, before decisions are taken, an analysis is made of the effects on women and men, respectively.

Strategic objective I.1.

Promote and protect the human rights of women, through the full imple-mentation of all human rights instruments, especially the Convention on the Elimination of All Forms of Discrimination against Women

Actions to be taken

230. By Governments:

(a) Work actively towards ratification of or accession to and implement international and regional human rights treaties;

(b) Ratify and accede to and ensure implementation of the Convention on the Elimination of All Forms of Discrimination against Women so that universal ratification of the Convention can be achieved by the year 2000;

(c) Limit the extent of any reservations to the Convention on the Elimination of All Forms of Discrimination against Women; formulate any such reservations as precisely and as narrowly as possible; ensure that no reservations are incompatible with the object and purpose of the Convention or otherwise incompatible with international treaty law and regularly review them with a view to withdrawing them; and with draw reservations that are contrary to the object and purpose of the Convention on the Elimination of All Forms of Discrimination against Women or which are otherwise incompatible with international treaty law;

(d) Consider drawing up national action plans identifying steps to improve the promotion and protection of human rights, including the human rights of women, as recommended by the World Conference on Human Rights;

(e) Create or strengthen independent national institutions for the protection and Promotion of these rights, including the human rights of women, as recommended by the World Conference on Human rights;

(f) Develop a comprehensive human rights education programme to raise awareness among women of their human rights and raise awareness among others of the human rights of women;

(g) If they are States parties, implement the Convention by reviewing all national laws, policies, practices and procedures to ensure that they meet the obligations set out in the Convention; all States should undertake a review of all national laws, policies, practices and procedures to ensure that they meet international human rights obligations in this matter;

(h) Include gender aspects in reporting under all other human rights conventions and instruments, including ILO conventions, to ensure analysis and review of the human rights of women;

(i) Report on schedule to the Committee on the Elimination of Discrimination against Women regarding the implementation of the Convention, following fully the guidelines established by the Committee and involving non-governmental organizations, where appropriate, or taking into account their contributions in the preparation of the report;

(j) Enable the Committee on the Elimination of Discrimination against Women fully to discharge its mandate by allowing for adequate meeting time through broad ratification of the revision adopted by the States parties to the Convention on the Elimination of All Forms of Discrimination against Women on 22 May 1995 relative to article 20, paragraph 1,[32] and by promoting efficient working methods;

(k) Support the process initiated by the Commission on the Status of Women with a view to elaborating a draft optional protocol to the Convention on the Elimination of All Forms of Discrimination against Women that could enter into force as soon as possible on a right of petition procedure, taking into consideration the Secretary-General's report on the optional protocol, including those views related to its feasibility;

(l) Take urgent measures to achieve universal ratification of or accession to the Convention on the Rights of the Child before the end of 1995 and full implementation of the Convention in order to ensure equal rights for girls and boys; those that have not already done so are urged to become parties in order to realize universal implementation of the Convention on the Rights of the Child by the year 2000;

(m) Address the acute problems of children, inter alia, by supporting efforts in the context of the United Nations system aimed at adopting efficient international measures for the prevention and eradication of female infanticide, harmful child labour, the sale of children and their organs, child prostitution, child pornography and other forms of sexual abuse and consider contributing to the drafting of an optional protocol to the Convention on the Rights of the Child;

(n) Strengthen the implementation of all relevant human rights instruments in order to combat and eliminate, including through international co-operation, organized and other forms of trafficking in women and children, including trafficking for the purposes of sexual exploitation, pornography, prostitution and sex tourism, and provide legal and social services to the victims; this should include provisions for international co-operation to prosecute and punish those responsible for organized exploitation of women and children;.

(o) Taking into account the need to ensure full respect for the human rights of indigenous women, consider a declaration on the rights of indigenous people for adoption by the General Assembly within the International Decade of the World's Indigenous People and encourage the participation of indigenous women in the working group elaborating the draft declaration, in accordance with the provisions for the participation of organizations of indigenous people.

231. By relevant organs, bodies and agencies of the United Nations system, all human rights bodies of the United Nations system, as well as the United Nations High Commissioner for Human Rights and the United Nations High Commissioner for Refugees, while promoting greater efficiency and effectiveness through better coordination of the various bodies, mechanisms and procedures, taking into account the need to avoid unnecessary duplication and overlapping of their mandates and tasks:

(a) Give full, equal and sustained attention to the human rights of women in the exercise of their respective mandates to promote universal respect for and protection of all human rights—civil, cultural, economic, political and social rights, including the right to development;

(b) Ensure the implementation of the recommendations of the World Conference on Human Rights for the full integration and mainstreaming of the human rights of women;

(c) Develop a comprehensive policy programme for mainstreaming the human rights of women throughout the United Nations system, including activities with regard to advisory services, technical assistance, reporting methodology, gender-impact assessments, coordination, public information and human rights education, and play an active role in the implementation of the programme;

(d) Ensure the integration and full participation of women as both agents and beneficiaries in the development process and reiterate the objectives established for global action for women towards sustainable and equitable development set forth in the Rio Declaration on Environment and Development;

(e) Include information on gender-based human rights violations in their activities and integrate the findings into all of their programmes and activities;

(f) Ensure that there is collaboration and co-ordination of the work of all human rights bodies and mechanisms to ensure that the human rights of women are respected;

(g) Strengthen co-operation and co-ordination between the Commission on the Status of Women, the Commission on Human Rights, the Commission for Social Development, the Commission on Sustainable Development, the Commission on Crime Prevention and Criminal Justice, the United Nations human rights treaty monitoring bodies, including the Committee on the Elimination of Discrimination against Women, and the United Nations Development Fund for Women, the International Research and Training Institute for the Advancement of Women, the United Nations Development Programme, the United Nations Children's Fund and other organizations of the United Nations system, acting within their mandates, in the promotion of the human rights of women, and improve cooperation between the Division for the Advancement of Women and the Centre for Human Rights;

(h) Establish effective co-operation between the United Nations High Commissioner for Human Rights and the United Nations High Commissioner for Refugees and other relevant bodies, within their respective mandates, taking into account the close link between massive violations of human rights, especially in the form of genocide, ethnic cleansing, systematic rape of women in war situations and refugee flows and other displacements, and the fact that refugee, displaced and returnee women may be subject to particular human rights abuse;

(i) Encourage incorporation of a gender perspective in national programmes of action and in human rights and national institutions, within the context of human rights advisory services programmes;

(j) Provide training in the human rights of women for all United Nations personnel and officials, especially those in human rights and humanitarian relief activities, and promote their understanding of the human rights of women so that they recognize and deal with violations of the human rights of women and can fully take into account the gender aspect of their work;

(k) In reviewing the implementation of the plan of action for the United Nations Decade for Human Rights Education (1995-2004), take into account the results of the Fourth World Conference on Women.

Strategic objective 1. 2.
Ensure equality and non-discrimination under the law and in practice

Actions to be taken

232. By Governments:

(a) Give priority to promoting and protecting the full and equal enjoyment by women and men of all human rights and fundamental freedoms without distinction of any kind as to race, colour, sex, language, religion, political or other opinions, national or social origins, property, birth or other status;

(b) Provide constitutional guarantees and/or enact appropriate legislation to prohibit discrimination on the basis of sex for all women and girls of all ages and assure women of all ages equal rights and their full enjoyment;

(c) Embody the principle of the equality of men and women in their legislation and ensure, through law and other appropriate means, the practical realization of this principle;

(d) Review national laws, including customary laws and legal practices in the areas of family, civil, penal, labour and commercial law in order to ensure the implementation of the principles and procedures of all relevant international human rights instruments by means of national legislation, revoke any remaining laws that discriminate on the basis of sex and remove gender bias in the administration of justice;

(e) Strengthen and encourage the development of programmes to protect the human rights of women in the national institutions on human rights that carry out programmes, such as human rights commissions or ombudspersons, according them appropriate status, resources and access to the Government to assist individuals, in particular women, and ensure that these institutions pay adequate attention to problems involving the violation of the human rights of women;

(f) Take action to ensure that the human rights of women, including the rights referred to in paragraphs 94 to 96 above, are fully respected and protected;

(g) Take urgent action to combat and eliminate violence against women, which is a human rights violation, resulting from harmful traditional or customary practices, cultural prejudices and extremism;

(h) Prohibit female genital mutilation wherever it exists and give vigorous support to effort among non-governmental and community organizations and religious institutions to eliminate such practices;

(i) Provide gender-sensitive human rights education and training to public officials, including, inter alia, police and military personnel, corrections officers, health and medical personnel, and social workers, including people who deal with migration and refugee issues, and teachers at all levels of the educational system, and make available such education and training also to the judiciary and members of parliament in order to enable them to better exercise their public responsibilities;

(j) Promote the equal right of women to be members of trade unions and other professional and social organizations;

(k) Establish effective mechanisms for investigating violations of the human rights of women perpetrated by any public official and take the necessary punitive legal measures in accordance with national laws;

(l) Review and amend criminal laws and procedures, as necessary, to eliminate any discrimination against women in order to ensure that criminal law and procedures guarantee women effective protection against, and prosecution of, crimes directed at or disproportionately affecting women, regardless of the relationship between the perpetrator and the victim, and ensure that women defendants, victims and/or witnesses are not revictimized or discriminated against in the investigation and prosecution of crimes;

(m) Ensure that women have the same right as men to be judges, advocates or other officers of the court, as well as police officers and prison and detention officers, among other things;

(n) Strengthen existing or establish readily available and free or affordable alternative administrative mechanisms and legal aid programmes to assist disadvantaged women seeking redress for violations of their rights;

(o) Ensure that all women and non-governmental organizations and their members in the field of protection and promotion of all human rights—civil, cultural, economic, political and social rights, including the right to development—enjoy fully all human rights and freedoms in accordance with the Universal Declaration of Human Rights and all other human rights instruments and the protection of national laws;

(p) Strengthen and encourage the implementation of the recommendations contained in the Standard Rules on the Equalization of Opportunities for Persons with Disabilities,[30] paying special attention to ensure non-discrimination and equal enjoyment of all human rights and fundamental freedoms by women and girls with disabilities, including their access to information and services in the field of violence against women, as well as their active participation in and economic contribution to all aspects of society;

(q) Encourage the development of gender-sensitive human rights programmes.

Strategic objective I. 3.
Achieve legal literacy

Actions to be taken

233. By Governments and non-governmental organizations, the United Nations and other international organizations, as appropriate:

(a) Translate, whenever possible, into local and indigenous languages and into alternative formats appropriate for persons with disabilities and persons at lower levels of literacy, publicize and disseminate laws and information relating to the equal status and human rights of all women, including the Universal Declaration of Human Rights, the International Covenant on Civil and Political Rights, the International Covenant on Economic, Social and Cultural Rights, the Convention on the Elimination of All Forms of Discrimination against Women, the International Convention on the Elimination of All Forms of Racial Discrimination,[33] the Convention on the Rights of the Child, the Convention against Torture and Other Cruel, Inhuman or Degrading Treatment or Punishment, the Declaration on the Right to Development[34] and the Declaration on the Elimination of Violence against Women, as well as the outcomes of relevant United Nations conferences and summits and national reports to the Committee on the Elimination of Discrimination against Women;

(b) Publicize and disseminate such information in easily understand-able formats and alternative formats appropriate for persons with disabilities, and persons at low levels of literacy;

(c) Disseminate information on national legislation and its impact on women, including easily accessible guidelines on how to use a justice system to exercise one's rights;

(d) Include information about international and regional instruments and standards in their public information and human rights education activities and in adult education and training programmes, particularly for groups such as the military, the police and other law enforcement personnel, the judiciary, and legal and health professionals to ensure that human rights are effectively protected;

(e) Make widely available and fully publicize information on the existence of national, regional and international mechanisms for seeking redress when the human rights of women are violated;

(f) Encourage, co-ordinate and co-operate with local and regional women's groups, relevant non-governmental organizations, educa-tors and the media, to implement programmes in human rights education to make women aware of their human rights;

(g) Promote education on the human and legal rights of women in school curricula at all levels of education and undertake public campaigns, including in the most widely used languages of the country, on the equality of women and men in public and private life, including their rights within the family and relevant human rights instruments under national and international law;

(h) Promote education in all countries in human rights and international humanitarian law for members of the national security and armed forces, including those assigned to United Nations peace-keeping operations, on a routine and continuing basis, reminding them and sensitizing them to the fact that they should respect the rights of women at all times, both on and off duty, giving special attention to the rules on the protection of women and children and to the protection of human rights in situations of armed conflict;

(i) Take appropriate measures to ensure that refugee and displaced women, migrant women and women migrant workers are made aware of their human rights and of the recourse mechanisms available to them.

J. Women and the media

234. During the past decade, advances in information technology have facilitated a global communications network that transcends national boundaries and has an impact on public policy, private attitudes and behaviour, especially of children and young adults. Everywhere the potential exists for the media to make a far greater contribution to the advancement of women.

235. More women are involved in careers in the communications sector, but few have attained positions at the decision-making level or serve on governing boards and bodies that influence media policy. The

lack of gender sensitivity in the media is evidenced by the failure to eliminate the genderbased stereotyping that can be found in public and private local, national and international media organizations.

236. The continued projection of negative and degrading images of women in media communications-electronic, print, visual and audio—must be changed. Print and electronic media in most countries do not provide a balanced picture of women's diverse lives and contributions to society in a changing world. In addition, violent and degrading or pornographic media products are also negatively affecting women and their participation in society. Programming that reinforces women's traditional roles can be equally limiting. The world-wide trend towards consumerism has created a climate in which advertisements and commercial messages often portray women primarily as consumers and target girls and women of all ages inappropriately.

237. Women should be empowered by enhancing their skills, knowledge and access to information technology. This will strengthen their ability to combat negative portrayals of women internationally and to challenge instances of abuse of the power of an increasingly important industry. Self-regulatory mechanisms for the media need to be created and strengthened and approaches developed to eliminate gender-biased programming. Most women, especially in developing countries, are not able to access effectively the expanding electronic information highways and therefore cannot establish networks that will provide them with alternative sources of information. Women therefore need to be involved in decision-making regarding the development of the new technologies in order to participate fully in their growth and impact.

238. In addressing the issue of the mobilization of the media, Governments and other actors should promote an active and visible policy of mainstreaming a gender perspective in policies and programmes.

Strategic objective J.1.

Increase the participation and access of women to expression and decision-making in and through the media and new technologies of communication

Actions to be taken

239. By Governments:

(a) Support women's education, training and employment to promote and ensure women's equal access to all areas and levels of the media;

(b) Support research into all aspects of women and the media so as to define areas needing attention and action and review existing media policies with a view to integrating a gender perspective;

(c) Promote women's full and equal participation in the media, including management, programming, education, training and research;

(d) Aim at gender balance in the appointment of women and men to all advisory, management, regulatory or monitoring bodies, including those connected to the private and State or public media;

(e) Encourage, to the extent consistent with freedom of expression, these bodies to increase the number of programmes for and by women to see to it that women's needs and concerns are properly addressed;

(f) Encourage and recognize women's media networks, including electronic networks and other new technologies of communication, as a means for the dissemination of information and the exchange of views, including at the international level, and support women's groups active in all media work and systems of communications to that end;

(g) Encourage and provide the means or incentives for the creative use of programmes in the national media for the dissemination of information on various cultural forms of indigenous people and the development of social and educational issues in this regard within the framework of national law;

(h) Guarantee the freedom of the media and its subsequent protection within the framework of national law and encourage, consistent with freedom of expression, the positive involvement of the media in development and social issues.

240. By national and international media systems:

Develop, consistent with freedom of expression, regulatory mecha-nisms, including voluntary ones, that promote balanced and diverse portrayals of women by the media and international communication systems and that promote increased participation by women and men in production and decision-making.

241. By Governments, as appropriate, or national machinery for the advancement of women:

(a) Encourage the development of educational and training programmes for women in order to produce information for the mass media, including funding of experimental efforts, and the use of the new technologies of communication, cybernetics space and satellite, whether public or private;

(b) Encourage the use of communication systems, including new technologies, as a means of strengthening women's participation in democratic processes;

(c) Facilitate the compilation of a directory of women media experts;

(d) Encourage the participation of women in the development of professional guidelines and codes of conduct or other appropriate self-regulatory mechanisms to promote balanced and non-stereotyped portrayals of women by the media.

242. By non-governmental organizations and media professional associations:

(a) Encourage the establishment of media watch groups that can monitor the media and consult with the media to ensure that women's needs and concerns are properly reflected;

(b) Train women to make greater use of information technology for communication and the media, including at the international level;

(c) Create networks among and develop information programmes for non-governmental organizations, women's organizations and professional media organizations in order to recognize the specific needs of women in the media, and facilitate the increased participation of women in communication, in particular at the international level, in support of South-South and North-South dialogue among and between these organizations, inter alia, to promote the human rights of women and equality between women and men;

(d) Encourage the media industry and education and media training institutions to develop, in appropriate languages, traditional, indigenous and other ethnic forms of media, such as story-telling, drama, poetry and song, reflecting their cultures, and utilize these forms of communication to disseminate information on development and social issues.

Strategic objective J.2.
Promote a balanced and non-stereotyped portrayal of women in the media

Actions to be taken

243. By Governments and international organizations, to the extent consistent with freedom of expression:

(a) Promote research and implementation of a strategy of information, education and communication aimed at promoting a balanced portrayal of women and girls and their multiple roles;

(b) Encourage the media and advertising agencies to develop specific programmes to raise awareness of the Platform for Action;

(c) Encourage gender-sensitive training for media professionals, including media owners and managers, to encourage the creation and use of non-stereotyped, balanced and diverse images of women in the media;

(d) Encourage the media to refrain from presenting women as inferior beings and exploiting them as sexual objects and commodities, rather than presenting them as creative human beings, key actors and contributors to and beneficiaries of the process of development;

(e) Promote the concept that the sexist stereotypes displayed in the media are gender discriminatory, degrading in nature and offensivre;

(f) Take effective measures or institute such measures, including appropriate legislation against pornography and the projection of violence against women and children in the media.

244. By the mass media and advertising organizations:

(a) Develop, consistent with freedom of expression, professional guidelines and codes of conduct and other forms of self-regulation to promote the presentation of non-stereotyped images of women;

(b) Establish, consistent with freedom of expression, professional guidelines and codes of conduct that address violent, degrading or pornographic materials concerning women in the media, including advertising;

(c) Develop a gender perspective on all issues of concern to communities, consumers and civil society;

(d) Increase women's participation in decision-making at all levels of the media.

245. By the media, non-governmental organizations and the private sector, in collaboration, as appropriate, with national machinely for the advancement of women:

(a) Promote the equal sharing of family responsibilities through media campaigns that emphasize gender equality and non-stereotyped gender roles of women and men within the family and that disseminate information aimed at eliminating spousal and child abuse and all forms of violence against women, including domestic violence;

(b) Produce and/or disseminate media materials on women leaders, *inter alia*, as leaders who bring to their positions of leadership many different life experiences, including but not limited to their experiences in balancing work and family responsibilities, as mothers, as professionals, as managers and as entrepreneurs, to provide role models, particularly to young women;

(c) Promote extensive campaigns, making use of public and private educational programmes, to disseminate information about and increase awareness of the human rights of women;

(d) Support the development of and finance, as appropriate, alternative media and the use of all means of communi cation to disseminate information to and about women and their concerns;

(e) Develop approaches and train experts to apply gender analysis with regard to media programmes.

K. Women and the Environment

246. Human beings are at the centre of concern for sustainable development. They are entitled to a healthy and productive life in harmony with nature. Women have an essential role to play in the development of sustainable and ecologically sound consumption and production patterns and approaches to natural resource management, as was recognized at the United Nations Conference on Environment and Development and the International Conference on Population and Development and reflected throughout Agenda 21. Awareness of resource depletion, the degradation of natural systems and the dangers of polluting substances has increased markedly in the past decade. These worsening conditions are destroying fragile ecosystems and displacing communities, especially women, from productive activities and are an increasing threat to a safe and healthy environ-ment. Poverty and environmental degradation are closely interrelated. While poverty results in certain kinds of environmental stress, the major cause of the continued deterioration of the global environment is the unsustainable pattern of consumption and production, particularly in industrialized countries, which is a matter of grave concern, aggravating poverty and imbalances. Rising sea levels as a result of global warming cause a grave and immediate threat to people living in island countries and coastal areas.The use of ozone-depleting substances, such as products with chloro fluorocarbons, halons and methyl bromides (from which plastics and

foams are made), are severely affecting the atmosphere, thus allowing excessive levels of harmful ultraviolet rays to reach the Earth's surface. This has severe effects on people's health such as higher rates of skin cancer, eye damage and weakened immune systems. It also has severe effects on the environment, including harm to crops and ocean life.

247. All States and all people shall co-operate in the essential task of eradicating poverty as an indispensable requirement for sustainable development, in order to decrease the disparities in standards of living and better meet the needs of the majority of the people of the world. Hurricanes, typhoons and other natural disasters and, in addition, the destruction of resources, violence, displacements and other effects associated with war, armed and other conflicts, the use and testing of nuclear weaponry, and foreign occupation can also contribute to environmental degradation. The deterioration of natural resources displaces communities, especially women, from income generating activities while greatly adding to unremunerated work. In both urban and rural areas, environmental degradation results in negative effects on the health, well-being and quality of life of the population at large, especially girls and women of all ages. Particular attention and recognition should be given to the role and special situation of women living in rural areas and those working in the agricultural sector, where access to training, land, natural and productive resources, credit, development programmes and cooperative structures can help them increase their participation in sustainable development. Environmental risks in the home and workplace may have a disproportionate impact on women's health because of women's different susceptibilities to the toxic effects of various chemicals. These risks to women's health are particularly high in urban areas, as well as in low-income areas where there is a high concentration of polluting industrial facilities.

248. Through their management and use of natural resources, women provide sustenance to their families and communities. As consumers and producers, caretakers of their families and educators, women play an important role in promoting sustainable development through their concern for the quality and sustainability of life for present and future generations. Governments have expressed their commitment to creating a new development paradigm that integrates environmental sustainability with gender equality and justice within and between generations as contained in chapter 24 of Agenda 21.[9]

249. Women remain largely absent at all levels of policy formulation and

decision-making in natural resource and environmental management, conservation, protection and rehabilitation, and their experience and skills in advocacy for and monitoring of proper natural resource management too often remain marginalized in policy-making and decision-making bodies, as well as in educational institutions and environment-related agencies at the managerial level. Women are rarely trained as professional natural resource managers with policy-making capacities, such as land-use planners, agriculturalists, foresters, marine scientists and environmental lawyers. Even in cases where women are trained as professional natural resource managers, they are often under represented in formal institutions with policy-making capacities at the national, regional and international levels. Often women are not equal participants in the management of financial and corporate institutions whose decision-making most significantly affects environmental quality. Furthermore, there are institutional weaknesses in co-ordination between women's non-governmental organizations and national institutions dealing with environmental issues, despite the recent rapid growth and visibility of women's non-governmental organizations working on these issues at all levels.

250. Women have often played leadership roles or taken the lead in promoting an environmental ethic, reducing resource use, and reusing and recycling resources to minimize waste and excessive consumption. Women can have a particularly powerful role in influencing sustainable consumption decisions. In addition, women's contributions to environmental management, including through grass-roots and youth campaigns to protect the environment, have often taken place at the local level, where decentralized action on environmental issues is most needed and decisive. Women, especially indige nous women, have particular knowledge of ecological linkages and fragile ecosystem management. Women in many communities provide the main labour force for subsistence production, including production of seafood; hence, their role is crucial to the provision of food and nutrition, the enhancement of the subsistence and informal sectors and the preservation of the environment. In certain regions, women are generally the most stable members of the community, as men often pursue work in distant locations, leaving women to safeguard the natural environment and ensure adequate and sustainable resource allocation within the household and the community.

251. The strategic actions needed for sound environmental management require a holistic, multidisciplinary and intersectoral approach.

Women's participation and leadership are essential to every aspect of that approach. The recent United Nations global conferences on development, as well as regional preparatory conferences for the Fourth World Conference on Women, have all acknowledged that sustainable development policies that do not involve women and men alike will not succeed in the long run. They have called for the effective participation of women in the generation of knowledge and environmental education in decision-making and management at all levels. Women's experiences and contributions to an ecologically sound environment must therefore be central to the agenda for the twenty-first century. Sustainable development will be an elusive goal unless women's contribution to environmental management is recognized and supported.

252. In addressing the lack of adequate recognition and support for women's contribution to conservation and management of natural resources and safeguarding the environment, Governments and other actors should promote an active and visible policy of mainstreaming a gender perspective in all policies and programmes, including, as appropriate, an analysis of the effects on women and men, respectively, before decisions are taken.

Strategic objective K.1.
Involve women actively in environmental decision-making at all levels

Actions to be taken

253. By Governments, at all levels, including municipal authorities, as appropriate:

(a) Ensure opportunities for women, including indigenous women, to participate in environmental decision-making at all levels, including as managers, designers and planners, and as implementers and evaluators of environmental projects;

(b) Facilitate and increase women's access to information and education, including in the areas of science, technology and economics, thus enhancing their knowledge, skills and opportunities for participation in environmental decisions;

(c) Encourage, subject to national legislation and consistent with the Convention on Biological Diversity,[35] the effective protection and use of the knowledge, innovations and practices of women of indigenous and local communities, including practices relating to traditional medicines, biodiversity and indigenous technologies, and endeavour to ensure that these are respected, maintained, promoted and preserved in an ecologically sustainable manner, and promote their wider application with the approval and involvement of the holders of such knowledge; in addition, safeguard the existing intellectual property rights of these women as protected under national and international law; work actively, where necessary, to find additional ways and means for the effective protection and use of such knowledge, innovations and practices, subject to national legislation and consistent with the Convention on Biological Diversity and relevant international law, and encourage fair and equitable sharing of benefits arising from the utilization of such knowledge, innovation and practices;

(c) Take appropriate measures to reduce risks to women from identified environmental hazards at home, at work and in other environments, including appropriate application of clean technologies, taking into account the precautionary approach agreed to in the Rio Declaration on Environment and Development;[18] Take measures to integrate a gender perspective in the design and implementation of, among other things, environmentally sound and sustainable resource management mechanisms, production techniques and infrastructure development in rural and urban areas;

(d) Take measures to empower women as producers and consumers so that they can take effective environmental actions, along with men, in their homes, communities and workplaces;

(e) Promote the participation of local communities, particularly women, in identification of public service needs, spatial planning and the provision and design of urban infrastructure.

254. By Governments and international organizations and private sector institutions, as appropriate:

(a) Take gender impact into consideration in the work of the Commission on Sustainable Development and other appropriate United Nations bodies and in the activities of international financial institutions;

(b) Promote the involvement of women and the incorporation of a gender perspective in the design, approval and execution of projects funded under the Global Environment Facility and other appropriate United Nations organizations;

(c) Encourage the design of projects in the areas of concern to the Global Environment Facility that would benefit women and projects managed by women;

(d) Establish strategies and mechanisms to increase the proportion of women, particularly at grass-roots levels, involved as decision makers, planners, managers, scientists and technical advisers and as beneficiaries in the design, development and implementation of policies and programmes for natural resource management and environmental protection and conservation;

(e) Encourage social, economic, political and scientific institutions to address environmental degradation and the resulting impact on women.

255. By non-governmental organizations and the private sector:

(b) Assume advocacy of environmental and natural resource management issues of concern to women and provide information to contribute to resource mobilization for environmental protection and conservation;

(b) Facilitate the access of women agriculturists, fishers and pastoralists to knowledge, skills, marketing services and environmentally sound technologies to support and strengthen their crucial roles and their expertise in resource management and the conservation of biological diversity.

Strategic objective K. 2.
Integrate gender concerns and perspectives in policies and programmes for sustainable development

Actions to be taken

256. By Governments:

(a) Integrate women, including indigenous women, their perspectives and knowledge, on an equal basis with men, in decision-making regarding sustainable resource management and the development of policies and programmes for sustainable development, including in particular those designed to address and prevent environmental degradation of the land;

(b) Evaluate policies and programmes in terms of environmental impact and women's equal access to and use of natural resources;

(c) Ensure adequate research to assess how and to what extent women are particularly susceptible or exposed to environmental degradation and hazards, including, as necessary, research and data collection on specific groups of women, particularly women with low income, indigenous women and women belonging to minorities;

(d) Integrate rural women's traditional knowledge and practices of sustainable resource use and management in the development of environmental management and extension programmes;

(e) Integrate the results of gender-sensitive research into mainstream policies with a view to developing sustainable human settlements;

(f) Promote knowledge of and sponsor research on the role of women, particularly rural and indigenous women, in food gathering and production, soil conservation, irrigation, watershed management, sanitation, coastal zone and marine resource management, integrated pest management, land-use planning, forest conservation and community forestry, fisheries, natural disaster prevention, and new and renewable sources of energy, focusing particularly on indigenous women's knowledge and experience;

(g) Develop a strategy for change to eliminate all obstacles to women's full and equal participation in sustainable development and equal access to and control over resources;

(h) Promote the education of girls and women of all ages in science, technology, economics and other disciplines relating to the natural environment so that they can make informed choices and offer informed input in determining local economic, scientific and environmental priorities for the management and appropriate use of natural and local resources and ecosystems;

(i) Develop programmes to involve female professionals and scientists, as well as technical, administrative and clerical workers, in environmental management, develop training programmes for girls and women in these fields, expand opportunities for the hiring and promotion of women in these fields and implement special measures to advance women's expertise and participation in these activities;

(j) Identify and promote environmentally sound technologies that have been designed, developed and improved in consultation with women and that are appropriate to both women and men;

(k) Support the development of women's equal access to housing infrastructure, safe water, and sustainable and affordable energy technologies, such as wind, solar, biomass and other renewable sources, through participatory needs assessments, energy planning and policy formulation at the local and national levels;

(l) Ensure that clean water is available and accessible to all by the year 2000 and that environmental protection and conservation plans are designed and implemented to restore polluted water systems and rebuild damaged watersheds.

257. By international organizations, non-governmental organizations and private sector institutions:

(a) Involve women in the communication industries in raising awareness regarding environmental issues, especially on the environmental and health impacts of products, technologies and industry processes;

(b) Encourage consumers to use their purchasing power to promote the production of environmentally safe products and encourage investment in environmentally sound and productive agricultural, fisheries, commercial and industrial activities and technologies;

(c) Support women's consumer initiatives by promoting the marketing of organic food and recycling facilities, product information and product labelling, including labelling of toxic chemical and pesticide containers with language and symbols that are understood by consumers, regardless of age and level of literacy.

Strategic objective K. 3.
Strengthen or establish mechanisms at the national, regional and international levels to assess the impact of development and environmental policies on women

Actions to be taken

258. By Governments, regional and international organizations and non-governmental organizations, as appropriate:

(a) Provide technical assistance to women, particularly in developing countries, in the sectors of agriculture, fisheries, small enterprises, trade and industry to ensure the continuing promotion of human resource development and the development of environmentally sound technologies and of women's entrepreneurship;

(b) Develop gender-sensitive databases, information and monitoring systems and participatory action-oriented research, methodologies and policy analyses, with the collaboration of academic institutions and local women researchers, on the following:

(i) Knowledge and experience on the part of women concerning the management and conservation of natural resources for incorporation in the databases and information systems for sustainable development;

(ii) The impact on women of environmental and natural resource degradation, deriving from, *inter alia*, unsustainable production and consumption patterns, drought, poor quality water, global warming, desertification, sea-level rise, hazardous waste, natural disasters, toxic chemicals and pesticide residues, radioactive waste, armed conflicts and its consequences;

(iii) Analysis of the structural links between gender relations, environment and development, with special emphasis on particular sectors, such as agriculture, industry, fisheries, forestry, environmental health, biological diversity, climate, water resources and sanitation;

(iv) Measures to develop and include environmental, economic, cultural, social and gender-sensitive analyses as an essential step in the development and monitoring of programmes and policies;

(v) Programmes to create rural and urban training, research and resource centres that will disseminate environmentally sound technologies to women;

(c) Ensure the full compliance with relevant international obligations, including where relevant, the Basel Convention and other conventions relating to the transboundary movements of hazardous wastes (which include toxic wastes) and the Code of Practice of the International Atomic Energy Agency relating to the movement of radioactive waste; enact and enforce regulations for environmentally sound management related to safe storage and movements; consider taking action towards the prohibition of those movements that are unsafe and insecure; ensure the strict control and management of hazardous wastes and radioactive waste, in accordance with relevant international and regional obligations and eliminate the exportation of such wastes to countries that, individually or through international agreements, prohibit their importation;

(g) Promote co-ordination within and among institutions to implement the Platform for Action and chapter 24 of Agenda 21 by, *inter alia,* requesting the Commission on Sustainable Development, through the Economic and Social Council, to seek input from the Commission on the Status of Women when reviewing the implementation of Agenda 21 with regard to women and the environment.

L. The Girl-Child

259. The Convention on the Rights of the Child recognizes that "States Parties shall respect and ensure the rights set forth in the present Convention to each child within their jurisdiction without discrimination of any kind, irrespective of the child's or his or her parent's or legal guardian's race, colour, sex, language, religion, political or other opinion, national, ethnic or social origin, property, disability, birth or status" (article 2, para. 1).[11] However, in many countries available indicators show that the girl-child is discriminated against from the earliest stages of life, through her childhood and into adulthood. In some areas of the world, men outnumber women by 5 in every 100. The reasons for the discrepancy include, among other things, harmful attitudes and practices, such as female genital mutilation, son preference —which results in female infanticide and prenatal sex selection early marriage, including child marriage, violence against women, sexual exploitation, sexual abuse, discrimination against girls in food allocation and other practices related to health and well-being. As a result, fewer girls than boys survive into adulthood.

260. Girls are often treated as inferior and are socialized to put themselves last, thus undermining their self-esteem. Discrimination and neglect in childhood can initiate a lifelong downward spiral of deprivation and exclusion from the social mainstream. Initiatives should be taken to prepare girls to participate actively, effectively and equally with boys at all levels of social, economic, political and cultural leadership.

261. Gender-biased educational processes, including curricula, educational materials and practices, teachers' attitudes and classroom interaction, reinforce existing gender inequalities.

262. Girls and adolescents may receive a variety of conflicting and confusing messages on their gender roles from their parents, teachers, peers and the media. Women and men need to work together with children and youth to break down persistent gender stereotypes, taking into account the rights of the child and the responsibilities, rights and duties of parents as stated in paragraph 267 below.

263. Although the number of educated children has grown in the past 20 years in some countries, boys have proportionately fared much better than girls. In 1990, 130 million children had no access to primary school; of these, 81 million were girls. This can be attributed to such factors as customary attitudes, child labour, early marriages, lack of funds and lack of adequate schooling facilities, teenage preg-

nancies and gender inequalities in society at large as well as in the family as defined in paragraph 29 above. In some countries the shortage of women teachers can inhibit the enrolment of girls. In many cases, girls start to undertake heavy domestic chores at a very early age and are expected to manage both educational and domestic responsibilities, often resulting in poor scholastic performance and an early drop-out from schooling.

264. The percentage of girls enrolled in secondary school remains significantly low in many countries. Girls are often not encouraged or given the opportunity to pursue scientific and technological training and education, which limits the knowledge they require for their daily lives and their employment opportunities.

265. Girls are less encouraged than boys to participate in and learn about the social, economic and political functioning of society, with the result that they are not offered the same opportunities as boys to take part in decisionmaking processes.

266. Existing discrimination against the girl-child in her access to nutrition and physical and mental health services endangers her current and future health. An estimated 450 million adult women in developing countries are stunted as a result of childhood protein-energy malnutrition.

267. The International Conference on Population and Development recognized, in paragraph 7.3 of the Programme of Action,[14] that "full attention should be given to the promotion of mutually respectful and equitable gender relations and particularly to meeting the educational and service needs of adolescents to enable them to deal in a positive and responsible way with their sexuality", taking into account the rights of the child to access to information, privacy, confidentiality, respect and informed consent, as well as the responsibilities, rights and duties of parents and legal guardians to provide, in a manner consistent with the evolving capacities of the child, appropriate direction and guidance in the exercise by the child of the rights recognized in the Convention on the Rights of the Child, and in conformity with the Convention on the Elimination of All Forms of Discrimination against Women. In all actions concerning children, the best interests of the child shall be a primary consideration. Support should be given to integral sexual education for young people with parental support and guidance that stresses the responsibility of males for their own sexuality and fertility and that help them exercise their responsibilities.

268. More than 15 million girls aged 15 to 19 give birth each year.

Motherhood at a very young age entails complications during pregnancy and delivery and a risk of maternal death that is much greater than average. The children of young mothers have higher levels of morbidity and mortality. Early child-bearing continues to be an impediment to improvements in the educational, economic and social status of women in all parts of the world. Overall, early marriage and early motherhood can severely curtail educational and employment opportunities and are likely to have a longterm adverse impact on their and their children's quality of life.

269. Sexual violence and sexually transmitted diseases, including HIV/AIDS, have a devastating effect on children's health, and girls are more vulnerable than boys to the consequences of unprotected and premature sexual relations. Girls often face pressures to engage in sexual activity. Due to such factors as their youth, social pressures, lack of protective laws, or failure to enforce laws, girls are more vulnerable to all kinds of violence, particularly sexual violence, including rape, sexual abuse, sexual exploitation, trafficking, possibly the sale of their organs and tissues, and forced labour.

270. The girl-child with disabilities faces additional barriers and needs to be ensured non-discrimination and equal enjoyment of all human rights and fundamental freedoms in accordance with the Standard Rules on the Equalization of Opportunities for Persons with Disabilities.[30]

271. Some children are particularly vulnerable especially the abandoned. homeless and displaced, street children, children in areas of conflict, and children who are discriminated against because they belong to an ethnic or racial minority group.

272. All barriers must therefore be eliminated to enable girls without exception to develop their full potential and skills through equal access to education and training, nutrition, physical and mental health care and related information.

273. In addressing issues concerning children and youth, Governments should promote an active and visible policy of ma;nstreaming a gender perspective into all policies and Programmes so that before decisions are taken an analysis is made of the effects on girls and boys, respectively.

Strategic objective L. 1.
Eliminte all forms of discrimination against the girl-child

Actions to be taken

274. By Governments:

(a) By States that have not signed or ratified the Convention on the Rights of the Child, take urgent measures towards signing and ratifying the Convention, bearing in mind the strong exhortation made at the World Conference on Human Rights to sign it before the end of 1995, and by States that have signed and ratified the Convention, ensure its full implementation through the adoption of all necessary legislative, administrative and other measures and by fostering an enabling environment that encourages full respect for the rights of children;

(b) Consistent with article 7 of the Convention on the Rights of the Child,[11] take measures to ensure that a child is registered immediately after birth and has the right from birth to a name, the right to acquire a nationality and, as far as possible, the right to know and be cared for by his or her parents;

(c) Take steps to ensure that children receive appropriate financial support from their parents, by, among other measures, enforcing child-support lawes.

(d) Eliminate the injustice and obstacles in relation to inherita faced by the girl-child so that all children may enjoy their right sence without discrimination, by *inter alia*, enacting, as appropriate, and enforcing legislation that guarantees equal right to succession and ensures equal right to inherit, regardless of the sex of the child;

(e) Enact and strictly enforce laws to ensure that marriage is only entered into with the free and full consent of the intending spouses; in addition, enact and strictly enforce laws concerning the minimum legal age of consent and the minimum age for marriage and raise the minimum age for marriage where necessary;

(f) Develop and implement comprehensive policies, plans of action and programmes for the survival, protection, development and advancement of the girl-child to promote and protect the full enjoyment of her human rights and to ensure equal opportunities for girls; these plans should form an integral part of the total development process;

(g) Ensure the disaggregation by sex and age of all data related to children in the health, education. and other sectors in order to include a gender perspective in planning, implementation and monitoring of such programmes

275. By Governments and international and non-governmental organizations:

(a) Disaggregate information and data on children by sex and age, undertake research on the situation of girls and integrate, as appropriate, the results in the formulation of policies, programmes and decision-making for the advancement of the girl-child;

(b) Generate social support for the enforcement of laws on the mini-mum legal age for marriage, in particular by providing educational pportunities for girls.

Strategic objective L. 2.
Eliminate negative cultural attitudes and practices against girls

Actions to be taken

276. By Governments:

(a) Encourage and support, as appropriate, non-governmental organizations and community-based organizations in their efforts to promote changes in negative attitudes and practices towards girls;

(b) Set up educational programmes and teaching materials and textbooks that will sensitize and inform adults about the harmful effects ofcertain traditional or customary practices on girl-children;

(c) Development and adopt curricula, teaching materials and textbooks to improve the self-image, lives and work opportunities of girls, particularly in areas where women have traditionally been under represented, such as mathematics, science and technology;

(d) Take steps so that tradition and religion and their expressions are not a basis for discrimination against girls.

277.By Governments and, as appropriate, international and non-governmental organizations:

(a) Promote an educational setting that eliminates all barriers that impede the schooling of married and/or pregnant girls and young mothers, including, as appropriate, affordable and physically accessible child-care facilities and parental education to encourage those who have responsibilities for the care of their children and siblings during their school years to return to, or continue with, and complete schooling;

(b) Encourage educational institutions and the media to adopt and project balanced and non-stereotyped images of girls and boys, and work to eliminate child pornography and degrading and violent portrayals of the girl-child;

(c) Eliminate all forms of discrimination against the girl-child and the root causes of son preference, which result in harmful and unethical practices such as prenatal sex selection and female infanticide; this is often compounded by the increasing use of technologies to determine foetal sex, resulting in abortion of female foetuses;

(d) Develop policies and programmes, giving priority to formal and informal education programmes that support girls and enable them to acquire knowledge, develop self-esteem and take responsibility for their own lives; and place special focus on programmes to educate women and men, especially parents, on the importance of girls' physical and mental health and well-being, including the elimina-tion of discrimination against girls in food allocation, early marriage, violence against girls, female genital mutilation, child prostitution, sexual abuse, rape and incest.

Strategic objective L. 3.
Promote and protect the rights of thegirl-child and increase awareness of her needs and potential

Actions to be taken

278. By Governments and international and non-governmental organizations:

(a) Generate awareness of the disadvantaged situation of girls among policy makers, planners, administrators and implementers at all levels, as well as within households and communities;

(b) Make the girl-child, particularly the girl-child in difficult circumstances, aware of her own potential, educate her about the rights guaranteed to her under all international human rights instruments, including the Convention on the Rights of the Child, legislation enacted for her and the various measures undertaken by both governmental and non-governmental organizations working to improve her status;

(c) Educate women, men, girls and boys to promote girls' status and encourage them to work towards mutual respect and equal partnership between girls and boys;

(d) Facilitate the equal provision of appropriate services and devices to girls with disabilities and provide their families with related support services, as appropriate.

Strategic objective L. 4.
Eliminate discrimination against girls in education, skills development and training

Actions to be taken

279. By Governments:

(a) Ensure universal and equal access to and completion of primary education by all children and eliminate the existing gap between girls and boys, as stipulated in article 28 of the Convention on the Rights of the Child;[11] similarly, ensure equal access to secondary education by the year 2005 and equal access to higher education, including vocational and technical education, for all girls and boys, including the disadvantaged and gifted;

(b) Take steps to integrate functional literacy and numeracy programmes, particularly for out-of-school girls in development programmes;

(c) Promote human rights education in educational programmes and include in human rights education the fact that the human rights of women and the girl-child are an inalienable. integral and indivisible part of universal human rights;

(d) Increase enrolment and improve retention rates of girls by allocating appropriate budgetary resources and by enlisting the support of the community and parents through campaigns and flexible school schedules, incentives. scholarships, access programmes for out-of-school girls and other measures;

(e) Develop training programmes and materials for teachers and educators, raising awareness about their own role in the educational process with a view to providing them with effective strategies for gender-sensitive teaching;

(f) Take actions to ensure that female teachers and professors have the same possibilities and status as male teachers and professors.

280. By Governments and international and non-governmental organizations:

(a) Provide education and skills training to increase girls' opportunities for employment and access to decision-making processes;

(b) Provide education to increase girls' knowledge and skills related to the functioning of economic, financial and political systems;

(c) Ensure access to appropriate education and skills-training for girl-children with disabilities for their full participation in life;

(d) Promote the full and equal participation of girls in extra curricular activities, such as sports, drama and cultural activities.

Strategic objective L.5.
Eliminate discrimination against girls in health and nutrition

Actions to be taken

281. By Governments and international and non-governmental organizations:

(a) Provide public information on the removal of discriminatory practices against girls in food allocation, nutrition and access to health services;

(b) Sensitize the girl-child, parents, teachers and society concerning good general health and nutrition and raise awareness of the health dangers and other problems connected with early pregnancies;

(c) Strengthen and reorient health education and health services, particularly primary health care programmes, including sexual and reproductive health, and design quality health programmes that meet the physical and mental needs of girls and that attend to the needs of young, expectant and nursing mothers;

(d) Establish peer education and outreach programmes with a view to strengthening individual and collective action to reduce the vulnerability of girls to H IV/AIDS and other sexually transmitted diseases, as agreed to in the Programme of Action of the International Conference on Population and Development and as established in the report of that Conference, recognizing the parental roles referred to in paragraph 267 of the present Platform for Action;

(e) Ensure education and dissemination of information to girls, especially adolescent girls, regarding the physiology of reproduction, reproductive and sexual health, as agreed to in the Programme of Action of the International Conference on Population and Development and as established in the report of that Conference, responsible family planning practice, family life, reproductive health, sexually transmitted diseases, HIV infection and AIDS prevention, recognizing the parental roles referred to in paragraph 267;

(f) Include health and nutritional training as an integral part of literacy programmes and school curricula starting at the primary level for the benefit of the girl-child;

(g) Emphasize the role and responsibility of adolescents in sexual and reproductive health and behaviour through the provision of appro- priate services and counselling, as discussed in paragraph 267;

(h) Develop information and training programmes for health planners and implementers on the special health needs of the girl-child;

(i) Take all the appropriate measures with a view to abolishing traditional practices prejudicial to the health of children, as stipulated in article 24 of the Convention on the Rights of the Child."

Strategic objective L. 6.

Eliminate the economic exploitation of child labour and protect young girls at work

Actions to be taken

282. By Governments:

(a) In conformity with article 32 of the Convention on the Rights of the Child,[11] protect children from economic exploitation and from performing any work that is likely to be hazardous or to interfere with the child's education, or to be harmful to the child's health or physical, mental, spiritual, moral or social development;

(b) Define a minimum age for a child's admission to employment in national legislation, in conformity with existing international labour standards and the Convention on the Rights of the Child, including girls in all sectors of activity;

(c) Protect young girls at work, *inter alia,* through:

(i) A minimum age or ages for admission to employment;

(ii) Strict monitoring of work conditions (respect for work time, prohibition of work by children not provided for by national legislation, and monitoring of hygiene and health conditions at work);

(iii) Application of social security coverage;

(iv) Establishment of continuous training and education;

(d) Strengthen, where necessary, legislation governing the work of children and provide for appropriate penalties or other sanctions to ensure effective enforcement of the legislation;

(e) Use existing international labour standards, including, as appropriate, ILO standards for the protection of working children, to guide the formulation of national labour legislation and policies.

Strategic objective L.7.
Eradicate violence against the girl-child

Actions to be taken

283. By Governments and, as appropriate, international and non-governmental organizations:

(a) Take effective actions and measures to enact and enforce legislation to protect the safety and security of girls from all forms of violence at work, including training programmes and support programmes, and take measures to eliminate incidents of sexual harassment ofgirls in educational and other institutions;

(b) Take appropriate legislative, administrative, social and educational measures to protect the girl-child, in the household and in society, from all forms of physical or mental violence, injury or abuse, neglect or negligent treatment, maltreatment or exploitation, including sexual abuse;

(c) Undertake gender sensitization training for those involved in healing and rehabilitation and other assistance programmes for girls who are victims of violence and promote programmes of informa-tion, support and training for such girls;

(d) Enact and enforce legislation protecting girls from all forms of violence, including female infanticide and prenatal sex selection, genital mutilation, incest, sexual abuse, sexual exploitation, child prostitution and child pornography and develop age-appropriate safe and confidential Programmes and medical, social and psychological support services to assist girls who are subjected to violence.

Strategic objective L. 8.
Promote the girl-childs awareness of and participation in social, economic and political life

Actions to be taken

284. By Governments and international

organizations:

(a) Provide access for girls to training, information and the media on social, cultural, economic and political issues and enable them to articulate their views;

(b) Support non-governmental organizations, in particular youth non-governmental organizations, in their efforts to promote the equality and participation of girls in society.

Strategic objective L.9.

Strengthen the role of the family* in improving the status of the girl-child

Actions to be taken

285. By Governments, in co-operation with non-governmental organizations:

(a) Formulate policies and programmes to help the family, as defined in paragraph 29 above, in its supporting, educating and nurturing roles, with particular emphasis on the elimination of intra-family discrimination against the girl-child;

(b) Provide an environment conducive to the strengthening of the family, as defined in paragraph 29 above, with a view to providing supportive and preventive measures which protect, respect and promote the potential of the girl-child;

(c) Educate and encourage parents and caregivers to treat girls and boys equally and to ensure shared responsibilities between girls and boys in the family, as defined in paragraph 29 above.

5. Institutional Arrangements

286. The Platform for Action establishes a set of actions that should lead to fundamental change. Immediate action and accountability are essential if the targets are to be met by the year 2000. Implementation is primarily the responsibility of Governments, but is also dependent on a wide range of institutions in the public, private and non-governmental sectors at the community, national; subregional/ regional and international levels.

287. During the United Nations Decade for Women (1976-1985), many institutions specifically devoted to the advancement of women were established at the national, regional and international levels. At the international level, the International Research and Training Institute for the Advancement of Women (INSTRAW), the United Nations Development Fund for Women (UNIFEM), and the Commit-

tee to monitor the Convention on the Elimination of All Forms of Discrimination against Women were established. These entities, along with the Commission on the Status of Women and its secretariat, the Division for the Advancement of Women, became the main institutions in the United Nations specifically devoted to women's advancement globally. At the national level, a number of countries established or strengthened national mechanisms to plan, advocate for and monitor progress in the advancement of women.

288. Implementation of the Platform for Action by national, subregional/regional and international institutions, both public and private, would be facilitated by transparency, by increased linkages between networks and organizations and by a consistent flow of information among all concerned. Clear objectives and accountability mechanisms are also required. Links with other institutions at the national, subregional/regional and international levels and with networks and organizations devoted to the advancement of women are needed.

289. Non-governmental and grass-roots organizations have a specific role to play in creating a social, economic, political and intellectual climate based on equality between women and men. Women should be actively involved in the implementation and monitoring of the Platform for Action.

290. Effective implementation of the Platform will also require changes in the internal dynamics of institutions and organizations, including values, behaviour, rules and procedures that are inimical to the advancement of women. Sexual harassment should be eliminated.

291. National, subregionaVregional and international institutions should have strong and clear mandates and the authority, resources and accountability mechanisms needed for the tasks set out in the Platform for Action. Their methods of operation should ensure efficient and effective implementation of the Platform. There should be a clear commitment to international norms and standards of equality between women and men as a basis for all actions.

292. To ensure effective implementation of the Platform for Action and to enhance the work for the advancement of women at the national, subregional/regional and international levels, Governments, the United Nations system and all other relevantorganizations should promote an active and visible policy of mainstreaming a gender perspective, *inter alia,* in the monitoring and evaluation of all policies

*As defined in paragraphy 29 above.

and programmes

A. National Level

293. Governments have the primary responsibility for implementing the Platform for Action. Commitment at the highest political level is essential to its implementation, and Governments should take a leading role in co-ordinating, monitoring and assessing progress in the advancement of women. The Fourth World Conference on Women is a conference of national and international commitment and action. This requires commitment from Governments and the international community. The Platform for Action is part of a continuing process and has a catalytic effect as it will contribute to programmes and practical outcomes for girls and women of all ages. States and the international community are encouraged to respond to this challenge by making commitments for action. As part of this process, many States have made commitments for action as reflected, inter alia, in their national statements·

294. National mechanisms and institutions for the advancement of women should participate in public policy formulation and encourage the implementation of the Platform for Action through various bodies and institutions, including the private sector, and, where necessary, should act as a catalyst in developing new programmes by the year 2000 in areas that are not covered by existing institutions

295. The active support and participation of a broad and diverse range of other institutional actors should be encouraged, including legislative bodies, academic and research institutions professional associations, trade unions, co-operatives, local community groups, nongovemmental organizations, induding women's organizat ions and feminist groups, the media, groups, youth organizations and cultural groups, as well as financial and non-profit organizations.

296. In order for the Platform for Action to be impiemented, it will be necessary for Governments to establish or improve the effectiveness of national machineries for the advancement of women at the highest political level, appropriate intra- and inter-ministerial procedures and Staffing, and other institutions with the mandate and capacity to broaden women's participation and inteerate gender analysis into policies and programmes. The first step in this process for all institutions should be to review their objectives, programmes and operational procedures in terms of the actions called for in the Platform. Akey activity should be to promote public awareness and support for the goals of the Platform fo, Action, *inter alia*, through the mass

media and public education.

297. As soon as possible, preferably by the end of 1995, Governments, in consultation with relevant institutions and non-governmental organizations, should begin to develop implementation strategies fo' the Platform and, preferably by the end of 1996, should have developed their strategies or plans of action This planning process should draw upon persons at the highest level of authority in government and relevant actors in civil society. These implementation strategies should be comprehensive, have time-bound targets and benchmarks for monitoring, and include proposals for allocating or reallocating resources fcr implementation. Where necessary, the support of the international community could be enlisted, including resources.

298. Non-governmental organizations should be encouraged to contribute to the design and implementation of these strategies or national plays of action They should also be encouraged to develop their own programmes to complement government efforts. Women's organizations and feminist in collaboration with other non-govemmental organizations, should be encouraged to organize networks, as necessary, and to advocate for and support the implementation of the Platform for Action by Governments and regional and international bodies.

299. Governments Should commit themselves to gender balance, *inter alia*, through the creation of special mechanisms, in all government-appointed committees, boards and other relevant official bodies, as appropriate, as well as in all international bodies, institutions and organization, notably by presenting and promoting more women candidates.

300. Regional and international organizations, in particular development institutions, especially INSTRAW, UNIFEM and bilateral donors, should provide financial and advisory assistance to national machinery in order to increase its ability to gather information, develop networks and carry out its mandate, in addition to strengthening international mechanisms to promote the advancement of women through their respective mandates, in co-operation with Governments.

B. SubregionaYregional Level

301. The regional commissions of the United Nations and other subregional/regional structures should promote and assist the pertinent national institutions in monitoring and implementing the global Platform for Action within their mandates. This should be done in co-

ordination with the implementation of the respective regional platforms or plans of action and in close collaboration with the Commission on the Status of Women, taking into account the need for a co-ordinated follow-up to United Nations conferences in the economic, social, human rights and related fields.

302. In order to facilitate the regional implementation, monitoring and evaluation process, the Economic and Social Council should consider reviewing the institutional capacity of the United Nations regional commissions within their mandates, including their women's units/focal points, to deal with gender issues in the light of the Platform for Action, as well as the regional platforms and plans of action. Consideration should be given, *inter alia,* and, where appropriate, to strengthening capacity in this respect.

303. Within their existing mandates and activities, the regional commissions should mainstream women's issues and gender perspectives and should also consider the establishment of mechanisms and processes to ensure the implementation and monitoring of both the Platform for Action and the regional platforms and plans of action. The regional commissions should, within their mandates, collaborate on gender issues with other regional intergovemmental organizations, non-governmental organizations, financial and research institutions and the private sector.

304. Regional offices of the specialized agencies of the United Nations system should as appropriate, develop and publicize a plan of action for implementing the Platform for Action, including the identification of timeframes and resources. Technical assistance and operational activities at the regional level should establish well-identified targets for the advancement of women. To this end, regular co-ordination should be undertaken among United Nations bodies and agencies.

305. Non-governmental organizations within the region should be supported in their efforts to develop networks to co-ordinate advocacy and dis-semination of information about the global Platform for Action and the respective regional platforms or plans of action.

C. International Level

1. United Nations

306. The Platform for Action needs to be implemented through the work of all of the bodies and organizations of the United Nations system during the period 1995-2000, specifically and as an integral part of

wider programming. An enhanced framework for international co-operation for gender issues must be developed during the period 1995-2000 in order to ensure the integrated and comprehensive implementation, follow-up and assessment of the Platform for Action, taking into account the results of global United Nations summits and conferences. The fact that at all of these summits and conferences, Governments have committed themselves to the empowerment of women in different areas, makes co-ordination crucial to the follow-up strategies for this Platform for Action. The Agenda for Development and the Agenda for Peace should take into account the Platform for Action of the Fourth World Conference on Women.

307. The institutional capacity of the United Nations system to carry out and co-ordinate its responsibility for implementing the Platform for Action, as well as its expertise and working methods to promote the advancement of women, should be improved.

308. Responsibility for ensuring the implementation of the Platform for Action and the integration of a gender perspective into all policies and programmes of the United Nations system must rest at the highest levels.

309. To improve the system's efficiency and effectiveness in providing support for equality and women's empowerment at the national level and to enhance its capacity to achieve the objectives of the Platform for Action, there is a need to renew, reform and revitalize various parts of the United Nations system. This would include reviewing and strengthening the strategies and working methods of different United Nations mechanisms for the advancement of women with a view to rationalizing and, as appropriate, strengthening their advisory, catalytic and monitoring functions in relation to mainstream bodies and agencies. Women/gender units are important for effective mainstreaming, but strategies must be further developed to prevent inadvertent marginalization as opposed to mainstreaming of the gender dimension throughout all operations.

310. In following up the Fourth World Conference on Women, all entities of the United Nations system focusing on the advancement of women should have the necessary resources and support to carry out follow-up activities. The efforts of gender focal points within organizations should be well integrated into overall policy, planning, programming and budgeting.

311. Action must be taken by the United Nations and other international organizations to eliminate barriers to the advancement of women within their organizations in accordance with the Platform for Action.

General Assembly

312. The General Assembly, as the highest intergovernmental body in the United Nations, is the principal policy-making and appraisal organ on matters relating to the follow-up to the Conference, and as such, should integrate gender issues throughout its work. It should appraise progress in the effective implementation of the Platform for Action, recognizing that these issues cut across social, political and economic policy. At its fiftieth session, in 1995, the General Assembly will have before it the report of the Fourth World Conference on Women. In accordance with its resolution 49/161, it will also examine a report of the Secretary-General on the follow-up to the Conference, taking into account the recommendations of the Conference. The General Assembly should include the follow-up to the Conference as part of its continuing work on the advancement of women. In 1996, 1998 and 2000, it should review the implementation of the Platform for Action.

Economic and Social Council

313. The Economic and Social Council, in the context of its role under the Charter of the United Nations and in accordance with General Assembly resolutions 45/264, 46/235 and 48/162, would oversee system-wide coordination in the implementation of the Platform for Action and make recommendations in this regard. Tne Council should be invited to review the implementation of the Platform for Action, giving due consideration to the reports of the Commission on the Status of Women. As co-ordinating body, the Council should be invited to review the mandate of the Commission on the Status of Women, taking into account the need for effective coordination with other related commissions and Conference follow-up. The Council should incorporate gender issues into its discussion of all policy questions, giving due consideration to recommendations prepared by the Commission. It should consider dedicating at least one high-level segment before the year 2000 to the advancement of women and implementation of the Platform for Action with the active involvement and participation, inter alia, of the specialized agencies, including the World Bank and IMF.

314. The Council should consider dedicating at least one coordination segment before the year 2000 to co-ordination of the advancement of women, based on the revised system-wide medium-term plan for the advancement of women.

315. The Council should consider dedicating at least one operational ac-

tivities segment before the year 2000 to the co-ordination of development activities related to gender, based on the revised system-wide medium-term plan for the advancement of women, with a view to instituting guidelines and procedures for implementation of the Platform for Action by the funds and programmes of the United Nations system.

316. The Administrative Committee on Co-ordination (ACC) should consider how its participating entities might best co-ordinate their activities, inter alia, through existing procedures at the inter-agency level for ensuring system-wide co-ordination to implement and help follow up the objectives of the Platform for Action.

Commission on the Status of Women

317. The General Assembly and the Economic and Social Council, in accordance with their respective mandates, are invited to review and strengthen the mandate of the Commission on the Status of Women, taking into account the Platform for Action as well as the need for synergy with other related commissions and Conference follow-up, and for a system-wide approach to its implementation.

318. As a functional commission assisting the Economic and Social Council, the Commission on the Status of Women should have a central role in monitoring, within the United Nations system, the implementation of the Platform for Action and advising the Council thereon. It should have a clear mandate with sufficient human and financial resources, through the reallocation of resources within the regular budget of the United Nations to carry the mandate out.

319. The Commission on the Status of Women should assist the Economic and Social Council in its co-ordination of the reporting on the implementation of the Platform for Action with the relevant organizations of the United Nations system. The Commission should draw upon inputs from other organizations of the United Nations system and other sources, as appropriate.

320. The Commission on the Status of Women, in developing its work programme for the period 1996-2000, should review the critical areas of concern in the Platform for Action and consider how to integrate in its agenda the follow-up to the World Conference on Women. In this context, the Commission on the Status of Women could consider how it could further develop its catalytic role in mainstreaming a gender perspective in United Nations activities.

Other Functional Commissions

321. Within their mandates, other functional commissions of the Economic and Social Council should also take due account of the Platform for Action and ensure the intergration of gender aspects in their respective work.

Committee on the Elimination of Discrimination against Women and other Treaty Bodies

322. The Committee on the Elimination of Discrimination against Women, in implementing its responsibilities under the Convention on the Elimination of All Forms of Discrimination against Women, should, within its mandate, take into account the Platform for Action when considering the reports submitted by States parties,

323. States parties to the Convention on the Elimination ofAII Forms of Discrimination against Women are invited, when reporting under article 18 of the Convention, to include information.On measures taken to implement the Platform for Action in order to facilitate the Committee on the Elimination of Discrimination against Women in monitoring effectively women's ability to enjoy the rights guaranteed by the Convention

324. The ability of the Committee on the Elimination of Discrimination against Women to monitor implementation of the Convention should be strengthened through the provision of human and financial resources within the regular budget of the United Nations, including expert legal assistance and, in accordance with General Assembly resolution 49/164 and the decision made by the meeting of States Parties to the Convention held in May 1995, sufficient meeting time for the Committee. The Committee should increase as co-ordination with other human rights treaty bodies, taking into account the recommendations in the Vienna Declaration and Programme of Action.

325. Within their mandate, other treaty bodies should also take due account of the implementation of the Platform for Action and ensure the integration of the equal status and human rights of women in their work.

UNITED NATIONS SECRETARIAT

Office ofthe Secretary-General

326. The Secretary-General is requested to assume responsibility for coordination of policy within the United Nations for the implementa-

tion of the Platform for Action and for the mainstreaming of a system-wide gender per-spective in all activities of the United Nations, taking into account the mandates of the bodies concerned. The Secretary-General should consider specific measures for ensuring effective co-ordination in the implementation of these objectives. To this end, the Secretary-General is invited to establish a high-level post in the office of the Secretary-General, using existing human and financial resources, to act as the Secretary-General's adviser on gender issues and to help ensure system-wide implementation of the Platform for Action in close co-operation with the Division for the Advancement of Women.

Division for the Advancement of Women

327. The primary function of the Division for the Advancement of Women of the Department for Policy Co-ordination and Sustainable Development is to provide substantive servicing to the Commission on the Status of Women and other intergovernmental bodies when they are concerned with the advancement of women, as well as to the Committee on the Elimination of Discrimination against Women. it has been designated a focal point for the implementation of the Nairobi Forward-looking Strategies for the Advancement of Women. In the light of the review of the mandate of the Commission on the Status of Women, as set out in paragraph 313 above, the functions of the Division for the Advancement of Women will also need to be assessed. The Secretary-General is requested to ensure more effective functioning of the Division by, *inter alia*, providing sufficient human and financial resources within the regular budget of the United Nations.

328. The Division should examine the obstacles to the advancement of women through the application of gender-impact analysis in policy studies for the Commission on the Status of Women and through support to other subsidiary bodies. After the Fourth World Conference on Women it should play a co-ordinating role in preparing the revision of the system-wide medium-term plan for the advancement of women for the period 1996-2001 and should continue serving as the secretariat for inter-agency coordination for the advancement of women. It should continue to maintain a flow of information with national commissions, national institutions for the advancement of women and non-governmental organizations with regard to implementation of the Platform for Action.

Other Units ofthe United Nations Secretariat

329. The various units of the United Nations Secretariat should examine their programmes to determine how they can best contribute to the coordinated implementation of the Platform for Action. Proposals for implementation of the Platform need to be reflected in the revision of the system-wide medium-term plan for the advancement of women for the period 1996-2001, as well as in the proposed United Nations medium-term plan for the period 1998-2002. The content of the actions will depend on the mandates ofthe bodies concerned.

330. Existing and new linkages should be developed throughout the, Secretariat in order to ensure that the gender perspective is introduced as a central dimension in all activities of the Secretariat.

331. The office of Human Resources Management should, in collaboration with programme managers worldwide, and in accordance with the Strategic plan of action for the improvement of the status of women in the Secretariat (1995-2000), continue to accord priority to the recruitment and promotion of women in posts subject to geographical distribution, particularly in senior policy-level and decision-making posts, in order to achieve the goals set out in General Assembly resolutions 45/125 and 45/239 C and reaffirmed in General Assembly resolutions 46/100, 47/93, 48/106 and 49/167. The training service should design and conduct regular gender-sensitivity training or include gender sensitivity training in all of its activities.

332. The Department of Public Information should seek to integrate a gender perspective in its general information activities and, within existing resources, strengthen and improve its Programmes on women and the girlchild. To this end, the Department should formulate a multimedia communications strategy to support the implementation of the Platform for Action.taking new technology fully into account. Regular outputs of the Department should promote the goals of the Platform, particularly in development.

333. The Statistical Division of the Department for Economic and Social Information and Policy Analysis should have an important coordinating role in international work in statistics, as described above in chapter IV, Strategic objective H. 3

International Research and Training Institute for the Advancemerrt ot Women

334. INSTRAW has a mandate to promote research and training on women's situation and development. In the light of the Platform for

Action, INSTRAW should review its work programme and develop a programme for implementing those aspects of the Platform for Action that fall within its mandate. It should identify those types of research and research methodologies to be given priority, strengthen national capacities to carry out women's studies and gender research, including that on the status of the girl-child, and develop networks of research institutions that can be mobilized for that purpose. It should also identify those types of education and training that can be effectively supported and promoted by the Institute.

340. Each organization should accord greater priority to the recruitment and promotion of women at the Professional level to achieve gender balance, particularly at decision-making levels. The paramount consideration in the employment of the staff and in the determination of the conditions of service should be the necessity of securing the highest standards of efficiency, competence and integrity. Due regard should be paid to the importance of recruiting the staff on as wide a geographical basis as possible. Organizations should report regularly to their governing bodies on progress towards this goal.

341. Coordination of United Nations operational activities for develop ment at the country level should be improved through the resident co-ordinator system in accordance with relevant resolutions of the General Assembly, in particular General Assembly resolution 47/199, to take full account of the Platform for Action.

Other International Institutions and Organizations

342. In implementing the Platform for Action, international financial institutions are encouraged to review and revise policies, procedures and staffing to ensure that investments and programmes benefit women and thus contribute to sustainable development. They are also encouraged to increase the number of women in high-level positions, increase staff training in gender analysis and institute policies and guidelines to ensure full consideration ofthe differential impact Of lending programmes and other activities on women and men. In this regard, the Bretton Woods institutions, the United Nations, as well as its funds and programmes and the specialized agencies, should establish regular and substantive dialogue, including dialogue at the field level, for more efficient and effective co-ordination of their assistance in order to strengthen the effectiveness of their programmes for the benefit of women and their families.

343. The General Assembly should give consideration to inviting the World Trade Organization to consider how it might contribute to

the implementation of the Platform forAction, including activities in co-operation with the United Nations system.

344. International non-governmental Organizations have an important role to play in implementing the Platform for Action. Consideration should be given to establishing a mechanism for collaborating with non-governmental organizations to promote the implementation of the Platform at various levels.

6. LINANCIAL ARRANGEMENTS

345. Financial and human resources have generally been insufficient for the advancement of women. This has contributed to the slow progress to date in implementing the Nairobi Forward-looking Strategies for the Advancement of Women. Full and effective implementation of the Platform for Action, including the relevant commitments made at previous United Nations summits and conferences, will require a political commitment to make available human and financial resources for the empowerment of women. This will require the integration of a gender perspective in budgetary decisions on policies and programmes, as well as the adequate financing of specific programmes for securing equality between women and men. To implement the Platform for Action, funding will need to be identified and mobilized from all sources and across all sectors. The reformulation of policies and reallocation of resources may be needed within and among programmes, but some policy changes may not necessarily have financial implications. Mobilization of additional resources, both public and private, including resources from innovative sources of funding, may also be necessary.

A. National Level

346. The primary responsibility for implementing the strategic objectives of the Platform for Action rests with Governments. To achieve these objectives, Governments should make efforts to systematically review how women benefit from public sector expenditures; adjust budgets to ensure equality of access to public sector expenditures, both for enhancing productive capacity and for meeting social needs; and achieve the gender-related commitments made in other United Nations summits and conferences. To develop successful national implementation strategies for the Platform for Action, Governments should allocate sufficient resources, including resources for undertaking gender-impact analysis. Governments should also encourage non-governmental organizations and private-sector and other insti-

tutions to mobilize additional resources.

347. Sufficient resources should be allocated to national machineries for the advancement of women as well as to all institutions, as appropriate, that can contribute to the implementation and monitoring of the Platform for Action.

348. Where national machineries for the advancement of women do not yet exist or where they have not yet been established on a permanent basis, Governments should strive to make available sufficient and continuing resources for such machineries.

349. To facilitate the implementatjon of the Platform for Action, Governments should reduce, as appropriate, excessive military expenditures and investments for arms production and acquisition, consistent with national security requirements.

350. Non-governmental organizations, the private sector and other actor of civil society should be encouraged to consider allocating the resources necessary for the, implementation of the Platform for Action. Governments should create a supportive ennronment for the mobilization of resources by non-governmental organizations, particularly women's organizations and networks, feminist group the private sector and other actors of civil society, to enable them to contribute towards this end. The capacity of nn-governmental organizations in this regard should be strengthened and enhanced.

B. Regional Level

351. Regional development banks, regional business associations and other regional institutions should be invited to contribute t,and help mobiolie resources in their lending and other activities for the implementation of the Platform for Action. They should also be encouraged to take account of the Platform for Action in their Policies and funding modalities.

352. The subregional and regional organizations and the United Nations regional commissions should, where appropriate and within their existing mandates, assist in the mobilization of funds for the implementation of the Platform for Action.

C. Interaational Level

353. Adequat, financial resources should be committed at the international level for the implementation of the Platform for Action in the developing countries, particularly in Africa and the least developed countries. Strengthening national capacities in developing countries, implement the Platform for Action will require striving for the fulfilment of the agreed target of 0.7 per cent of the gross national

Product of developed countries for overall official developmen assistance as soon as possible, as well as increasing the share of funding for activities designed to implement the Platform for Action. Furthermore, countries involved in development cooperation should conduct a critical analysis of their assistance programmes so as to improve the quality and effectiveness of aid through the integration of a gender approach.

354. International financial institutions, including the World Bank, the International Monetary Fund, the International Fund for Agricultural Development and the regional development banks, should be invited to examine their grants and lending and to allocate loans and grants to programmes for implementing the Platform for Action in developing countries, especially in Africa and the least developed countries.

355. The United Nations system should provide technical cooperation and other forms of assistance to the developing countries, in particular in Africa and the least developed countries, in implementing the Platform for Action.

356. Implementation of the Platform for Action in the countries with economies in transition will require continued international cooperation and assistance. The organizations and bodies of the United Nations system, including the technical and sectoral agencies, should facilitate the efforts of those countries in designing and implementing policies and programmes for the advancement of women. To this end, the International Monetary Fund and the World Bank should be invited to assist those efforts.

357. The outcome of the World Summit for Social Development regarding debt management and reduction as well as other United Nations world summits and conferences should be implemented in order to facilitate the realization of the objectives of the Platform for Action.

358. To facilitate implementation of the Platform for Action, interested developed and developing country partners, agreeing on a mutual commitment to allocate, on average, 20 per cent of official development assistance and 20 per cent of the national budget to basic social programmes should take into account a gender perspective.

359. Development funds and programmes of the United Nations system should undertake an immediate analysis of the extent to which their programmes and projects are directed to implementing the Platform for Action and, for the next programming cycle, should ensure the adequacy of resources targeted towards eliminating disparities between women and men in their technical assistance and funding

activities.

360. Recognizing the roles of United Nations funds, programmes and specialized agencies, in particular the special roles of UNIFEM and INSTRAW, in the promotion of the empowerment to women and therefore in the implèmentation of the Platform for Action within their respective empowerment of women, and there mandates, *inter alia*, in research, training and information activities for the advancement of women as well as technical and financial assistance to incorporate a gender perspective in development efforts, the resources provided by the international community need to be sufficient and should be maintainedat and adequate level.

361. To improve the efficiency and effectiveness of the United Nations system in its efforts to Promote the advancement of women and to enhance its capacity to further the objectives of the Platform for Action, there is a need to renew, reform and revitalize various parts of the United Nations system, especially the Division for the Advancement of Women of the United Nations Secretariate, as well as other units and subsidiary bodies that have a specific mandate to promote the advancement of women. In this regard, relevant goveering bodies within the United Nations system are encouraged to give special consideration to the effective implementation of the, Platform for Action and to review their policies, programmes, budgets and activities in order to achieve the most effective and efficient use of funds to this end. Allocation of additional resources from within the United Nations regular budget in order to impiement the Platform for Action will also be necessarly.

Notes

1. *Report of the World Conference to Review and Appraise the Achievements of the United Nations Decade for Women: Equality, Development and Peace, Nairobi, 15-26 July 1985* (United Nations publication, Sales No. E.85.IV.10) chap. I, sect. A.
2. *Report of the World Conference on Human Rights, Vienna, 14-25 June 1993* (A/CONF. 157/24 (Part I)), chap. III.
3. General Assembly resolution 34/180, annex.
4. General Assembly resolution 45/164.
5. General Assembly resolution 44/82.
6. General Assembly resolution 48/126.
7. *A/47/308-E/1992/97*, annex.
8. General Assembly resolution 48/104.
9. Vienna Declaration and Programme of Action, *Report of the World Conference on Human Rights ...*, chap. III, pa. 5.
10. See *The Results of the Uruguay Round of Multilateral Trade Negotiations: The Legal Texts* (Geneva, GATT secretariat, 1994).

General Assembly resolution 44/25, annex.

12. *Final Report of the World Conference on Education for All: Meeting Basic Learning Needs, Jomtien, Thailand, 5-9 March 1990,* Inter-Agency Commission (UNDP, UNESCO, UNICEF, World Bank) for the World Conference on Education for All, New York, 1990, appendix I.
13. General Assembly resolution 2200 A (XXI), annex.
14. *Report of the International Conference on Population and Development, Cairo, 5-13 September 1994,* (United Nations publication, Sales No.E.95.XIII.18), chap. I, resolution 1, annex.
15. *Report of the World Summit for Social Development, Copenhagen, 6-12 March 1995* (A/CONF. 166/9), chap. I, resolution 1, annexes I and II.
16. Unsafe abortion is defined as a procedure for terminating an unwanted pregnancy either by persons lacking the necessary skills or in an environment lacking the minimal medical standards or both (based on World Health Organization, *The Prevention and Management of Unsafe Abortion,* Report of a Technical Working Group, Geneva, April 1992 (WHO/ MSM/92.5)).
17. *Final Report of the International Conference on Nutrition, Rome,. 5-11 December 1992* (Rome, Food and Agriculture Organization of the United Nations, 1993), Part II.
18. *Report of the United Nations Conference* on *Environment and Developnent, Rio de Janeiro, 3-14 june 1992,* vol. I, *Resolution Adopted by The Conference* (United Nations publication, Sales No. E.93. I. 8 and corrigenda), resolution 1, annex I.
19. Ibid. resolution 1, annex II
20. *General Assembly resolution* 317 (IV), annex.
21. General Assembly resolution 217A (III).
22. General Assembly resolution 39/46, annex.
23. *Official Record of the General Assembly, Forty-seventh Session,* Supplement No- *38 (A/47/38),* chap. I.
24. United Nations, *Treaty Series,* vol. 75, No. 973 p. 287.
25. *Report of the World Conference* on *Human Rights...., chap. III,* sect. II, *para.* 38.
26. See *The United Nations Disarmament Yearbook,* vol. 5: *1980 (United* Nations publication, Sales No. *E. 81. IX. 4), appendix* VII.
27. General Assembly resolution 260 A (III), annex.
28. United Nations, *Treaty* Series, vol. *189,* No. 2545.
29. Ibid., vol. 606, No. *8791.*
30. General Assembly resolution 48/96, annex.
31. GeneralAssembly resolution 1386 (XIV).
32. See CEDAW/SP/1995/2 .
33. General Assembly resolution 2106 A(XX), annex.
34. General Assembly resolution 41/128, annex.
35. United Nations Environment Programme, *Convention* on *Biological Diversity* (Environmental Law and Institutions Programme Activity Centre), June 1992.